Dietitians of Canada

Cook!

275 recipes
celebrate food from field to table

Mary Sue Waisman, MSc, RD

Robert
ROSE

For complete cataloguing information, see page 373.

Disclaimer
The recipes in this book have been carefully tested by our kitchen and our tasters. To the best of our knowledge, they are safe and nutritious for ordinary use and users. For those people with food or other allergies, or who have special food requirements or health issues, please read the suggested contents of each recipe carefully and determine whether or not they may create a problem for you. All recipes are used at the risk of the consumer.

We cannot be responsible for any hazards, loss or damage that may occur as a result of any recipe use.

For those with special dietary needs, allergies, requirements or health problems, in the event of any doubt, please contact your medical adviser prior to the use of any recipe.

Design and Production: Daniella Zanchetta/PageWave Graphics Inc.
Editors: Sue Sumeraj and Jennifer MacKenzie
Proofreader: Sheila Wawanash
Indexer: Gillian Watts
Photographer: Colin Ericson
Associate Photographer: Matt Johannsson
Food Stylist: Kathryn Robertson
Prop Stylist: Charlene Ericson

Cover image: Maple-Glazed Pork Tenderloin (page 212)

We acknowledge the financial support of the Government of Canada through the Book Publishing Industry Development Program (BPIDP) for our publishing activities.

Published by Robert Rose Inc.
120 Eglinton Avenue East, Suite 800, Toronto, Ontario, Canada M4P 1E2
Tel: (416) 322-6552 Fax: (416) 322-6936
www.robertrose.ca

Printed and bound in Canada

1 2 3 4 5 6 7 8 9 TCP 19 18 17 16 15 14 13 12 11

Contents

Acknowledgments

Just as good recipes come from a great team of ingredients, so too is *Cook!* the result of great teamwork. Our goal was to build a book that celebrated all the wonderful food available to us here in Canada, and to inspire Canadian families to cook with it every day.

Sincere thanks to Mary Sue Waisman for giving this book its soul and unique personality. Mary Sue is an experienced dietitian, a great chef and a talented writer. Her passion for food, her desire to keep taste paramount in healthful cooking and her unwavering aspiration to teach others to nourish their bodies through delicious food are at the heart of this book. We thank her for creating the inspiring content, for testing recipes and for contributing many delicious original recipes.

Thanks also to Adam Hudson, dietetic intern, for his contribution by testing selected recipes.

A special thanks to the Review Committee for volunteering their time to review the text and ensure the accuracy of the content. Dietitians of Canada (DC) members participating in the Review Committee are:

Shani Gillespie, Prince Edward Island
Anna Leiper, Nova Scotia
Christina Blais, Quebec
Nancy Saunders, Quebec
Honey Bloomberg, Ontario
Krystal Taylor, Ontario
Marcia Cooper, Ontario
Margaret Howard, Ontario
Carolyn Chu, Saskatchewan
Desiree Nielsen, British Columbia
Heather McColl, British Columbia

Hats off to Caroline Dubeau, Nutrition Month Manager, Dietitians of Canada, who led and managed the project with *une main de maître*.

Thanks to Janice Macdonald, Director, Communications, Dietitians of Canada, for her guidance and support. Our thanks also to Sharyn Joliat of Info Access (1988) Inc. for analyzing the recipes.

Dietitians of Canada recognizes the Nutrition Month 2011 Official Sponsors for their contribution:

- Compass Group Canada
- Dairy Farmers of Canada

Our advice, disseminated through DC products and services, is based on sound science and the professional expertise and experience of our members. Materials are written by dietitians with experience in that topic area. DC maintains full editorial control of materials.

Dietitians of Canada makes a point of being transparent regarding sources of revenue. We do this through acknowledgments on our website, on specific educational tools and resources and at meetings. However, the acknowledgment is not an endorsement of the products or services of the contractor, sponsor or advertiser. Dietitians of Canada does not endorse or promote any commercial products or services.

We also want to thank our publisher, Robert Rose Inc., and in particular Bob Dees and Marian Jarkovich for their sound advice. Thanks, too, to editors Sue Sumeraj and Jennifer MacKenzie; to Daniella Zanchetta at PageWave Graphics for her contribution to the design and production of the book; and to food stylist Kathryn Robertson, prop stylist Charlene Erricson, associate photographer Matt Johannsson and photographer Colin Erricson for the wonderful photographs.

Finally, thanks to the dietitians and members of the public who shared recipes and tips for this book. Without your creative and tasty recipes, *Cook!* would not exist.

About Dietitians of Canada

Dietitians of Canada
Les diététistes du Canada

Dietitians of Canada (DC) is the national professional association for dietitians, representing almost 6,000 members at the local, provincial and national levels.

As the recognized leaders of dietetic practice, we advance health through food and nutrition, providing trusted information to Canadians and advising government and others at the federal and provincial/territorial levels on best practices in nutrition.

Dietitians of Canada is also one of the largest organizations of dietetics professionals in the world and actively facilitates the global advancements of dietetics.

As part of our commitment to evidence-based practice, in 1991 we established the Canadian Foundation of Dietetic Research. To support food and nutrition research, consider a donation; look for details at www.cfdr.ca.

For trusted advice on food and nutrition, including information to help you Plan, Shop and Cook healthy, visit our website, www.dietitians.ca. Whether you're looking for advice on a wellness program at work, individual nutrition counseling, a consultant in food service management or a media-savvy dietitian with expertise in nutrition and health, this website will also help you find a dietitian in your area.

Nutrition Month and National Dietitians Day

Nutrition Month celebrates 30 years in March 2011, and the introduction of this cookbook is one way dietitians are marking the event. During Nutrition Month, dietitians across Canada unite to organize events and communications to reinforce the importance of healthy eating.

In 2011, we also celebrate the second anniversary of Dietitians Day. Once a year, on the third Wednesday in March, we honor dietitians as health care professionals who use their specialized food and nutrition knowledge and skills every day to improve the health of Canadians. Dietitians Day raises the profile of dietitians and helps encourage and attract others to this worthy, satisfying and respected profession.

MARCH IS NUTRITION MONTH
WWW.DIETITIANS.CA

Introduction

Cook! is a celebration of Canadian foods. It contains 275 recipes, contributed by families from across Canada, that showcase the variety of nutrient-rich foods provided by and available in our wonderful country. It is also a call to action for Canadian families. With more and more of us finding that we have less and less time available for cooking, there's a good chance that our children won't be learning to prepare food at home from basic ingredients. We invite Canadian families to get into the kitchen and teach their children about food and cooking: where food comes from and how to prepare delicious meals that will nourish them and preserve the art of food preparation for generations to follow.

Notable Facts about Canadian Foods

We have much to celebrate when it comes to Canadian foods. Our land is vast and diverse and our coastline is the longest in the world, providing great abundance for the people who call Canada home. It's no surprise, then, that the foods available to us — especially in the spring, summer and fall — collectively provide all the nutrients we need for proper growth and development, to promote health and to ward off disease.

Did You Know?

The wide variety of Canadian foods, listed in *Eating Well with Canada's Food Guide*, provides most Canadians with all the nutrition their bodies need, although at certain times and stages of life, additional nutrients in the form of supplements might be required.

We also import many foods that we are unable to produce ourselves, and enjoy the benefits of the increased diversity. Imported foods, along with home-preserved foods and canned products, become particularly important in the winter, when our climate precludes us from producing enough fresh fruits and vegetables to meet population demands.

Eating Well with Canada's Food Guide identifies how many servings we need each day from each of four food groups: Vegetables and Fruit; Grain Products; Milk and Alternatives; and Meat and Alternatives. Listed below are some noteworthy facts about Canadian-grown or Canadian-produced foods from each of these groups, details on the nutrients and health benefits they provide and information on imported foods we can use to supplement and enhance our diet.

Vegetables and Fruit

Vegetables and fruit provide a great variety of vitamins and minerals, as well as dietary fiber and health-promoting antioxidants, which are known to help prevent heart disease and some types of cancer.

Canadian Crops

- A wide range of vegetables, from asparagus to zucchini, are grown in Canada. In 2009, in terms of acreage, sweet corn and green peas were the largest crops grown.

- We grow a *lot* of potatoes! In 2006, the potato crop accounted for 35% of all vegetable farm cash receipts, producing close to 5 million metric tons. This makes Canada the 12th-largest potato producer in the world. Canada's smallest province, Prince Edward Island, produces the most potatoes, followed by Manitoba, Alberta and New Brunswick.

- Fruits grown in Canada include apples, apricots, blueberries, cherries, cranberries, grapes, peaches, pears, plums, raspberries and strawberries, to name but a few.

Did You Know?

Cranberries grow in clusters on vines that are planted in natural or man-made peat bogs or sand beds. During harvesting, the bogs are flooded and the berries are shaken loose, landing softly in the water. Cranberries float, which makes them easy to collect either by hand or with harvesting machines. In Canada, cranberries are grown mainly in British Columbia and Quebec.

- With proper storage, some Canadian fruits (such as apples) and vegetables (such as carrots, potatoes and squash) remain available during our long winter months. But the availability of many other fresh fruits and vegetables is reduced, so consumers need to rely on frozen or canned supplies (either preserved at home or store-bought) or fresh produce imported from other countries.

Did You Know?

Many fruits and vegetables can be stored just as they are for weeks, or even months, in a root cellar, without any additives or preservatives. It's the ideal way to get fresh local produce in the winter months!

Imports

- In the winter months, Canada is quite reliant on imports to meet the domestic demand for vegetables and fruits, even those grown in Canada during warmer seasons.

- Fruits and vegetables that are not commonly grown in Canada, such as avocados, bananas, citrus fruits, mangos, papayas, pineapples, bamboo shoots, cassava, daikon radishes, plantains and yams, can add variety, delicious flavor and nutrition to meals and snacks all year round.

Canadian Sources of Vitamin C

Citrus fruits, such as oranges, grapefruit, lemons and limes, grow in hot climates and are valued for their high vitamin C content. However, many vegetables and fruits grown in Canada contain ample vitamin C for Canadians of all ages. Consider that 1/2 cup (125 mL) of orange juice contains 50 mg of vitamin C — more than half the recommended dietary allowance — then compare that with these alternative Canadian sources:

Canadian-Grown Food	Vitamin C Content	% DV
1/2 cup (125 mL) chopped raw yellow bell pepper	145 mg	240%
1/2 cup (125 mL) chopped raw red bell pepper	100 mg	165%
1/2 cup (125 mL) chopped raw green bell pepper	65 mg	110%
1/2 cup (125 mL) fresh sliced strawberries	50 mg	85%
1/2 cup (125 mL) cooked Brussels sprouts	50 mg	85%
1/2 cup (125 mL) chopped raw broccoli	40 mg	65%

- The United States was the source of nearly 60% of all fruit and vegetable imports in 2008. Mexico provided just over 9%, and other countries, such as Chile, China and Costa Rica, provided the remaining 31%.

Grain Products

Grain products provide a host of vitamins and minerals, along with valuable dietary fiber, which aids in digestion.

Canadian Crops

- Grain crops grown in Canada include wheat, corn, rye, oats, barley, buckwheat and wild rice.
- Field corn (which is different from edible sweet corn) is one of Canada's most important crops. It's the third-largest field crop, after wheat and barley. It is used for a multitude of products ranging from animal fodder to a variety of food products (including corn syrup and cornstarch) to industrial plastics and ethyl alcohol (used for fuel). Field corn is grown in every province in Canada, with the bulk of production in Ontario and Quebec.
- Buckwheat has been grown on the eastern Prairies for over a century. Most often, it's milled into flour, either light or dark, and used in baked products and a variety of other foods. Buckwheat groats (crushed buckwheat, with the husk removed) are often eaten as breakfast cereal.
- Canada grows an abundance of durum wheat and exports it to many of the world's top pasta producers, such as Italy and Turkey.
- The province of Manitoba grows about 25% of Canada's wild rice.

Did You Know?

Wild rice is not actually rice at all, but an aquatic grass. It grows primarily in shallow water along the shores of rivers, streams and lakes, and is native to North America. Grains of wild rice are about $\frac{1}{2}$ inch (1 cm) long, thin, hard and dark brown. When cooked, the grains become tender and the ends split open, revealing a lighter interior. Wild rice takes longer to cook than regular rice and is delicious in pilafs and stuffing.

Imports

- More than 2,000 varieties of rice are grown worldwide, serving as a staple grain for much of the world. Most of the world's rice production is based in Asia, with smaller amounts grown in Europe, North Africa and the United States.

Milk and Alternatives

Dairy products, such as milk, yogurt and cheese, provide protein and an assortment of vitamins and minerals, including those needed for bone health, such as calcium and vitamin D. As part of a balanced daily meal plan, dairy products may also help to prevent colon cancer and high blood pressure. Drink fortified soy beverages if you do not drink milk.

Canadian Products

- Just under 1 million dairy cows on over 13,000 farms supply Canadians with milk. Annually, Canada produces around 75 million hectoliters of milk, which is processed at about 450 plants across the country.
- There are 667 distinct varieties of Canadian cheese: 477 varieties are produced in Quebec (72%), 125 varieties are produced in Ontario (19%) and 65 varieties are produced in other provinces

(10%). Unique Canadian cheeses include Oka and cheese curds. Canadian cheeses made from 100% Canadian milk can be found by looking for the blue cow label.

- Many fortified soy beverages are produced in Canada.

> ## Did You Know?
>
> Milk, especially chocolate milk, is an ideal beverage after vigorous exercise: the liquid and electrolytes replenish the body's fluid, the carbohydrate replaces the energy used, and the protein repairs and builds muscles.

Imports

- Choose Canadian! We produce a wide variety of Canadian Milk and Alternatives.

Meat and Alternatives

Meats and meat alternatives provide high-quality protein to help build muscles and repair any worn-out or damaged tissues. Red meats, such as beef and pork, are a source of many vitamins, particularly B vitamins, and minerals, such as iron, magnesium, potassium and phosphorus. Chicken, the most popular poultry product in Canada, also provides a variety of vitamins and minerals, including niacin, B_6, potassium and phosphorus.

There is ample nutrition in one handy little egg! It is often said that eggs contain the perfect protein for humans, as they provide all the essential amino acids required for building and repairing body tissues. They also supply a variety of vitamins and minerals.

> ## Did You Know?
>
> All of the fat and cholesterol in eggs is found in the yolk, which is why some people choose to avoid yolks and use only the white part of the egg. If you do this, know that you also lose about half of the protein provided by the egg.

Fish such as salmon, herring, char, sardines, trout and mackerel have omega-3 fats, which help promote heart health and can aid in proper brain, nerve and eye development in infants.

Pulses (dried beans, peas and lentils), also known as legumes, are not only an inexpensive source of protein, but also provide dietary fiber, which aids in digestion. Some of their components may also help prevent cell damage that could lead to cancer.

Canadian Products

- Canada's red meat and meat products industry includes beef, pork, lamb, venison and bison. Beef is produced in all provinces, by about 83,000 farmers and ranchers. In 2007, it contributed $25 billion to the Canadian economy.

- Canadian farmers produced 1.2 million tons of poultry meat in 2009. Chicken, including stewing hens, accounts for 86% of all poultry meat produced. Turkey production stood at 167,000 tons in 2009.

- Canada produced over 620 million dozen eggs in 2009 — that's a staggering 7.4 billion eggs in one year! Most of Canada's egg production occurs in Ontario and Quebec.

> ## Did You Know?
>
> Chicken breasts contain less fat than the dark meat found in legs and thighs. Most of the fat found in chicken is in the skin. To reduce the amount of fat you consume, either remove the skin before cooking or cook chicken with the skin on and then remove it before eating.

- Canada boasts the world's longest coastline (244,000 km), representing 25% of the world's coastlines. Our lakes and seas provide us with more than 160 species of fish and seafood.

- Canada is a large producer and exporter of pulses, including dried peas, beans, lentils and chickpeas.

- Soybean production has increased in Canada in recent decades, although Canada is still a small player in international soybean trade. Grown in small quantities in several provinces, soybeans are valued for their nutritional merits (they contain a complete protein) and versatility. Common soybean products include tofu, soy sauce, soy beverage and tempeh.

Imports

- While certain regions of Canada produce peanuts and other nuts, such as hazelnuts, most nuts — including almonds, walnuts, pecans and cashews — are grown in other countries.

Other Canadian Products

Canola Oil

Canola, a descendant of rapeseed, was developed in the 1960s and 1970s by plant breeders in Saskatchewan and Manitoba, who named the new seed "canola," an abbreviation of "Canadian oil, low acid." It is Canada's only truly Canadian crop. Canola oil's parent, rapeseed oil, was once treasured as a lamp oil and as a lubricant for steam engines and other machines; in fact, rapeseed was first grown in Canada during the Second World War as an emergency measure when European and Asian supplies were cut off. But while rapeseed oil has many undesirable qualities as a food oil, canola oil's neutral flavor, favorable nutritional profile and high smoke point make it a great choice for both cooking and baking. Canola oil supplies essential fatty acids, as well as monounsaturated fat.

Maple Syrup

Pure maple syrup is a Canadian treasure! As the name implies, it's a product of maple trees, specifically the sap of sugar maple trees, found predominantly in Quebec, Ontario, and some Maritime provinces. While there have been technological advances in production, the basic process remains the same: sap is collected from trees and then concentrated to produce the syrup. Maple syrup is graded according to color and flavor, as the composition of sugars and other compounds within the syrup change over the course of maple syrup season. Generally speaking, at the beginning of the season, in early spring, the syrup is lighter in color and only slightly sweet. As the season progresses, the flavor takes on more caramel flavor. Lighter syrup is generally preferred for table use, such as on pancakes, while darker syrup is favored for baking and cooking.

Maple syrup should be differentiated from pancake syrup, which is usually made from corn syrup flavored with real or artificial maple flavoring. Pure maple syrup is more expensive than pancake syrup.

Other Imports

Coffee, tea, chocolate and most spices are not produced in Canada. While none of these common food items is essential to a healthy way of eating, they do provide variety and pleasure. We are fortunate to have a ready supply of these products in most parts of the country.

Mealtime Is Family Time

Though we are blessed with an abundance of nutrient-rich fresh foods, many modern Canadian families say they have very little time to prepare meals as they try to balance work, play, school and leisure time. We increasingly rely on prepared foods — from takeout and delivery to semi- or fully prepared products made by grocery stores and food companies — instead of cooking at home, from scratch. As a result, food culture and cooking skills may not be handed down in the traditional way: from parent or grandparent to child. Observational data suggest that Canada could be heading toward a "cooking crisis," in which future generations have little knowledge of basic cooking skills that enable them to choose and prepare meals consistent with a healthy way of eating.

How can we avoid this crisis? As we navigate our busy days, we prioritize certain activities, making sure to find time for them. Cooking at home and eating together yield substantial benefits for the entire family, so it makes sense to make mealtime a valued part of your day. Anything worth having requires a little dedication.

Why Cook at Home?

Using the tremendous variety of nutritious ingredients available in Canada to prepare appetizing, healthy meals and snacks has many benefits. Cooking at home provides us with an opportunity to control ingredient quality and quantity, spend time with our family, learn about food economics and pass down family food culture, all while we're teaching our children valuable cooking skills and respect for natural ingredients.

Cooking at home means planning meals that meet the nutritional needs of your family, shopping for affordable, healthy ingredients and assembling those ingredients into dishes your family will enjoy. It does not mean *never* using a convenience food such as reduced-sodium canned soup or semi-prepared items such as prewashed lettuce or sliced chicken; healthy versions of convenience items can be significant time savers, and if they help you achieve your goal of cooking at home as a family, use them on occasion, so long as you don't fall into the habit of opening cans or boxes of prepared foods on a daily basis!

Why Eat Together?

Sitting around the table as a family, enjoying a delicious meal prepared with Canada's finest ingredients, allows you to connect with your loved ones and discover what's going on in their lives. You'll hear about everyone's day, solve problems together, make plans for future activities and create lasting memories. A family meal also gives you the opportunity to be a positive role model for your children by demonstrating healthy food choices and portion sizes, and provides the perfect environment to teach children about food customs and traditions.

A personal story serves as an excellent example of the value of the family meal. My grandfather Joe immigrated from Italy in the early 1900s. His father had taught him how to grow beefsteak tomatoes, and after moving to Canada, Joe learned to successfully grow them in his backyard. His son-in-law, Chet — my father — adored Grandpa's tomatoes, both fresh off the vine and in the delicious tomato sauce canned by my grandmother. When Dad went off to serve in the Second World War, he survived on canned meats and other products, with few fresh fruits or vegetables. While eating his war rations, he would often daydream about picking a tomato off the vine or savoring homemade pasta sauce at a fall dinner table. When he came home from the war, the first meal he asked for was pasta with homemade tomato sauce.

When I was a child, I was mesmerized when my dad and grandfather told this story. It taught me the value of working with the land and the joy of eating a home-grown tomato, freshly picked from the vine. I learned that home canning is an economical way to preserve that delicious flavor so it can be enjoyed all year round, and that happy memories can sustain you through difficult times far from home. But the best part was simply spending time with my parents, siblings and grandparents, listening to this story and many others while we gobbled up my grandmother's pasta sauce, still made with home-grown

tomatoes. My children, in turn, also heard this story around the dinner table, and I hope the tradition will continue through future generations.

Getting Your Family Involved in Meal Preparation

When the whole family participates in meal preparation, some amazing things happen. Because many hands make light work, the cooking process suddenly seems like less of a chore and more of a joy, and the work goes faster, especially as children get older and can help more. But even more importantly, spending this quality time together, teaching and learning, joking around, catching up or simply working side by side in a comfortable silence, bonds you as a family, providing memories that will last a lifetime.

There are a number of ways to encourage your family to get involved. It all starts with the right attitude: if you value mealtime together and view cooking as fun, your kids will too. The next step is to make learning about food a family project: have frequent conversations about food, plant a garden and visit a farmers' market. Go grocery shopping together and experiment with new foods and cuisines. You might even consider taking a cooking class together. And when it's time to get into the kitchen and start cooking, assign a task, big or small, to each family member, so that everyone feels like they have an important role to play in this family activity.

Fun Recipes to Inspire Your Kids

Need proof that cooking can be fun? These recipes are a case in point.

- Piggy Pancakes (page 46). Even little kids can help measure, scoop and stir the ingredients for these adorable pancakes, which look just like wee piglets.
- Four Perfect Chicken Panini (page 72). Let older kids experiment with their own creative panini fillings. Then you can grill up their special sandwiches.
- Sushi Sandwich Wraps (page 67) and Super-Easy Crab and Sweet Potato Sushi Rolls (page 111). Sushi is one of the hottest food trends right now, and your fashion-conscious tweens and teens will get a kick out of having a sushi-making party with their friends.

Get Everyone Talking About Food

Stir up enthusiasm for mealtime by having interesting discussions about food and cooking. Here are some conversation starters:

- What are your favorite foods? Why?
- What foods do you dislike? Why?
- What different tastes can your tongue distinguish? There are only five: sweet, sour, salty, bitter and umami. Select and try various foods with these different tastes.

Did You Know?

Umami is a word of Japanese origin that means "delicious flavor." It is a way of describing the flavor of certain savory foods, such as seafood, meats, cheeses and some vegetables.

- Where do your favorite foods come from? Are they grown in the ground? Raised on the land? Fished from the sea? What part of Canada do they come from? Do they come from nearby or far away?

- What foods come from the part of Canada where you live? What foods do you see at your local farmers' market? Have you ever talked to the farmer about how the foods are grown or raised? Have you ever visited a working farm?

Did You Know?

Agriculture and Agri-Food Canada have launched a new website to help inform Canadians about farmers' markets. Visit www.farmersmarketscanada.ca.

- What foods do our bodies need to stay healthy? Visit www.healthcanada.gc.ca/foodguide and download a free copy of *Eating Well with Canada's Food Guide*. Look at it often to refresh your memory on how much and what types of food you need each day to help maintain optimum health. Health Canada's site also contains lots of other helpful information about food and nutrition basics that can spark lively discussions.

- How many different ways can you think of to cook a certain food? For example, a potato can be baked in the oven with the skin on and eaten as is; it can be peeled, boiled and turned into mashed potatoes;

it can be cut into slices, chunks or strips and baked or fried; leftover mashed potatoes can be turned into potato pancakes; and so on. What about other foods, like tomatoes, corn or carrots?

- How do fruits and vegetables get processed into other familiar products? How do tomatoes get turned into ketchup? How does corn get turned into tortillas? How does a cacao pod get turned into a chocolate bar?

- What was cooking like for your parents or grandparents? What foods did they eat every day? How often did they eat out or eat prepared food purchased at the grocery store?

- What foods have important meaning to your family? Why?

- What food traditions are important to your family? Which ones will you keep? What new traditions will you create?

- Where will you go on vacation this year? What regional foods will you try when you get there? When traveling in Canada, try partridgeberries from Newfoundland and Labrador, fiddleheads from Nova Scotia, Malpeque oysters from Prince Edward Island, pure maple syrup from New Brunswick, local cheese from Quebec, heirloom tomatoes from Ontario, wild rice from Manitoba, Saskatoon berries from Saskatchewan, bison from Alberta, spot prawns from British Columbia, moose from the Yukon, caribou from the Northwest Territories or arctic char from Nunavut.

- How can we all be gentler to the earth so it can continue to produce food for centuries to come?

Plant a Garden

Nothing teaches you as much about a food as growing it yourself, and nothing makes you value it more. You can plant a vegetable garden in your backyard, if you have space.

You can grow certain vegetables and fruits, such as tomatoes, bell peppers, lettuce and strawberries, in pots on a deck, balcony or terrace. You can even grow potted herbs on a sunny windowsill. If none of these options work for you, look for a local community garden and find out how to get a plot. If there are no community gardens in your area, consider starting one!

However big or small your garden, encourage your children to help care for it, with designated tasks ranging from planting and watering to weeding and harvesting.

Did You Know?

Community-supported agriculture (CSA) is a way for you to "own" part of a farm without doing the farming. You pay the farmer a specified amount of money; in return, the farmer provides you with produce throughout the year. You're directly supporting local agriculture, farms and farmers, and investing in your community. You often don't know what will arrive in your weekly basket, and you can consider that an opportunity to learn about new foods and think up creative ways to prepare them. The fact that you pay up front can also help with family budgeting.

Visit a Farmers' Market

A family excursion to a local farmers' market can be far more than a shopping trip: farmers have a wealth of knowledge about the foods they grow and the animals they raise. While you're there, take the time to talk with farmers about

- how their food is produced;

- their suggestions on how to prepare the foods they produce;

- what it's like to live on a farm;

- what time they get up in the morning and go to bed at night;

- how their animals are fed and raised;
- how their fruits and vegetables are grown, irrigated and harvested;
- what they do to keep their soil healthy and their land sustainable.

When you're ready to move on, make sure to thank the farmers for being so generous with their time and for providing healthy, delicious foods.

Did You Know?

When you visit a farmers' market, it's best to take along your own reusable shopping bags. Although most farmers will have plastic bags available, your own large, sturdy bags will make it much easier to carry your purchases, and you'll lessen your impact on the environment. If you're planning to buy meat or other perishable foods, take a cooler to keep the food safe on the ride home. Be sure to wash your shopping bags and cooler after each use.

Take Your Family Shopping

Getting your family involved in grocery shopping can save time and effort and ensure that everyone gets to eat some of their favorite foods. Grocery shopping can also be a good way for kids to learn about health and nutrition. Here are some tips to make sure you get the most out of your family shopping trip:

- When a family member says, "We have nothing to eat," encourage him or her to add a couple of healthy items to the grocery list.
- Minimize stress by choosing a shopping time that works for everyone. You'll all be a lot happier if you shop on a full stomach and are not in a hurry.

- Ask your children to help you find healthy foods that offer good value for the price. Have them review key information on the Nutrition Facts table and compare different package sizes and prices.
- Encourage children to choose a healthy item they've never eaten before, such as a new local fruit or vegetable.

Did You Know?

Many grocery stores offer nutrition tours, including some specifically designed for children. See if you can find one in your area and attend as a family.

Eat with the Seasons

At the start of each new season, sit down as a family and talk about foods in your area that are coming into season. For example, in many parts of Canada,

- lettuce, asparagus and fiddleheads are plentiful, fresh and affordable in the spring;
- strawberries grace the fields in June;
- peaches, beans and corn are ready by August;
- apples, root vegetables and squash are plentiful starting in October and November.

Pick out your favorites, and be sure to choose some new foods you'd like to try. The types of foods that are plentiful often determine what kind of cooking we do. For example, in spring, the availability of fresh lettuce and spinach prompts us to prepare fresh salads. As summer arrives, it's time to fire up the barbecue and grill some corn on the cob alongside grilled pork tenderloin, or make fresh berry smoothies, cobblers or roasted fruit. With the onset of the fall harvest, vegetables take center stage, appearing in everything from side dishes and salads to homemade preserves. Finally, the cold days of winter make us long for warm, simmering stews and casseroles filled with foods preserved from the seasons just passed.

> ### Did You Know?
> Most produce tastes best and contains the most nutrients when it's harvested at the peak of ripeness.

Preserve the Harvest

Learning how to safely preserve fresh foods for year-round enjoyment can be a fun activity for the whole family. With a boiling water canner, some mason jars, a bounty of produce and a free afternoon, you can work together to create any number of home preserves, including pickles, salsas, chutneys, jams, jellies and marmalades. It's very important to preserve safely, so be sure to use current recipes from a reliable source. A trusted resource for information on safe preserving is www.homecanning.ca.

If you're not quite up for making preserves, try freezing fruits and vegetables for long-term storage instead. Some fruits, such as berries and grapes, can simply be frozen in airtight containers without any additional preparation. Fruits that tend to brown when chopped benefit from being tossed with lemon juice before freezing. Vegetables should be blanched before they are stored in the freezer.

> ### Did You Know?
> Some fruits and vegetables don't freeze all that well. These include citrus fruits, pears, celery, cucumbers, eggplant, garlic, leafy greens, mushrooms and onions.

Take Cooking Classes

Many grocery stores, community organizations and local high schools and community colleges offer cooking classes that you can attend as a family. If your kids show a particular interest in learning how to cook, you can even look for summer or holiday cooking camps in your region.

If a formal class is not your family's style, why not ask a parent or grandparent to teach you how to make one of their favorite recipes? You'll all get great satisfaction out of keeping a family tradition alive, and you're sure to pick up some good cooking tips while listening to stories about the "good old days."

Experiment with Recipes

We all get into a cooking rut sometimes, making the same few meals over and over again because we know everyone likes them. But variety is the spice of life, so when it's time to shake things up, get your whole family involved in choosing new recipes to try. Here are some easy ways to expand your cooking repertoire:

- Ask everyone in the family to flip through this book and other cookbooks, flagging recipes that appeal to them. Make sure to give everyone's choices an equal chance. Go shopping together to gather the ingredients, then work as a team to create the meal.

- When you discover a new food you want to try, but you're not sure how to cook it, challenge everyone to find a recipe for it by looking through cookbooks and searching online. Vote on the best one, then prepare the recipe together.

- Select a region of Canada and make a regional meal. For example, find a recipe for pea soup from Quebec, rappie pie from the Acadian shores in Nova Scotia or goldeye fish from Manitoba.

- Choose an international cuisine and have a theme night. Prepare an ethnic dish or two, and challenge each family member to learn an interesting fact about the relevant region or culture to share at the dinner table.

Assign Kitchen Tasks

The entire family can participate in all aspects of meal preparation, from setting the table to cooking to cleaning. Older children can help with just about anything, as long as you teach them how to use knives and kitchen gadgets safely; younger children can perform simple tasks with ingredients you've already prepared. Here are some tips on how family members can help in the kitchen:

- Keep the menu for the week posted on the fridge and the evening's recipe on the counter. Whoever gets home first can get the meal started.

- Children of all ages can help set the table. Preschoolers will have fun carrying placemats, utensils and unbreakable cups to the table.

- Invite children to read recipes aloud and help collect the ingredients and utensils needed to prepare them.

- Children as young as two or three can help scrub potatoes or tear lettuce leaves for a salad. When they're a little older, they can help scoop, measure, mix and stir ingredients that are not on the stove. Remind them to clean their hands before and after touching food.

- If you don't mind children standing on a chair beside you at the stove, they can add ingredients to the saucepan, stir soups and stews or just watch what you are doing.

- Ask your kids to taste your recipe and tell you what they think of it. Do they like the taste, the color, the texture? If they don't, ask them what they don't like about it. Encourage older children to give you suggestions on how to improve it, then take their advice — even if they're wrong, you'll all learn something about what *not* to do!

- Let kids help prepare their own sandwiches and wraps: they can spread ingredients, add toppings, choose their own condiments and roll up wraps.

- Older children can have full responsibility for preparing a component of the meal, such as a vegetable platter with dip, a salad or even dessert.

- Assign older kids an easy baking project after school. Have them try making Cranberry Pumpkin Cookies (page 342) or Apricot Oatmeal Bran Muffins (page 321).

- Just about everyone can help clear the table, wash and dry the dishes or load the dishwasher.

Let's Get Cooking!

Now that you've rallied your troops, it's time to get into the kitchen. But before you pull out those pots and pans, there are a few important steps that can make the cooking experience more efficient and more enjoyable. First, you'll want to organize your kitchen so it's easy to use. Once your kitchen is shipshape, you can head to the grocery store, shopping list in hand, to purchase everything you need to prepare healthy, satisfying meals with Canada's best ingredients. An organized kitchen and sensible shopping won't just make cooking easier, but will also help you avoid waste. The next step is to make sure you know how to read and follow recipes: they have their own language, which we've decoded for you on page 22. Finally, you're ready to cook with ease and confidence, with the help of our handy tips on timing, prep work and making your meals as healthy as possible.

Make Your Kitchen Easy to Use

To pull together tasty, healthy meals and snacks in short order, you need a kitchen that's ready for action. If it's disorganized, you might be tempted to order in or eat out. Not only is this more expensive and likely less healthy, it can actually take longer than making a meal yourself. You also miss out on all the rewards that come from making a meal at home — the delicious aromas wafting through the house, the satisfaction of knowing your family ate a nutritious meal and the great leftovers that make future meal preparation a breeze.

The whole family can help organize the kitchen. Here are some steps for getting your kitchen in tip-top shape:

Organize Your Fridge

- Discard expired items, old condiments that won't be used and leftovers that have been in there for more than three days.

- Place similar items in the same part of the fridge so it's easy to find what you're looking for.

> ### Did You Know?
> The shelves on the door are the warmest part of the fridge, so they're not a good place for dairy products or eggs. It's fine to store condiments and juice on these shelves, though.

- The back of the fridge is the coldest part, so push the most perishable items, such as meat and fish, to the back.

- Keep your fruits and vegetables in the crispers designed to hold them: the crispers have a higher humidity level to help keep your produce from withering.

- Place ready-to-go healthy items near the front for easy access.

- Keep leftovers near the front so you're less likely to forget them.

Organize Your Cupboards and Drawers

- If you have extra canned foods or items that you won't be using, donate them to a local food bank.

- Keep like items grouped together: baking supplies (flour, baking soda, baking powder, etc.), spices, canned goods, pasta and rice, healthy snacks and breakfast cereals can each have their own area.

- Place older cans and packages in front of more recent purchases so they get used first.

- Keep healthy snacks at the front and within easy reach. Store special treats out of sight and out of reach.

- Relegate rarely used pots, pans and kitchen appliances to the backs of cupboards, or even to that hard-to-reach cupboard, so you have ample space for more frequently used items and can pull them out easily.

- Designate a shelf or drawer for storage containers and supplies. Keep lids in one container and stack the bottoms in another.

- Ask your children for tips on what storage solutions would make it easier for them to pack their own lunches.

> ### Did You Know?
> In days gone by, pie safes (pie cupboards or cabinets) and jelly cupboards were specialized pieces of furniture designed to store pies and jellies, jams and spices, respectively. It's thought that they were introduced to North America by the Pennsylvania Dutch.

Be a Smart Shopper

We've all done it: headed off to the grocery store with no real idea of what we're going to buy when we get there, then wandered up and down the aisles, adding things we like to our carts with little thought about how we'll use those items to make meals. This strategy — or rather, lack thereof — costs us both time and money and often creates a lot of waste.

Taking a little time to make a plan, in the form of a shopping list, before you head for the store will help you purchase ingredients that will combine into healthy, affordable, easy-to-prepare meals. Once you're at the store, use the information on food labels to help you make the best choices.

Make a Shopping List

Knowing what you want before you go shopping saves you time and can prevent you from making impulse purchases that might be less nutritious or more expensive or may not get used. And with a list in hand, you're far less likely to forget anything.

- Keep a notepad in your kitchen and jot down items as they run low.

- Review the recipes you intend to make and add the ingredients to your list, making sure to include the amounts required.

- Sort the items on your list by the store departments: produce, meat, bakery, dairy and so on — it will save you backtracking time.

> ### Did You Know?
> Shopping the perimeter of the store helps you focus on buying fresh meats, dairy products, breads and produce. But don't forget about the aisles filled with dried beans, 100% fruit juices, whole-grain cereals and other healthy choices. Just try to skip the chips aisle and any others that might tempt you to purchase less healthy foods.

Keep Healthy Meals Affordable

Eating well doesn't have to be expensive. Many nutritious foods, such as bulk beans and grains, large packages of oatmeal and brown rice, in-season fresh produce, eggs, legumes, powdered milk and sale-priced frozen or canned fruits, vegetables and fish, are quite affordable. Here are some tips for keeping your grocery bills down:

- Stick to your list, to prevent or reduce impulse purchases.

- Read flyers and look for weekly specials. Plan your menus around them or use them to stock your freezer.

- Use discount coupons, but make sure they're for products you will actually use. If you don't need it, a sale item is an added expense, not a savings.

- If freezer space allows, buy meat and bread on sale and freeze them for later use. Take the time to separate large packages of meat into meal-sized portions and date them before putting them in the freezer.

- If you have extra shelf space, stock up on staples such as canned beans or fish when they are on sale.

- Buy lots of in-season vegetables and fruits when they are most affordable and preserve or freeze them for later use (see page 16).

> ## Did You Know?
> Frozen or canned produce may be cheaper than fresh at certain times of the year. Choose those without added salt, sugar or rich sauces.

- Check best-before dates to make sure the product won't expire before you're able to use it up.

- Buy bigger packages of frequently used products. You can then repackage into smaller amounts and freeze. But don't buy bigger packages just because they are cheaper. If you have no space to store the food, or if having extra food will cause you to overindulge, the sale price isn't a bargain.

- Compare the cost per serving, listed on shelf tags, to ensure that you're buying the most economical size.

Use Convenience Food to Your Advantage

When shopping, keep an eye out for nutritious time savers. Here are some of our favorites:

- Washed and ready-to-eat produce can make short work of prep time. Most grocery stores carry a good selection of salad mixes, vegetable platters with dip and chopped vegetables for stir-fries. Keep in mind that any prep done to food before it is packaged increases its cost, and that many of the packaging materials cannot be recycled.

- Rotisserie-cooked chicken or oven-roasted beef is occasionally the perfect way to jumpstart a meal. Add our Fresh Slaw (page 152), made the day before and stored in the refrigerator, some leftover Poultry Stuffing (page 315) and an ice-cold glass of milk for a delicious meal.

- Precut fresh meat for stews or stir-fries saves time at home. Get to know the meat department staff — they will often cut meat and fish the way you want!

> ## Did You Know?
> While prepared foods can be convenient on occasion, many of them have added salt and sugar. Be sure to check the ingredient list and Nutrition Facts table.

- Frozen chopped vegetables are nutritious, and the prep work is done, so you can simply add them to soups, stews and stir-fries. Likewise, frozen chopped fruits can be used to make smoothies or pies, or thawed for a quick dessert. These items are likely to be more expensive than fresh, though, so decide whether the extra cost justifies the added convenience.

- Canned fruit in its own juice is a great start to a fruit salad.

- Peeled and cored pineapple makes a healthy dessert or a refreshing snack. You can also put it on the grill for a delicious accompaniment to barbecued meats.

- Frozen partially baked bread can be popped in the oven for a fresh-baked treat.

- Frozen pizza dough makes homemade pizza an easy option.

- Reduced-sodium or no-salt-added tomato sauce can be enriched with vegetables and meat at home.

- Reduced-sodium or no-salt-added soup can be used as a base; boost flavor and nutrition by adding vegetables, pasta or rice at home.

Become a Label Reader

Nutrition labeling is mandatory on most food packages. The labels help you figure out the nutritional value of foods, compare the nutritional content of products, manage special diets and increase or decrease your intake of a particular nutrient.

The Nutrition Facts table on food labels has a standardized format and must include information on amount of food; calories; total fat; saturated and trans fats; cholesterol; sodium; carbohydrate, fiber and sugars; protein; vitamin A; vitamin C; calcium; and iron. Here's some advice on using the Nutrition Facts table to your best advantage:

- Compare products with similar amounts of food.

- Choose foods with the least amount of saturated fat and no trans fats.

- Check the sodium content. You might be surprised by how high it can be in foods that don't even taste salty, such as breads and cereals.

- Check the amount of food the nutrition information is based on. The amount of food is not a recommended serving, but rather a reference amount for the nutrition information.

- Remember that many nutrient-rich foods, such as fresh fruits, vegetables and meats, are not required to have food labels. To learn about the nutrients in foods without labels, check out www.eatracker.ca.

Did You Know?

The percent Daily Value (% DV) in the Nutrition Facts table can help you compare foods to see whether they have a little or a lot of a nutrient. For example, 1 tbsp (15 mL) of light cream cheese provides 2% DV of calcium — a little calcium — whereas 1 cup (250 mL) of milk provides 30% DV of calcium — a lot of calcium. Remember, 5% DV or less is a little; 15% DV or more is a lot. This applies to all nutrients.

For more information, visit www.healthcanada.gc.ca/dailyvalue.

How to Use the Nutrient Analyses in This Book

In this book, each recipe is accompanied by a nutrient analysis that provides a snapshot of how many calories, energy-producing macronutrients (protein, fat and carbohydrate) and selected key micronutrients are in one serving. As you plan your meals, be conscious of portion size and look for dishes that give you many nutrients for few calories. Gradually, as you get in the habit of checking nutrient analyses, it will become second nature to choose recipes that provide a range of healthful nutrients.

Avoid Waste

There's much we can do to purchase only the food we need and minimize waste. A little planning goes a long way.

- Plan your weekly menu.
- Plan your grocery shopping around your weekly menu.
  - Buy only as much fresh product (fresh fruits and vegetables) as you will use. This may mean that you need to shop for fresh items twice a week to avoid spoilage.
  - Buy only what you need to replenish your shelves.
  - Be bargain-wise — it's only a good deal if you can use the product.
  - Stick to your list! It may be tempting to purchase foods that seem like a bargain, look attractive or smell divine, but if you can't use them, they'll just go to waste.
- Cook only as much as you will be able to eat now or save for another time. Big-batch cooking can be a time-saving technique, but be sure to store the extras safely. If you have more than you can use or freeze, take extras to a neighbor.
- Stay on top of foods.
  - Have a "Check Your Fridge Day," typically three or four days after a major grocery shopping trip. Look at what's on its last legs and do something with it so it's not wasted. Older leafy greens can be tossed into soups; older carrots and zucchini can be used to make muffins or quick breads; older berries and tender fruits can be puréed and added to smoothies. Practice food safety at all times. If a food begins to look moldy, don't use it. As always, when in doubt, throw it out.

- Check foods that are on your counter or in dry storage bins often. If bananas are getting overripe, freeze them for later use in breads or muffins. Stale (not moldy) bread can be cut into cubes, toasted and used as croutons or frozen and used to make stuffing.
- Check your freezer frequently. Better yet, keep a list of what's in it so you aren't surprised by freezer-burned mystery food tucked away at the back or bottom. When you store leftovers, be sure to label them, identifying the contents and the date you froze them, and try to use them up within three months.

Did You Know?

Food waste is a big problem in Canada. Some researchers estimate that as much as much as 40% of all food produced in Canada goes to waste.

- Compost organic matter. Everything from vegetable peelings and fruit rinds to coffee grounds, teabags, eggshells and lobster shells can be composted. If you live in an area that has a city-wide composting system, use it! If not, you can create your own compost pile/bin system: learn how on a reputable ecology website.

Learn How to Read and Follow a Recipe

Well-written recipes give you good guidance on how ingredients go together. But they have their own language, which you need to learn to follow a recipe successfully. Here are some tips, followed by a sample recipe (from page 276), with instructions on how to interpret the ingredient list and preparation instructions.

- The very first step in cooking is to read the recipe all the way through, from beginning to end. That way, you'll know you have all the ingredients and tools on hand, and you'll have a sense of the timing and the order in which tasks need to happen.

- A recipe usually indicates the number of servings it will make, based on average healthy portion sizes. Before starting to cook, check the number of servings. If the recipe makes more than you need, plan for leftovers. If it makes less, consider doubling it. For example, the sample recipe makes 8 servings. If you're a family of four, you'll have enough left over for another full meal.

- In this book, any special equipment you might need is listed at the top of the recipe.

- In a well-written recipe, ingredients are listed in the order they are used.

- Recipes are just guidelines, but when you're making one for the first time, it's important to follow the measurements exactly and measure accurately. As you become more experienced in cooking or after you have made a recipe a couple of times, you can try making adjustments to suit your tastes.

Did You Know?

When a recipe calls for a tablespoon or teaspoon, you're meant to use actual measuring utensils, not the spoons you use for eating and serving.

- In a recipe where both imperial and metric measurements are given, use either all metric or all imperial. Mixing and matching might compromise the success of the recipe.

- Even the order of words in an ingredient list is important, as it tells you something about how the foods should be prepared. For instance, if a recipe calls for "1 cup (250 mL) nuts, chopped," that is different from "1 cup (250 mL) chopped nuts." In the first case, you should measure 1 cup (250 mL) of shelled nuts, then chop them. In the second case, the nuts should be chopped first, then measured.

- Many recipes, including the ones in this book, make certain assumptions in the ingredient list. Common assumptions include: eggs are large unless otherwise specified; butter is salted unless otherwise indicated; all produce is medium-size and is washed before preparation, and inedible portions are discarded during prep.

- Look for any tips that accompany the recipe, as they can be very helpful. They might tell you where to find ingredients or how to prepare them, clarify an instruction or explain how to store the finished dish if you want to make it ahead. The tip in our sample recipe tells you an easy way to peel squash.

Did You Know?

The Dietitians of Canada website, www.dietitians.ca, has lots of ideas to help you plan, shop for and cook your meals.

Slow Cooker Squash Couscous

- **Minimum 5-quart slow cooker**

1	butternut squash (about 1$\frac{1}{2}$ lbs/750 g)	1
3 cups	cooked or rinsed drained canned chickpeas	750 mL
2 cups	chopped yellow summer squash or zucchini	500 mL
$\frac{1}{2}$ cup	thinly sliced onion	125 mL
$\frac{1}{2}$ cup	raisins	125 mL
2 tbsp	granulated sugar	30 mL
2 tsp	ground ginger	10 mL
$\frac{1}{2}$ tsp	ground turmeric	2 mL
$\frac{1}{2}$ tsp	freshly ground black pepper	2 mL
4 cups	reduced-sodium vegetable broth	1 L
2 tbsp	non-hydrogenated margarine	30 mL
1$\frac{1}{2}$ cups	couscous	375 mL
$\frac{1}{4}$ cup	coarsely chopped fresh parsley	60 mL

1. Peel butternut squash and cut the flesh into 1-inch (2.5 cm) cubes; you should have 4 to 5 cups (1 to 1.25 L) cubed squash.

2. In slow cooker stoneware, combine butternut squash, chickpeas, summer squash, onion, raisins, sugar, ginger, turmeric, pepper, broth and margarine. Cover and cook on Low for 4 to 5 hours or until vegetables are tender.

3. Uncover, increase heat to High and cook for 15 minutes or until liquid is reduced slightly. Using a slotted spoon, remove vegetable mixture to a large bowl. Cover and keep warm.

4. Place couscous in a large bowl and pour in 1$\frac{1}{2}$ cups (375 mL) of the hot broth from the slow cooker. Cover with plastic wrap and let stand for 5 to 10 minutes or until couscous is plumped. Fluff with a fork.

5. Spoon vegetable mixture over couscous and ladle the remaining broth over top. Sprinkle with parsley.

What the Ingredient list Says	What It Means
1 butternut squash (about 1½ lbs/750 g)	Buy a butternut squash that weighs about 1½ lbs (750 g). It's okay if it's a little under or over that weight.
3 cups (750 mL) cooked or rinsed drained canned chickpeas	You can either soak and cook dried chickpeas (see page 257) or use canned chickpeas, which you'll drain and rinse before measuring. Either way, you need to end up with 3 cups (750 mL).
2 cups (500 mL) chopped yellow summer squash or zucchini	You can use either yellow summer squash (also known as yellow zucchini) or green zucchini. Chop the squash first, then measure 2 cups (500 mL). Since the size of the chop is not specified, assume that you are meant to cut it into uniform bite-size pieces.
½ cup (125 mL) thinly sliced onion	Since the recipe does not specify a type of onion, you can assume that a yellow cooking onion is intended. Thinly slice the onion, then measure ½ cup (125 mL).
½ cup (125 mL) raisins	The type of raisin is not specified, so you can use either dark or golden raisins, whichever you prefer.
2 tbsp (30 mL) granulated sugar	Use white granulated sugar, not brown sugar or any other type.
2 tsp (10 mL) ground ginger	You're intended to use the packaged spice ground ginger. If fresh ginger was intended, the ingredient would read "minced gingerroot."
½ tsp (2 mL) ground turmeric	Use the packaged spice ground turmeric.
½ tsp (2 mL) freshly ground black pepper	For the best flavor, grind black peppercorns yourself. If you don't have a pepper mill, you can use preground black pepper.
4 cups (1 L) reduced-sodium vegetable broth	When you're at the grocery store, read the labels on different brands of vegetable broth and choose the one that's lowest in sodium.
2 tbsp (30 mL) non-hydrogenated margarine	Read the labels on different brands of margarine and choose one that's non-hydrogenated.
1½ cups (375 mL) couscous	You're meant to use raw couscous; otherwise, "cooked couscous" would be specified.
¼ cup (60 mL) coarsely chopped fresh parsley	Purchase fresh parsley, not dried. Pick the leaves off the stems, discarding the stems. Coarsely chop the leaves first, then measure.

What the Preparation Instructions Say	What They Mean
1. Peel butternut squash and cut the flesh into 1-inch (2.5 cm) cubes; you should have 4 to 5 cups (1 to 1.25 L) cubed squash.	After peeling the squash, do your best to cut it into even 1-inch (2.5 cm) cubes; the cooking time is based on pieces of this size. Since you've purchased a 1½-lb (750 g) squash, you should end up with somewhere between 4 and 5 cups (1 and 1.25 L) of cubes. If you're a little shy of 4 cups (1 L) or slightly over 5 cups (1.25 L), the recipe will still work.
2. In slow cooker stoneware, combine butternut squash, chickpeas, summer squash, onion, raisins, sugar, ginger, turmeric, pepper, broth and margarine. Cover and cook on Low for 4 to 5 hours or until vegetables are tender.	After combining the specified ingredients in the slow cooker, place the lid on top and turn the dial to the Low setting. Because slow cookers vary in power, it might take as little as 4 hours or as much as 5 hours for the vegetables to cook. After 4 hours, check to see how tender they are. If they're tender, move on to the next step. If not, keep cooking for up to another hour, checking once or twice, until they're ready.
3. Uncover, increase heat to High and cook for 15 minutes or until liquid is reduced slightly. Using a slotted spoon, remove vegetable mixture to a large bowl. Cover and keep warm.	Remove the lid and increase the heat so that some of the liquid boils off, thickening the sauce. Remove the vegetables, leaving the liquid in the slow cooker. Covering the vegetables will help keep them warm so they're enjoyable in the finished dish.
4. Place couscous in a large bowl and pour in 1½ cups (375 mL) of the hot broth from the slow cooker. Cover with plastic wrap and let stand for 5 to 10 minutes or until couscous is plumped. Fluff with a fork.	To rehydrate the couscous, ladle hot liquid from the slow cooker into a liquid measuring cup to measure 1½ cups (375 mL), then pour the liquid over the couscous. Use a large bowl, to make sure the couscous has enough room to expand as it absorbs the water. To help that process, the bowl needs to be covered and not disturbed. When the couscous is plumped, fluff it with a fork.
5. Spoon vegetable mixture over couscous and ladle the remaining broth over top. Sprinkle with parsley.	Use a large spoon to arrange the reserved vegetables on top of the couscous, then use a ladle to scoop up the remaining broth from the slow cooker and pour it over the mixture. Sprinkling the finished dish with parsley makes it even more attractive.

Cook with Ease and Confidence

Once you know how to read a recipe, your cooking skills will develop gradually as you practice and gain experience. You'll soon discover that being organized helps a lot in the kitchen, as in most things, so figure out the timing involved and have everything prepared and ready to go before you start a recipe. Before long, you'll be able to make little tweaks to recipes, adjusting them to your taste or to make them healthier.

Get a Handle on Timing

How many times have you started a recipe, only to realize there's no way it will be finished by the time everyone arrives at the dinner table? Timing is one of the reasons it's so important to read a recipe all the way through before starting to prepare it. As you read the recipe, you'll want to think about how much time each step will take, figure out whether any of them can be done simultaneously, then add it all up to come up with a total time. You can start by making written notes about timing; after a while, mental notes will likely suffice.

The steps to consider might include how long it will take to prepare the ingredients (is there a lot of chopping involved, or do you just have to measure?); how much cooking time is involved (there may be several stages of cooking, such as browning, then sautéing, then baking); and whether you need to allow time for steps such as marinating, rising (as with breads), resting (as with roasts), cooling (as with cakes) or chilling (as with dips).

As an example, have a look at the sample recipe on page 24. When you read the ingredient list, one of the first things you'll see is that you need cooked or canned chickpeas. If you decide to use canned chickpeas, no big deal: it will only take a couple of minutes to open the can, drain off the liquid and rinse the chickpeas. But if you want to use cooked chickpeas, that's a whole different scenario. The process of soaking and cooking dried legumes can take anywhere from $1\frac{1}{2}$ hours to overnight, depending on what methods you use, so that's a big chunk of time you'll need to figure in.

Next, you'll note that you have to chop two kinds of squash and thinly slice some onion. Depending on your knife skills, this will probably take about 15 or 20 minutes. Add another 5 minutes or so for measuring out the remaining ingredients. The cooking time itself takes 4 to 5 hours plus 15 minutes, then you reconstitute the couscous for 5 to 10 minutes. You can chop the parsley while the couscous is plumping. To be on the safe side, tack on another 5 or 10 minutes to account for the small miscellaneous tasks you need to perform here and there throughout.

Assuming you decide to use canned chickpeas, you're looking at a minimum total time of $4\frac{3}{4}$ hours and a maximum total time of 6 hours — you'll know which is more accurate as you get to know your slow cooker and how quickly you are able to perform each task. If you want to have dinner on the table around 6:00 p.m., you'll need to start cooking by 1:45 at the latest and possibly as early as noon. (Of course, the beauty of the slow cooker is that, for most of that time, you don't actually have to be attentive to the cooking process; you're only needed for a little while at the beginning and the end.)

Did You Know?

In the early 1900s, women spent as much as 44 hours a week preparing meals! These days, it's common to spend as little as 15 minutes getting a meal on the table.

Get Everything Ready

The French term *mise en place* is chef talk for "having everything in place, ready to go." Getting organized in advance, before you start cooking, will streamline the process, make cooking easier and make it more likely that you'll end up with a successful dish.

Start with a clean kitchen — there is nothing more frustrating than trying to cook when your counters are cluttered and the utensils you need are dirty. Next, set out everything you'll need to prepare the recipe. Mise en place can include:

- preparing bowls, pots and pans (setting out containers of the right size, greasing pans, etc.);
- setting out all the utensils and tools you'll need (there's nothing worse than being in the middle of a recipe and realizing you need the food processor, which is buried at the back of a cupboard);
- having towels handy to wipe up spills;
- preparing ingredients (chopping vegetables, fruit and herbs, trimming meat, etc.);
- measuring ingredients into cups or bowls;
- having a waste area nearby for compost and other garbage;
- having a sink ready with hot water and soap for washing your hands and equipment.

Did You Know?

When you watch a cooking show, and the chef has all the ingredients chopped, measured and laid out in individual bowls, that's mise en place in action!

Add Taste, Not Fat or Salt

You can add flavor to your meals without adding fat or salt by using herbs and spices to season foods. For instance, a sprinkling of finely chopped fresh dill makes a fillet of grilled fish spring to life, as does a dollop of horseradish on a slice of beef. You can also create your own salt-free spice mixture.

Make Recipes Healthier

The recipes in *Dietitians of Canada Cook!* are dietitian-approved and nutritious. But when you're following a recipe from another source, you might be able to modify it to boost the nutritional value. Even small changes can sometimes create big savings in fat, sugar or calories. There are also simple ways to add fiber to your favorite recipes.

Reduce Fat

- Use low-fat plain yogurt instead of sour cream in dips, dressings and baked products.
- Substitute skim, 1% or 2% milk for whole milk in baked items such as muffins or quick breads.
- Reduce the amount of oil in baking recipes by up to a third and replace it with an equal amount of unsweetened applesauce, pumpkin purée (not pie filling), mashed banana or prune purée (baby food).
- Bake or broil meats and vegetables rather than frying them.
- Moisten absorbent toweling with a small amount of oil and lightly coat the bottom of the pan before you sauté foods.
- Use a smaller quantity of a stronger-tasting cheese to replace a mild cheese. For example, substitute Parmesan, old Cheddar or Asiago for mozzarella or brick.
- Drain fat after browning ground meats.
- Try vegetarian ground round in place of ground meat in chilis, casseroles and stews.
- Substitute vegetables for some of the meat. If a stew calls for 2 lbs (1 kg) of meat, use 1½ lbs (750 g) and make up the difference with extra vegetables or legumes.

- Cook poultry stuffing in a separate dish, outside the bird, so it won't soak up fat in the cooking process.

- Skim fat off gravy with a gravy separator or, better still, chill the gravy. The fat will rise to the surface and harden, making it easier to skim off. You can then reheat the gravy before serving.

- Season vegetables with lemon juice, herbs and vinegar instead of butter or margarine.

- Add plain yogurt to a baked potato instead of butter and sour cream.

Did You Know?

Small, gradual changes in how you shop, cook and eat can make a big difference to your nutritional health. Soon, your new habits will become a way of life and healthy eating will be easy.

Reduce Sugar

- Reduce sugar by a third in recipes such as cookies, muffins, squares and quick breads. Use extra cinnamon, nutmeg or cloves (just add a little, to taste).

- Use canned fruits packed in their own juice instead of syrup.

Increase Fiber

- Add ground flaxseed, wheat bran or oatmeal to quick breads.

- Replace up to half of the all-purpose flour with whole wheat flour when making muffins, cookies, bars or quick breads.

- Choose brown or wild rice instead of white rice.

- Choose whole wheat pasta or white pasta with added fiber instead of white pasta.

Did You Know?

There are two types of fiber: soluble fiber, found in foods like apples, carrots and legumes; and insoluble fiber (commonly known as "roughage"), found in foods like wheat bran, whole flax seeds and the skins of fruits and vegetables. Both types are important for health. Choose a range of whole-grain products daily, along with legumes, fruits and vegetables, to meet your daily fiber needs.

Food Topics on the Minds of Canadians

With the renewed interest in food and cooking in Canada, many Canadians have questions about some hot topics. Here are the answers to your frequently asked questions.

Can I be a locavore in Canada?

"Locavore" was the 2007 *New Oxford American Dictionary* Word of the Year. Combining "local" and the suffix "-vore," meaning "eater" (think of "herbivore" and "carnivore"), it refers to the trend of using locally grown and seasonally available foods.

Depending on where you live in Canada, being a locavore year-round can present a challenge when it comes to fresh fruits and vegetables, as most of the country freezes through the winter months. Take advantage of the local harvest to eat delicious, nutritious vegetables and fruits when they are in season. When they're at their peak, freeze or preserve them so you'll have a ready and steady supply of local produce throughout the winter.

Choosing locally produced meat, dairy and grain products is easier to do year-round. A great place to start is at a farmers' market, where you can ask farmers of cattle, chickens, hogs, fish or game how they raise the animals, the type of feed they use, the type of farming practices they employ and so on. Ask egg, dairy and grain farmers whether their products are organic, how far they travel to the market and any other questions that interest you.

You can also ask the manager of your grocery store what local foods they stock.

Are locally produced fruits and vegetables more nutritious?

While this is a commonly held premise, there is limited evidence to back it up. Several factors that affect the nutritional quality of produce prevent us from making the generalization that locally produced fruits and vegetables contain more nutrients than their counterparts from afar. These factors include:

- **Crop variety.** Some crops have been bred for specific characteristics, but the benefits of this type of breeding sometimes come at the expense of nutrient content. For example, some research indicates that higher-yielding tomato plants produce tomatoes that are lower in nutrients.

- **Ripeness at harvest and handling, storage and transportation post-harvest.** Most produce tastes best and contains the most nutrients when it's harvested at the peak of ripeness, but inappropriate handling and long storage of ripe produce post-harvest can diminish nutrient quality. So, to retain the maximum nutrients, produce should be picked at its peak; carefully handled to prevent bruising; chilled quickly to remove field heat, to prevent further ripening; and kept at the optimal temperature and humidity during

transport. A breakdown in any of these processes can diminish nutrient content, regardless of whether the produce is grown locally and brought to a farmers' market or transported from a great distance. (But it sure makes a case for growing strawberries in your own backyard and picking them in the morning to enjoy on your cereal!)

Tempting as it may be, there is no conclusive evidence to support the claim that locally grown foods are more nutritious than foods produced and imported from farther away. But don't let that stop you from supporting local farmers, as there are many other good reasons to do so.

Are canned and frozen fruits and vegetables nutritious?

Canned and frozen fruits and vegetables are typically harvested and packed when nutrients are at their peak. If they contain no added sugar, fat or salt, they are healthy choices, and are sometimes more affordable than fresh produce. They're also practical options for people who live in remote areas, and they allow all Canadians to enjoy a variety of produce year-round.

If I buy locally grown food, does that mean it's organic?

No. "Locally grown" and "organic" have different meanings. Not all locally produced foods are organically grown, and not all organically grown foods are locally produced. When you're shopping at a farmers' market, ask farmers about their growing practices.

Are organic foods more nutritious?

Evidence shows that some organic foods may be higher in certain nutrients, such as vitamin C, but current data are not consistent enough to make conclusive statements about other nutrients. Purchasing organic food is a personal choice that may depend upon its availability, price and appearance, as well as your personal values, such as a preference for this food production method and a desire to safeguard the environment.

Are there growth hormones in the milk I drink in Canada?

No. The growth hormone rBST (recombinant bovine somatotropin) is not legal in Canada and is therefore not used in dairy production.

How can I get a healthy meal on the table for minimal cost?

Cost is very important for many Canadians when they're shopping for food. To keep costs down while providing the best nutrition for your family, select foods that pack a big nutrient punch for a small price. For example, choose meat alternatives such as eggs, beans and lentils more often. Canned or frozen fruits and vegetables and some dried fruits (such as raisins) can also be lower-cost options. Locally grown fruits and vegetables are often less expensive than their imported counterparts. See page 19 for more ideas on keeping healthy meals affordable.

What does it mean when a food is labeled "Product of Canada"?

The "Product of Canada" label means that all major ingredients in the product must come from Canada and any labor needed to create the product must be done in Canada. The product can contain minor additions, such as spices, food additives, vitamins or minerals, that are produced outside Canada.

Why are there preservatives and other food additives in processed foods?

Food manufacturers and processers use food additives for various reasons, such as to preserve foods or improve their appearance. Here are examples of some preservatives and food additives, and their functions:

- **Anti-caking agents** keep powdered or granulated foods running freely (e.g., calcium silicate in table salt).

- **Enzymes** help produce desired chemical reactions (e.g., rennet helps curdle milk in the cheesemaking process).

- **Preservatives** inhibit the growth of molds, yeasts and bacteria (e.g., calcium propionate in bread).

- **Texture-modifying agents** create a desired consistency (e.g., carrageenan in ice cream).

- **Salt** and ingredients containing sodium preserve the quality and safety of foods by inhibiting the growth of bacteria, yeasts and molds, helping to prevent spoilage. The foods most commonly preserved with salt are cured ready-to-eat meats and processed cheese products. In fermented foods, such as pickles, salt suppresses spoilage organisms and allows lactic acid bacteria to produce acid; the increased acidity contributes to flavor and helps limit further microbial growth. While salt plays a valuable role in food preservation, consumers should limit their intake of sodium, as it is known to affect blood pressure.

What is "healthy food"?

There is no commonly accepted definition of "healthy food." Foods that contain high amounts of nutrients while providing reasonable amounts of energy are usually considered healthy. But really, all foods can be a part of healthy eating. Indeed, "healthy eating" is a more useful term than "healthy food": it means that you eat a variety of nutrient-rich foods to meet your daily energy needs and choose foods with few nutrients and many calories only occasionally.

Breakfast and Brunch

It's no wonder this is the most important meal of the day, as it literally means to "break the fast." After many hours of sleep, with no energy fueling the body, it's time to rev up your body with food. The benefits of breakfast are well known. Not only does a morning meal help you feel alert, but eating breakfast on a regular basis can help adults manage their weight. Children who eat breakfast are more alert in school and are a healthier weight than those who skip it. If you go without breakfast, you also miss out on an opportunity to get important nutrients, and it can be difficult to make up for that over the rest of the day.

So, Just What Makes a "Good" Breakfast?

A general guideline is to include foods from at least three of the four food groups, always including a source of protein. Protein gives staying power to your morning and keeps you from feeling hungry too soon. Examples of protein-rich foods include eggs, milk, cheese, yogurt, peanut butter, beans, fortified soy beverages, meat, fish and poultry.

But... chicken for breakfast? Why not? While a standard Canadian breakfast may include poached or boiled eggs, milk- or soy-based smoothies or cereal with milk, there's no rule that says leftover baked chicken or pot roast, black bean soup, stir-fried tofu, pizza or grilled cheese sandwiches can't be eaten at breakfast. What's most important is to find a delicious, protein-rich food that you and your family enjoy.

It's a great habit to sit down, relax and enjoy your breakfast. Sometimes, though, that's just not possible and it's necessary to have breakfast on the go. If you find yourself at risk of missing this important meal altogether, try a little nighttime planning:

- Set out your breakfast cereal, bowl and spoon.
- Have fresh fruit cut up in the fridge, ready to eat.
- Boil eggs and keep them in the fridge.
- Prepare and cook extra pancakes, French toast or waffles and freeze them. In the morning, pop one in the toaster and enjoy it with a glass of juice and a boiled egg.
- Portion out a favorite leftover and reheat it in the microwave.

You can also plan to take something with you on the go. Ideal take-along breakfasts include:

- A peanut butter (or other nut butter) and jam sandwich on whole-grain bread, a handful of grapes and unsweetened 100% juice in an insulated container.
- A leftover slice of homemade pizza on whole-grain crust, a banana and milk in an insulated container.
- Leftover homemade vegetable soup in an insulated container, a whole-grain bun and a few cubes of cheese.
- Yogurt and granola in a reusable container and an apple.
- A fruit and yogurt smoothie in an insulated container and a homemade muffin.

You get the idea!

All About Oats

Perfect oatmeal depends on the type of oats you use, so it's best to follow the instructions on the food package or carton. You can get a nutritional boost by using milk or soy beverage as the liquid, instead of water. You can also top oatmeal with a variety of fresh or dried fruits, nuts and seeds. Remember, the best nutrition comes from the oats that have been processed the least.

- **Groats** are the least processed oats: the grain is washed and only the outer husk is removed. They are also generally toasted.
- **Steel-cut oats** are groats that have been cut into two or three pieces; they are not rolled.
- **Rolled oats** are just that: after being steamed, the groats are flattened by huge rollers. These are also called old-fashioned oats.
- **Quick-cooking rolled oats** result when the groats are cut into several pieces before being steamed and flattened. The smaller pieces cook much more quickly than regular rolled oats. Old-fashioned rolled oats and quick-cooking rolled oats can often be used interchangeably in recipes, but it's still best to follow the recipe guidelines.
- **Instant oats** have been precooked and dried before cutting and rolling, so that when hot liquid is added they instantly turn into a hot cereal. Do not substitute instant oats in recipes calling for rolled or quick-cooking oats.

Boning Up for Breakfast!

Foods in the Milk and Alternatives group, such as milk, cheese, yogurt and fortified soy beverage, are often included in a typical Canadian breakfast. They are a delicious way to get calcium, vitamin D and many other vitamins and minerals that your body needs every day. Calcium and vitamin D play important roles in keeping bones strong and healthy, and you need these important nutrients throughout your life. When choosing Milk and Alternatives:

- Know how much you need every day. *Eating Well with Canada's Food Guide* recommends that Canadians age two and older have 2 cups (500 mL) of milk every day. Depending on your age and sex, you may need additional servings.

Drink fortified soy beverage if you do not drink milk.

- Know what constitutes a serving size. Examples include:
  - 1 cup (250 mL) milk or reconstituted powdered milk
  - ½ cup (125 mL) canned evaporated milk
  - 1 cup (250 mL) fortified soy beverage — check to make sure your brand is fortified
  - ¾ cup (175 mL) yogurt — yogurts made with vitamin D–fortified milk may contain a significant amount of vitamin D; look for brands that say they contain more than 15% of the daily value (% DV) for vitamin D
  - 1½ oz (45 g) cheese (about the size of 3 dominoes)

Family Cooking Lesson

Hard-Cooked Eggs

Eggs provide the perfect protein and are very versatile. Having hard-cooked eggs on hand in the refrigerator provides a great start to breakfast on the go, a quick snack or the beginnings of a great lunch: they can be the basis of egg salad or a great topping for spinach salad.

What You Need

6-cup (1.5 L) bowl	1 cup (250 mL) ice	Small saucepan
Water	6 eggs	Slotted spoon

How to Hard-Cook Eggs

1. Fill the 6-cup (1.5 L) bowl with water and ice and set it aside. (This will be the ice bath in which to place the cooked eggs.)

2. Carefully place the eggs in the bottom of the saucepan. Add enough water to cover them. Bring to a boil, then remove from the heat, cover and let stand for 18 to 23 minutes.

3. Transfer the eggs to the prepared ice bath (this will prevent them from cooking further). When the eggs are cool enough to handle, peel them and use as desired, or place them in a small bowl, cover and refrigerate for up to 5 days.

Note: When eggs are overcooked, they get a green ring around the yolk. They are still safe to eat, but many people find the color unappetizing.

✔ Kid Approved

Here's a quick breakfast that kids can easily make for themselves in the morning. You can help them measure out the ingredients the night before.

Variations

Add nuts and/or fresh or dried fruits of your choice.

Stir in fortified soy beverage or low-fat milk.

Sweeten with brown sugar or maple syrup.

Serving Idea

For a wholesome breakfast, serve with nuts, fruit and milk or soy beverage on the side.

Hot Breakfast Cereal Mix

David Shaikh, Ontario

2 tbsp	old-fashioned rolled oats	30 mL
2 tbsp	wheat bran	30 mL
1 tbsp	wheat germ	15 mL
1 tbsp	soy beverage powder	15 mL

1. In a small, microwave-safe cup, stir together oats, bran, wheat germ and soy beverage powder. Stir in $\frac{1}{2}$ cup (125 mL) water. Microwave on High for 1 to $1\frac{1}{2}$ minutes or until oats are tender.

> David suggests enjoying this with a cup of ginger tea. Simply fill a microwave-safe mug with water and add 2 thin slices of peeled gingerroot. Microwave on High for 2 minutes. Remove the ginger and stir in 1 tsp (5 mL) liquid honey, if desired.

Nutrients per serving

Calories	114
Fat	1.8 g
Saturated fat	0.4 g
Sodium	5 mg (0% DV)
Carbohydrate	19 g
Fiber	6 g (24% DV)
Protein	9 g
Calcium	44 mg (4% DV)
Iron	2.9 mg (21% DV)

Very high in: Magnesium

High in: Zinc and thiamine

Diabetes Food Choice Values:

1   Carbohydrate

**Makes 10 cups
(2.5 L)**

Serving size: ½ cup
(125 mL)

✔ Kid Approved

Joanne has been making
this granola for years
and always keeps a big
jar on her kitchen island.
Her teenage sons are
elite athletes and can eat
mountains of it.

Tips

If you can't find barley flakes,
use 6 cups (1.5 L) old-fashioned
rolled oats.

To easily stir the oat-honey
mixture, use clean hands
lightly coated with oil.

Nutrients per serving

Calories	315
Fat	14.6 g
Saturated fat	1.4 g
Sodium	8 mg (0% DV)
Carbohydrate	43 g
Fiber	7 g (28% DV)
Protein	9 g
Calcium	59 mg (5% DV)
Iron	2.5 mg (18% DV)

Very high in: Magnesium

High in: Zinc, folate and
thiamine

Diabetes Food Choice Values:

2½ Carbohydrates
½ Meat & Alternatives
3 Fats

Great Grains, Fruit and Nut Granola with Honey and Almond Butter

Joanne Rankin, Dietitian, British Columbia

- **Preheat oven to 325°F (160°C)**
- **Rimmed baking sheet**

½ cup	walnut halves	125 mL
½ cup	hazelnuts	125 mL
½ cup	almonds	125 mL
⅔ cup	almond butter or other natural nut butter	150 mL
½ cup	liquid honey	125 mL
2 tbsp	canola oil	30 mL
3 cups	old-fashioned rolled oats	750 mL
3 cups	barley flakes	750 mL
1 cup	wheat germ	250 mL
½ cup	ground flax seeds (flaxseed meal)	125 mL
1 tsp	vanilla extract	5 mL
½ cup	chopped dried apricots	125 mL
½ cup	raisins	125 mL
½ cup	chopped dates	125 mL

1. Spread walnuts, hazelnuts and almonds on baking sheet. Toast in preheated oven for about 15 minutes or until fragrant and lightly browned. Check often and stir during the final 5 minutes to avoid burning. Remove from oven, leaving oven on, and transfer nuts to a cutting board. Let cool completely, then coarsely chop.

2. In a medium, microwave-safe bowl, stir together almond butter, honey and oil. Microwave on High for about 1 minute or until bubbly. Set aside.

3. In a large bowl, stir together oats, barley flakes, wheat germ and flax seeds. Stir in hot honey mixture. Spread evenly on baking sheet.

4. Bake for 30 minutes. Every 10 minutes, remove from oven to stir, bringing grains from the outside to the center. Let cool completely on baking sheet on a wire rack.

5. Return to the bowl, sprinkle with vanilla and stir to combine. Stir in chopped nuts, apricots, raisins and dates.

> *Eating Well with Canada's Food Guide* considers nuts a meat alternative. A quarter cup (60 mL) is considered one serving. Nuts contain ample amounts of fat, so pay attention to portion size. For example, one handful of shelled roasted peanuts (about ½ cup/125 mL) provides just over 400 calories, with about three-quarters of the calories coming from fat.

Tips

While it's baking, be sure to stir the oat mixture every 10 minutes to prevent the edges from burning. If you prefer larger chunks of granola, do not stir after it comes out of the oven for the final time.

To store, divide granola among airtight containers and store at room temperature for up to 1 month.

Variation

You can vary the nuts and dried fruits, depending on preference and availability. This is also delicious with dried blueberries, cranberries and cherries.

Serving Idea

Make yogurt parfaits: Place ¼ cup (60 mL) granola in a parfait or sundae glass. Layer with ½ cup (125 mL) chopped fresh fruit and ¾ cup (175 mL) yogurt. Sprinkle 2 tsp (10 mL) granola on top.

These eggs are a unique alternative for your weekend brunch — or even for supper. If you're only serving two people, prepare the full recipe of beans anyway and reserve half to make burritos the next day.

Tip

A standard 19-oz (540 mL) can of beans yields about 2 cups (500 mL) drained and rinsed beans. If you have smaller or larger cans, you can use the volume called for or just add the amount from your can. To help remove excess sodium, drain canned beans in a colander and rinse thoroughly under cold running water before adding them to your recipe.

Nutrients per serving

Calories	349
Fat	13.6 g
Saturated fat	5.0 g
Sodium	539 mg (22% DV)
Carbohydrate	41 g
Fiber	8 g (32% DV)
Protein	18 g
Calcium	156 mg (14% DV)
Iron	2.6 mg (19% DV)

Very high in: Magnesium, folate, vitamin B_{12} and niacin

High in: Zinc, vitamin A, thiamine and riboflavin

Diabetes Food Choice Values:

2	Carbohydrates
2	Meat & Alternatives
1	Fat

Hearty Tex-Mex Brunch Eggs

Desiree Nielsen, Dietitian, British Columbia

- Preheat broiler
- Baking sheet

Bean Mixture

1 cup	canned or cooked black beans, drained and rinsed (see tip, at left)	250 mL
2 cups	frozen corn kernels	500 mL
2 cups	cherry tomatoes, halved	500 mL
2 tsp	finely chopped jalapeño pepper	10 mL
1 tsp	curry powder	5 mL
1 tsp	chili powder	5 mL

Tortilla Crackers

2	large whole wheat tortillas	2
2 tsp	butter, softened	10 mL

Eggs

1 tsp	canola oil	5 mL
4	eggs	4
½ cup	shredded part-skim mozzarella or Cheddar cheese	125 mL

1. *Bean mixture:* In a large saucepan, combine beans, corn, tomatoes, jalapeño, curry powder, chili powder and ¼ cup (60 mL) water. Bring to a boil over medium-high heat. Reduce heat and simmer, stirring occasionally, for 20 minutes.

2. *Crackers:* Meanwhile, spread tortillas with butter. Place on baking sheet and broil for about 45 seconds or until golden and crisp. Set aside.

3. *Eggs:* In a large nonstick skillet, heat oil over medium-high heat. Fry eggs to desired consistency (they may be left sunny side up or turned over).

4. Divide bean mixture evenly among four large soup bowls. Top each with 1 cooked egg and 2 tbsp (30 mL) shredded cheese. Serve each with half a tortilla cracker.

Tortillas are a Mexican flatbread made from ground maize (corn) or wheat flour. You can find flour tortillas in most grocery stores, often flavored with ingredients such as sun-dried tomatoes or pesto.

Tips

The bean mixture will freeze well if there's any left over. Transfer cooled beans to an airtight container and freeze for up to 3 months.

Be sure to watch the tortilla crackers while they bake, as they can burn quickly.

Variations

Vary the heat in the bean mixture to your liking by adjusting the amount of jalapeño pepper used.

For added kick, use Monterey Jack cheese with jalapeño peppers in place of the mozzarella.

✔ **Kid Approved**

These colorful eggs use ingredients that are readily available in most parts of Canada.

Tips

You can use canola oil or butter in this recipe. Butter provides added flavor but is from an animal source and therefore contains saturated fat. Canola oil contains unsaturated fat.

If you're short on time, you can use store-bought tzatziki instead of homemade.

Serving Idea

Serve for brunch along with a Kid-Friendly Garden Salad (page 155) and whole-grain toast.

Nutrients per serving

Calories	204
Fat	11.7 g
Saturated fat	4.5 g
Sodium	261 mg (11% DV)
Carbohydrate	10 g
Fiber	1 g (4% DV)
Protein	12 g
Calcium	240 mg (22% DV)
Iron	1.5 mg (11% DV)

Very high in: Folate, vitamin B_{12} and riboflavin

High in: Zinc, vitamin A, vitamin C and niacin

Diabetes Food Choice Values:

1	Carbohydrate
1	Meat & Alternatives
½	Fat

Local Veggie Scrambled Eggs

Mary Sue Waisman, Dietitian, Nova Scotia

8	eggs	8
¼ cup	Homemade Tzatziki (see box, below)	60 mL
½ cup	crumbled feta cheese	125 mL
1 tsp	dried oregano	5 mL
½ tsp	freshly ground black pepper	2 mL
2 tsp	canola oil or butter	10 mL
½ cup	finely chopped green onions	125 mL
½ cup	chopped cooked potato	125 mL
½ cup	chopped roasted red bell peppers	125 mL
½ cup	chopped lightly steamed asparagus	125 mL

1. In a medium bowl, whisk together eggs, tzatziki, feta, oregano and pepper; set aside.

2. In a large nonstick skillet, heat oil over medium heat. Sauté green onions and potato for 4 to 5 minutes or until lightly browned. Add roasted peppers and asparagus; sauté until heated through.

3. Pour in egg mixture and cook, stirring with a wooden spoon, for 2 to 3 minutes or until eggs form soft, thick curds.

Homemade Tzatziki

Line a sieve with cheesecloth and set over a bowl. Pour in 2 cups (500 mL) plain yogurt (gelatin- and starch-free). Cover and refrigerate; let drain for 1 to 3 hours or until yogurt is thickened. Discard liquid in bowl. In a small bowl, combine drained yogurt, ½ cup (125 mL) drained grated cucumber and 2 cloves pressed garlic. Cover tightly with plastic wrap and refrigerate for at least 30 minutes or for up to 1 day.

Spinach and Pesto Crustless Quiche

Daphna Gale, Ontario

● **Preheat oven to 350°F (180°C)**
● **9-inch (23 cm) glass pie plate, lightly greased**

5	eggs	5
½ cup	2% evaporated milk	125 mL
⅓ cup	basil pesto	75 mL
1	package (10 oz/300 g) frozen spinach, thawed, drained and squeezed dry	1
1 cup	shredded part-skim mozzarella cheese	250 mL
½ cup	crumbled feta cheese	125 mL

1. In a medium bowl, whisk together eggs, evaporated milk and pesto. Stir in spinach, mozzarella and feta. Transfer to prepared baking dish.

2. Bake in preheated oven for 25 to 30 minutes or until center is firm. Let rest for 5 minutes before serving.

Nutrients per serving

Calories	165
Fat	11.4 g
Saturated fat	4.6 g
Sodium	367 mg (15% DV)
Carbohydrate	5 g
Fiber	1 g (4% DV)
Protein	11 g
Calcium	252 mg (23% DV)
Iron	1.1 mg (8% DV)

Very high in: Vitamin A and vitamin B_{12}

High in: Magnesium, folate and riboflavin

Diabetes Food Choice Values:

1   Meat & Alternatives
1   Fat

Makes 12 mini quiches

Serving size: 1 mini quiche

✔ Kid Approved

Kids can choose and combine their own filling for these mini quiches, which are perfect for brunch or lunch. They're a brilliant way to please children and adults with different taste preferences.

Tips

For picky eaters, omit the filling and simply top the egg mixture with shredded regular or light Cheddar cheese.

If everyone wants cheese, you can mix it in with the eggs instead of adding it to each muffin tin.

Personalized Crustless Mini Quiches

Connie Mallette, Ontario

- **Preheat oven to 350°F (180°C)**
- **12-cup muffin pan, lightly greased**

10	eggs	10
¼ cup	1% milk	60 mL
½ tsp	dry mustard	2 mL
½ tsp	additional seasonings, such as dried basil, dried oregano or chili powder (optional)	2 mL
¼ tsp	salt (optional)	1 mL
¼ tsp	freshly ground black pepper	1 mL

Filling

Greek: finely chopped onions, tomatoes and black olives, crumbled light feta cheese

Veggie: finely chopped bell peppers, onions and mushrooms, shredded regular or light Cheddar cheese

Green: frozen chopped spinach or broccoli, thawed and well drained, finely chopped onion, shredded light Cheddar cheese

---

Nutrients per serving (Greek Mini Quiche)

Calories	82
Fat	5.4 g
Saturated fat	1.9 g
Sodium	137 mg (6% DV)
Carbohydrate	2 g
Fiber	0 g (0% DV)
Protein	7 g
Calcium	46 mg (4% DV)
Iron	0.5 mg (4% DV)

High in: Vitamin B_{12}

Diabetes Food Choice Values:
1   Meat & Alternatives

Nutrients per serving (Veggie Mini Quiche)

Calories	81
Fat	5.4 g
Saturated fat	2.1 g
Sodium	75 mg (3% DV)
Carbohydrate	1 g
Fiber	0 g (0% DV)
Protein	6 g
Calcium	54 mg (5% DV)
Iron	0.5 mg (4% DV)

High in: Vitamin B_{12}

Diabetes Food Choice Values:
1   Meat & Alternatives

Nutrients per serving (Green Mini Quiche)

Calories	75
Fat	4.6 g
Saturated fat	1.5 g
Sodium	86 mg (4% DV)
Carbohydrate	2 g
Fiber	0 g (0% DV)
Protein	7 g
Calcium	55 mg (5% DV)
Iron	0.5 mg (4% DV)

High in: Vitamin B_{12}

Diabetes Food Choice Values:
1   Meat & Alternatives

1. In a large bowl, whisk together eggs, milk, mustard, seasonings (if using), salt (if using) and pepper.
2. Place 2 tbsp (30 mL) filling in each muffin cup. Divide egg mixture evenly among muffin cups. Top with cheese, if using.
3. Bake in preheated oven for 20 minutes or until a knife inserted in the center comes out clean.

Quiche is a tart that traditionally has a pastry crust and a custard filling. Cheese and other savory ingredients are often added for a range of diverse flavors. Quiche Lorraine originated in the Lorraine region of France and is made with eggs, cream and bacon or lardons. Soon after the Second World War, quiche became popular in North America. Eliminating the pastry, for a crustless version, reduces the calories and fat.

Tip

Cooked mini quiches can be cooled, transferred to an airtight container and frozen for up to 1 month. To reheat, place on a baking sheet and bake at 350°F (180°C) for 15 minutes or until heated through. If you're in a hurry, defrost in the microwave and reheat on Medium (50%) until warm.

Serving Idea

If you're preparing these for a brunch party, make a variety of flavors. Set them out with labels on the buffet table so guests can choose their favorites. Add our Seasonal Fruit Platter with Honey Yogurt Dip (page 56) and Marla's Pumpkin Walnut Bran Muffins (page 319) to complete a lovely brunch menu.

Makes 7 large
waffles

Serving size: $\frac{1}{2}$ waffle

✔ **Kid Approved**

The nutty taste of whole
wheat flour offers a
delicious taste alternative
to regular waffles.

Tips

Young children can break
the eggs for the batter. With
supervision, older children can
help pour the batter onto the
waffle maker.

To ease cleanup, be sure to
wipe any spills off the waffle
maker after making each
waffle.

Depending on the size and
shape of your waffle maker,
the number of waffles you get
from this recipe may vary.

Serving Idea

Serve topped with fresh
berries and Berry Canadian
Maple Sauce (page 55).

Nutrients per serving

Calories	211
Fat	9.8 g
Saturated fat	1.3 g
Sodium	166 mg (7% DV)
Carbohydrate	25 g
Fiber	2 g (8% DV)
Protein	6 g
Calcium	130 mg (12% DV)
Iron	1.4 mg (10% DV)

High in: Folate

Diabetes Food Choice Values:

1½ Carbohydrates

2 Fats

Weekend Wheaty Waffles

Kim Knott, Dietitian, Manitoba

- Preheat oven to 200°F (100°C)
- Belgian waffle maker, preheated to medium-high

2 cups	all-purpose flour	500 mL
1 cup	whole wheat flour	250 mL
2 tbsp	baking powder	30 mL
2 tbsp	granulated sugar	30 mL
3	eggs	3
3 cups	1% milk	750 mL
½ cup	canola oil	125 mL
	Vegetable cooking spray	

1. In a large bowl, combine all-purpose flour, whole wheat flour, baking powder and sugar.

2. In another large bowl, whisk together eggs, milk and oil. Add to flour mixture and stir until well blended.

3. Spray preheated waffle maker lightly with cooking spray. Pour ¾ cup (175 mL) batter onto waffle maker (or an amount appropriate for your waffle maker) and cook for 3 minutes or until golden brown. Transfer to a plate and keep warm in preheated oven. Repeat with the remaining batter, spraying waffle maker between batches as needed.

Serving size:
2 pancakes

✔ Kid Approved

Janice started making these pancakes over 30 years ago! They are the fluffiest ones she's ever made, and her grown children now make them even more often than she does.

Tip

To make these pancakes quickly in the morning, stir together the dry ingredients and wet ingredients in separate bowls the night before. Be sure to refrigerate the wet ingredients.

Serving Idea

Serve with a wedge of Canadian cheese and Canadian Summertime Fruit Salad with Vanilla Maple Yogurt Dressing (page 142).

Nutrients per serving

Calories	184
Fat	3.7 g
Saturated fat	0.8 g
Sodium	231 mg (10% DV)
Carbohydrate	31 g
Fiber	2 g (8% DV)
Protein	7 g
Calcium	132 mg (12% DV)
Iron	1.5 mg (11% DV)

High in: Folate, thiamine and riboflavin

Diabetes Food Choice Values:

2 Carbohydrates
½ Fat

Fluffy Pancakes

Janice Macdonald, Dietitian, British Columbia

● **Preheat oven to 200°F (100°C)**

1¼ cups	all-purpose flour	300 mL
¾ cup	whole wheat flour	75 mL
2 tbsp	granulated sugar	30 mL
1 tbsp	baking powder	15 mL
¼ tsp	salt	1 mL
1	egg	1
1¾ cups	1% milk	425 mL
1 tbsp	canola oil	15 mL
	Vegetable cooking spray	

1. In a large bowl, combine all-purpose flour, whole wheat flour, sugar, baking powder and salt.

2. In a medium bowl, whisk together egg, milk and oil. Add to flour mixture and stir to combine.

3. Heat a griddle or large nonstick skillet over medium heat. Spray lightly with cooking spray. For each pancake, pour ¼ cup (60 mL) batter onto griddle and cook for about 2 minutes or until bubbly around the edges. Flip and cook for 2 minutes or until golden brown. Transfer to a plate and keep warm in preheated oven. Repeat with the remaining batter, spraying griddle and adjusting heat between batches as needed.

Serving size:
1 pancake

✔ Kid Approved

Kids will get a kick out of making these adorable pancakes, and even teenagers will smile when they see them!

Tip

Freeze any leftover pancakes and warm them up in the toaster oven on a busy morning.

Nutrients per serving

Calories	250
Fat	11.5 g
Saturated fat	2.3 g
Sodium	268 mg (11% DV)
Carbohydrate	31 g
Fiber	3 g (12% DV)
Protein	8 g
Calcium	135 mg (12% DV)
Iron	1.8 mg (13% DV)

High in: Magnesium, folate, riboflavin and niacin

Diabetes Food Choice Values:

2   Carbohydrates
2   Fats

Piggy Pancakes

Sue Mah, Dietitian, and her daughter Abbey Chan, Ontario

- **Preheat oven to 200°F (100°C)**
- **Plastic squeeze bottle**

1 cup	all-purpose flour	250 mL
1 cup	whole wheat flour	250 mL
2 tbsp	ground flax seeds (flaxseed meal)	30 mL
1 tbsp	baking powder	15 mL
½ tsp	baking soda	2 mL
Pinch	salt	Pinch
2	eggs	2
1¾ cups	1% milk	425 mL
¼ cup	canola oil	60 mL
	Vegetable cooking spray	
¼ cup	blueberries (approx.)	60 mL
¼ cup	chocolate chips (approx.)	60 mL

1. In a large bowl, combine all-purpose flour, whole wheat flour, flax seeds, baking powder, baking soda and salt.

2. In a medium bowl, whisk together eggs, milk and oil. Add to flour mixture and stir to combine. Pour batter into a plastic squeeze bottle (a funnel may help with this).

3. Heat a griddle or large nonstick skillet over medium heat. Spray lightly with cooking spray. For each piggy, squeeze out enough batter to form one large circle, about 5 inches (12.5 cm) in diameter, and two smaller circles, each 1½ to 2 inches (4 to 5 cm) in diameter. Cook for about 2 minutes or until bubbly around the edges. Flip and cook for 2 minutes or until golden brown. Transfer to a plate and keep warm in preheated oven. Repeat with the remaining batter, spraying griddle and adjusting heat between batches as needed.

4. To form a piggy, place the large pancake in the middle of a plate. Cut one of the small circles in half and use the halves as the pig's ears, with the cut end facing out. Position the other small circle in the middle of the large circle to form the snout. Use 2 blueberries for the nostrils and 2 chocolate chips for the eyes.

> Flax seeds contain an essential omega-3 fatty acid called ALA. Our bodies can't make ALA, but we require it to function normally, so it's important to eat foods rich in ALA, such as flax, canola and soy. (Salmon and other fatty fish contain different omega-3s known as EPA and DHA, which are important for heart health and for the development of the brain, nerves and eyes in infants.)

Variations
Use other fruits, such as raspberries or blackberries, for the eyes.

Add a smile to the face with a sliver of dried apricot.

Serving Idea
Serve with an assortment of fresh berries, a drizzle of maple syrup and a light dusting of confectioners' (icing) sugar.

Pumpkin Pancakes

Karen Omichinski, Dietitian, Manitoba

Karen Omichinski, Dietitian, Manitoba

Makes eighteen 3- to 4-inch (7.5 to 10 cm) pancakes

Serving size:
2 pancakes

✔ Kid Approved

Both kids and adults love the spiced pumpkin taste of these pancakes — it's sort of like pumpkin pie for breakfast! They are delicious on a fall morning, topped with warm spiced applesauce.

Tips

You can cook your own pie pumpkin to make the purée for this recipe or you can use canned pumpkin purée; just be sure not to use pumpkin pie filling, which is sweetened.

The chemical reaction of baking soda and vinegar makes this pancake batter particularly fluffy. Work quickly.

Nutrients per serving

Calories	179
Fat	4.7 g
Saturated fat	0.8 g
Sodium	300 mg (13% DV)
Carbohydrate	30 g
Fiber	3 g (12% DV)
Protein	6 g
Calcium	103 mg (9% DV)
Iron	1.9 mg (14% DV)

Very high in: Vitamin A
High in: Folate

Diabetes Food Choice Values:

2	Carbohydrates
1	Fat

● **Preheat oven to 200°F (100°C)**

1 cup	all-purpose flour	250 mL
1 cup	whole wheat flour	250 mL
3 tbsp	lightly packed brown sugar	45 mL
2 tsp	baking powder	10 mL
1 tsp	baking soda	5 mL
1 tsp	ground allspice	5 mL
1 tsp	ground cinnamon	5 mL
1/2 tsp	ground ginger	2 mL
1/4 tsp	salt	1 mL
1	egg	1
1 1/2 cups	1% milk	375 mL
1 cup	pumpkin purée (see tip, at left)	250 mL
2 tbsp	canola oil	30 mL
1 tbsp	white vinegar	15 mL
	Vegetable cooking spray	

1. In a large bowl, combine all-purpose flour, whole wheat flour, brown sugar, baking powder, baking soda, allspice, cinnamon, ginger and salt.

2. In another large bowl, whisk together egg, milk, pumpkin purée, oil and vinegar. Add to flour mixture and stir to combine.

3. Heat a griddle or large nonstick skillet over medium heat. Spray lightly with cooking spray. For each pancake, pour 1/4 cup (60 mL) batter onto griddle and cook for about 2 minutes or until bubbly around the edges. Flip and cook for 2 minutes or until golden brown. Transfer to a plate and keep warm in preheated oven. Repeat with the remaining batter, spraying griddle and adjusting heat between batches as needed.

> Pie pumpkins, used to make pumpkin purée, are smaller and sweeter than the large pumpkins used for decoration during the fall season.

Hearty Tex-Mex Brunch Eggs (page 38)

Pumpkin Pancakes (page 48)

Open-Face Tuna Sandwich
with Pesto (page 79)

Indian Curry Chicken Salad (page 85)

Appetizer Endive Salad (page 102)

Rainbow Lettuce Wraps
(page 103)

Crab-Stuffed Baby Tomatoes (page 112)

Roasted Cauliflower and
Red Pepper Soup (page 124)

Corn and Zucchini Pancakes

Leslie Gareau, Dietitian, Alberta

Leslie Gareau, Dietitian, Alberta

Makes twelve 3-inch (7.5 cm) pancakes

Serving size: 2 pancakes

✔ **Kid Approved**

Leslie and her family love Alberta corn, and even though her son doesn't care much for zucchini, he thoroughly enjoys these unique pancakes.

Tips

Be sure to squeeze the zucchini well to remove as much water as possible.

The easiest way to remove corn from the cob is to break the cob in half so you have a flat end. Stand the cob half on the flat end and slice the kernels off.

If a few corn kernels fall off a pancake when you're cooking it, be sure to remove them from the pan and discard them before you cook the next batch.

Nutrients per serving

Calories	181
Fat	5.3 g
Saturated fat	0.9 g
Sodium	85 mg (4% DV)
Carbohydrate	31 g
Fiber	4 g (16% DV)
Protein	6 g
Calcium	20 mg (2% DV)
Iron	1.2 mg (9% DV)

Very high in: Folate
High in: Magnesium and thiamine

Diabetes Food Choice Values:

2   Carbohydrates
1   Fat

• **Preheat oven to 200°F (100°C)**

3 cups	cooked corn kernels (3 to 4 cobs)	750 mL
1 cup	shredded zucchini, squeezed to remove excess moisture	250 mL
½ cup	cornmeal	125 mL
2	eggs, beaten	2
1 tbsp	1% milk	15 mL
1 tsp	ground cumin	5 mL
Pinch	salt	Pinch
½ tsp	freshly ground black pepper	2 mL
1 tbsp	canola oil, divided	15 mL

1. In a medium bowl, combine corn, zucchini, cornmeal, eggs, milk, cumin, salt and pepper.

2. In a large skillet, heat 1 tsp (5 mL) oil over medium heat. For each pancake, pour ¼ cup (60 mL) batter onto griddle and cook for about 2 minutes or until bubbly around the edges. Flip and cook for 2 to 3 minutes or until golden brown. Transfer to a plate and keep warm in preheated oven. Repeat with the remaining batter, adding oil and adjusting heat between batches as needed.

> Corn has played a significant role in the food history and culture of South America and Mexico, having been cultivated as far back as 2700 BC.

Cornmeal Crêpes with Avocado Filling

Laura Glenn, Dietetic Student, Quebec

Makes 4 to 6 crêpes

Serving size: 1 crêpe

Thicker than ordinary crêpes but thinner than pancakes, these cornmeal treats offer a unique taste and texture, resembling soft tacos.

Tips

Select an avocado that is firm to the touch yet yields with gentle pressure.

If the batter is too thick to spread, add another 1 tbsp (15 mL) milk.

- **6-inch (15 cm) crêpe pan or nonstick skillet**

Cornmeal Crêpes

½ cup	all-purpose flour	125 mL
⅓ cup	cornmeal	75 mL
1 tsp	baking powder	5 mL
1 tsp	granulated sugar	5 mL
¼ tsp	salt	1 mL
2	eggs	2
1 cup	low-fat plain yogurt	250 mL
3 tbsp	2% milk	45 mL
2 tbsp	melted non-hydrogenated margarine	30 mL
	Vegetable cooking spray	

Avocado Filling

1	large ripe avocado	1
2 tsp	freshly squeezed lemon or lime juice	10 mL
2	ripe tomatoes, seeded and finely chopped	2
½ cup	chopped green onions	125 mL
1 tsp	chile and garlic sauce	5 mL
¼ tsp	salt	1 mL
¼ tsp	freshly ground black pepper	1 mL
¼ cup	low-fat sour cream (optional)	60 mL

1. *Crêpes:* In a large bowl, combine flour, cornmeal, baking powder, sugar and salt.

2. In another large bowl, whisk together eggs, yogurt, milk and margarine. Make a well in the center of the flour mixture and gradually add the egg mixture, whisking until batter is blended and smooth. Cover and let rest at room temperature for 10 minutes.

Nutrients per serving

Calories	235
Fat	12.7 g
Saturated fat	2.3 g
Sodium	355 mg (15% DV)
Carbohydrate	24 g
Fiber	4 g (16% DV)
Protein	8 g
Calcium	131 mg (12% DV)
Iron	1.2 mg (9% DV)

Very high in: Folate

High in: Vitamin D, vitamin B$_{12}$ and riboflavin

Diabetes Food Choice Values:

1 Carbohydrate
2½ Fats

3. Heat crêpe pan over medium heat. Spray lightly with cooking spray. Lift the pan and pour in about $1/3$ cup (75 mL) batter. Swirl the pan so the batter reaches the edges. Return to heat and cook for about 1 minute or until crêpe is no longer shiny on top and is very light golden on the bottom. Flip and cook for 30 to 60 seconds or until starting to turn golden. Transfer to a plate, cover with foil and keep warm. Repeat with the remaining batter, spraying pan and adjusting heat between batches as needed.

4. *Filling:* In a small bowl, mash avocado. Sprinkle with lemon juice. Gently stir in tomatoes, green onions, chile and garlic sauce, salt and pepper.

5. Divide filling among crêpes. Fold bottom edge of crêpe over filling, then fold top edge over bottom edge. Transfer to a serving plate, seam side down. Serve with a dollop of sour cream, if desired.

> Avocados are one of the few fruits that contain a substantial amount of fat. But unlike coconut (the fruit of the tropical palm tree), which contains mostly saturated fat, avocados provide mainly monounsaturated fat.

Tip

If you find you cannot swirl the batter quickly enough for it to reach the edges of the pan, simply use more batter.

Variation

Fill these crêpes with black beans, salsa and cheese in place of the avocado filling.

Buckwheat offers a
delicious nutty flavor that
works best with savory
fillings.

Tips

Some of the ingredients in this
batter tend to settle to the
bottom, so stir it often while
you're using it.

The batter may be made a
day in advance, covered and
refrigerated. Let it warm to
room temperature before
using it.

Serving Idea

Fill each crêpe with a
thin slice of warmed back
bacon, a few slices of thinly
sliced onion, 2 tbsp (30 mL)
chopped arugula and 2 tbsp
(30 mL) chopped figs. Serve
drizzled with a sweet onion
vinaigrette, if desired.

Nutrients per serving

Calories	109
Fat	4.6 g
Saturated fat	1.3 g
Sodium	68 mg (3% DV)
Carbohydrate	13 g
Fiber	1 g (4% DV)
Protein	4 g
Calcium	57 mg (5% DV)
Iron	0.8 mg (6% DV)

High in: Vitamin D

Diabetes Food Choice Values:

1	Carbohydrate
½	Fat

Buckwheat Crêpes

Dianna Bihun, Dietitian, British Columbia

- **6-inch (15 cm) crêpe pan or nonstick skillet**

2 cups	2% milk	500 mL
1½ tbsp	white vinegar	22 mL
¾ cup	all-purpose flour	175 mL
¾ cup	buckwheat flour	175 mL
Pinch	salt	Pinch
3	eggs	3
3	egg yolks	3
2 tbsp	light (fancy) molasses	30 mL
2 tbsp	melted non-hydrogenated margarine	30 mL
	Vegetable cooking spray	

1. In a large bowl, combine milk and vinegar; set aside for 10 minutes.

2. In another large bowl, combine all-purpose flour, buckwheat flour and salt.

3. Add eggs, egg yolks and molasses to the milk mixture. Beat with an electric mixer for 1 minute. Add margarine and beat for 20 seconds. Make a well in the flour mixture and gradually add the egg mixture, whisking until batter is blended and smooth. Cover and let rest at room temperature for 30 minutes.

4. Heat crêpe pan over medium heat. Spray lightly with cooking spray. Lift the pan and pour in about ⅓ cup (75 mL) batter. Swirl the pan so the batter reaches the edges. Return to heat and cook for about 1 minute or until crêpe is no longer shiny on top and is very light golden on the bottom. Flip and cook for 30 to 60 seconds or until starting to turn golden. Transfer to a plate, cover with foil and keep warm. Repeat with the remaining batter, spraying pan and adjusting heat between batches as needed.

> Buckwheat is not wheat at all; in fact, it's not even a grain! Rather, it is a broad-leaf plant that grows well in the eastern prairies of Canada. Buckwheat seeds are used to make groats (hulled and crushed kernels), which can be toasted to make kasha, often used to make hot cereal or pilafs. When milled into flour, buckwheat can be used to make crêpes or the famous Russian blini (thin pancakes classically served with caviar and sour cream).

Serving size: 1 crêpe

This crêpe recipe is simple and works perfectly every time.

Tips

To avoid overcooking crêpes, cook them only until they lose their raw appearance, when the batter turns from wet-looking to dry-looking.

These crêpes can be made ahead and frozen. If you place waxed paper between them before freezing, it's easier to thaw them one at a time. To thaw, transfer to the refrigerator 1 to 2 hours before use.

Variation

Add a sprig of fresh dill and a sprinkle of lemon juice on top of the salmon before folding.

Nutrients per serving

Calories	131
Fat	4.9 g
Saturated fat	2.2 g
Sodium	301 mg (13% DV)
Carbohydrate	12 g
Fiber	1 g (4% DV)
Protein	9 g
Calcium	69 mg (6% DV)
Iron	1.2 mg (9% DV)

Very high in: Vitamin D, folate and vitamin B_{12}

High in: Vitamin A and niacin

Diabetes Food Choice Values:

1 Carbohydrate
1 Meat & Alternatives

Crêpes with Smoked Salmon

Martine Laroche, Alberta

● **6-inch (15 cm) crêpe pan or nonstick skillet**

Crêpes

2	eggs	2
1¼ cups	1% milk	300 mL
Pinch	salt	Pinch
1 cup	all-purpose flour	250 mL
	Vegetable cooking spray	

Filling

3 tbsp	herb-and-garlic-flavored cream cheese, divided	45 mL
1 cup	packed baby spinach leaves	250 mL
8 to 10	thin slices smoked salmon	8 to 10

1. *Crêpes:* In a small bowl, whisk together eggs, milk and salt. Whisk in flour until batter is blended and smooth. Cover and let rest at room temperature for 30 minutes.

2. Heat crêpe pan over medium heat. Spray lightly with cooking spray. Lift the pan and pour in about ¼ cup (60 mL) batter. Swirl the pan so the batter reaches the edges. Return to heat and cook for about 30 seconds or until crêpe is no longer shiny on top and is very light golden on the bottom. Flip and cook for 20 to 30 seconds or until starting to turn golden. Transfer to a plate, cover with foil and keep warm. Repeat with the remaining batter, spraying pan and adjusting heat between batches as needed.

3. *Filling:* Spread 1 tsp (5 mL) cream cheese over each crêpe. Place a few spinach leaves in the middle, followed by 1 slice smoked salmon. Fold bottom edge of crêpe over salmon, then fold top edge over bottom edge. Transfer to a serving plate, seam side down.

> Smoked salmon is either hot-smoked (a high smoking temperature for a short duration) or cold-smoked (a cooler smoking temperature for a longer duration, often a day or even weeks). In hot-smoking, the salmon may take on some of the flavor of the wood used to smoke it, such as maple or applewood. In both cases, the fish is cured first by the addition of salt to help remove moisture and kill bacteria.

Pork, Apple and Sage Patties

Mary Sue Waisman, Dietitian, Nova Scotia

- **Preheat oven to 375°F (190°C)**
- **Rimmed baking sheet, greased**

1 tsp	canola oil	5 mL
12 oz	lean ground pork	375 g
¾ cup	finely chopped onions	175 mL
½ cup	finely chopped peeled apple	125 mL
1	slice raisin or whole wheat bread, torn into small pieces	1
1	egg, lightly beaten	1
¼ cup	finely diced dried apricots	60 mL
1 tbsp	pure maple syrup	15 mL
½ tsp	dried savory	2 mL
½ tsp	dried marjoram	2 mL
1 tsp	ground sage	5 mL
¼ tsp	salt	1 mL

1. In a large nonstick skillet, heat oil over medium heat. Sauté pork, breaking it up with a spoon, for about 8 minutes or until no longer pink. Add onions and apple; sauté for about 5 minutes or until softened.

2. Transfer pork mixture to a large bowl and stir in bread, egg, apricots, maple syrup, savory, marjoram, sage and salt. Using about ¼ cup (60 mL) mixture, form into ½-inch (1 cm) thick patties and place about 2 inches (5 cm) apart on prepared baking sheet.

3. Bake in preheated oven, turning once, for 15 to 20 minutes or until an instant-read thermometer inserted in the center of a patty registers 160°F (71°C).

Lean ground pork contains about 11 g fat per 2½-oz (75 g) serving, while the same size serving of medium ground pork provides almost 16 g. When possible, purchase lean ground pork.

Makes 5 cups (1.25 L)

Serving size: 2 tbsp (30 mL)

✔ **Kid Approved**

Kim developed this sauce for her clients with diabetes as it has a lower carbohydrate content than straight maple syrup. Serve it warm atop pancakes or waffles. It was a huge hit with our tasting panel!

Tips

Children can help cut up the strawberries and mix the cornstarch with water — they love seeing the cornstarch disappear in the cold water.

Freeze extra sauce in ice cube trays. Once frozen, place the cubes in a freezer bag. Defrost in the microwave as needed.

Variation

Add a few splashes of lemon juice with the vanilla to enhance the berry flavor.

Nutrients per serving

Calories	25
Fat	0.1 g
Saturated fat	0.0 g
Sodium	1 mg (0% DV)
Carbohydrate	6 g
Fiber	1 g (4% DV)
Protein	0 g
Calcium	8 mg (1% DV)
Iron	0.1 mg (1% DV)

Very high in: Riboflavin

Diabetes Food Choice Values:
½ Carbohydrate

Berry Canadian Maple Sauce

Kim Knott, Dietitian, Manitoba

● **Food processor or blender**

1	apple, peeled, cored and sliced	1
4 cups	chopped strawberries	1 L
½ cup	cold water	125 mL
1½ tbsp	cornstarch	22 mL
¾ cup	pure maple syrup	175 mL
¼ tsp	vanilla extract	1 mL

1. In a medium saucepan, bring 1½ cups (375 mL) water to a boil over high heat. Add apple, reduce heat and simmer for 2 to 3 minutes or until tender. Add strawberries, increase heat to high and return to a boil. Reduce heat and simmer for 2 minutes. Remove from heat and let cool slightly.

2. Carefully transfer hot fruit mixture to food processor and purée until smooth. Return to saucepan and bring to a simmer over medium heat.

3. In a small bowl, stir together cold water and cornstarch until smooth. Add to fruit mixture and cook, stirring, for 2 to 3 minutes or until thickened. Stir in maple syrup and vanilla. Remove from heat and let cool slightly to serve warm or let cool completely. Store cooled sauce in an airtight container in the refrigerator for up to 4 days.

Makes 6 servings

✔ **Kid Approved**

A fresh fruit platter makes a colorful addition to your Sunday brunch table.

Tips

Keep your cutting surface dry so your knife does not slip.

In the summertime, keep a fruit platter on hand in the fridge to serve as a delicious, nutritious afternoon treat.

Variations

Vary the fruits to your liking and the season.

Thread the fruit pieces onto skewers to make kebabs.

Seasonal Fruit Platter with Honey Yogurt Dip

Caroline Dubeau, Dietitian, Ontario

2	fresh peaches, halved and pitted	2
½	honeydew melon, peeled and seeded	½
1 cup	blueberries	250 mL
18	strawberries, hulled	18
Honey Yogurt Dip		
¾ cup	low-fat plain yogurt	175 mL
2 tbsp	liquid honey	30 mL
1 tsp	vanilla extract	5 mL

1. Place peach halves flesh side down on a cutting board and cut into 3 to 4 slices per half. Cut melon into slices, then into rough cubes.

2. Starting at one end of a serving platter, arrange fruit as follows: peaches, blueberries, melon, strawberries.

3. *Dip:* In a small bowl, stir together yogurt, honey and vanilla. Serve with fruit for dipping.

Nutrients per serving

Calories	116
Fat	0.7 g
Saturated fat	0.3 g
Sodium	42 mg (2% DV)
Carbohydrate	27 g
Fiber	3 g (12% DV)
Protein	3 g
Calcium	70 mg (6% DV)
Iron	0.5 mg (4% DV)

Very high in: Vitamin C
High in: Folate

Diabetes Food Choice Values:
1½ Carbohydrate

Makes 3¹/₂ to 4 cups (875 mL to 1 L)

Serving size: 1 cup (250 mL)

✔ **Kid Approved**

Frozen fruits add intense flavor to a smoothie and keep it cold longer.

Tip

Freeze leftover smoothies in ice pop containers for a quick frozen treat.

Variation

Vary the frozen fruits, yogurt and juice to suit your taste. For example, try a combination of frozen mangos, frozen peaches, peach-flavored yogurt and orange juice.

Serving Idea

Pour the smoothie into attractive wineglasses and garnish each with a fresh strawberry to serve at a weekend brunch.

Nutrients per serving

Calories	153
Fat	1.0 g
Saturated fat	0.4 g
Sodium	45 mg (2% DV)
Carbohydrate	33 g
Fiber	3 g (12% DV)
Protein	4 g
Calcium	119 mg (11% DV)
Iron	0.5 mg (4% DV)

Very high in: Vitamin C

Diabetes Food Choice Values:
2 Carbohydrate

Berry Smoothie

Joëlle Zorzetto, Dietitian, Ontario

● **Blender**

1	banana, broken into chunks	1
2 cups	mixed frozen berries (strawberries, blueberries, blackberries, raspberries)	500 mL
1 cup	low-fat strawberry-flavored yogurt	250 mL
1 cup	unsweetened orange, strawberry and banana juice	250 mL

1. In blender, on high speed, blend banana, berries, yogurt and juice for 30 seconds or until smooth.

When selecting a yogurt, it's helpful to know the % M.F. — the percentage of milk fat in the product. If a yogurt container says 3.5% M.F., it means that 100 g of the yogurt has 3.5 g of fat. Note that % M.F. does not indicate the percentage of calories from fat provided by the product. Yogurts labeled 2% M.F. or lower are considered low-fat options.

Lunches

Lunch is a vital part of your day, so take some time to plan and make a delicious, healthy lunch for your family, referring to *Eating Well with Canada's Food Guide* for guidance. Aim to include at least one food from each of the four food groups. Include a protein-rich food (cheese, meat, poultry, fish, beans, eggs, nut butters or nut butter alternatives) and fiber-rich foods (whole grains, nuts and seeds, vegetables and fruits), as protein and fiber help us feel full for longer periods of time and energized for the afternoon's activities.

Kid-Approved Lunches

"That was an awesome lunch, Mom — thanks!" Wouldn't that be wonderful to hear? The best way to ensure lunch success is to make it a team effort: get your children involved, from planning the menu and grocery shopping to preparing the meal and helping with cleanup. Generally speaking, the more involved children are in the process, the more likely that they will eat and enjoy lunch.

Avoid Processed Meats

Use leftover cooked chicken, beef or other meats for sandwiches or salads. To reduce the risk of developing colorectal cancer, eat few, if any, processed meats (meat preserved by smoking, curing or salting, or with added chemical preservatives). Processed meats also generally contain a lot of sodium.

Tips for Packing Lunches

- Make lunches the night before and store them in the fridge.

- Pack supper leftovers for lunch; that way, you only need to clean up the kitchen once.

- Get the gear: lunch boxes come in all shapes and sizes. When possible, let kids pick out their own.

- Practice food safety. Use insulated containers to keep hot foods hot; use cold packs to keep cold foods well chilled. Thoroughly wash out lunch boxes daily.

- Avoid foods that are messy, get mushy or have a strong smell.

- Set up a lunch drawer that contains all your packaging needs: insulated containers, reusable containers, plastic wrap, baggies, stickers, napkins, plastic cutlery, etc. Dedicate a shelf or area in the refrigerator for lunch foods. Having everything you need in one place will make lunch prep a breeze!

- If your kids complain about soggy lunches, consider using partitioned containers to keep the ingredients separate. These reusable containers will also help you go along with the litterless lunch initiatives undertaken by some schools.

- Know school policies on the use of peanuts and other possible food allergens.

Family Cooking Lesson

Measuring Ingredients

There are three common ways to measure ingredients: by weight, by volume or by count.

- Meats, fish and poultry are commonly measured by **weight**, either as ounces and pounds (in the imperial measurement system) or as grams and kilograms (in the metric measurement system). If you don't have a kitchen scale, buy meats that have been weighed in the grocery store; check the package label for the weight.

- **Volume** refers to the amount of space occupied by an ingredient. In the imperial system, volume is measured in teaspoons, tablespoons, cups, pints and quarts; in the metric system, it is measured in milliliters or liters.

- **Count** is a simple way to measure an ingredient: 3 eggs, 4 cloves garlic, etc.

It's best to measure ingredients as the recipe says, by weighing, measuring volume or counting. For volume, use liquid measuring cups for wet ingredients (they generally have a lip or spout to facilitate easy pouring) and dry measuring cups for dry ingredients. Use actual measuring spoons; household teaspoons and tablespoons will not give accurate results.

Family Cooking Lesson

Kitchen Tools and Equipment

To get the best results for your recipes, it's important to know and use the proper tools and equipment in a home kitchen. Here's a partial listing and description of household tools.

Knives

- **Chef's knife (French knife):** An all-purpose knife with a sturdy handle and tapered blade that can be used for a variety of cutting and chopping jobs.

- **Utility knife:** An all-purpose knife with a narrower blade than a chef's knife. It's especially good for cutting produce and carving poultry.

- **Boning knife:** A knife with a slim, curved blade, generally 6 to 8 inches (15 to 20 cm) long, used to cut raw meat away from bones.

- **Paring knife:** A handy small knife used for small cutting tasks. The blade is generally only 2 to 4 inches (5 to 10 cm) long.

Hand Tools

- **Ladle:** A long-handled tool with a scoop at the end, useful for portioning liquids such as soup. Ladles come in a variety of sizes.

- **Scoop:** A lever-operated tool that is very useful for measuring doughs or serving uniform portions. Scoops come in a variety of sizes.

- **Dry measuring cups:** Sold in a standard set of sizes (usually 1/4, 1/3, 1/2 and 1 cup, or 60 mL, 75 mL, 125 mL and 250 mL). Use these measuring cups for ingredients such as flour, sugar, peanut butter and margarine, filling them right to the top, then leveling them off with a straight edge.

- **Liquid measuring cups:** Generally sold in three sizes (1 cup, 2 cups or 4 cups, or 250 mL, 500 mL or 1 L). The top of the cup has a spout to facilitate pouring.

- **Measuring spoons:** Sold as a set in either imperial or metric measures and designed for measuring small volumes.

- **Whisk:** A long-handled tool designed to incorporate air into a product while hand-mixing.

- **Wooden spoons:** These spoons of varying lengths are ideal for stirring and mixing.

Most Breads Don't Taste Salty, But...

Many people are surprised to learn that commercial breads, buns, rolls and pitas contain a lot of sodium. Most don't taste salty, but if you read the ingredient list, you'll sometimes see both salt and other sodium-containing ingredients listed. With the current emphasis on reducing daily sodium intake, many food manufacturers are working diligently to reduce sodium in prepared foods. Check the Nutrition Facts table and the ingredient list and choose a bread with the lowest percent Daily Value (% DV) of sodium.

- **Spatulas:** Rubber, silicone or metal spatulas come in varying lengths. Some are designed for incorporating items, as in folding; others are designed for lifting.

Cookware

- **Pots:** Large, round cooking vessels with straight sides and two looped handles for easy lifting; also called "saucepots."
- **Saucepans:** Round cooking vessels with one long handle and either straight or sloped sides; often just called "pans."
- **Skillets:** Long-handled, round, shallow pans; also called "fry pans" or "frying pans."
- **Wok:** A large cooking vessel with a rounded bottom and curved sides, ideal for sautéing and stir-frying.
- **Strainer:** A metal mesh container or a metal or plastic container with holes, used to drain liquid from foods, drain washed fruits and vegetables, etc.
- **Sieve:** A small fine-mesh container that strains liquid or small, fine particles of dry ingredients out of mixtures.

Small Electric Equipment

- **Blender:** Designed to liquefy or purée foods; ideally suited to making smoothies and milkshakes and puréeing soup, fruit and vegetables.
- **Food processor:** Similar in function to a blender, but designed to purée larger batches of food. Some food processors have attachments that can slice or shred ingredients.
- **Immersion blender:** A handheld tool with a spinning blade at the end. It can be immersed in a pot to purée foods such as soups or vegetables. Also called a "stick blender" or a "hand blender."
- **Stand mixer:** Designed for mixing cakes, cookies and other items that require more work than hand-mixing. Some stand mixers come with attachments for grinding meats, kneading breads and rolling and cutting fresh pasta.
- **Hand mixer:** Similar in function to a stand mixer, but handheld and designed for smaller jobs, such as whipping cream and eggs and making soft doughs, such as for quick breads.

Makes 2 servings

Enjoy this quick, tasty meal when peppers are at their peak in the fall. It is satisfying for lunch or dinner, and it never disappoints.

Tip

Cooking the peppers covered over a low heat draws out their moisture and flavor. The key is to make sure they don't brown. If you need to add liquid to prevent the peppers from browning, you can add wine instead of water, if desired.

Serving Idea

Serve with Green Salad with Apple Balsamic Vinaigrette (page 146).

Nutrients per serving

Calories	288
Fat	15.4 g
Saturated fat	3.8 g
Sodium	384 mg (16% DV)
Carbohydrate	22 g
Fiber	3 g (12% DV)
Protein	16 g
Calcium	102 mg (9% DV)
Iron	2.2 mg (16% DV)

Very high in: Vitamin A, vitamin C, folate, vitamin B_{12} and riboflavin

High in: Magnesium, zinc, vitamin D, vitamin B_6, thiamine and niacin

Diabetes Food Choice Values:

1	Carbohydrate
2	Meat & Alternatives
1	Fat

Sautéed Peppers and Eggs

Francy Pillo-Blocka, Dietitian, Ontario

2 tsp	olive oil	10 mL
2	red bell peppers, sliced into thin strips	2
4	eggs	4
Pinch	salt	Pinch
	Freshly ground black pepper	
2	multigrain buns, split and toasted	2

1. In a large skillet, heat oil over medium-low heat. Spread red peppers evenly in pan, cover and simmer, stirring occasionally, for 15 to 20 minutes or until peppers are very tender, but not browned. (If peppers start turning brown, add 1 to 2 tbsp/15 to 30 mL water and cover again.)

2. In a small bowl, whisk together eggs, salt and pepper to taste. Stir into skillet, cover and cook, stirring occasionally, for 2 to 3 minutes or until eggs are just set.

3. Place toasted multigrain bun halves on serving plates and spoon egg mixture over top.

Serving size:
3 meatballs

✔ **Kid Approved**

This recipe was created by our youngest contributor, seven-year-old Eben! Eben and his grandmother enjoy cooking together, as it's fun and gives them time together. When they prepare this recipe, Eben is the chef and his grandmother is the sous-chef: she does the chopping and shredding and handles the oven. They both wear aprons and do all the cleanup together.

Tip

Make these meatballs on the weekend, then warm them up when your kids come home for lunch for "Meatball Monday."

Serving Idea

Serve with a whole-grain bun, cucumber slices and carrot sticks.

Nutrients per serving

Calories	182
Fat	10.5 g
Saturated fat	5.4 g
Sodium	330 mg (14% DV)
Carbohydrate	3 g
Fiber	0 g (0% DV)
Protein	18 g
Calcium	131 mg (12% DV)
Iron	1.5 mg (11% DV)

Very high in: Zinc, vitamin B$_{12}$ and niacin

Diabetes Food Choice Values:

2½ Meat & Alternatives

Eben's Special Meatballs

Eben Thorpe-Keith, British Columbia

- Preheat oven to 350°F (180°C)
- Rimmed baking sheet, lined with parchment paper

1 lb	extra-lean ground beef	500 g
1	egg, beaten	1
1 cup	finely chopped onion	250 mL
1 cup	shredded old Cheddar cheese	250 mL
1 tbsp	Worcestershire sauce	15 mL
½ tsp	salt	2 mL
½ tsp	freshly ground black pepper	2 mL
Dipping Sauce		
½ cup	ketchup	125 mL
¼ cup	prepared yellow mustard	60 mL

1. In a large bowl, combine beef, egg, onion, cheese, Worcestershire sauce, salt and pepper. Shape into 1½-inch (4 cm) round meatballs and place at least 1 inch (2.5 cm) apart on prepared baking sheet. Bake in preheated oven for 25 to 30 minutes or until no longer pink inside.

2. *Sauce:* In a small bowl, combine ketchup and mustard. Divide among individual serving bowls and serve with meatballs for dipping.

Serving size: 2 buns

✔ **Kid Approved**

Teach kids to make dough at a birthday party. Start the dough at the beginning of the party, and ask the birthday child to punch down the dough after each of the two risings. The children can then fill their own buns.

Tips

Be sure to remove the vegetables from the heat before adding the cheese, so the cheese doesn't melt.

This recipe works well halved, for a smaller crowd.

Nutrients per serving

Calories	311
Fat	8.5 g
Saturated fat	2.6 g
Sodium	308 mg (13% DV)
Carbohydrate	42 g
Fiber	5 g (20% DV)
Protein	18 g
Calcium	86 mg (8% DV)
Iron	3.3 mg (24% DV)

Very high in: Zinc, folate, vitamin B_{12} and niacin

High in: Magnesium, thiamine and riboflavin

Diabetes Food Choice Values:

2½ Carbohydrates
1½ Meat & Alternatives

Hamburger Pizza Buns

Lindsay McGregor, Dietitian, Saskatchewan

● **Baking sheets, lightly greased**

Bun Dough

½ cup	granulated sugar	125 mL
2 tbsp	quick-rising yeast	30 mL
1 tsp	salt	5 mL
2	eggs, beaten	2
3 cups	warm water	750 mL
¼ cup	canola oil	60 mL
5 cups	whole wheat flour	1.25 L
4 cups	all-purpose flour	1 L

Filling

2 lb	lean ground beef	1 kg
2 cups	finely chopped mushrooms	500 mL
1½ cups	finely chopped onions	375 mL
1 cup	finely chopped green bell pepper	250 mL
1	can (14 oz/398 mL) tomato sauce	1
3 cups	shredded light Cheddar cheese	750 mL
1 tbsp	dried oregano	15 mL
	Freshly ground black pepper	

1. *Dough:* In a large bowl, combine sugar, yeast, salt, eggs, warm water and oil. Gradually stir in whole wheat flour and all-purpose flour until incorporated.

2. Turn dough out onto a floured surface and knead for about 5 minutes or until smooth. Place in lightly greased large bowl, cover with plastic wrap and let rise in a warm, draft-free place for about 45 minutes or until doubled in bulk. Punch dough down, cover and let rise again for about 45 minutes or until doubled in bulk. Meanwhile, preheat oven to 350°F (180°C).

3. *Filling:* Meanwhile, in a large skillet, over medium-high heat, cook beef, breaking it up with the back of a spoon, for about 8 minutes or until no longer pink. Using a slotted spoon, transfer beef to a bowl. Drain off all but 2 tsp (10 mL) fat from the pan.

4. Reduce heat to medium. Add mushrooms, onions and green pepper to the skillet and sauté for 4 to 5 minutes or until softened. Remove from heat and stir in reserved beef, tomato sauce, cheese, oregano and pepper to taste.

5. Punch dough down. Pinch off a piece of dough about the size of a golf ball and roll it out on a floured surface to a 3- to 3½-inch (7.5 to 9 cm) circle. Place about 1½ tbsp (22 mL) filling in center of dough, wrap dough around filling and firmly pinch edges together to seal. Place seam side down on a prepared baking sheet (do not let rise). Repeat with the remaining dough and filling, placing buns about 2 inches (5 cm) apart.

6. Bake one sheet at a time in preheated oven for 20 to 25 minutes or until buns are lightly browned.

> Cup for cup, whole wheat flour provides over three times as much fiber as all-purpose flour.

Tip
Use your imagination for the fillings. Try cooked broccoli and shredded cheese, or pesto and cooked chicken, in place of the ground beef mixture.

Serving Idea
For a child's birthday party, serve with fresh veggies and Legume Guacamole (page 95). Finish the meal with the Seasonal Fruit Platter with Honey and Yogurt Dip (page 56) and the Chocolate Lava Cupcake Tower (page 350).

Scrambled Egg Pizza

Justyne Tirrell-Kanji, Alberta

- **Preheat broiler**
- **Baking sheet, lightly greased**

1	10-inch (25 cm) whole wheat flour tortilla	1
2 tbsp	drained rinsed canned kidney beans, mashed	30 mL
2 tbsp	salsa	30 mL
1 tsp	canola oil	5 mL
½ cup	chopped vegetables (see tip, at left)	125 mL
3	eggs	3
1 tbsp	1% milk	15 mL
Pinch	salt	Pinch
¼ tsp	freshly ground black pepper	1 mL
¼ cup	shredded Cheddar cheese	60 mL

1. Place tortilla on prepared baking sheet. In a small bowl, combine mashed beans and salsa. Spread over tortilla and set aside.

2. In a medium nonstick skillet, heat oil over medium heat. Sauté vegetables for 3 to 5 minutes or until softened.

3. In a small bowl, whisk together eggs and milk. Season with salt and pepper. Pour over vegetable mixture and cook, stirring occasionally, for about 1 minute or until eggs form soft, thick curds.

4. Spread cooked eggs evenly over tortilla and sprinkle with cheese. Broil for 1 minute or until cheese melts. Cut tortilla into quarters and serve.

✔ **Kid Approved**

These tempting sushi wraps san be assembled the night before for a delicious lunch or after-school snack.

Tips

Use a very sharp knife to get clean, even cuts.

Children love to help prepare and roll sushi, but should be supervised when using a knife.

Make a variety of sushi wraps and keep them in the refrigerator for snacks.

Variations

Omit the fish for people who don't like it.

Dress these up for a special event by using 4 thin slices of smoked salmon.

Nutrients per serving

Calories	144
Fat	6.2 g
Saturated fat	1.1 g
Sodium	241 mg (10% DV)
Carbohydrate	20 g
Fiber	3 g (12% DV)
Protein	4 g
Calcium	31 mg (3% DV)
Iron	1.4 mg (10% DV)

Very High in: Vitamin A
High in: Folate

Diabetes Food Choice Values:
1   Carbohydrate
1   Fat

Sushi Sandwich Wraps

Natascha Park, Ontario

4	10-inch (25 cm) spinach-flavored flour tortillas	4
2 tbsp	light herb-and-garlic-flavored cream cheese, softened	30 mL
4	large romaine lettuce leaves	4
1	avocado, cut into thin strips	1
1	large carrot, cut into thin 6-inch (15 cm) long strips	1
½	English cucumber, cut into thin 6-inch (15 cm) long strips	½
½ cup	imitation crab (crab-flavored pollock pieces) (optional)	125 mL

1. Place tortillas on a work surface and spread each with one-quarter of the cream cheese, making sure to spread all the way to the top edge to help seal the wrap.

2. On the bottom third of each, place 1 lettuce leaf and one-quarter each of the avocado strips, carrot strips, cucumber strips and crab. Starting at the bottom edge, roll up as you would a jelly roll, tucking ingredients in tightly as you roll and leaving the sides open. Press the top edge to seal with cream cheese.

3. Wrap each roll in plastic wrap and refrigerate for at least 1 hour or overnight. Remove plastic wrap, slice off ends of rolls and discard. Cut evenly into four 2-inch (5 cm) pieces and stand up on a plate.

> Sushi is traditionally made of cooked and/or raw fish rolled or formed with short-grain rice seasoned with rice vinegar. It originated in Japan, where it was first created as a means to preserve fish. There are many types of sushi, including temaki (which is hand-rolled into a conical shape), maki (which is rolled into a cylinder and cut into small pieces) and nigiri (a hand-pressed rice ball with cooked or raw fish). It takes years of training to become an experienced sushi chef.

This recipe was given to Debra by her grandmother. She says her mom always disliked the smell of canned salmon, but she enjoyed eating this as long as she didn't have to cook it!

Tip
Much of the sodium in this recipe comes from the English muffins and the canned salmon. To reduce the sodium, serve the salmon mixture over steamed brown rice. Using 1¼ cups (300 mL) leftover cooked flaked salmon instead of canned will also help.

Variation
Use canned tuna instead of salmon.

Serving Idea
Add a crisp green salad and serve for a light weekend lunch.

Nutrients per serving

Calories	221
Fat	6.5 g
Saturated fat	1.4 g
Sodium	534 mg (22% DV)
Carbohydrate	23 g
Fiber	3 g (12% DV)
Protein	19 g
Calcium	392 mg (36% DV)
Iron	1.7 mg (12% DV)

Very high in: Vitamin D, vitamin B_{12} and niacin

High in: Magnesium, zinc, vitamin C, thiamine and riboflavin

Diabetes Food Choice Values:
1½ Carbohydrates
1½ Meat & Alternatives

Creamed Salmon on English Muffins

Debra Palfreyman, Alberta

1	can (7½ oz/213 g) salmon	1
2 tsp	canola oil	10 mL
1 tbsp	finely chopped shallots	15 mL
1 tbsp	thinly sliced green onions	15 mL
2 tsp	all-purpose flour	10 mL
¼ tsp	freshly ground black pepper	1 mL
Pinch	salt	Pinch
1 cup	2% evaporated milk	250 mL
¼ cup	thawed frozen green peas	60 mL
1 tsp	minced fresh dill	5 mL
2	whole wheat English muffins, split and toasted	2

1. Drain liquid from salmon, reserving liquid. Transfer salmon to a bowl and flake with a fork. Set both aside.

2. In a large nonstick skillet, heat oil over medium-high heat. Sauté shallots and green onions for about 1 minute or until softened. Reduce heat to medium and add flour, pepper and salt; sauté for 1 minute, making sure flour does not burn.

3. Gradually stir in milk and reserved liquid from salmon, stirring until smooth. Reduce heat to low and stir in salmon and peas; simmer until heated through. Stir in dill.

4. Place toasted English muffin halves on serving plates and spoon salmon mixture over top.

✔ **Kid Approved**

French Canadians will recognize this as a *guédille*, a salad mixture served in a hot dog bun. This is one of Caroline's favorite summer lunches, and she still likes it best when her mom makes it!

Tips

It's best to use lettuce that has some crunch, so romaine hearts are perfect. You can substitute iceberg lettuce, if you prefer.

You can also use a panini grill to toast the buns.

Variation

Add diced leftover cooked chicken or turkey to the salad mixture.

Serving Idea

Serve with cheese curds or a piece of Canadian Cheddar cheese.

Nutrients per serving

Calories	210
Fat	7.7 g
Saturated fat	1.3 g
Sodium	423 mg (18% DV)
Carbohydrate	33 g
Fiber	5 g (20% DV)
Protein	6 g
Calcium	77 mg (7% DV)
Iron	1.5 mg (11% DV)

High in: Magnesium, folate and niacin

Diabetes Food Choice Values:

1½ Carbohydrates
1   Fat

Veggie Roll

Caroline Dubeau, Dietitian, Ontario

1 cup	finely diced English cucumber (unpeeled)	250 mL
1 cup	coarsely chopped plum (Roma) tomatoes	250 mL
½ cup	finely chopped romaine lettuce hearts	125 mL
½ cup	thinly sliced red radishes	125 mL
¼ cup	finely chopped red onion	60 mL
¼ cup	light mayonnaise	60 mL
1 tbsp	1% milk	15 mL
1 tsp	dry mustard	5 mL
1 tsp	liquid honey or granulated sugar	5 mL
	Salt and freshly ground black pepper	
4	whole wheat hot dog buns	4

1. In a medium bowl, combine cucumber, tomatoes, lettuce, radishes and red onion.

2. In a small bowl, combine mayonnaise and milk. Stir in mustard and honey. Season to taste with salt and pepper; mix well. Add dressing to vegetables and stir gently until well coated.

3. In a nonstick skillet, over medium heat, lightly toast cut sides of buns, using a spatula to flatten them. Divide the vegetable mixture among the buns and serve warm.

It's always a great idea to have a few hard-cooked eggs ready to go in the refrigerator. Here's a quick lunch idea for them.

Tips

For instructions on hard-cooking eggs, see page 34.

Gherkins are tiny, immature cucumbers preserved in vinegar. In French cooking, they are known as cornichons.

Variation

Use 3 tbsp (45 mL) sweet relish in place of the gherkins and capers.

Serving Idea

To make an attractive appetizer, cut the rolls into 1-inch (2.5 cm) slices. Thread half a gherkin, then an egg roll slice, onto a cocktail skewer.

Nutrients per serving

Calories	226
Fat	12.5 g
Saturated fat	2.9 g
Sodium	545 mg (23% DV)
Carbohydrate	18 g
Fiber	2 g (8% DV)
Protein	10 g
Calcium	47 mg (4% DV)
Iron	1.5 mg (11% DV)

Very high in: Folate and vitamin B_{12}

High in: Magnesium, vitamin A, thiamine and riboflavin

Diabetes Food Choice Values:

1	Carbohydrate
1	Meat & Alternatives
1½	Fats

Egg Salad Roll

Caroline Dubeau, Dietitian, Ontario

4	hard-cooked eggs, peeled	4
2 tbsp	finely chopped drained gherkins	30 mL
1 tbsp	chopped drained capers	15 mL
1 tbsp	finely chopped fresh parsley	15 mL
1 tbsp	finely snipped fresh chives	15 mL
¼ cup	light mayonnaise	60 mL
4	6-inch (15 cm) whole wheat tortillas	4
4	romaine or Boston lettuce leaves	4

1. In a medium bowl, mash eggs with a fork. Stir in gherkins, capers, parsley, chives and mayonnaise until well combined. Spread mixture evenly over tortillas. Top with lettuce and roll up.

Chives are one of the easiest herbs to grow. A member of the onion family, they provide a subtle but distinct onion flavor. Chive blossoms, which are light pink or purple, are also edible. They make an attractive garnish for salads or other recipes that contain chives.

✔ Kid Approved

This is a terrific way to use up leftover cooked chicken. The apple and dried cranberries add a nice sweetness to the chicken mixture.

Tips

You can also use a panini grill to toast the buns.

The chicken filling can be prepared up to 1 day in advance. Cover and refrigerate.

Variation

Substitute cooked turkey for the chicken and add ¼ tsp (1 mL) dried sage to the mixture.

Chicken on a Roll

Caroline Dubeau, Dietitian, Ontario

1 cup	cubed or shredded cooked chicken	250 mL
½	apple, finely diced	½
2 tbsp	finely chopped dried cranberries	30 mL
2 tbsp	finely chopped green onion	30 mL
¼ cup	light mayonnaise	60 mL
1 tsp	cider vinegar	5 mL
	Salt and freshly ground black pepper	
4	whole wheat hot dog buns	4

1. In a bowl, combine chicken, apple, cranberries and green onion. Stir in mayonnaise and vinegar. Season to taste with salt and pepper.

2. In a nonstick skillet, over medium heat, lightly toast cut sides of buns, using a spatula to flatten them. Divide the chicken mixture among the buns and serve warm.

> Skip toasting the bun and add this sandwich to a lunch box, along with carrot sticks, 100% apple juice and yogurt. Be sure to keep the sandwich chilled safely with an ice pack.

Nutrients per serving

Calories	270
Fat	10.0 g
Saturated fat	1.9 g
Sodium	443 mg (18% DV)
Carbohydrate	33 g
Fiber	4 g (16% DV)
Protein	15 g
Calcium	63 mg (6% DV)
Iron	1.8 mg (13% DV)

Very high in: Niacin

High in: Magnesium, zinc and vitamin B_6

Diabetes Food Choice Values:

2	Carbohydrates
1½	Meat & Alternatives
1	Fat

Four Perfect Chicken Panini

For panini, a popular way to make grilled sandwiches, a variety of fillings are placed between 2 slices of bread or panini buns and grilled in a panini grill. If you don't have a panini grill, you can simply grill the sandwich in a skillet over medium heat, using a spatula to flatten it and turning to grill both sides.

Preparing the Chicken

Chicken breast is a very popular panini ingredient. Here, we teach you to properly prepare a chicken breast fillet to make it "grill-ready."

1. Remove and discard the cartilage or connective tissue (the white strips that seem to hold the breast muscles together) from one large (8 oz/250 g) boneless skinless chicken breast. This fiber is tough when cooked.

2. If it's present, remove the tenderloin muscle. (This will look like a "chicken finger," and indeed is what true chicken fingers are made from.) Freeze these tenderloins to make chicken strips another time.

3. Starting from the thicker end of the breast, cut the chicken breast in half horizontally so that each half is about $\frac{1}{2}$ inch (1 cm) thick.

Marinating the Chicken

There are two types of marinades: wet and dry. Wet marinades are typically made of some type of acid (wine, vinegar, lemon juice), herbs and/or spices and oil (which helps release or carry the flavors of the herbs and/or spices). Dry marinades, often called "rubs," are a mixture of dried herbs and/or spices that is rubbed onto the item before cooking. Here, we give you two wet marinades, each of which makes enough for 2 large chicken breasts (4 fillets).

Mediterranean Marinade

1	clove garlic, finely minced	1
2 tsp	dried basil	10 mL
2 tsp	dried oregano	10 mL
1 tsp	hot pepper flakes	5 mL
$\frac{1}{2}$ tsp	freshly ground black pepper	2 mL
2 tbsp	canola or olive oil	30 mL
2 tbsp	water	30 mL
2 tsp	freshly squeezed lemon juice	10 mL

1. In a small bowl, whisk together garlic, basil, oregano, hot pepper flakes, black pepper, oil, water and lemon juice.

2. Place 4 chicken fillets (from 2 large breasts) in a glass or ceramic plate or sealable plastic bag. Pour marinade over chicken and coat both sides. Cover and refrigerate for at least 30 minutes or for up to 2 hours. When ready to cook chicken, drain off and discard excess marinade.

Cajun Marinade

1	clove garlic, finely minced	1
2 tsp	chili powder	10 mL
2 tsp	ground cumin	10 mL
2 tsp	ground coriander	10 mL
½ tsp	freshly ground black pepper	2 mL
2 tbsp	canola oil	30 mL
2 tbsp	water	30 mL
4 tsp	freshly squeezed lime juice	20 mL

1. In a small bowl, whisk together garlic, chili powder, cumin, coriander, pepper, oil, water and lime juice.

2. Place 4 chicken fillets (from 2 large breasts) in a glass or ceramic plate or sealable plastic bag. Pour marinade over chicken and coat both sides. Cover and refrigerate for at least 30 minutes or for up to 2 hours. When ready to cook chicken, drain off and discard excess marinade.

Grilling the Chicken

To grill chicken breasts, preheat barbecue grill to medium-high. Grill chicken, turning once, for 3 to 4 minutes per side or until no longer pink inside and an instant-read thermometer inserted in the thickest part of a fillet registers 165°F (74°C).

If using a panini grill, preheat grill to medium-high. Grill chicken for 5 to 6 minutes or until no longer pink inside and an instant-read thermometer inserted in the thickest part of a fillet registers 165°F (74°C). Watch the heat on your panini grill; if the chicken starts to darken too quickly, reduce the temperature.

Versatile Panini Spread

Keep this tasty spread on hand for panini and other types of sandwiches.

Makes about ¼ cup (60 mL)
Serving size: 1 tsp (5 mL)

¼ cup	low-fat cream cheese, softened	60 mL
½ tsp	minced garlic	2 mL
1 tbsp	finely chopped fresh basil	15 mL
1 tbsp	finely chopped drained oil-packed sun-dried tomatoes, patted dry	15 mL
½ tsp	freshly ground black pepper	2 mL

1. In a small bowl, combine cream cheese, garlic, basil, sun-dried tomatoes and pepper; stir well.

2. Use immediately or cover and refrigerate for up to 3 days.

Caramelized Onions

These add terrific flavor to panini and other sandwiches. They are typically prepared with a lot of oil, but with low heat and slow cooking, you can use much less.

Makes 1 cup (250 mL)
Serving size: 1 tbsp (15 mL)

1½ tbsp	canola or olive oil	22 mL
2	onions, very thinly sliced	2
1 tbsp	balsamic vinegar	15 mL
¼ tsp	freshly ground black pepper	1 mL

1. In a large nonstick skillet, heat oil over medium-high heat, swirling to coat. Add onions and stir to coat with oil. Sauté until onions turn slightly brown. Reduce heat to medium-low and cook, stirring every 3 to 4 minutes, for 15 minutes or until golden brown (do not let burn).

2. Stir in vinegar and pepper. Cook, stirring every 3 to 4 minutes, for 8 to 10 minutes or until onions are very soft and dark golden brown.

3. Use immediately or let cool, transfer to an airtight container and refrigerate for up to 5 days.

Assembling and Grilling the Panini

For all of these panini, you'll first need to preheat the panini grill to medium-high. Each of these sandwiches is 1 serving.

Chicken Panini à la Med

1/4 tsp	canola oil or non-hydrogenated margarine	1 mL
2	slices whole-grain bread (or 1 panini bun, split)	2
2 oz	grilled Mediterranean chicken breast (1/2 of fillet, page 72)	60 g
2 tsp	Versatile Panini Spread (page 74)	10 mL
3	arugula leaves	3

1. Lightly brush oil over one side of each bread slice (or outsides of bun). Flip bread over and spread each slice with half the panini spread. Arrange chicken and arugula on one slice. Cover with the other slice, oiled side up. Press gently to pack.

2. Place sandwich in preheated grill, close the top plate and cook for 2 to 3 minutes or until golden brown. Serve immediately.

Nutrients per serving

Calories 325	**Sodium** 464 mg (19% DV)	**Protein** 21 g
Fat 9.4 g	**Carbohydrate** 41 g	**Calcium** 108 mg (10% DV)
Saturated fat 2.1 g	**Fiber** 6 g (24% DV)	**Iron** 3.6 mg (26% DV)

Very high in: Magnesium, vitamin B$_6$, folate and niacin / **High in:** Zinc, thiamine and riboflavin

Diabetes Food Choice Values: 2 1/2 Carbohydrates / 2 Meat & Alternatives

Chicken Panini with Pesto and Jack Cheese

1/4 tsp	canola oil or non-hydrogenated margarine	1 mL
2	slices whole-grain bread (or 1 panini bun, split)	2
1 tsp	basil pesto	5 mL
2 oz	grilled Mediterranean chicken breast (1/2 of fillet, page 72)	60 g
1/2 oz	Monterey Jack cheese, sliced	15 g

1. Lightly brush oil over one side of each bread slice (or outsides of bun). Flip bread over and spread each slice with half the pesto. Arrange chicken and cheese on one slice. Cover with the other slice, oiled side up. Press gently to pack.

2. Place sandwich in preheated grill, close the top plate and cook for 2 to 3 minutes or until golden brown and cheese is melted. Serve immediately.

(see over for nutrient analysis)

Nutrients per serving (Chicken Panini with Pesto and Jack Cheese)

Calories 374	Sodium 571 mg (24% DV)	Protein 24 g
Fat 13.9 g	Carbohydrate 40 g	Calcium 203 mg (18% DV)
Saturated fat 4.2 g	Fiber 6 g (24% DV)	Iron 3.5 mg (25% DV)

Very high in: Magnesium, vitamin B$_6$, folate and niacin / **High in:** Zinc, vitamin B$_{12}$, thiamine and riboflavin

Diabetes Food Choice Values: 2 Carbohydrates / 2 Meat & Alternatives / 1 Fat

Cajun Chicken Panini with Roasted Bell Peppers

1/4 tsp	canola oil or non-hydrogenated margarine	1 mL
2	slices whole-grain bread (or 1 panini bun, split)	2
2 tsp	Versatile Panini Spread (page 74)	10 mL
2 oz	grilled Cajun chicken breast (1/2 of fillet, page 73)	60 g
1/2	roasted red bell pepper (see box, page 124)	1/2

1. Lightly brush oil over one side of each bread slice (or outsides of bun). Flip bread over and spread each slice with half the panini spread. Arrange chicken and roasted pepper on one slice. Cover with the other slice, oiled side up. Press gently to pack.

2. Place sandwich in preheated grill, close the top plate and cook for 2 to 3 minutes or until golden brown. Serve immediately.

Nutrients per serving

Calories 337	Sodium 469 mg (20% DV)	Protein 21 g
Fat 9.7 g	Carbohydrate 43 g	Calcium 102 mg (9% DV)
Saturated fat 2.1 g	Fiber 6 g (24% DV)	Iron 4.0 mg (29% DV)

Very high in: Magnesium, vitamin C, vitamin B$_6$, folate, thiamine and niacin / **High in:** Zinc, vitamin A and riboflavin

Diabetes Food Choice Values: 2 1/2 Carbohydrates / 2 Meat & Alternatives

Cajun Chicken Panini with Hummus

¼ tsp	canola oil or non-hydrogenated margarine	1 mL
2	slices whole-grain bread (or 1 panini bun, split)	2
2 tsp	hummus	10 mL
2 oz	grilled Cajun chicken breast (½ of fillet, page 73)	60 g
1	romaine lettuce leaf	1

1. Lightly brush oil over one side of each bread slice (or outsides of bun). Flip bread over and spread each slice with half the hummus. Arrange chicken and lettuce on one slice. Cover with the other slice, oiled side up. Press gently to pack.

2. Place sandwich in preheated grill, close the top plate and cook for 2 to 3 minutes or until golden brown. Serve immediately.

Nutrients per serving

Calories 321	**Sodium** 473 mg (20% DV)	**Protein** 21 g
Fat 8.9 g	**Carbohydrate** 42 g	**Calcium** 94 mg (9% DV)
Saturated fat 1.3 g	**Fiber** 6 g (24% DV)	**Iron** 3.9 mg (28% DV)

Very high in: Magnesium, vitamin B$_6$, folate, thiamine and niacin / **High in:** Zinc and riboflavin

Diabetes Food Choice Values: 2½ Carbohydrates / 2 Meat & Alternatives

✔ **Kid Approved**

Corinne has been making these sandwiches — a great use for leftover corn on the cob — for years. Now in their late teens, her daughters make them themselves when they're looking for childhood comfort.

Tips

Use Jonagold or Cortland apples, as they are less likely to turn brown when shredded.

You can reduce or vary the type of cheese to your liking.

This is a terrific after-school treat when a more substantial snack is needed.

Open-Face Quirky Grilled Cheese

Corinne Eisenbraun, Dietitian, Manitoba

● **Preheat broiler**

1	apple, peeled and shredded	1
¼ cup	finely chopped red onion	60 mL
¾ cup	cooked or frozen corn kernels (thawed and drained if frozen)	175 mL
1½ cups	shredded Cheddar cheese	375 mL
1 to 2 tsp	Worcestershire sauce	5 to 10 mL
6	slices dark rye or pumpernickel bread	6

1. In a large bowl, combine apple, red onion, corn, cheese and Worcestershire sauce to taste.

2. Place bread on a baking sheet. Broil until toasted on one side.

3. Divide corn mixture evenly on untoasted side of bread slices. Broil for 3 to 4 minutes or until cheese is melted and bubbly.

> Pumpernickel bread, made from both rye and wheat flour, gets its dark brown color from the molasses added to the dough.

Nutrients per serving

Calories	212
Fat	10.4 g
Saturated fat	6.2 g
Sodium	348 mg (14% DV)
Carbohydrate	21 g
Fiber	2 g (8% DV)
Protein	10 g
Calcium	225 mg (20% DV)
Iron	1.1 mg (8% DV)

High in: Folate

Diabetes Food Choice Values:

1	Carbohydrate
1	Meat & Alternatives
1	Fat

This may sound like an odd combination, but give it a try — it's delicious!

Tips

Check the weight of bread slices: *Canada's Food Guide* uses 35 g as 1 bread serving, but many bread slices weigh 45 g or more.

Check the sodium content of sliced bread on the Nutrition Facts table. Although bread doesn't taste salty, many sliced breads contain a lot of sodium. Look for those with the lowest "% DV" (percent daily value) per serving.

You can use purchased or homemade pesto in this recipe.

Variation

Vary the cheese to your liking. For example, try Havarti with jalapeño peppers or Oka.

Nutrients per serving

Calories	216
Fat	6.9 g
Saturated fat	2.3 g
Sodium	476 mg (20% DV)
Carbohydrate	22 g
Fiber	3 g (12% DV)
Protein	17 g
Calcium	151 mg (14% DV)
Iron	2.2 mg (16% DV)

Very high in: Vitamin B_{12} and niacin

High in: Magnesium, vitamin B_6 and folate

Diabetes Food Choice Values:

1	Carbohydrate
2	Meat & Alternatives

Open-Face Tuna Sandwich with Pesto

Sandra Smith, Dietitian, Manitoba

2 tbsp	basil pesto	30 mL
4	slices whole-grain or multigrain bread, toasted	4
1	can (7½ oz/213 g) water-packed light tuna, drained and flaked	1
1	large tomato, cut into 4 slices	1
4	thin slices red onion (optional)	4
½ cup	shredded part-skim mozzarella cheese	125 mL

1. Spread 1½ tsp (7 mL) pesto over each bread slice. Divide tuna evenly on top. Top each with 1 tomato slice, 1 red onion slice (if using) and one-quarter of the cheese.

2. Broil until tuna is heated through and cheese is melted.

> The fish used in canned light tuna is generally younger and smaller and has significantly less mercury than fresh or frozen tuna, so, for the most part, Canadians don't need to be concerned about consuming canned tuna. The exception is canned white albacore tuna, which comes from larger fish.

Makes 4 servings

The ginger marmalade is the key ingredient, giving a little zip to this sandwich. Serve it for lunch with a crisp green salad.

Tips

Stir the salmon mixture gently if you like your salad flaky; stir vigorously for a smoother texture.

More than half the sodium in this recipe comes from the bun. Look for buns with the lowest % DV of sodium per serving.

Variation

Use canned tuna instead of salmon.

Nutrients per serving

Calories	343
Fat	8.9 g
Saturated fat	1.5 g
Sodium	588 mg (25% DV)
Carbohydrate	49 g
Fiber	4 g (16% DV)
Protein	17 g
Calcium	182 mg (17% DV)
Iron	2.9 mg (21% DV)

Very high in: Vitamin D and vitamin B$_{12}$
High in: Niacin

Diabetes Food Choice Values:
3   Carbohydrates
2   Meat & Alternatives

Open-Face Salmon Salad Sandwich with Apple and Ginger

Mary Sue Waisman, Dietitian, Nova Scotia

● **Preheat broiler**

1	can (7½ oz/213 g) salmon, drained	1
¼ cup	light mayonnaise	60 mL
2 tbsp	finely chopped green onion	30 mL
¼ cup	finely chopped apple	60 mL
1 tbsp	freshly squeezed lemon juice	15 mL
1 tsp	finely grated gingerroot	5 mL
2 tsp	curry powder	10 mL
½ tsp	cayenne pepper	2 mL
4	thin whole-grain hamburger buns, split	4
3 tbsp	ginger marmalade	45 mL
1	apple, peeled and cut into 8 slices (optional)	1
1 tbsp	liquid honey (optional)	15 mL

1. In a small bowl, combine salmon, mayonnaise, green onion, chopped apple, lemon juice, ginger, curry powder and cayenne.

2. Place hamburger buns cut side up on a baking sheet. Spread each with about 1 tsp (5 mL) ginger marmalade. Divide salmon mixture evenly on top. If desired, place 1 apple slice on top of salmon mixture and brush with honey.

3. Broil for 4 to 5 minutes or until salmon mixture is warm.

> Gingerroot, commonly known as ginger, has an important place in food history, with its use dating back to 500 to 600 BC in Southeast Asia. The underground root of the plant is used in cooking. Sliced, minced or grated gingerroot is often used to enhance flavor in Indian and Asian dishes. It is also used to make ginger ale, ginger beer and ground ginger, commonly used in baking to flavor items such as gingerbread, ginger snaps and molasses cookies.

Two Open-Face Portobello Sandwiches

Portobello mushroom caps make the ideal base for open-face sandwiches and are a nice alternative to bread. To prepare the mushroom cap, cut the stem flush with the cap. Discard the stem or save it for another use. Brush the top of the mushroom cap with a paper towel to remove excess dirt. Using a spoon, lightly scrape off the gills on the underside of the cap and discard them. Lightly brush each side of the mushroom cap with $1/2$ tsp (2 mL) canola oil. Grill on a preheated panini grill for 2 to 3 minutes, or on a barbecue grill over medium heat for 2 to 3 minutes per side.

Brie and Walnut Portobello Sandwich

Spread 1 tbsp (15 mL) cherry jam over a 4-inch (10 cm) grilled mushroom cap. Top with 1 oz (30 g) thinly sliced Brie cheese and 2 tsp (10 mL) finely chopped walnuts.

Nutrients per serving

Calories 219	**Sodium** 190 mg (8% DV)	**Protein** 9 g
Fat 13.7 g	**Carbohydrate** 17 g	**Calcium** 63 mg (6% DV)
Saturated fat 5.4 g	**Fiber** 2 g (8% DV)	**Iron** 0.7 mg (5% DV)

Very high in: Riboflavin / **High in:** Folate, vitamin B_{12} and niacin

Diabetes Food Choice Values: 1 Carbohydrate / 1 Meat & Alternatives / 2 Fats

Roast Beef and Caramelized Onion Portobello Sandwich

Spread 1 tbsp (15 mL) caramelized onions (see page 74) over a 4-inch (10 cm) grilled mushroom cap. Top with 2 oz (60 g) thinly sliced lean roast beef and 2 tsp (10 mL) crumbled herbed feta cheese.

Nutrients per serving

Calories 183	**Sodium** 109 mg (5% DV)	**Protein** 22 g
Fat 8.4 g	**Carbohydrate** 4 g	**Calcium** 39 mg (4% DV)
Saturated fat 2.7 g	**Fiber** 1 g (4% DV)	**Iron** 2 mg (17% DV)

Very high in: Zinc, vitamin B_{12}, riboflavin and niacin

Diabetes Food Choice Values: 2 Meat & Alternatives

Lentils are very versatile and work well with both savory and sweet salads. This one has the added sweetness of fresh oranges and dried cranberries.

Tip

Instead of using canned lentils, you can cook dried lentils. Place ½ cup (125 mL) dried green or yellow lentils in a saucepan with 1½ cups (375 mL) water. Bring to a boil, then reduce heat and simmer for 20 to 30 minutes or until tender. Check near the end of cooking and add more water if the lentils become dry. Drain well. Makes about 1¼ cups (300 mL) cooked lentils.

Serving Idea

Serve this salad on top of mixed greens for a refreshing lunch. Add a glass of cold milk and some chopped fresh fruit.

Nutrients per serving

Calories	186
Fat	7.3 g
Saturated fat	0.6 g
Sodium	258 mg (11% DV)
Carbohydrate	25 g
Fiber	5 g (20% DV)
Protein	8 g
Calcium	50 mg (5% DV)
Iron	2.6 mg (19% DV)

Very high in: Vitamin C and folate

High in: Magnesium

Diabetes Food Choice Values:

1   Carbohydrate
1   Meat & Alternatives
1   Fat

Refreshing Lentil Salad

Julie Aubé, Dietitian, Quebec

2	plum (Roma) tomatoes, seeded and diced	2
2	oranges, peeled and cut into segments	2
1	can (19 oz/540 mL) lentils, drained and rinsed	1
½ cup	sliced green onions	125 mL
¼ cup	coarsely chopped fresh cilantro	60 mL
3 tbsp	coarsely chopped dried cranberries	45 mL
⅓ cup	freshly squeezed lemon juice	75 mL
2 tbsp	canola oil	30 mL
½ tsp	freshly ground black pepper	2 mL
¼ tsp	salt	1 mL
¼ cup	toasted slivered almonds (see page 139)	60 mL

1. In a large bowl, combine tomatoes, oranges, lentils, green onions, cilantro and cranberries. Drizzle with lemon juice and oil; toss to coat. Sprinkle with pepper and salt. Top with toasted almonds.

Makes 6 servings

This delicious salad, complete with vegetables, cheese and beans, is as pretty as a picture! Serve it for a weekend lunch with friends and save any leftovers for workday or school lunches.

Tips

If served as a side salad at a potluck supper, this dish will serve 10 people.

To make this dish in a snap, enlist the help of family members to chop, drain and crumble the ingredients.

Variation

For a different taste, try Oka, blue cheese or Havarti instead of the mozzarella and/or the feta.

Nutrients per serving

Calories	243
Fat	12.0 g
Saturated fat	5.1 g
Sodium	559 mg (23% DV)
Carbohydrate	25 g
Fiber	5 g (20% DV)
Protein	11 g
Calcium	225 mg (20% DV)
Iron	1.5 mg (11% DV)

Very high in: Vitamin C, vitamin B$_6$ and folate

High in: Magnesium, zinc, vitamin A, vitamin B$_{12}$ and riboflavin

Diabetes Food Choice Values:

1	Carbohydrate
1	Meat & Alternatives
1½	Fats

Tomato, Cheese and Chickpea Salad

Adapted from Dairy Farmers of Canada (www.dairygoodness.ca)

2	shallots, finely chopped	2
1	can (19 oz/540 mL) chickpeas, drained and rinsed	1
2 cups	cherry tomatoes, cut in half	500 mL
1 cup	chopped yellow bell peppers	250 mL
1 cup	chopped red bell peppers	250 mL
¾ cup	diced part-skim mozzarella cheese	175 mL
⅔ cup	crumbled feta cheese	150 mL
¼ cup	chopped fresh basil	60 mL
¼ cup	freshly squeezed lemon juice	60 mL
2 tbsp	extra virgin olive oil	30 mL
½ tsp	freshly ground black pepper	2 mL
¼ tsp	salt	1 mL

1. In a large bowl, combine shallots, chickpeas, tomatoes, yellow peppers, red peppers, mozzarella, feta and basil.

2. In a small bowl, whisk together lemon juice, oil, pepper and salt. Pour dressing over salad and toss gently to coat.

✔ Kid Approved

This vibrantly colored salad is a hit with kids of all ages.

Tip

To prevent the cooked pasta from sticking together, have all the other salad ingredients ready to add as soon as it's drained.

Variations

Omit the arugula and serve the salad on a bed of lettuce.

Use canned salmon instead of tuna and add 2 tsp (10 mL) chopped fresh dill.

Serving Idea

Serve some cut-up fresh fruit with low-fat flavored yogurt for dessert.

Nutrients per serving

Calories	160
Fat	3.0 g
Saturated fat	0.6 g
Sodium	304 mg (13% DV)
Carbohydrate	22 g
Fiber	3 g (12% DV)
Protein	11 g
Calcium	72 mg (7% DV)
Iron	1.4 mg (10% DV)

Very high in: Vitamin B_{12} and niacin

High in: Magnesium and vitamin C

Diabetes Food Choice Values:

1   Carbohydrate
1   Meat & Alternatives

Whole Wheat Pasta and Tuna Salad

Melissa Kazan, Quebec

8 oz	whole wheat fusilli pasta	250 g
2	cans (each 6 oz/170 g) water-packed flaked tuna, drained	2
¾ cup	finely chopped red, green or yellow bell pepper (or a combination)	175 mL
¾ cup	finely chopped red onion	175 mL
¾ cup	coarsely chopped arugula	175 mL
½ cup	cooked green peas	125 mL
1 cup	low-fat plain yogurt	250 mL
¼ cup	light mayonnaise	60 mL
1½ tsp	Dijon mustard	7 mL
1 tsp	tarragon vinegar	5 mL
½ tsp	freshly ground black pepper	2 mL
¼ tsp	salt	1 mL

1. In a large pot of boiling salted water, cook pasta according to package directions. Drain and transfer to a large bowl.

2. Add tuna, bell pepper, onion, arugula and peas to pasta and stir to combine. Let cool slightly.

3. In a small bowl, whisk together yogurt, mayonnaise, mustard, vinegar, pepper and salt. Add to pasta mixture and stir well to coat noodles. Cover and refrigerate for at least 4 hours or for up to 8 hours before serving.

Yogurt provides tang, hot mango chutney supplies heat, and dried fruits lend sweetness, making this dish a favorite among adults and children alike.

Tips

When you're making a chicken dish, cook 2 extra breasts to use the next day to prepare this salad.

To reduce the sugar content, omit the apricots and/or dates.

Serving Idea

Serve as a salad on a bed of spinach or use as a filling in a whole wheat pita for lunch or a quick dinner.

Nutrients per serving

Calories	279
Fat	12.9 g
Saturated fat	2.4 g
Sodium	432 mg (18% DV)
Carbohydrate	27 g
Fiber	3 g (12% DV)
Protein	16 g
Calcium	57 mg (5% DV)
Iron	1.5 mg (11% DV)

Very high in: Niacin

High in: Magnesium and vitamin B$_6$

Diabetes Food Choice Values:

1½ Carbohydrates

2 Meat & Alternatives

1 Fat

Indian Curry Chicken Salad

Abbey Fitzpatrick, Ontario

½ cup	light mayonnaise	125 mL
¼ cup	low-fat Greek-style yogurt	60 mL
⅓ cup	hot mango chutney	75 mL
1 tsp	curry powder	5 mL
½ tsp	freshly ground black pepper	2 mL
Pinch	salt	Pinch
2 cups	diced cooked chicken	500 mL
1 cup	chopped celery	250 mL
1 cup	seedless grapes, cut in half	250 mL
½ cup	chopped dried apricots	125 mL
¼ cup	chopped dates	60 mL
¼ cup	sliced green onions	60 mL
¼ cup	toasted slivered almonds (see page 139)	60 mL

1. In a large bowl, whisk together mayonnaise, yogurt, chutney, curry powder, pepper and salt. Gently stir in chicken, celery, grapes, apricots, dates, green onions and almonds.

> In North America, Greek-style yogurt usually refers to a thick plain yogurt that is used to make dips, dressings and sauces. It is also available in low-fat varieties.

Snacks, Dips and Appetizers

Appetizers are intended to stimulate your appetite, getting you ready for the main course. It's also common nowadays to have appetizer parties, or to use appetizers as snacks. Three square meals a day used to be the mantra of healthy eating, but the value of snacks is now recognized. A mid-morning snack can help quell hunger and get you through until lunch, and a mid-afternoon snack can stave off hunger until suppertime. It is, however, important to choose your snacks wisely. This chapter includes a variety of appetizers and snacks chosen for their delicious flavor and nutritious ingredients.

Lighten Up!

Many traditional appetizers use large amounts of high-fat ingredients, such as mayonnaise, sour cream, cream cheese and cheese. But there are lower-fat varieties of most of these products, and fat-free varieties of some. Another option is to substitute a lower-fat ingredient, such as yogurt. Here are some tips on how to use these alternatives.

Mayonnaise

Commercial regular mayonnaise is made with oil, egg yolks and lemon juice or vinegar, and usually provides about 100 calories per tbsp (15 mL), with 11 g fat. Reduced-fat versions contain about 50 calories per tbsp (15 mL) and about 5 g fat. You can generally replace the regular version with the light version when making dips, devilled eggs or salads and still have a tasty product.

> Using a lower-fat product in a recipe can sometimes create a different texture or flavor than would have been the case with the regular ingredient — just be aware that this might happen and adjust your taste buds!

Sour Cream

To make sour cream, specially cultured bacteria are added to pasteurized, homogenized light cream to "sour" it. (In days gone by, cream was left to sour on top of a warm stove.) Take a look at the energy and fat content of the various sour creams, and at those of low-fat plain yogurt, in the table below.

Light sour cream contains less fat but a bit more carbohydrate than regular. It works well as a substitute in dips and dressings.

Fat-free sour cream contains no fat and about half the amount of calories as regular, with most of the calories coming from carbohydrate. It usually works to substitute fat-free sour cream for regular in dips and dressings, but they may taste sweeter and be a bit thinner.

Low-fat plain yogurt can be an acceptable substitute for regular sour cream in dips and dressings and in quick breads and cakes. Its tart taste is similar to that of regular sour cream, and it is not as sweet as lower-fat sour creams, which have added sugars. As a bonus, it has more calcium.

Per 1 cup (250 mL)	Calories (kcal)	Protein (g)	Fat (g)	Carbohydrate (g)
Regular sour cream (14% milk fat)	440	17	34	17
Light sour cream (5% milk fat)	360	9	28	19
Fat-free sour cream	200	8	0	42
1% to 2% plain yogurt	160	14	4	18

Cream Cheese

Cream cheese, made from cow's milk, is a fresh, unripened cheese with a minimum of 30% milk fat. The table below compares the various cream cheeses.

As with sour cream, lower-fat versions of cream cheese can generally be substituted in dips, dressings or spreads.

Per 1 tbsp (15 mL)	Calories (kcal)	Protein (g)	Fat (g)	Carbohydrate (g)
Regular cream cheese	50	1	5	1
Low-fat or light cream cheese	30	1	2	1
Fat-free cream cheese	20	2	0	1

Cheese

While most cheeses provide ample protein and calcium, they also have substantial calories and fat per serving. Lower-fat varieties of some cheeses are available. The table below compares three Cheddar cheeses.

Per 1½ oz (50 g)	Calories (kcal)	Protein (g)	Fat (g)	Carbohydrate (g)
Regular Cheddar cheese (32% milk fat)	200	12	17	1
Reduced-fat Cheddar cheese (18% milk fat)	140	14	9	1
Low-fat Cheddar cheese (7% milk fat)	85	12	4	1

The reduced-fat and low-fat varieties are good alternatives to regular cheese for snacks and sandwiches. However, they melt very differently from regular cheese, producing a tough, stringy result when used, for example, in a casserole or as a pizza topping. Rather than making a complete switch to lower-fat cheese in cooking, try using less regular cheese or using half regular and half lower-fat cheese. You could also use a smaller amount of a stronger-tasting cheese, such as Asiago or Parmesan, to get a big flavor boost with a moderate portion size.

Family Cooking Lesson

Common Cooking Terms

Chopping when you're supposed to mince and mincing when you're supposed to chop can have unpleasant consequences in a recipe. Here's the lowdown on common cooking terms:

- **Chop:** To cut into uneven pieces. Generally speaking, coarsely chopped pieces are $\frac{3}{4}$ to 1 inch (2 to 2.5 cm) in size, chopped pieces are $\frac{1}{2}$ to $\frac{3}{4}$ inch (1 to 2 cm), and finely chopped pieces are $\frac{1}{4}$ to $\frac{1}{2}$ inch (0.5 to 1 cm).

- **Cube:** To cut into uniform cubes about $\frac{1}{2}$ inch (1 cm) on each side.

- **Dice:** To cut into small, uniform cubes, about $\frac{1}{4}$ inch (0.5 cm) on each side.

- **Mince:** To cut into very small, uneven pieces, generally $\frac{1}{8}$ inch (3 mm) or less.

- **Stir or combine:** To mix ingredients with a spoon until they are evenly distributed.

- **Beat:** To vigorously stir ingredients, either with a spoon or with an electric mixer. Beating is generally done to incorporate air into a mixture or to develop gluten.

- **Blend:** To mix ingredients with a blender until they form a homogeneous mixture, with the parts indistinguishable.

- **Cream:** To combine sugar and fat (such as butter), creating a uniform mixture where the sugar is evenly dispersed in the fat. Generally used in baking recipes (e.g., for cookies and cakes).

- **Whisk:** To use a wire whisk to combine ingredients or incorporate air.

- **Whip:** To use a wire whisk or an electric mixer to vigorously beat ingredients, generally to incorporate air, as with egg whites.

- **Fold:** To gently combine two or more ingredients, usually with a rubber spatula, to create a uniform mixture.

- **Knead:** To press, fold and stretch a dough, using either your hands or the dough hook on an electric mixer, to help stretch the gluten in flour.

- **Sauté:** To cook stirring constantly or frequently.

- **Heat until steaming:** To heat a liquid or food until steam rises from the surface and small bubbles form but do not rise and break the surface.

- **Simmer:** To cook a liquid or food while small bubbles break the surface at a slow but constant pace.

- **Boil gently:** To cook a liquid or food while larger bubbles break the surface at a moderate pace. If stirred, bubbles will subside slightly, then resume as soon as stirring stops.

- **Boil:** To cook a liquid or food while large bubbles break the surface at a rapid pace. If stirred, bubbles will continue to break the surface, but slightly more slowly.

Jennifer gives these nuts
as Christmas gifts instead
of chocolates and always
gets rave reviews. She
credits her mom with this
tasty recipe.

Tip

Nuts contain a lot of oil and
can burn easily, so be careful
with the heat and adjust it if
the nuts get too dark before
the sugar caramelizes.

Variation

Use walnuts or pecans instead
of almonds.

Serving Idea

These make a nice
accompaniment to a cheese
tray after dinner.

Nutrients per serving

Calories	292
Fat	21.9 g
Saturated fat	1.7 g
Sodium	154 mg (6% DV)
Carbohydrate	20 g
Fiber	4 g (16% DV)
Protein	8 g
Calcium	84 mg (8% DV)
Iron	1.7 mg (12% DV)

Very high in: Magnesium

Diabetes Food Choice Values:

1	Carbohydrate
1	Meat & Alternatives
3 1/2	Fats

Spicy Almonds

Jennifer House, Dietitian, Alberta

● **Baking sheet, lined with parchment paper**

2 tsp	ground cumin	10 mL
2 tsp	hot pepper flakes	10 mL
1/2 tsp	salt	2 mL
2 tbsp	canola oil	30 mL
2 cups	blanched whole almonds	500 mL
1/2 cup	granulated sugar	125 mL

1. In a large bowl, combine cumin, pepper flakes and salt; set aside.

2. In a large skillet, heat oil over medium-high heat. Sauté nuts for 1 minute to coat well. Sprinkle sugar over nuts and sauté until nuts are golden and sugar starts to caramelize.

3. Immediately add nuts to spice mixture and stir well to combine. Spread out on prepared baking sheet and let cool.

Roasted Chickpeas

Jaclyn Pritchard, Dietitian, Ontario

Makes about 1¹/₂ cups (375 mL)

Serving size: 2 tbsp (30 mL)

✔ Kid Approved

Roasted chickpeas make a nice savory snack alternative to chips. Kids love the crunch, but be sure they're old enough that these do not pose a choking hazard.

Tips

Be sure to drain and rinse the beans to remove excess sodium. Pat them dry so the coating adheres.

These can be stored in an airtight container at room temperature for 1 week, but they likely won't last that long!

Variation

Vary the spices to your liking; added cayenne pepper will give them a hot kick.

- **Preheat oven to 350°F (180°C)**
- **Baking sheet, lined with foil**

1	can (19 oz/540 mL) chickpeas, rinsed, drained and patted dry	1
1 tbsp	canola oil	15 mL
¹/₂ tsp	chili powder	2 mL
¹/₄ tsp	garlic powder	1 mL
¹/₄ tsp	ground cumin	1 mL

1. In a small bowl, combine chickpeas, oil, chili powder, garlic powder and cumin. Stir to coat well. Spread evenly on preparing baking sheet.

2. Bake in preheated oven, stirring occasionally, for 60 to 75 minutes or until crisp. Let cool on pan on a wire rack.

Nutrients per serving

Calories	55
Fat	1.6 g
Saturated fat	0.2 g
Sodium	98 mg (4% DV)
Carbohydrate	9 g
Fiber	2 g (8% DV)
Protein	2 g
Calcium	11 mg (1% DV)
Iron	0.5 mg (4% DV)

Diabetes Food Choice Values:

¹/₂   Carbohydrate
¹/₂   Fat

These are the perfect accompaniment to guacamole, instead of fried nacho chips.

Tips

For ease in cutting, stack 2 to 3 pitas together before cutting them into wedges.

These chips will stay crisp in a sealable plastic bag or airtight container for up to 7 days.

Serving Idea

Serve with Warm Green Goddess Dip (page 97) or Legume Guacamole (page 95).

Holy Smokes Pita Chips

Mary Sue Waisman, Dietitian, Nova Scotia

● **Preheat oven to 375°F (190°C)**

2	cloves garlic, finely minced	2
2 tsp	ground cumin	10 mL
½ tsp	chili powder	2 mL
½ tsp	paprika	2 mL
½ tsp	curry powder	2 mL
½ tsp	freshly ground black pepper	2 mL
¼ tsp	salt	1 mL
1 to 2 tbsp	canola oil	15 to 30 mL
2 to 3	drops hot pepper sauce	2 to 3
6	6-inch (15 cm) whole wheat pitas	6

1. In a small bowl, combine garlic, cumin, chili powder, paprika, curry powder, black pepper, salt, oil and hot pepper sauce to taste.

2. Using a pastry brush, coat both sides of each pita with spice mixture and cut each into 8 wedges. Spread wedges in a single layer on two baking sheets.

3. Bake in preheated oven, turning once, for 8 to 10 minutes or until pitas are brown and crisp. Let cool completely on pans on a wire rack.

Nutrients per serving

Calories	98
Fat	2.1 g
Saturated fat	0.2 g
Sodium	220 mg (9% DV)
Carbohydrate	18 g
Fiber	3 g (12% DV)
Protein	3 g
Calcium	10 mg (1% DV)
Iron	1.2 mg (9% DV)

Diabetes Food Choice Values:

1	Carbohydrate
½	Fat

Baked Masala Puri

Shefali Raja, Dietitian, British Columbia

✔ **Kid Approved**

The sesame seeds in these puri provide a wonderful nutty flavor once baked; they are a nice change from crackers. Kids can help roll them out.

Tip

For an evenly browned color on the puri, place the baking sheet on the middle rack of the oven and bake one sheet at a time.

Variation

If a stronger sesame taste is desired, use 1½ tsp (7 mL) each sesame oil and canola oil.

Serving Idea

These puri are great on their own as a snack, but also make great entertaining fare when paired with a dip or spread.

● **Preheat oven to 325°F (160°C)**

½ cup	whole wheat flour	250 mL
1 tbsp	canola oil	15 mL
2 tsp	sesame seeds	10 mL
½ tsp	ground cumin	2 mL
½ tsp	freshly ground black pepper	2 mL
¼ tsp	ground turmeric	1 mL
¼ tsp	salt	1 mL
¼ cup	chopped fresh cilantro (optional)	60 mL
2 tbsp	water (approx.)	30 mL

1. In a medium bowl, combine whole wheat flour, oil, sesame seeds, cumin, pepper, turmeric, salt and cilantro (if using). Add a small amount of water and mix with your hands to form a stiff dough.

2. Turn dough out onto a floured surface and knead for 2 to 3 minutes or until dough is soft and smooth. Leave dough on floured surface and cover with large bowl. Let rest for 10 minutes.

3. Divide dough into 25 equal portions. On a lightly floured surface, roll out each portion into a thin round, about 2 inches (5 cm) in diameter. Prick with a fork and place at least 2 inches (5 cm) apart on baking sheets.

4. Bake in preheated oven for 15 minutes. Flip puri over and bake for 10 minutes or until golden brown. Remove from oven and let cool.

> Puri (often spelled "poori") are unleavened breads of Indian origin. They are traditionally large breads that are fried and then filled with curries; here, Shefali has made them into small, cracker-type morsels and baked them to reduce the fat content.

Nutrients per serving

Calories	15
Fat	0.7 g
Saturated fat	0.1 g
Sodium	23 mg (1% DV)
Carbohydrate	2 g
Fiber	0 g (0% DV)
Protein	0 g
Calcium	2 mg (0% DV)
Iron	0.1 mg (1% DV)

Diabetes Food Choice Values:

1   Extra

This dish is both sweet and spicy, which makes for a great flavor combination.

Tips

Shefali's recipe calls for tamarind chutney, but since it is not readily available, we substituted hot mango chutney, which provides a very pleasant taste.

For the best texture, use a tart apple, such as Granny Smith or Cortland.

Variation

Use the dhai ingredients to make a delicious potato salad, perfect for a summer barbecue. Combine the potato mixture with the remaining ingredients. Serve the salad on its own or place about 4 puri on a plate and evenly distribute the potato mixture over top.

Nutrients per serving

Calories	91
Fat	0.7 g
Saturated fat	0.1 g
Sodium	81 mg (3% DV)
Carbohydrate	20 g
Fiber	2 g (8% DV)
Protein	2 g
Calcium	36 mg (3% DV)
Iron	1.1 mg (8% DV)

Diabetes Food Choice Values:

1   Carbohydrate

Dhai Puri

Shefali Raja, Dietitian, British Columbia

6	baby potatoes (each about 2 inches/5 cm)	6
½ tsp	hot pepper flakes	2 mL
¼ cup	plain yogurt or light sour cream	60 mL
1 tsp	ground cumin	5 mL
1	apple, peeled and finely chopped	1
½ cup	cooked or canned chickpeas, rinsed and drained	125 mL
½ cup	coarsely chopped fresh cilantro	125 mL
¼ cup	finely chopped onion	60 mL
2 tbsp	hot mango chutney	30 mL
25	Baked Masala Puri (page 93)	25

1. Place baby potatoes in a saucepan and add enough cold water to cover. Bring to a boil over high heat. Reduce heat and boil gently for about 15 minutes or until fork-tender. Drain and let cool. Cut into small cubes. Place in a small bowl and toss with hot pepper flakes.

2. In another small bowl, combine yogurt and cumin. Place apple, chickpeas, cilantro, onion and chutney in separate small bowls. Place puri in the center of the table, surrounded by the small bowls, and let everyone top their own dhal puri, using the desired ingredients.

Cilantro and coriander are not the same ingredient, though many people think they are. Cilantro is the leafy herb of the *Coriandrum sativum* plant; coriander is the spice made from the seed or ground seed of the same plant. They each offer a distinct flavor and are used differently in recipes, so read the ingredient lists carefully.

Legume Guacamole

Mary Sue Waisman, Dietitian, Nova Scotia

**Makes about
1¹/₂ cups (375 mL)**

Serving size: 2 tbsp
(30 mL)

Puréed peas mimic the color of mashed avocado and help reduce the overall fat content of this popular snack dip.

Tip

Vary the heat and flavor intensity by adjusting the amounts of lime juice, jalapeño and hot pepper sauce.

Variation

If you dislike cilantro, use chopped fresh parsley instead.

Serving Idea

Use this as a spread on grilled vegetable sandwiches.

Nutrients per serving

Calories	50
Fat	3.4 g
Saturated fat	0.5 g
Sodium	76 mg (3% DV)
Carbohydrate	5 g
Fiber	2 g (8% DV)
Protein	1 g
Calcium	11 mg (1% DV)
Iron	0.5 mg (4% DV)

Diabetes Food Choice Values:
1   Fat

● **Food processor or blender**

1 cup	frozen baby peas	250 mL
1	ripe avocado	1
3	cloves garlic, minced	3
1	jalapeño pepper, seeded and coarsely chopped	1
¼ cup	coarsely chopped fresh cilantro	60 mL
2 tbsp	chopped red onion	30 mL
3 tbsp	freshly squeezed lime or lemon juice	45 mL
2 tbsp	light mayonnaise	30 mL
1 tsp	ground cumin	5 mL
½ tsp	chili powder	2 mL
½ tsp	freshly ground white pepper	2 mL
¼ tsp	salt	1 mL
1 cup	coarsely chopped plum (Roma) tomatoes	250 mL
½ to 1 tsp	hot pepper sauce (optional)	2 to 5 mL

1. In a small saucepan, bring ¼ cup (60 mL) water to a boil over high heat. Add peas and return to a boil. Reduce heat to low, cover and simmer for 4 minutes. Remove from heat and let cool.

2. Peel avocado and scoop flesh into food processor. Add cooled peas (along with any remaining liquid from the pan), garlic, jalapeño, cilantro, red onion, lime juice, mayonnaise, cumin, chili powder, pepper and salt; pulse until chopped. Purée for about 1 minute or until mostly smooth with some small bits remaining.

3. Transfer to a bowl and gently stir in tomatoes. Season to taste with hot pepper sauce (if using).

> While avocados contain a healthy type of fat, they do have a lot of it, which adds to the calorie content of a recipe. Substituting a legume that mimics the color for some of the avocado helps to reduce the fat and still provides a smooth, flavorful product.

Serving size: 2 tbsp
(30 mL)

Make yogurt cheese
from plain yogurt for a
delicious, rich-tasting
dip. The endive spears
reminded Honey of
spoons, so she thought
they'd make perfect
dippers.

Tips

For the best texture, when
choosing yogurt for this recipe,
read the label carefully and
make sure it doesn't contain
any gelatin or starch.

You can let the yogurt drain
for up to 1 day. The longer
it drains, the thicker it will
become.

Serving Idea

This dip would make a
delicious topping for grilled
chicken.

Yogurt Dill Dip with Belgian Endive

Honey Bloomberg, Dietitian, Ontario

- **Colander or strainer**
- **Cheesecloth**

3 cups	low-fat plain yogurt (see tip, at left)	750 mL
1	clove garlic, finely minced	1
2 tbsp	chopped fresh dill	30 mL
¼ tsp	salt	1 mL
¼ tsp	freshly ground white pepper	1 mL
1 tsp	extra virgin olive oil or canola oil	5 mL
	Grated zest and juice of 1 lemon	
2	heads Belgian endive, leaves separated	2

1. Line colander with a double layer of cheesecloth and set over a large bowl. Place yogurt in colander, cover and refrigerate. Let drain for 3 to 5 hours or until yogurt is thickened and resembles soft cream cheese. Discard liquid in bowl.

2. Place yogurt cheese in a medium bowl. Stir in garlic, dill, salt, pepper, oil, lemon zest and lemon juice. Serve with endive leaves for dipping.

Nutrients per serving

Calories	25
Fat	0.7 g
Saturated fat	0.3 g
Sodium	56 mg (2% DV)
Carbohydrate	3 g
Fiber	0 g (0% DV)
Protein	0 g
Calcium	73 mg (7% DV)
Iron	0.1 mg (1% DV)

Diabetes Food Choice Values:
1   Extra

Warm Green Goddess Dip

Mary Sue Waisman, Dietitian, Nova Scotia

Serving size: 2 tbsp (30 mL)

✔ Kid Approved

Warm from the oven, this dip is sure to impress guests with its flavor and texture.

Tip

To thaw frozen spinach, remove it from the package, place it in a microwave-safe bowl and defrost in the microwave until thawed, stirring occasionally. When thawed, drain and squeeze out excess water.

Variation

If you prefer a very smooth dip, purée the ingredients in a blender or food processor instead of combining them by hand.

Serving Idea

Serve with Holy Smokes Pita Chips (page 92) or a platter of cut-up fresh vegetables.

Nutrients per serving

Calories	71
Fat	4.0 g
Saturated fat	1.7 g
Sodium	201 mg (8% DV)
Carbohydrate	6 g
Fiber	2 g (8% DV)
Protein	4 g
Calcium	98 mg (9% DV)
Iron	0.5 mg (4% DV)

High in: Vitamin A

Diabetes Food Choice Values:
1   Fat

- **Preheat oven to 375°F (190°C)**
- **8-inch (20 cm) square glass baking dish, greased**

1 tbsp	canola oil	15 mL
1 cup	finely chopped onion	250 mL
½ cup	finely chopped green onion	125 mL
¼ cup	finely chopped red bell pepper	60 mL
3	cloves garlic, finely minced	3
1	can (14 oz/398 mL) artichoke hearts, drained, patted dry and coarsely chopped	1
1	package (10 oz/300 g) frozen chopped spinach, thawed, squeezed dry and coarsely chopped	1
¼ cup	finely chopped fresh parsley, divided	60 mL
½ cup	light sour cream	125 mL
½ cup	light herb-and-garlic-flavored cream cheese	125 mL
2 tbsp	light mayonnaise	30 mL
¼ tsp	salt	1 mL
¼ tsp	freshly ground black pepper	1 mL
½ cup	shredded part-skim mozzarella cheese	125 mL
¼ cup	freshly grated Parmesan cheese	60 mL

1. In a medium skillet, heat oil over medium-high heat. Sauté onion, green onion and red pepper for 3 to 5 minutes or until softened. Add garlic and sauté for 30 seconds. Remove from heat and let cool.

2. In a large bowl, combine artichoke hearts, spinach, 2 tbsp (30 mL) of the parsley, sour cream, cream cheese, mayonnaise, salt and pepper. Stir in the cooled onion mixture. Transfer to prepared baking dish.

3. Bake in preheated oven for about 20 minutes or until heated through. Remove from oven and sprinkle with the remaining parsley and the mozzarella and Parmesan. Bake for about 5 minutes or until cheese is slightly melted.

> Although cream cheese is made from cow's milk, it is not considered a Milk and Alternatives in *Eating Well with Canada's Food Guide*, as its nutrients do not meet the standard for this food group.

Makes 1¹/₂ cups (375 mL)

Serving size: 2 tbsp (30 mL)

If you're looking for a snack with some heat, this is it! This dip also makes a delicious spread for sandwiches, as an alternative to mayonnaise.

Tip

It's best to start by adding just one pepper to the dip, then you can add more to taste.

Variation

For Asian flair, add a few drops of sesame oil and garnish this dip with sesame seeds.

Serving Idea

Spread some of this piquant dip inside a whole wheat pita pocket and fill it with roasted eggplant, zucchini, onions and peppers.

Piquant White Bean and Parsley Dip

Mary Sue Waisman, Dietitian, Nova Scotia

● **Food processor or blender**

2	green onions, coarsely chopped	2
2	cloves garlic, minced	2
1 to 2	jalapeño peppers, seeded and coarsely chopped	1 to 2
1	can (19 oz/540 mL) white kidney beans, drained and rinsed	1
¹/₂ cup	loosely packed chopped fresh parsley	125 mL
¹/₄ cup	freshly squeezed lemon juice	60 mL
1 tbsp	canola oil	15 mL
1 tsp	ground cumin	5 mL

1. In food processor, combine green onions, garlic, jalapeños to taste, beans, parsley, lemon juice, oil and cumin; process until smooth.

2. Transfer to a bowl, cover and refrigerate for at least 1 hour, until chilled, or for up to 1 day.

> There are two types of parsley (a perennial herb) commonly grown in Canada and used widely by cooks: flat-leaf (Italian) parsley and curly parsley.

Nutrients per serving

Calories	48
Fat	1.4 g
Saturated fat	0.1 g
Sodium	104 mg (4% DV)
Carbohydrate	7 g
Fiber	3 g (12% DV)
Protein	2 g
Calcium	20 mg (2% DV)
Iron	0.7 mg (5% DV)

Diabetes Food Choice Values:

¹/₂ Carbohydrate

Roasted Red Pepper and Feta Hummus

Trisha Wood, Dietitian, Ontario

● **Food processor or blender**

2	red bell peppers, roasted and peeled (see box, page 124)	2
2	cloves garlic, minced	2
1	can (19 oz/540 mL) chickpeas, drained and rinsed	1
½ cup	crumbled feta cheese	125 mL
2 tbsp	chopped fresh parsley	30 mL
2 tbsp	tahini	30 mL
2 tbsp	freshly squeezed lemon juice	30 mL
1 tbsp	canola oil	15 mL
¼ tsp	cayenne pepper	1 mL
½	lemon	½

1. In food processor, combine roasted peppers, garlic, chickpeas, feta, parsley, tahini, 2 tbsp (30 mL) lemon juice, 2 tbsp (30 mL) water, oil and cayenne; process until smooth.

2. Transfer to a bowl, cover and refrigerate for at least 1 hour, until chilled, or for up to 1 day. Squeeze fresh lemon juice over dip before serving.

> Tahini is a paste or butter made from crushed sesame seeds. It has a distinctive nutty taste and coarse texture. It is frequently used in Middle Eastern cooking.

Makes ½ cup (125 mL)

Serving size: 1 tbsp (15 mL)

Three simple ingredients give big taste to this chunky spread.

Tips

Don't mash the sardines too much, or you'll end up with more of a paste than a spread.

Try Mediterranean-style or lemon-flavored sardines.

Serving Idea

Serve with crudités, whole-grain crackers or toasted French baguette slices.

Sardine and Pesto Spread

Claude Gamache, Dietitian, Quebec

1	can (3½ oz/106 g) sardines, drained	1
2 tbsp	basil pesto	30 mL
1 tbsp	freshly squeezed lime juice	15 mL

1. In a small bowl, mash sardines with a fork. Stir in pesto and lime juice until just blended.

> Sardines are an often overlooked food. They are a good choice for people trying to increase their intake of vitamin B_{12}. Sardines are also one of the types of fish that *Eating Well with Canada's Food Guide* recommends enjoying often for their health-promoting omega-3 fats.

Nutrients per serving

Calories	37
Fat	2.5 g
Saturated fat	0.4 g
Sodium	98 mg (4% DV)
Carbohydrate	1 g
Fiber	0 g (0% DV)
Protein	3 g
Calcium	48 mg (4% DV)
Iron	0.4 mg (3% DV)

Very high in: Vitamin B_{12}

Diabetes Food Choice Values:
½   Meat & Alternatives

Beet Jelly

Michèle LaFramboise, Ontario

Makes about 7 to 8 cups (1.75 to 2 L)

Serving size: 1 tbsp (15 mL)

✔ **Kid Approved**

Michèle's husband helps grate the beets for this dish, which she prepares annually. When her children were young, she coaxed them into eating beets with this recipe! Now, her married children ask for beet jelly every year, and she also trades it for pickles made by her nieces. Our taste testers were asking for more!

Tip

Beets can temporarily stain counters and your hands, so wear plastic gloves, work carefully and wipe up spills quickly.

Serving Idea

Serve with light cream cheese spread on crackers or crudités or alongside roasted meats or poultry.

5 lbs	whole medium beets	2.5 kg
2 cups	granulated sugar	500 mL
½ cup	all-purpose flour	125 mL
1 tsp	dry mustard	5 mL
Pinch	salt	Pinch
2 cups	white vinegar	500 mL

1. Place beets in a large pot and add enough cold water to cover. Bring to a boil over high heat. Reduce heat and boil gently for 45 to 60 minutes or until fork-tender. Drain and rinse under cold water. When cool enough to handle, peel off and discard skins. On the coarse side of a box grater, grate beets into a large bowl; set aside.

2. In a clean large pot, combine sugar, flour, mustard and salt. Whisk in vinegar. Heat over medium heat, stirring often, until bubbling and sauce thickens. Remove from heat. Pour over grated beets and stir to combine.

3. Cover and refrigerate for 24 hours. Use immediately or place 1-cup (250 mL) portions of beet jelly in freezer bags and freeze flat for up to 1 year. Let thaw before using.

Nutrients per serving

Calories	23
Fat	0.0 g
Saturated fat	0.0 g
Sodium	14 mg (1% DV)
Carbohydrate	6 g
Fiber	0 g (0% DV)
Protein	0 g
Calcium	3 mg (0% DV)
Iron	0.1 mg (1% DV)

Diabetes Food Choice Values:
½ Carbohydrate

Simple ingredients create a festive look in these pretty appetizers.

Variation

Make this into a salad. Break endive leaves into bite-size pieces and toss with the other ingredients. If desired, drizzle with 1 to 2 tbsp (15 to 30 mL) olive oil and 1 tbsp (15 mL) white wine vinegar.

Appetizer Endive Salad

Heather McColl, Dietitian, British Columbia

2	pears (unpeeled), diced	2
1 tsp	grated orange zest	5 mL
1 tbsp	freshly squeezed orange juice	15 mL
2 to 3 oz	blue cheese, crumbled	60 to 90 g
½ cup	chopped toasted walnuts (see page 139)	125 mL
	Seeds from 1 pomegranate	
4	heads Belgian endive, separated into leaves (about 30)	4

1. In a medium bowl, toss pears with orange zest and orange juice. Add blue cheese, walnuts and pomegranate seeds; toss gently to combine.

2. Divide filling evenly among endive leaves.

Nutrients per serving

Calories	62
Fat	3.7 g
Saturated fat	1.0 g
Sodium	54 mg (2% DV)
Carbohydrate	7 g
Fiber	1 g (4% DV)
Protein	2 g
Calcium	29 mg (3% DV)
Iron	0.1 mg (1% DV)

Diabetes Food Choice Values:
½   Carbohydrate
½   Fat

**Makes about
2 cups (500 mL)
filling**

Serving size: 2 wraps

✔ **Kid Approved**

Lettuce wraps are a fresh alternative to bread-based wraps. These are best assembled individually at the table. Three 18-year-old taste testers finished this entire recipe off in no time at all!

Tips

You could also use cooled cooked cabbage leaves as the wraps.

Children enjoy filling and rolling their own wraps.

Variation

Ground beef, pork or vegetarian ground round can be used in place of turkey.

Serving Idea

These would be great served at a teen's birthday party.

Nutrients per serving

Calories	69
Fat	3.1 g
Saturated fat	0.7 g
Sodium	95 mg (4% DV)
Carbohydrate	5 g
Fiber	1 g (4% DV)
Protein	6 g
Calcium	13 mg (1% DV)
Iron	0.7 mg (5% DV)

High in: Vitamin C

Diabetes Food Choice Values:

1   Meat & Alternatives

Rainbow Lettuce Wraps

Heather McColl, Dietitian, British Columbia

1 lb	lean ground turkey or chicken	500 g
1 tbsp	grated gingerroot	15 mL
2 tsp	canola oil	10 mL
¾ cup	finely chopped red bell pepper	175 mL
¾ cup	finely chopped yellow bell pepper	175 mL
½ cup	finely chopped onion	125 mL
2	cloves garlic, minced	2
1	can (8 oz/227 mL) sliced water chestnuts, drained and chopped	1
¼ cup	hoisin sauce	60 mL
¾ tsp	Chinese five-spice powder	3 mL
¼ to ½ tsp	hot pepper flakes	1 to 2 mL
½ cup	shredded carrot	125 mL
1	head butter lettuce, leaves separated	1

1. In a large nonstick skillet, over medium heat, brown turkey and ginger, breaking up turkey with a spoon, for 5 to 6 minutes or until no longer pink. Transfer to a bowl and set aside.

2. In the same skillet, heat oil over medium heat. Sauté red pepper, yellow pepper and onion for 4 to 5 minutes or until vegetables are softened. Add garlic and sauté for 30 seconds. Return turkey to skillet and stir in water chestnuts, hoisin sauce, ¼ cup (60 mL) water, five-spice powder and hot pepper flakes to taste; cook, stirring often, for 3 to 4 minutes or until heated through. Transfer to a serving bowl.

3. Arrange carrot and lettuce leaves on a large platter and set out with the turkey mixture. Top each lettuce leaf with 2 tbsp (30 mL) of the turkey mixture, then carrot. Wrap lettuce to enclose filling.

> Butter lettuce is a type of head lettuce that has, as the name implies, a smooth, buttery texture. Varieties of butter lettuce include Boston and Bibb.

✔ **Kid Approved**

These delicious vegetarian appetizers, filled with fresh flavor and color, would also make a nice after-school snack.

Tip

For guaranteed success with an herb garden, start by growing mint. It grows well in most climates and grows wild in many parts of Canada.

Variations

Use black beans or kidney beans instead of chickpeas.

Add some heat to the mixture with minced jalapeño or a few drops of hot pepper sauce.

Serving Idea

Add a wedge of cheese and a piece of fresh fruit to turn this snack into a wholesome lunch.

Bulgur and Vegetable Lettuce Wraps

Leila Smaily, Dietitian, Ontario

¾ cup	bulgur	175 mL
¾ cup	warm water	175 mL
1 cup	diced tomatoes	250 mL
½ cup	cooked or canned chickpeas, drained and rinsed	125 mL
¼ cup	chopped fresh parsley	60 mL
2 tbsp	chopped green onion	30 mL
2 tbsp	chopped red onion	30 mL
1 tbsp	chopped fresh mint	15 mL
2 tbsp	canola oil	30 mL
1 tbsp	freshly squeezed lemon juice	15 mL
¼ tsp	salt	1 mL
½ tsp	freshly ground black pepper	2 mL
1	head butter lettuce, leaves separated	1

1. In a large bowl, combine bulgur and warm water. Let stand for 30 minutes, until bulgur is softened and liquid is absorbed.

2. Add tomatoes, chickpeas, parsley, green onion, red onion, mint, oil, lemon juice, salt and pepper. Stir well to combine.

3. Top each lettuce leaf with 2 tbsp (30 mL) bulgur mixture. Wrap lettuce to enclose filling.

People often confuse cracked wheat with bulgur. Cracked wheat is simply whole wheat grains that are crushed or cracked into smaller bits, while bulgur is wheat kernels that have been parched, steamed and dried. Bulgur is often used in Middle Eastern cooking, in dishes such as tabbouleh.

Nutrients per serving

Calories	50
Fat	2.0 g
Saturated fat	0.2 g
Sodium	39 mg (2% DV)
Carbohydrate	7 g
Fiber	1 g (4% DV)
Protein	2 g
Calcium	12 mg (1% DV)
Iron	0.5 mg (4% DV)

Diabetes Food Choice Values:
½ Carbohydrate
½ Fat

✔ **Kid Approved**

Pumpkin seeds are a unique alternative to pine nuts in the pesto that fills these yummy hors d'oeuvres.

Tip

If you need a last-minute appetizer, use purchased basil pesto to make these super-easy appetizers.

Variation

To give these appetizers a cheesy twist, combine half the pesto with ¼ cup (60 mL) softened goat cheese. Pipe into cored tomatoes. Cover and refrigerate the remaining pesto for up to 2 days for another use.

Pesto-Stuffed Tomatoes

Heather McColl, Dietitian, British Columbia

- **Food processor or blender**
- **Piping bag with medium-size round tip**

2	cloves garlic, minced	2
1 cup	packed fresh basil leaves	250 mL
⅓ cup	green pumpkin seeds (pepitas), toasted and cooled (see page 139)	75 mL
¼ tsp	salt	1 mL
¼ tsp	freshly ground black pepper	1 mL
3 tbsp	extra virgin olive oil	45 mL
24	cherry tomatoes, cored	24

1. In food processor, combine garlic, basil, pumpkin seeds, salt, pepper and oil; process until smooth.
2. Transfer pesto to piping bag and pipe into cherry tomatoes; do not overfill. Cover and refrigerate until chilled, for up to 4 hours.

> Green pumpkin seeds are also known as pepitas. They are often toasted to bring out their nutty flavor. Be sure to use hulled pumpkin seeds in this recipe.

Nutrients per serving

Calories	30
Fat	2.7 g
Saturated fat	0.3 g
Sodium	25 mg (1% DV)
Carbohydrate	1 g
Fiber	1 g (4% DV)
Protein	1 g
Calcium	7 mg (1% DV)
Iron	0.3 mg (2% DV)

Diabetes Food Choice Values:
½ Fat

Serving size: 2 half
peppers

Jalapeño peppers take on a smoky flavor when grilled on the barbecue.

Tip

Wear disposable gloves when working with jalapeños so the hot oils do not touch your skin.

Variation

In place of the hummus, stuff peppers with a mixture of $\frac{1}{4}$ cup (60 mL) light cream cheese, 2 tsp (10 mL) finely minced shallots, 2 tsp (10 mL) freshly squeezed lime juice, 1 tsp (5 mL) finely minced garlic and $\frac{1}{4}$ tsp (1 mL) freshly ground black pepper.

Grilled Stuffed Jalapeño Peppers

Adam Hudson, Dietitian, Ontario

- **Preheat barbecue grill to medium**

| 4 | jalapeño peppers, halved lengthwise and seeded | 4 |
| $\frac{1}{4}$ cup | chile pepper–flavored hummus or other hummus | 60 mL |

1. Fill each jalapeño half with $1\frac{1}{2}$ tsp (7 mL) hummus. Place on preheated barbecue, filling side up, and grill for 4 to 5 minutes or until grill marks form on underside of pepper.

> Jalapeño peppers are just one of over 100 varieties of chile peppers; despite their reputation, they are only considered medium-hot on the heat scale, as many other chiles can claim higher heat. Chipotle peppers are dried and smoked jalapeños.

Nutrients per serving

Calories	24
Fat	1.2 g
Saturated fat	0.2 g
Sodium	46 mg (2% DV)
Carbohydrate	2 g
Fiber	1 g (4% DV)
Protein	1 g
Calcium	6 mg (1% DV)
Iron	0.4 mg (3% DV)

Diabetes Food Choice Values:
1   Extra

Serving size: 3 pyrohy

✔ **Kid Approved**

Make pyrohy on a chilly Saturday, inviting the kids and grandkids over to help and then enjoy the meal together.

Tips

For the fruit, try any combination of berries, plums and/or cherries.

If you use frozen fruit, do not thaw it. Sweeten it slightly, if desired, and toss with up to ½ cup (125 mL) all-purpose flour to keep the juices from running out as the fruit thaws.

The pyrohy dough can be left out, covered, for several hours. It becomes softer with resting.

Variation

Instead of the fruit filling, try using a purchased poppy seed filling.

Nutrients per serving

Calories	141
Fat	1.5 g
Saturated fat	0.1 g
Sodium	23 mg (1% DV)
Carbohydrate	29 g
Fiber	2 g (8% DV)
Protein	3 g
Calcium	13 mg (1% DV)
Iron	1.5 mg (11% DV)

Very high in: Folate
High in: Thiamine

Diabetes Food Choice Values:
2   Carbohydrates
½   Fat

Fruit Pyrohy

Dianna Bihun, Dietitian, British Columbia

Dough

3 cups	all-purpose flour (approx.)	750 mL
Pinch	salt	Pinch
1 tbsp	canola oil	15 mL
1½ cups	warm water	375 mL

Fruit Filling

4 cups	finely chopped fresh seasonal fruit (see tips, at left)	1 L
	Granulated sugar (optional)	

Topping

2 tbsp	granulated sugar	30 mL
1 tsp	ground cinnamon	5 mL

1. *Dough:* In a large bowl, combine flour and salt. Gradually add oil, then warm water, incorporating flour with a wooden spoon as you pour. Stir until mixture holds together. Transfer to a lightly floured work surface and knead for about 10 minutes, until a soft and pliable dough forms, adding more flour as necessary to prevent sticking. Invert the bowl over the dough and let rest for at least 10 minutes.

2. *Filling:* In a bowl, combine fruit and sugar to taste (if using).

3. Pinch off a ball of dough about the diameter of a two-dollar coin. On a clean, lightly floured surface, roll out the dough until it is very thin (no thicker than about ⅛ inch/3 mm) and 2 to 2½ inches (5 to 6 cm) in diameter. Place the circle in the palm of your hand and place about 1 tsp (5 mL) filling in the center. Fold the circle in half and press the edges together with your fingers, making sure no filling has seeped through to the edges. Place pyrohy on a lightly floured board or work surface and cover with a clean tea towel. Do not let them stick together. Repeat with remaining dough and filling.

4. In a large pot of boiling water, boil 10 to 15 pyrohy at a time, stirring gently with a wooden spoon to separate and prevent sticking, for 3 to 5 minutes or until puffed. Using a slotted spoon, transfer pyrohy to a serving dish.

5. *Topping:* In a small bowl, combine sugar and cinnamon. Sprinkle over pyrohy.

✔ Kid Approved

We were thrilled to receive
this Eastern European
recipe, as it's great to
see food culture being
handed down through
the generations. Don't
be intimidated by this
recipe; the ingredients are
simple, and with a little
practice, you can master
the technique of rolling
them thinly.

Tips

The pyrohy dough can be left
out, covered, for several hours.
It becomes softer with resting.

The cooking time of the pyrohy
will vary depending on their
size and the thickness of the
dough.

Nutrients per serving

Calories	213
Fat	5.0 g
Saturated fat	0.7 g
Sodium	36 mg (2% DV)
Carbohydrate	34 g
Fiber	2 g (8% DV)
Protein	8 g
Calcium	34 mg (3% DV)
Iron	1.5 mg (11% DV)

Very high in: Folate
High in: Thiamine and niacin

Diabetes Food Choice Values:
2   Carbohydrates
1   Fat

Potato and Cheese Pyrohy

Dianna Bihun, Dietitian, British Columbia

Dough

3 cups	all-purpose flour (approx.)	750 mL
Pinch	salt	Pinch
1 tbsp	canola oil	15 mL
1½ cups	warm water	375 mL

Potato and Cheese Filling

4	medium baking potatoes, peeled and chopped	4
1 cup	shredded Cheddar cheese or dry-pressed cottage cheese	250 mL
2 tbsp	canola oil	30 mL
2 tbsp	finely chopped onion	30 mL
	Salt and freshly ground black pepper (optional)	

Topping

1 tbsp	canola oil	15 mL
½ cup	finely chopped onion	125 mL
½ cup	light sour cream	125 mL

1. *Dough:* In a large bowl, combine flour and salt. Gradually add oil, then warm water, incorporating flour with a wooden spoon as you pour. Stir until mixture holds together. Transfer to a lightly floured work surface and knead for about 10 minutes, until a soft and pliable dough forms, adding more flour as necessary to prevent sticking. Invert the bowl over the dough and let rest for at least 10 minutes.

2. *Filling:* Meanwhile, fill a large pot with water and bring to a boil over high heat. Add potatoes, reduce heat and boil gently for about 15 minutes or until fork-tender. Drain and transfer to a large bowl. Mash until fairly smooth. If using Cheddar cheese, stir it in now so it will melt, then let the mixture cool.

3. In a small skillet, heat oil over medium-high heat. Sauté onion for about 3 minutes or until softened. Stir into mashed potatoes. If using cottage cheese, stir it in now. Season to taste with salt and pepper (if using). Let cool completely.

4. Pinch off a ball of dough about the diameter of a two-dollar coin. On a clean, lightly floured surface, roll out the dough until it is very thin (no thicker than about $\frac{1}{8}$ inch/3 mm) and 2 to $2\frac{1}{2}$ inches (5 to 6 cm) in diameter. Place the circle in the palm of your hand and place about 1 tsp (5 mL) filling in the center. Fold the circle in half and press the edges together with your fingers, making sure no filling has seeped through to the edges. Place pyrohy on a lightly floured board or work surface and cover with a clean tea towel. Do not let them stick together. Repeat with remaining dough and filling.

5. In a large pot of boiling water, boil 10 to 15 pyrohy at a time, stirring gently with a wooden spoon to separate and prevent sticking, for 3 to 5 minutes or until puffed. Using a slotted spoon; transfer pyrohy to a serving dish.

6. *Topping:* Meanwhile, in a small skillet, heat oil over medium heat; sauté onion for about 8 minutes or until lightly browned. Add to pyrohy and toss gently to coat. Serve with sour cream on the side.

> Pyrohy, also known as pirozhki and pierogi, are dumplings of Eastern European origin. Many cultures make a dumpling-like food: Asian potstickers, Japanese gyoza, Italian ravioli and Swedish palt, for example.

Variations
Instead of the potato mixture, try filling each pyrohy with 1 tsp (5 mL) finely chopped sautéed mushrooms.

Fill each pyrohy with 1 tsp (5 mL) sauerkraut with sautéed onions in place of the potato filling.

Serving Idea
Serve alongside other traditional Eastern European foods, such as cabbage rolls.

In this unique appetizer, polenta (made from cornmeal) gets a protein boost from tofu (made from soybeans). Desiree's husband wasn't a tofu fan, so to get him to eat it, she had to get creative with presentation. With its layers of color and texture, this dish makes an elegant vegetarian first course.

Tips

Be patient when browning the tofu, as turning it too soon may cause it to break. An even browning will give the dish great texture.

This recipe can also be served as an entrée, with two towers per plate.

Variation

Use feta in place of the goat cheese.

Nutrients per serving

Calories	196
Fat	9.8 g
Saturated fat	2.1 g
Sodium	265 mg (11% DV)
Carbohydrate	16 g
Fiber	2 g (8% DV)
Protein	12 g
Calcium	150 mg (14% DV)
Iron	2.6 mg (19% DV)

Diabetes Food Choice Values:

1	Carbohydrate
1	Meat & Alternatives
1	Fat

Mediterranean Tofu Strata

Desiree Nielsen, Dietitian, British Columbia

- **Preheat oven to 200°F (100°C)**
- **Ovenproof plate**

2 tbsp	canola oil, divided	30 mL
1	roll precooked polenta (16 oz/500 g), sliced into 16 rounds	1
2 cups	coarsely chopped mushrooms	500 mL
1 cup	coarsely chopped zucchini (about 1 medium)	250 mL
⅛ tsp	hot pepper flakes	0.5 mL
3	cloves garlic, minced	3
2 cups	unsalted diced canned tomatoes	500 mL
1 tsp	chopped fresh thyme	5 mL
1	sprig fresh rosemary	1
1 lb	pressed firm tofu, cut crosswise into 16 slices	500 g
½ cup	crumbled goat cheese (chèvre)	125 mL

1. In a large nonstick skillet, heat 2 tsp (10 mL) of the oil over medium-high heat. In batches as necessary, brown polenta for 2 to 3 minutes per side or until crisp. Transfer to ovenproof plate and keep warm in preheated oven.

2. In the same skillet, over medium heat, heat 2 tsp (10 mL) of the oil. Sauté mushrooms, zucchini and hot pepper flakes for 4 to 5 minutes or until tender. Add garlic and sauté for 30 seconds. Stir in tomatoes, thyme and rosemary; bring to a boil. Reduce heat and simmer, stirring occasionally, for 20 minutes. Discard rosemary.

3. Meanwhile, in another nonstick skillet, heat the remaining oil over medium-high heat. Fry 8 of the tofu slices for 3 to 4 minutes per side or until lightly browned. Add browned tofu to the ovenproof plate and keep warm while browning the remaining tofu.

4. On each of eight serving plates, alternately layer 2 slices of polenta and 2 slices of tofu to build a tower. Evenly distribute the vegetable mixture over each tower. Crumble goat cheese over the top of each.

Makes 8 servings

✔ **Kid Approved**

This is a great way to introduce people to sushi, as the possible fillings are endless. And because these rolls are easy to eat with your fingers, they make great party snacks!

Tip

Keep a bowl of warm water near you as you work; you'll find it handy for cleaning your hands and knife, as the rice is very sticky.

Variations

Replace the crab with drained canned tuna or salmon mixed with an additional 1 tbsp (30 mL) light mayonnaise.

Instead of the sweet potato and avocado, try slices of cucumber, cooked carrot, red or green bell pepper or asparagus.

Nutrients per serving

Calories	267
Fat	5.5 g
Saturated fat	0.8 g
Sodium	113 mg (5% DV)
Carbohydrate	45 g
Fiber	4 g (16% DV)
Protein	9 g
Calcium	33 mg (3% DV)
Iron	0.8 mg (6% DV)

Very high in: Vitamin A and vitamin B$_{12}$
High in: Zinc, folate and niacin

Diabetes Food Choice Values:

3	Carbohydrates
1	Fat

Super-Easy Crab and Sweet Potato Sushi Rolls

Patricia Chuey, Dietitian, British Columbia

2 cups	sushi rice	500 mL
2 tbsp	rice vinegar	30 mL
1	sweet potato, peeled	1
8	sheets nori (dried seaweed)	8
2 tbsp	light mayonnaise	30 mL
1	avocado, cut into 16 slices	1
1 cup	chopped cooked crabmeat or imitation crab	250 mL
	Sodium-reduced soy sauce, wasabi and ginger (optional)	

1. Prepare rice according to package directions. Let cool. Stir in rice vinegar.

2. Slice sweet potato into 16 long strips, each about $\frac{1}{2}$ inch (1 cm) wide. Place in a microwave-safe dish and add a splash of water. Cover with plastic wrap, leaving one corner open for a vent, and microwave on High for 2 to 3 minutes or until just tender. Let cool.

3. Place 1 nori sheet on a work surface. Spread one-eighth of the rice in a thin layer over the bottom third of the sheet. Spread about $\frac{3}{4}$ tsp (3 mL) mayonnaise on top. Place 2 strips of sweet potato, 2 slices of avocado and one-eighth of the crab along the rice, extending the width of the nori sheet.

4. Gently lift the bottom end of the nori sheet and roll it up over the rice and filling, as you would roll a burrito. Roll slowly and tightly. When you are about 1 inch (2.5 cm) from the end, lightly moisten the remaining nori with a few drops of water and continue rolling to seal the roll. Set aside and repeat with the remaining nori sheets, rice, mayonnaise, sweet potato, avocado and crab. Slice into 2-inch (5 cm) rolls and, if desired, serve with small bowls of soy sauce, wasabi and ginger.

Sweet potatoes and yams are botanically unrelated and have many differences. Yams are grown on vines throughout the Caribbean, are less sweet and can weigh up to 40 lbs (18 kg). Sweet potatoes are grown as a root vegetable and are much smaller and sweeter.

Crab-Stuffed Baby Tomatoes

Mary Sue Waisman, Dietitian, Nova Scotia

Makes 6 servings

Serve these morsels of two-bite deliciousness on a serving platter lined with kale or other dark green leaves. If you're short on time, simply make the filling and serve it as a dip for crudités.

Tips

You can use imitation crab (crab-flavored pollock) instead of crabmeat, if you prefer.

Use a very sharp knife to get clean cuts in the tomato.

Variation

Add a few drops of hot pepper sauce or $\frac{1}{2}$ tsp (2 mL) curry powder to the crab mixture.

12	cocktail-size or large cherry tomatoes	12
1	can (5$\frac{1}{2}$ oz/156 g) crabmeat, drained	1
2 tbsp	light cream cheese (plain or flavored)	30 mL
2 tbsp	light mayonnaise	30 mL
1 tbsp	finely diced red onion	15 mL
1 tbsp	freshly squeezed lemon juice	15 mL
$\frac{1}{2}$ tsp	prepared horseradish	2 mL
1 tbsp	finely snipped chives	15 mL

1. Cut a very thin slice from the bottom of the tomatoes so they stand upright. Cut $\frac{1}{8}$ to $\frac{1}{4}$ inch (3 to 5 mm) from the tops and scoop out flesh; save for another use or discard. Turn tomatoes upside down on a plate lined with paper towels and let drain.

2. Pick through crabmeat to remove any shell or cartilage. In a small bowl, combine crab, cream cheese, mayonnaise, red onion, lemon juice and horseradish. Fill each tomato with about 2 tsp (10 mL) crab filling. Serve garnished with chives.

Nutrients per serving

Calories	53
Fat	2.8 g
Saturated fat	0.9 g
Sodium	194 mg (8% DV)
Carbohydrate	3 g
Fiber	1 g (4% DV)
Protein	4 g
Calcium	21 mg (2% DV)
Iron	0.7 mg (5% DV)

Diabetes Food Choice Values:
$\frac{1}{2}$ Meat & Alternatives

Plump sea scallops make an elegant first course. The small bit of butter is a key flavor ingredient.

Tip

Avoid soggy scallops by making sure they are well dried before breading them.

Variations

Season the bread crumbs with chopped herbs, such as fresh dill, parsley or cilantro, or with a spice such as curry powder.

Replace the lemon juice or the grapefruit juice with orange juice.

Serving Idea

Place 2 scallops and a bit of juice in a clean scallop shell and serve with a crusty whole-grain baguette slice.

Nutrients per serving

Calories	157
Fat	4.1 g
Saturated fat	2.0 g
Sodium	324 mg (14% DV)
Carbohydrate	9 g
Fiber	0 g (0% DV)
Protein	20 g
Calcium	42 mg (4% DV)
Iron	0.7 mg (5% DV)

Very high in: Magnesium and vitamin B$_{12}$
High in: Niacin

Diabetes Food Choice Values:
½ Carbohydrate
2 Meat & Alternatives

Simple Citrus Scallops

Mary Sue Waisman, Dietitian, Nova Scotia

8	large sea scallops (about 1 lb/500 g)	8
Pinch	salt	Pinch
Pinch	freshly ground black pepper	Pinch
¼ cup	fine dry bread crumbs	60 mL
1 tbsp	butter	15 mL
2 tbsp	freshly squeezed lemon juice	30 mL
2 tbsp	freshly squeezed grapefruit juice	30 mL
1 tbsp	finely snipped chives	15 mL

1. Place scallops on a dish lined with paper towels, cover with another towel and pat dry. Season scallops lightly with salt and pepper.

2. Place bread crumbs in a small dish. Dip scallops in bread crumbs, turning to coat evenly and shaking off excess. Discard excess bread crumbs.

3. In a large nonstick skillet, melt butter over medium-high heat, swirling to coat pan. When bubbles subside, place scallops in pan, being sure not to crowd the pan. Reduce heat to medium and cook for about 2 minutes or until bottom is lightly browned. Turn scallops over and cook for 2 minutes. Add lemon juice and grapefruit juice; cook until liquid is reduced by half and scallops are just firm and opaque throughout. Serve garnished with chives.

Five Fast and Fabulous Appetizers

Goat Cheese and Grape Skewers

Cut large red and green seedless grapes in half. For each appetizer, make a $1/2$-inch (1 cm) ball of plain or cranberry-flavored goat cheese and roll it in finely chopped toasted walnuts or pistachios. Thread a red grape half, a goat cheese ball and a green grape half onto each cocktail skewer.

Two-Bite Apricots

For each appetizer, make a 1- by $1/4$-inch (2.5 by 0.5 cm) disk of goat cheese and roll it in a mixture of finely chopped dried cranberries and toasted pistachios. Place each disk on a dried apricot half. Secure with a cocktail skewer, if desired.

Tortellini Skewers

Thread the following onto each cocktail skewer: a fresh basil leaf, a pitted black olive, a cooked tortellini, a grape tomato and another fresh basil leaf. (If desired, the tomatoes and tortellini could first be marinated in your favorite Italian vinaigrette.) For an attractive presentation, stand the skewers in a glass serving dish or a drinking glass.

Caramelized Pear with Brie

Peel a pear and cut it into 8 slices. In a nonstick skillet, melt 1 tsp (5 mL) butter over medium-high heat. Add 1 tsp (5 mL) pure maple syrup and swirl to coat pan. Add pear slices and cook, turning once or twice, for about 5 minutes or until caramelized. Place a small slice of Brie or Camembert cheese on a French baguette slice and top with a slice of caramelized pear.

Spicy Apple Slices

Thinly slice a Jonagold, Gala or Cortland apple. Top each slice with 1 to 2 arugula leaves and a thin slice of old Cheddar cheese.

Five Butter-Free Phyllo Appetizers

To prepare phyllo pastry appetizers or desserts, such as baklava, it is common to brush many layers of the paper-thin dough with butter. We found a way to use this popular pastry in a variety of appetizers without added butter.

Lay 2 sheets of phyllo on a clean work surface. Cover the remaining phyllo with a damp paper towel to prevent it from drying out as you work. Lightly spray phyllo with cooking spray. Cut phyllo in half lengthwise, then crosswise into 2-inch (5 cm) wide strips. You should have 14 pieces of dough. Place the desired filling (see suggestions, below) at the bottom of each strip. Fold the bottom corner diagonally over the filling and roll up, flag style, to create small triangular pouches. Lightly spray tops with cooking spray. Place on a lightly greased baking sheet. Bake in a 400°F (200°C) oven for 10 to 12 minutes or until pastry is golden and filling is hot.

Fillings

1. A $1/2$-inch (1 cm) ball of goat cheese rolled in finely minced dried cranberries and walnuts.
2. 1 thin slice of rare roast beef and $1^1/2$ tsp (7 mL) caramelized onions.
3. $1/2$ fresh strawberry, $1/2$ fresh mint leaf and a $1/2$-inch (1 cm) ball of goat cheese.
4. $1/2$ to 1 tsp (2 to 5 mL) Versatile Panini Spread (page 74).
5. A $1/2$-inch (1 cm) cube of Brie cheese rolled in finely minced dried apricots and pistachios.

Soups

Nothing says "comfort food" quite like a delicious homemade soup. Soups can have just a few simple ingredients or be brimming with a variety of vegetables, legumes and meats. Most soups are intended to be eaten hot, but a chilled soup, such as our Chilled Four-Berry Soup, can be very refreshing on a scorching hot day. Soup can be a starter course for an elegant meal, as with Roasted Pear and Parsnip Soup, or a meal in itself, like our Chicken Tortellini Soup. Cook up a batch of soup on the weekend and use it for lunches in the days to come.

What's All the Fuss About Salt?

Canadians eat too much salt — or, more precisely, too much sodium, which is found in salt. According to the Canadian Community Health Survey, Cycle 2.2 (Nutrition), Canadians currently ingest about 3,400 mg of sodium every day, which is much more than our bodies need. Eating too much sodium on a regular basis can increase your risk of developing high blood pressure, which, in turn, can increase the risk of heart disease, including heart attack, and stroke.

Most of the sodium we eat comes, not from the salt shaker, but from processed foods such as canned soups, deli meats, pizza, hot dogs and commercially prepared baked goods including breads. The Sodium Working Group (a multi-stakeholder group established by the Minister of Health to develop a population health strategy for reducing sodium intake among Canadians) recommends that all Canadians reduce their intake of sodium, and they hope to see the population's average daily intake reduced to 2,300 mg by 2016.

10 Ways to Lower Your Sodium Intake

1. Eat fresh foods most of the time. Prepare home-cooked meals. Look for quick, easy, lower-salt recipes and plan your meals ahead of time.

2. Season foods with lemon or lime juice, vinegar, wine, fresh garlic, herbs and spices. Avoid seasonings that contain salt, such as garlic salt or seasoning salt.

3. Avoid using salt at the table and use as little as possible in your cooking.

4. Read food labels for sodium content — it can vary significantly between different brands of the same food. For most foods, a low-sodium choice would be 140 mg or 5% DV or less per serving (or reference amount). Look for foods with the lowest percent Daily Value (% DV) for sodium.

5. Choose foods labeled "reduced sodium," "low sodium" or "no salt added." Continue to read the label. Many reduced-sodium foods, while better than the original, still have a lot of sodium. Remember, 5% DV or less is a little, 15% DV or more is a lot.

6. Limit portions of processed foods, and how often you eat them. These foods include, but are not limited to: canned or packaged soups; packaged pasta or rice with sauce; "instant" foods such as soup and noodles; processed cheese slices and spreads; processed, cured or smoked meats, such as sausage, wieners, ham, bacon, pepperoni and smoked fish and seafood; canned vegetables, meats and fish (though rinsing with water can reduce the sodium of these items); and tomato and vegetable juices.

7. Limit salted snack foods, such as chips, crackers, popcorn and nuts.

8. Limit pickled foods, relishes, salsa, dips, chutney, sauerkraut and olives.

9. Use small quantities of higher-salt condiments such as ketchup, mustard, soy sauce, salad dressing, barbecue sauce and other sauces.

10. Eat out less often. While many fast-food outlets and restaurants offer low-sugar and low-fat choices, their foods are often still high in sodium. Ask to see the nutrition information for the menu items and choose those with the lowest sodium content. Ask your server if menu items can be prepared without added salt, and ask for sauces and dressings to be served on the side.

Types of Salt

- **Table salt** is a fine-grained salt mined from salt mines. It usually contains an anti-caking agent, such as calcium silicate, to keep it free-flowing. In the 1920s, iodine was added to table salt to prevent goiter, which was common in many areas of North America where iodine was very low in the local food supply. Today, iodine deficiency is rare, but table salt is still iodized. Table salt is 99% sodium chloride.

- **Sea salt** is made by the evaporation of seawater. It is sometimes named after the sea it comes from. Gourmet cooks can often distinguish between varieties of sea salt because of their distinctive qualities, which can create subtle differences in flavor and finish. Unrefined sea salt contains 95% to 98% sodium chloride and 2% to 5% trace minerals.

- **Kosher salt** is basically table salt, but it contains no additives and has a coarse grain. It is used to prepare meat according to Jewish dietary regulations.

- **Pickling salt** is used for brines to make pickled foods. It is usually coarser than table salt, but unlike table salt, doesn't contain iodine or anti-caking ingredients, which would make the brine cloudy.

All of the above salts contain about 2,300 mg of sodium per teaspoon (5 mL).

Family Cooking Lesson

Add Flavor and Skip the Salt

It's all too common to flavor savory foods such as meats and vegetables by picking up the salt shaker and tossing on a few grains of salt. Instead, try one of these alternative flavor combinations for various meats and vegetables.

Meats and Alternatives	Flavors That Enhance the Food
Beans, peas, lentils	Parsley, savory, garlic, thyme, black pepper, mushrooms, cumin, curry powder, rosemary, sage, lemon juice or zest
Beef	Garlic, onions, thyme, bay leaf, black pepper, parsley, mushrooms
Chicken	Basil, bay leaf, cinnamon, garlic, ginger, lemon, parsley, rosemary, tarragon, thyme
Eggs	Black or white pepper, spinach, a variety of herbs and spices, onions, nutmeg
Fish	Dill, parsley, lemon juice, fennel, ginger, lemongrass
Lamb	Basil, bay leaf, cardamom, cinnamon, coriander, cumin, curry powder, fennel, garlic, ginger, lemon, mint, orange, oregano, parsley, black pepper, rosemary, sage, tarragon, thyme
Pork	Apples, ginger, sage, peaches, rosemary, bay leaf, thyme

Alternatives to Salt

- Salt-free seasoning blends can be used instead of salt to flavor food. They are a mixture of flavorful dried herbs and spices that don't contain sodium chloride.

- Salt substitutes replace some or all of the sodium in salt with another mineral such as potassium or magnesium. Potassium chloride is a common salt substitute.

- Season your food with herbs and spices instead of salt. See the suggestions above for inspiration.

Vegetables	Flavors That Enhance the Food
Beets	Chives, dill, lemon, orange juice or zest, shallots, tarragon, vinegars
Bell peppers	Basil, garlic, thyme
Broccoli	Chile peppers, garlic, lemon, tarragon, sesame seeds, sesame oil
Brussels sprouts	Garlic, lemon, parsley, black pepper, thyme, nutmeg, cider vinegar
Cabbage, white	Caraway seeds, garlic, juniper berries, black pepper, thyme
Cabbage, red	Apples, bay leaf, lemon, black pepper, balsamic vinegar
Carrots	Chervil, chile peppers, ginger, lemon, maple syrup, orange juice, parsley
Cauliflower	Curry, dill, garlic, lemon, mint, black pepper
Green beans	Basil, onions, parsley, savory, tomatoes, lemon juice or zest, orange juice or zest
Mushrooms	Garlic, parsley, rosemary, sage
Peas	Chervil, mint, sage, tarragon
Spinach	Dill, garlic, nutmeg, black pepper, sesame seeds
Squash	Allspice, cinnamon, cloves, nutmeg, sage, thyme
Zucchini	Basil, garlic, lemon, marjoram, parsley, thyme, black pepper

On a hot summer day, this soup is incredibly refreshing.

Tip

The soup can also be left unstrained if you don't mind some seeds.

Variation

Any combination of fresh or frozen berries can be used.

Serving Idea

This soup is a lovely first course for a summer barbecue or dinner party.

Chilled Four-Berry Soup

Mary Sue Waisman, Dietitian, Nova Scotia

- **Food processor, blender or immersion blender**
- **Fine-mesh sieve**

4 cups	thawed frozen 4-berry mix	1 L
½ cup	granulated sugar	125 mL
½ cup	crisp white wine, such as Sauvignon Blanc	125 mL
½ cup	orange, strawberry and banana juice	125 mL
1	4-inch (10 cm) cinnamon stick	1
¾ cup	low-fat strawberry yogurt	175 mL

1. In a large saucepan, combine berries, sugar, 1 cup (250 mL) water, wine, juice and cinnamon stick; bring to a boil over high heat. Reduce heat and simmer for 10 minutes. Discard cinnamon stick and let soup cool slightly.

2. Working in batches, transfer soup to food processor (or use immersion blender in pot) and purée until very smooth. Set the sieve over a bowl and strain soup, pressing slightly if necessary. Discard seeds.

3. Stir yogurt into strained soup. Cover and refrigerate for at least 4 hours, until chilled, or for up to 1 day.

> Sauvignon Blanc is a white grape varietal originally grown in France. It is now grown in many parts of the world to make this very popular white wine.

Nutrients per serving

Calories	167
Fat	0.7 g
Saturated fat	0.2 g
Sodium	23 mg (1% DV)
Carbohydrate	37 g
Fiber	3 g (12% DV)
Protein	2 g
Calcium	73 mg (7% DV)
Iron	0.8 mg (6% DV)

Diabetes Food Choice Values:
2   Carbohydrates

Spinach Soup

Carmelina Salomone, Ontario

1 tbsp	canola oil	15 mL
1 cup	chopped onion	250 mL
2	cloves garlic, minced	2
1	package (10 oz/300 g) baby spinach, roughly chopped	1
4 cups	reduced-sodium chicken broth	1 L
½ cup	peperini, orzo or other tiny pasta	125 mL
	Freshly ground black pepper	
¼ cup	freshly grated Parmesan cheese	60 mL

✔ Kid Approved

This quick, easy soup is a delicious way to add spinach to your day. Carmelina's young daughter washes and rinses the spinach for her. Pack some soup in insulated containers for your kids to take for school lunch.

Tip

Chopping the spinach before adding it to the pot makes it easier to eat and disperses the color throughout the soup more evenly.

Variation

Add leftover chopped cooked chicken or other chopped vegetables to make it a more complete meal.

1. In a large pot, heat oil over medium heat. Sauté onion for 3 to 4 minutes or until softened. Add garlic and sauté for 30 seconds. Add spinach and cook, stirring, for 2 to 3 minutes or until spinach is tender and reduced in volume by at least half.

2. Add broth, increase heat to high and bring to a boil. Stir in pasta, reduce heat and simmer for 5 to 7 minutes or until pasta is tender. Ladle into bowls, sprinkle with pepper to taste and garnish with cheese.

If you're feeling confident about your cooking skills, you can make a unique and pleasant finish for this soup. As the soup is cooking, in a small bowl, combine 1 beaten egg and 1 tbsp (15 mL) of the Parmesan, whisking until cheese is incorporated. Gradually whisk in 2 tbsp (30 mL) hot broth from the soup. Remove soup from the heat and very, very gradually add the egg mixture to the pot, stirring as you add it. Ladle into bowls and sprinkle with the remaining cheese. The resulting broth will be velvety in texture.

Note: It's important to add a bit of soup to the egg mixture so that the temperature of the egg mixture is close to that of the soup. Otherwise, the heat of the soup will scramble the egg when you add it.

Nutrients per serving

Calories	122
Fat	3.9 g
Saturated fat	0.9 g
Sodium	491 mg (20% DV)
Carbohydrate	16 g
Fiber	2 g (8% DV)
Protein	7 g
Calcium	126 mg (11% DV)
Iron	2.2 mg (16% DV)

Very high in: Vitamin A and folate

High in: Magnesium

Diabetes Food Choice Values:
½ Carbohydrate
1 Fat

Makes 6 servings

The flavors in this soup are a winning combination, especially if you can find fresh peas. Fresh tarragon is a key ingredient.

Tips

Be sure not to brown the shallots or you will have unpleasant brown bits in your soup.

This soup may be strained after it is puréed. The resulting soup will be very thin, and much of the fibrous pea matter will be removed.

Serving Idea

This soup makes a pleasant first course before a beef- or pork-based dinner.

Green Pea and Tarragon Soup

Mary Sue Waisman, Dietitian, Nova Scotia

● **Food processor, blender or immersion blender**

1 tsp	canola oil	5 mL
¼ cup	finely chopped shallots	60 mL
¼ cup	loosely packed chopped fresh tarragon	60 mL
1	star anise	1
4 cups	fresh or frozen green peas (thawed if frozen)	1 L
4 cups	reduced-sodium chicken broth	1 L
½ tsp	freshly ground white pepper	2 mL
½ tsp	salt (optional)	2 mL

1. In a large pot, heat oil over medium heat. Sauté shallots for about 3 minutes or until softened, being careful not to brown them. Add tarragon and sauté for 30 seconds. Add star anise, peas and broth; bring to boil. Reduce heat and simmer for about 20 minutes or until peas are very tender. Discard star anise.

2. Working in batches, transfer soup to food processor (or use immersion blender in pot) and purée until smooth. Return soup to pot (if necessary) and stir in pepper and salt (if using).

> Star anise has a pleasant licorice flavor similar to anise. It is the seed of a Chinese evergreen tree and is one of the ingredients in Chinese five-spice powder.

Nutrients per serving

Calories	101
Fat	1.0 g
Saturated fat	0.1 g
Sodium	398 mg (17% DV)
Carbohydrate	16 g
Fiber	6 g (24% DV)
Protein	7 g
Calcium	39 mg (4% DV)
Iron	1.5 mg (11% DV)

Very high in: Folate
High in: Magnesium and thiamine

Diabetes Food Choice Values:
½ Carbohydrate

Broccoli Cheese Soup

Laura Robinson, Ontario

This hearty soup would make a perfect lunch or supper on a cold day. The cream cheese adds both a smooth texture and wonderful flavor.

Tips

Stirring constantly when you're adding the cheese to the soup allows for even distribution and reduces the chance that the cheese will clump or stick to the bottom of the pot.

For a thicker soup, use up to 1 cup (250 mL) potato flakes.

One serving of this soup provides about the same amount of calcium as 1 serving (1 cup/250 mL) of milk.

Nutrients per serving

Calories	227
Fat	9.8 g
Saturated fat	4.8 g
Sodium	481 mg (20% DV)
Carbohydrate	24 g
Fiber	4 g (16% DV)
Protein	13 g
Calcium	336 mg (31% DV)
Iron	1.1 mg (8% DV)

Very high in: Vitamin A, vitamin C and vitamin D

High in: Magnesium, vitamin B_6, folate and riboflavin

Diabetes Food Choice Values:

1	Carbohydrate
½	Meat & Alternatives
1	Fat

• **Food processor, blender or immersion blender**

1 tbsp	canola oil	15 mL
5 cups	coarsely chopped broccoli florets	1.25 L
2 cups	coarsely chopped carrots	500 mL
1 cup	finely chopped onion	250 mL
3	cloves garlic, minced	3
2 cups	reduced-sodium chicken or vegetable broth	500 mL
1	can (370 mL) 2% evaporated milk	1
¾ cup	instant potato flakes	175 mL
½ tsp	freshly ground black pepper	2 mL
½ cup	light herb-and-garlic-flavored cream cheese	125 mL
½ cup	shredded old Cheddar cheese	125 mL

1. In a large pot, heat oil over medium heat. Sauté broccoli, carrots and onion for 3 to 4 minutes or until onions are softened. Add garlic and sauté for 30 seconds.

2. Add broth and 2 cups (50 mL) water; increase heat to high and bring to a boil. Reduce heat and simmer for 20 to 25 minutes or until broccoli and carrots are very tender. Remove from heat.

3. Working in batches, transfer soup to food processor (or use immersion blender in pot) and pulse 3 to 4 times, until vegetables are of uniform texture but not puréed.

4. Return soup to pot (if necessary) and place pot over medium heat. Stir in evaporated milk, potato flakes and pepper; heat until flakes are softened. Stir in cream cheese and Cheddar; heat, stirring constantly, until cheeses are melted and smooth. (Do not let boil or soup may curdle.)

You can purchase evaporated milk as whole (7.8% milk fat), partly skimmed (2% milk fat) or skim (0.2% milk fat). Using partly skimmed or skim evaporated milk is a great way to get the smooth texture of a cream soup without all the fat of whipping cream.

This soup not only offers
great flavor, but the
colors and textures are
attractive as well. Roasting
intensifies the flavors of
the vegetables.

Tip

Cutting the cauliflower into
bite-size florets makes for
easy eating.

Variations

Use a combination of
cauliflower and broccoli,
keeping the total amount at
5 cups (1.25 L).

To make this soup vegan,
substitute vegetable broth
for the chicken broth.

Serving Idea

Serve with half a Canadian
Cheddar cheese sandwich and
unsweetened canned fruit for
a light lunch.

Nutrients per serving

Calories	61
Fat	2.6 g
Saturated fat	0.2 g
Sodium	314 mg (13% DV)
Carbohydrate	8 g
Fiber	3 g (12% DV)
Protein	3 g
Calcium	28 mg (3% DV)
Iron	0.4 mg (3% DV)

Very high in: Vitamin A and
vitamin C

High in: Folate

Diabetes Food Choice Values:
½ Fat

Roasted Cauliflower and Red Pepper Soup

Mary Sue Waisman, Dietitian, Nova Scotia

- **Preheat oven to 425°F (220°C)**
- **Rimmed baking sheet, lined with foil**

5 cups	bite-size cauliflower florets	1.25 L
4 tsp	canola oil, divided	20 mL
1 cup	finely chopped onion	250 mL
1 cup	finely chopped carrots	250 mL
2	cloves garlic, minced	2
4 cups	reduced-sodium chicken broth	1 L
2	roasted red bell peppers (see box, below), finely chopped	2
2	sprigs fresh thyme	2
	Freshly ground black pepper	

1. Place cauliflower on prepared baking sheet and drizzle with 2 tsp (10 mL) of the oil. Roast in preheated oven, turning once, for 20 to 25 minutes or until florets start to caramelize and are lightly browned.

2. Meanwhile, in a large pot, heat the remaining oil over medium heat. Sauté onion and carrots for 3 to 4 minutes or until softened. Add garlic and sauté for 30 seconds. Stir in caramelized cauliflower, broth, roasted peppers and thyme; increase heat to high and bring to a boil. Reduce heat and simmer for 10 minutes to blend the flavors. Discard thyme sprigs. Season to taste with pepper.

How to Roast Red Peppers

To roast your own red peppers, quarter peppers and remove seeds. Place skin side up on a rimmed baking sheet in a 450°F (230°C) oven and roast for 10 minutes. Turn peppers over and roast for 10 to 15 minutes or until skins are blackened. Transfer peppers to a small bowl, cover tightly and let stand for about 15 minutes. When cool enough to handle, peel off blackened skin and discard.

Makes 6 servings

Caramelizing the onions and roasting the mushrooms adds tremendous flavor to this soup.

Tips

Marsala is a fortified wine (i.e., it has brandy or another spirit added to it) made from Sicilian grapes.

Be sure to remove the rosemary and thyme sprigs before serving so that there are no hard, woody parts in the soup.

Serving Idea

For an elegant first course for your next dinner party, ladle soup into bowls and top with 1 slice of toasted French bread and 1 tsp (5 mL) Parmesan cheese.

Nutrients per serving

Calories	102
Fat	4.8 g
Saturated fat	0.4 g
Sodium	399 mg (17% DV)
Carbohydrate	11 g
Fiber	2 g (8% DV)
Protein	4 g
Calcium	27 mg (2% DV)
Iron	1.2 mg (9% DV)

High in: Vitamin D

Diabetes Food Choice Values:
1   Fat

Caramelized Onion and Roasted Mushroom Soup

Mary Sue Waisman, Dietitian, Nova Scotia

- Preheat oven to 425°F (220°C)
- Rimmed baking sheet

1 lb	mushrooms, quartered	500 g
2 tbsp	canola oil, divided	30 mL
4	sprigs fresh rosemary, divided	4
4	sprigs fresh thyme, divided	4
1 tsp	freshly ground black pepper, divided	5 mL
2 cups	coarsely chopped onions	500 mL
¼ cup	coarsely chopped shallots	60 mL
¼ cup	Marsala wine	60 mL
4 cups	reduced-sodium chicken broth	1 L
1	bay leaf	1

1. Place mushrooms on baking sheet and drizzle with 1 tbsp (15 mL) of the oil. Add 2 sprigs each of rosemary and thyme. Sprinkle with ½ tsp (2 mL) pepper. Roast in preheated oven, stirring occasionally, for 20 to 25 minutes or until mushrooms are golden brown. Discard rosemary and thyme sprigs. Set mushrooms aside.

2. Meanwhile, in a large pot, heat the remaining oil over medium heat. Sauté onions and shallots for 2 minutes. Reduce heat to low and cook, stirring frequently, for about 15 minutes or until onions are caramelized (dark golden brown).

3. Add Marsala and deglaze the pot, scraping up any brown bits stuck to the bottom. Add roasted mushrooms, broth, bay leaf and the remaining rosemary, thyme and pepper; increase heat to high and bring to a boil. Reduce heat and simmer for 15 minutes to blend the flavors. Discard rosemary and thyme sprigs and bay leaf.

**Makes 6 to
8 servings**

This winning flavor combination is made even better when the vegetables and fruit are roasted in advance.

Tips

This is a very thick soup, so it's best to keep portion sizes small.

The caramelized parsnips and pears would also make a delicious side dish on their own.

Variation

To make a vegan soup, substitute vegetable broth for the chicken broth.

Serving Idea

This makes a delicious first course for Thanksgiving dinner.

Nutrients per serving

Calories	104
Fat	2.7 g
Saturated fat	0.3 g
Sodium	305 mg (13% DV)
Carbohydrate	19 g
Fiber	3 g (12% DV)
Protein	3 g
Calcium	39 mg (4% DV)
Iron	0.5 mg (4% DV)

High in: Folate

Diabetes Food Choice Values:
½   Carbohydrate
½   Fat

Roasted Pear and Parsnip Soup

Mary Sue Waisman, Dietitian, Nova Scotia

- **Preheat oven to 425°F (220°C)**
- **Rimmed baking sheet, lined with foil**
- **Food processor, blender or immersion blender**

1 lb	parsnips, cut lengthwise into quarters	500 g
2	Bosc pears, peeled and sliced	2
4 tsp	canola oil, divided	20 mL
2 tsp	pure maple syrup	10 mL
½ cup	finely chopped onion	125 mL
1	clove garlic, minced	1
4 cups	reduced-sodium chicken broth	1 L
½ cup	unsweetened apple juice	125 mL
2 tbsp	light sour cream	15 mL
	Ground cinnamon	

1. Place parsnips and pears on prepared baking sheet and drizzle with 2 tsp (10 mL) of the oil and the maple syrup. Roast in preheated oven, stirring once, for 20 to 25 minutes or until parsnips and pears start to caramelize and are lightly browned.

2. Meanwhile, in a large pot, heat the remaining oil over medium-high heat. Sauté onions for 3 to 4 minutes or until softened. Add garlic and sauté for 30 seconds. Add caramelized parsnips and pears, breaking them up with a spoon. Stir in broth and apple juice; bring to a boil. Reduce heat and simmer for 10 minutes to blend the flavors. Remove from heat.

3. Working in batches, transfer soup to food processor (or use immersion blender in pot) and purée until very smooth. Ladle into bowls and top each with a dollop of sour cream and a pinch of cinnamon.

Pear trees are long-lived and can bear fruit for up to 100 years.

Makes 8 servings

✔ **Kid Approved**

When daylight hours are short and you have some time on your hands, let the warmth and aromas of this soup fill your home.

Tips

Teach children about all the different vegetables as they help you peel them!

For the best consistency, cut the potatoes, sweet potatoes and turnips into ½-inch (1 cm) cubes.

You can also use a pressure cooker and cook the soup for 8 minutes instead of simmering it in step 2.

Variation

If you like a smooth texture, purée this soup in small batches in a food processor or blender (or using an immersion blender in the pot).

Nutrients per serving

Calories	156
Fat	3.7 g
Saturated fat	0.3 g
Sodium	488 mg (20% DV)
Carbohydrate	27 g
Fiber	4 g (16% DV)
Protein	5 g
Calcium	56 mg (5% DV)
Iron	1.0 mg (7% DV)

Very high in: Vitamin A
High in: Vitamin B$_6$ and folate

Diabetes Food Choice Values:

1   Carbohydrate
½   Fat

Winter Root Vegetable Soup

Kathleen Martin, Nova Scotia

2 tbsp	canola oil	30 mL
1½ cups	coarsely chopped onions	375 mL
1½ cups	coarsely chopped mushrooms	375 mL
3	cloves garlic, minced	3
½ cup	dry red wine	125 mL
2 cups	coarsely chopped parsnips	500 mL
2 cups	coarsely chopped carrots	500 mL
2 cups	cubed peeled potatoes	500 mL
2 cups	cubed peeled sweet potatoes	500 mL
1 cup	cubed turnips	250 mL
6 cups	reduced-sodium chicken or vegetable broth	1.5 L

1. In a large pot, heat oil over medium heat. Sauté onions and mushrooms for 4 to 5 minutes or until softened. Add garlic and sauté for 30 seconds.

2. Add wine and deglaze the pot, scraping up any brown bits stuck to the bottom. Boil for about 10 minutes to reduce wine slightly. Stir in parsnips, carrots, potatoes, sweet potatoes, turnips and broth; bring to a boil. Reduce heat and simmer for 20 to 30 minutes or until vegetables are tender.

> Parsnips are sometimes called "white carrots," as they resemble carrots in shape. Since they have no orange color, however, they contain no beta-carotene.

✔ **Kid Approved**

Tanya created this soup one night when she needed to make a quick supper for her kids. She noticed she had a couple of sweet potatoes on hand, then looked in her fridge and cupboards for inspiration. The result was a pleasant surprise.

Tips

Kids can help peel the sweet potato.

This soup makes great leftovers, as the flavors improve with time.

Serving Idea

Enjoy this soup with a whole-grain bun and a piece of cheese for a light supper.

Nutrients per serving

Calories	94
Fat	0.2 g
Saturated fat	0.0 g
Sodium	410 mg (17% DV)
Carbohydrate	21 g
Fiber	2 g (8% DV)
Protein	3 g
Calcium	37 mg (3% DV)
Iron	0.5 mg (4% DV)

Very high in: Vitamin A

High in: Magnesium, vitamin C, vitamin B$_6$, folate, thiamine

Diabetes Food Choice Values:

1   Carbohydrate

Sweet Potato Orange Ginger Soup

Tanya Lorimer-Charles, Nova Scotia

● **Food processor, blender or immersion blender**

1	red onion, thinly sliced	1
2 cups	thinly sliced peeled sweet potato	500 mL
2 tbsp	ginger marmalade	30 mL
4 cups	reduced-sodium chicken broth	1 L
1 tbsp	grated orange zest	15 mL
½ cup	freshly squeezed orange juice	125 mL
½ tsp	freshly ground white pepper (or to taste)	2 mL
½ tsp	ground cumin	2 mL
½ tsp	salt (optional)	2 mL

1. In a large pot, combine red onion, sweet potato, marmalade and broth; bring to a boil over medium-high heat. Reduce heat and simmer for about 30 minutes or until sweet potato is fork-tender.

2. Working in batches, transfer soup to food processor (or use immersion blender in pot) and purée until smooth.

3. Return soup to pot (if necessary) and place over low heat. Stir in orange zest, orange juice, pepper, cumin and salt (if using); simmer, stirring occasionally, for 10 minutes to blend the flavors.

White beans give this soup a protein boost and help thicken it too!

Tip

To reduce the sodium in this soup, use our homemade vegetable broth (page 256) or look for a reduced-sodium brand.

Variation

Use acorn squash instead of butternut.

Nutrients per serving

Calories	138
Fat	3.1 g
Saturated fat	0.3 g
Sodium	526 mg (22% DV)
Carbohydrate	25 g
Fiber	7 g (28% DV)
Protein	6 g
Calcium	76 mg (7% DV)
Iron	1.9 mg (14% DV)

Very high in: Vitamin A

High in: Magnesium and folate

Diabetes Food Choice Values:

1	Carbohydrate
½	Fat

Curried Butternut Squash and Bean Soup

Rosie Dhaliwal, Dietitian, British Columbia

- **Food processor, blender or immersion blender**

1 tbsp	canola oil	15 mL
½ cup	coarsely chopped onion	125 mL
½ cup	coarsely chopped carrot	125 mL
½ cup	coarsely chopped celery	125 mL
2	cloves garlic, minced	2
1 tsp	minced gingerroot	5 mL
2 tsp	curry powder	10 mL
1½ tsp	ground cumin	7 mL
1	can (19 oz/540 mL) white kidney beans, drained and rinsed	1
2 cups	mashed cooked butternut squash (see box, below)	500 mL
2 cups	vegetable broth	500 mL
	Salt and freshly ground black pepper	

1. In a large pot, heat oil over medium high heat. Sauté onion, carrot and celery for 4 to 5 minutes or until softened. Add garlic, ginger, curry powder and cumin; sauté for 30 seconds. Stir in beans, squash, broth and 2 cups (500 mL) water; bring to a boil. Reduce heat and simmer, stirring occasionally, for 30 minutes to blend the flavors.

2. Working in batches, transfer soup to food processor (or use immersion blender in pot) and purée until smooth. Return soup to pot (if necessary) and season to taste with salt and pepper.

> To make 2 cups (500 mL) mashed cooked butternut squash, use 1 medium squash. Cut it in half lengthwise and scoop out the seeds. Place it cut side down on a lightly greased baking sheet and prick the skin several times with a fork. Bake in a 375°F (190°C) oven for about 30 minutes or until fork-tender. Let cool, then scoop out the flesh and discard the skin. If you have more flesh than you need, reserve the extra for another use.

This hearty, warming soup is a delicious way to get some great soluble fiber from beans. It's perfect for a cold Canadian winter weeknight supper. Make the soup on the weekend and reheat it to serve during the week.

Tips

The tomatoes and onions can be broiled up to 1 day in advance. Let cool, cover and refrigerate until ready to use.

This soup gets the prize for having the most dietary fiber of all our soups! At 11 g per serving, it's a great way to boost your fiber intake.

Nutrients per serving

Calories	257
Fat	7.6 g
Saturated fat	2.1 g
Sodium	388 mg (16% DV)
Carbohydrate	37 g
Fiber	11 g (44% DV)
Protein	13 g
Calcium	122 mg (11% DV)
Iron	2.8 mg (20% DV)

Very high in: Magnesium and folate

High in: Zinc, vitamin B_6, thiamine and niacin

Source of: Vitamin A, vitamin C and riboflavin

Diabetes Food Choice Values:

1½ Carbohydrates
1   Meat & Alternatives
1   Fat

Pinto Bean Tortilla Soup

Heather McColl, Dietitian, British Columbia

- **Rimmed baking sheet**
- **Food processor or blender**

1½ cups	dried pinto beans	375 mL
1	large onion, cut into 6 wedges	1
5	plum (Roma) tomatoes, quartered	5
4 tsp	canola oil, divided	20 mL
4	5-inch (12.5 cm) corn tortillas, divided	4
2	cloves garlic, minced	2
1	jalapeño pepper, seeded and finely minced	1
2 tsp	ground cumin	10 mL
1 tsp	ground coriander	5 mL
4 cups	reduced-sodium chicken broth	1 L
1	bay leaf	1
2 tbsp	tomato paste	30 mL
1 cup	frozen corn kernels	250 mL
Pinch	salt	Pinch
½	avocado, chopped	½
½ cup	shredded Cheddar cheese	125 mL

1. Place beans in a large bowl and add enough cold water to cover by at least 3 inches (7.5 cm). Cover and let soak overnight. Drain soaked beans and rinse well under cold water. Discard any shriveled beans or those that did not swell.

2. Place beans in a large pot and add enough fresh cold water to cover by 3 inches (7.5 cm). Bring to a boil over high heat. Reduce heat and simmer for 30 to 35 minutes or until beans are tender. Drain and set aside.

3. Meanwhile, preheat broiler. Place onion and tomatoes on baking sheet and brush with 1 tsp (5 mL) of the oil. Broil, turning every 5 minutes, for about 15 minutes or until charred. Transfer to food processor and process until smooth. Set aside. Reduce oven temperature to 350°F (180°C).

4. Cut tortillas into 2- by ¼-inch (5 by 0.5 cm) strips.

5. In a clean large pot, heat 2 tsp (10 mL) oil over medium heat. Add half the tortilla strips, garlic and jalapeño; sauté for 3 minutes. Stir in cumin and coriander. Add broth and deglaze the pot, scraping up any brown bits stuck to the bottom. Add bay leaf and bring to a boil. Stir in puréed onion mixture and tomato paste; return to a boil. Reduce heat and simmer, stirring occasionally, for 20 minutes. Stir in corn and cooked pinto beans; simmer for 10 minutes to blend the flavors. Discard bay leaf.

6. Meanwhile, gently toss the remaining tortilla strips with the remaining oil and the salt. Spread on a baking sheet. Bake for about 10 minutes or until crisp.

7. Ladle soup into bowls and garnish with baked tortilla strips, avocado and cheese.

It's impossible to tell the hotness of a jalapeño pepper by looking at it. One way to test for hotness is to place the tip of your finger on a cut piece of jalapeño and touch your finger to your tongue. Be sure to wash your hand afterward, and don't touch your eyes.

Variations

We made this soup with Jacob's cattle beans, which are grown in Nova Scotia, and it worked equally well.

Increase the heat of this soup by adding hot pepper sauce to taste with the corn and beans.

The evaporated milk in this delicious, creamy soup gives it a richness that suggests it is higher in fat than it actually is. The addition of sweet potato and red pepper helps increase your intake of beta carotene and vitamin C.

Variations

This soup works just as well without the chicken. Try replacing it with drained canned clams for variety. With clams, a little hot pepper sauce makes a nice addition.

Ask your family what other ingredients they would like to add to customize the soup.

Chicken and Corn Chowder

Eileen Campbell, Ontario

1 tbsp	non-hydrogenated margarine	15 mL
1 cup	finely chopped onion	250 mL
1 cup	diced celery	250 mL
½ cup	finely chopped red bell pepper	125 mL
1	boneless skinless chicken breast (about 4 oz/125 g), cubed	1
4 cups	reduced-sodium chicken broth	1 L
1 cup	diced peeled sweet potato	250 mL
1 cup	frozen corn kernels, thawed	250 mL
1	can (370 mL) 2% evaporated milk	1
1 tbsp	chopped fresh parsley	15 mL

1. In a large saucepan, melt margarine over medium heat. Sauté onion, celery and red pepper until softened, about 5 minutes.

2. Add chicken, broth, sweet potato and corn; bring to a boil. Reduce heat, cover and simmer for 25 minutes or until chicken and potatoes are cooked through. Add evaporated milk and parsley; heat over low heat (do not boil or milk will curdle).

Nutrients per serving

Calories	118
Fat	2.7 g
Saturated fat	0.8 g
Sodium	362 mg (15% DV)
Carbohydrate	14 g
Fiber	1 g (4% DV)
Protein	10 g
Calcium	145 mg (13% DV)
Iron	0.5 mg (4% DV)

Very high in: Vitamin A and vitamin C

High in: Vitamin D and niacin

Diabetes Food Choice Values:

½ Carbohydrate
1 Meat & Alternatives

Chicken Tortellini Soup

Laurie Barker Jackman, Dietitian, Nova Scotia

Leftover chicken? Not a problem — add it to this delicious soup, which makes a balanced meal for an easy supper or a hearty lunch. Laurie's husband and daughter love it, and they help with the chopping, assembling and stirring!

Tip

Using half broth and half water in this soup helps keep the amount of sodium in check. If you want to further reduce the sodium, use 2 cups (500 mL) cooked whole wheat rotini pasta instead of the tortellini.

Serving Idea

Serve with Fresh Slaw (page 152) to add some crunch to this meal.

1 tbsp	canola oil	15 mL
2 cups	coarsely chopped mushrooms	500 mL
1 cup	coarsely chopped onion	250 mL
1 cup	coarsely chopped carrots	250 mL
½ cup	coarsely chopped zucchini	125 mL
¾ cup	finely chopped red bell pepper	175 mL
3	cloves garlic, minced	3
1	can (28 oz/796 mL) diced tomatoes	1
4 cups	reduced-sodium chicken broth	1 L
1	package (12 oz/340 g) cheese-filled tortellini	1
2 cups	cubed or shredded cooked chicken	500 mL
2 cups	loosely packed fresh spinach leaves	500 mL
¼ cup	freshly grated Parmesan cheese	60 mL

1. In a large pot, heat oil over medium heat. Sauté mushrooms, onion, carrots, zucchini and red pepper for 4 to 5 minutes or until softened. Add garlic and sauté for 30 seconds.

2. Add tomatoes, broth and 4 cups (1 L) water; bring to a boil. Stir in pasta and boil for 10 minutes or until pasta is al dente (tender to the bite).

3. Stir in chicken and spinach; simmer, stirring occasionally, for 10 minutes or until chicken is heated through and spinach is wilted. Ladle into bowls and garnish with cheese.

Nutrients per serving

Calories	266
Fat	8.0 g
Saturated fat	1.5 g
Sodium	693 mg (29% DV)
Carbohydrate	31 g
Fiber	3 g (12% DV)
Protein	19 g
Calcium	128 mg (12% DV)
Iron	2.9 mg (21% DV)

Very high in: Vitamin A, vitamin C and niacin

High in: Magnesium, zinc, vitamin B_6, folate, thiamine and riboflavin

Diabetes Food Choice Values:

1½   Carbohydrates
2   Meat & Alternatives

This savory soup is
simultaneously everyday
and exotic — and it's
good for you too!

Variations

Replace the chicken with
8 oz (250 g) tofu strips.

Instead of the chicken, use
thin strips of skinless fish
fillets or medium shrimp,
peeled and deveined. Cook
fish until it is opaque and
flakes easily with a fork; cook
shrimp until pink and opaque.

Nutrients per serving

Calories	177
Fat	1.6 g
Saturated fat	0.4 g
Sodium	695 mg (29% DV)
Carbohydrate	19 g
Fiber	3 g (12% DV)
Protein	21 g
Calcium	48 mg (4% DV)
Iron	1.8 mg (13% DV)

Very high in: Vitamin A and
niacin

High in: Vitamin B$_6$

Diabetes Food Choice Values:
½ Carbohydrate
2 Meat & Alternatives

Asian Chicken Soup Bowl

Adapted from Green Giant from General Mills
(www.lifemadedelicious.ca)

2 cups	medium egg noodles	500 mL
1 tbsp	minced gingerroot	15 mL
1 tsp	grated lemon zest	5 mL
1 tsp	grated lime zest	5 mL
3½ cups	reduced-sodium chicken broth	875 mL
2 tbsp	reduced-sodium soy sauce	30 mL
1 tsp	hot chili paste	5 mL
12 oz	boneless skinless chicken breasts, cut into thin strips	375 g
1	package (14 oz/400 g) frozen baby vegetables	1
1 tsp	freshly squeezed lime juice	5 mL
¼ cup	chopped fresh cilantro	60 mL

1. In a large pot of boiling salted water, cook egg noodles according to package directions. Drain well.

2. Meanwhile, in a large saucepan, combine ginger, lemon zest, lime zest, broth, 2½ cups (625 mL) water, soy sauce and chili paste. Bring to a boil over medium-high heat. Add chicken and vegetables; reduce heat and boil gently for 5 minutes or until chicken is no longer pink inside and vegetables are heated through.

3. Add noodles and simmer for 2 to 3 minutes to blend the flavors. Stir in lime juice. Ladle into bowls and sprinkle with cilantro.

Makes 8 to 10 servings

Dorraine could not find a low-sodium turkey soup recipe for her slow cooker, so she created one herself. As the wonderful aromas start to fill the kitchen, you'll say, "It smells like turkey dinner!"

Variation

Use long-grain brown rice instead of wild rice.

Serving Idea

Serve with Golden Beet Salad (page 158) for a delicious supper.

Nutrients per serving

Calories	125
Fat	4.9 g
Saturated fat	1.1 g
Sodium	287 mg (12% DV)
Carbohydrate	10 g
Fiber	1 g (4% DV)
Protein	11 g
Calcium	31 mg (3% DV)
Iron	1.1 mg (8% DV)

High in: Vitamin A and niacin

Diabetes Food Choice Values:

½ Carbohydrate
1 Meat & Alternatives

Turkey Wild Rice Soup

Dorraine Hayward, Saskatchewan

● **Minimum 4-quart slow cooker**

2 tsp	canola oil	10 mL
1 lb	lean ground turkey	500 g
1	clove garlic, minced	1
1 cup	coarsely chopped onion	250 mL
1 cup	coarsely chopped celery	250 mL
1 cup	coarsely chopped carrots	250 mL
½ cup	wild rice	125 mL
4 cups	reduced-sodium chicken broth	1 L
½ tsp	ground sage	2 mL
½ tsp	dried savory	2 mL
½ tsp	dried thyme	2 mL
½ tsp	dried marjoram	2 mL
½ tsp	freshly ground black pepper	2 mL
½ tsp	salt (optional)	2 mL
2 to 3 tbsp	chopped fresh parsley	30 to 45 mL

1. In a large nonstick skillet, heat oil over medium heat. Brown turkey, breaking it up with a spoon, for about 8 minutes or until no longer pink. Drain off excess fat.

2. Transfer turkey to slow cooker stoneware and stir in garlic, onion, celery, carrots, wild rice, broth, 2 cups (500 mL) water, sage, savory, thyme, marjoram, pepper and salt (if using). Cover and cook on High for 4 to 5 hours or until vegetables and rice are tender. Ladle into bowls and garnish with parsley to taste.

Mini Meatball Soup

Adam Hudson, Dietitian, Ontario

This soup tastes like spaghetti and meatballs and contains foods from three of the four food groups in *Eating Well with Canada's Food Guide*. Add a cold glass of milk to complete the meal.

Tips

Kids can help roll the meatballs, but be sure they wash their hands well after handling the raw meat.

Incorporate the ingredients gently when mixing the meatballs, and let them brown in the pot before turning them. This loving care will ensure that they stay soft and retain all their flavor.

Meatballs

8 oz	lean ground beef	250 g
8 oz	lean ground pork	250 g
2	cloves garlic, minced	2
1	egg	1
1/3 cup	fine dry bread crumbs	75 mL
1 tsp	dried oregano	5 mL
1/2 tsp	dried basil	2 mL
1/4 tsp	chili powder	1 mL
1/4 tsp	hot pepper flakes	1 mL
Pinch	cayenne pepper	Pinch
2 tsp	canola oil, divided	10 mL

Soup

1 tsp	canola oil	5 mL
1 cup	finely chopped onion	250 mL
1 cup	finely chopped carrots	250 mL
1 cup	finely chopped celery	250 mL
1	clove garlic, minced	1
1	can (28 oz/796 mL) diced tomatoes	1
1	bay leaf	1
1	sprig fresh thyme	1
4 cups	reduced-sodium beef broth	1 L
1 tbsp	tomato paste	15 mL
1/2 cup	peperini, orzo or other tiny pasta	125 mL
1 1/2 cups	lightly packed coarsely chopped fresh spinach	375 mL
1/4 cup	freshly grated Parmesan cheese	60 mL

1. *Meatballs:* In a large bowl, gently combine beef, pork, garlic, egg, bread crumbs, oregano, basil, chili powder, hot pepper flakes and cayenne. Using the palms of your hands, gently roll small pieces of the mixture into 3/4-inch (2 cm) meatballs. Set aside on a plate.

Nutrients per serving

Calories	248
Fat	10.7 g
Saturated fat	3.6 g
Sodium	586 mg (24% DV)
Carbohydrate	20 g
Fiber	3 g (12% DV)
Protein	18 g
Calcium	120 mg (11% DV)
Iron	2.9 mg (21% DV)

Very high in: Zinc, vitamin A, folate, vitamin B_{12}, thiamine and niacin

High in: Magnesium, vitamin B_6 and riboflavin

Diabetes Food Choice Values:

1	Carbohydrate
2	Meat & Alternatives

2. In a large pot, heat 1 tsp (5 mL) of the oil over medium-high heat. Add half the meatballs and brown on all sides, adjusting heat as needed to ensure meatballs do not burn. Transfer to a clean dry plate. Heat the remaining oil and repeat with the remaining meatballs. Discard any fat remaining in the bottom of the pot, leaving any brown bits. Set meatballs aside.

3. *Soup:* In the same pot, heat oil over medium-high heat. Sauté onion, carrots and celery, scraping up brown bits from bottom of pot, for 4 to 5 minutes or until softened. Add garlic and sauté for 30 seconds.

4. Stir in cooked meatballs, tomatoes, bay leaf, thyme, broth and tomato paste; bring to a boil. Reduce heat and simmer for 30 minutes. Stir in pasta and simmer for 5 to 7 minutes or until pasta is tender. Discard bay leaf and thyme sprig. Stir in spinach until wilted. Ladle into bowls and garnish with cheese.

How to Make Your Own Dry Bread Crumbs

Tear day-old bread or buns into small pieces and spread out on an ungreased baking sheet. Place in a 200°F (100°C) oven to dry out. Let cool completely. Pulse in a food processor to form crumbs or place between two sheets of waxed paper or in a sealable plastic bag and roll with a rolling pin.

Tip
Do not overcrowd the pan when cooking meatballs or they will stew instead of browning.

Variation
Use lean ground chicken or turkey to make the meatballs.

Serving Idea
This soup definitely stands on its own, but it's also wonderful with crusty bread or a salad.

Salads

Salads are one of the most versatile menu items. They can be as simple as a few fresh greens adorned with a simple dressing or can be very complex, with many ingredients. They can be used as an appetizer, side dish or main course, or even served after a main course. What's important is that the ingredients work together in harmony, bound by a dressing, to create delicious flavor, an interesting texture and beautiful color. All of the recipes in this chapter meet these requirements, and all are packed with nutrition.

Choosing Fats

When it comes to choosing fats, either for use in salad dressings or in general cooking, let clear oils be the clear choice. Oils you can see through, such as canola, olive and soybean, are ideal choices for food preparation, as they are higher in unsaturated fats. Canola and peanut oil also have a higher smoke point, meaning they don't burn easily. Extra virgin olive oil can burn at high heat, but refined olive oil can safely be used for sautéing and frying.

Extra virgin olive oil usually has a noticeable olive flavor and is ideal for recipes where you want this flavor to stand out, such as in salads or some appetizers. Nut and seed oils, such as walnut, almond or sesame, are nice additions to salad dressings, though their flavor is quite strong, so only a small amount is needed. These oils have lower smoke points and are not recommended for high-heat cooking.

Toasting Nuts and Seeds

Toasting is a great way to bring out the flavor of nuts and seeds. But because they contain a lot of oil, when you add heat they can easily burn, so you'll need to watch them carefully. To toast nuts and seeds, heat a skillet over medium-high heat. Add a single layer of nuts or seeds. Cook, stirring, for 1 minute. Flip nuts or seeds over and cook, stirring and flipping as needed, for 1 to 2 minutes, adjusting heat if necessary to make sure they don't burn. The goal is a light golden "toasty" color. Remove from heat and transfer the nuts or seeds to a clean plate or sheet of waxed paper or parchment paper so they don't cook any further in the hot skillet. Let them cool a bit before using them in a recipe.

Turning a Side Salad into an Entrée

If you're serving a salad as a main dish for lunch or supper, remember to add a source of protein. Leftover cooked chicken, shrimp or salmon are ideal toppings for entrée salads. Other alternatives include chopped hard-cooked eggs, shredded cheese, cubed tofu and cooked beans, lentils or chickpeas. Nuts and seeds are also protein-rich additions, but they're higher in fat, so moderation rules.

Balsamic Vinegar

Balsamic vinegar means "vinegar-like balm." It adds wonderful flavor and, since it doesn't contain any fat, is particularly useful when you're trying to eat healthy. It is a much loved salad dressing ingredient, but here are some other ideas on how to use it:

- Mix 1 to 2 drops with $1/4$ cup (60 mL) extra virgin olive oil to make a dip for crusty Italian bread.
- Stir 1 tbsp (15 mL) into gravy for a roast — it will really improve the flavor!
- Stir into roasted vegetables such as onions, tomatoes, fennel, bell peppers and eggplant.
- Sprinkle over white fish after steaming, grilling or broiling
- Add to fresh tomato sauce and toss with pasta.
- Add a few drops to lemonade.

Family Cooking Lesson

Vinaigrette Salad Dressings

Traditional vinaigrettes use a ratio of three parts oil to one part vinegar, which produces a rather oily dressing. To create flavorful lower-fat vinaigrettes, you can replace some of the fat with water, juice or concentrated juice and add flavorful extras. You can also use another acid (such as orange juice, lemon juice or lime juice) instead of vinegar. The method remains the same:

1. In a small bowl, combine oil, acid and water/juice. Whisk, stir vigorously with a fork or cover and shake until well blended.
2. Add sweetener and/or add-ins and stir until well combined.
3. Cover and store in the refrigerator for up to 5 days (3 days if you've added garlic). Shake before using.

Here are some delicious vinaigrette salad dressing options:

Asian Vinaigrette

Oil: 2 tbsp (30 mL) sesame oil
Acid: $\frac{1}{2}$ cup (125 mL) rice vinegar
Water/juice: $\frac{1}{4}$ cup (60 mL) unsweetened apple juice
Sweetener: 1 tsp (5 mL) granulated sugar
Add-ins: 2 chopped green onions, 2 tbsp (30 mL) reduced-sodium soy sauce, 1 tbsp (15 mL) grated gingerroot, 1 tsp (5 mL) Dijon mustard
Yield: About $1\frac{1}{3}$ cups (325 mL)
Suggested serving size: 1 tbsp (15 mL)
Delicious on: A salad of steamed edamame, toasted corn kernels and chopped red bell peppers

Blueberry Vinaigrette

Oil: 2 tbsp (30 mL) canola oil
Acid: $\frac{1}{4}$ cup (60 mL) balsamic vinegar
Water/juice: 2 tbsp (30 mL) water
Sweetener: $\frac{1}{3}$ cup (75 mL) liquid honey
Add-ins: $\frac{1}{2}$ cup (125 mL) fresh or thawed frozen blueberries, mashed
Yield: About $1\frac{1}{3}$ cups (325 mL)
Suggested serving size: 1 tbsp (15 mL)
Delicious on: A salad of mesclun mix, fresh blueberries and strawberries and toasted pecans

Raspberry Orange Vinaigrette

Oil: $\frac{1}{4}$ cup (60 mL) olive oil
Acid: $\frac{1}{4}$ cup (60 mL) orange juice, 2 tbsp (30 mL) raspberry vinegar
Water/juice: $\frac{1}{4}$ cup (60 mL) water
Add-ins: 2 tbsp (30 mL) chopped fresh parsley
Yield: About 1 cup (250 mL)
Suggested serving size: 1 tbsp (15 mL)
Delicious on: Fruit or cottage cheese salads

Citrus Chive Dressing

Oil: 2 tbsp (30 mL) canola oil
Acid: 2 cups (500 mL) orange juice, heated to evaporate liquid so that $\frac{2}{3}$ cup (150 mL) remains
Water/juice: 2 tbsp (30 mL) freshly squeezed lemon juice
Sweetener: 1 tbsp (15 mL) liquid honey
Add-ins: 2 tbsp (30 mL) chopped fresh chives, salt and freshly ground black pepper to taste
Yield: About 1 cup (250 mL)
Suggested serving size: 1 tbsp (15 mL)
Delicious on: A salad of romaine lettuce, cooked shelled peas and fresh mint

Grapefruit and Poppy Seed Dressing

Oil: 3 tbsp (45 mL) canola oil
Acid: 2 cups (500 mL) grapefruit juice, heated to evaporate liquid so that ²/₃ cup (150 mL) remains
Water/juice: 2 tbsp (30 mL) water
Sweetener: 1 to 2 tbsp (15 to 30 mL) liquid honey
Add-ins: 1 tbsp (15 mL) poppy seeds
Yield: About 1 cup (250 mL)
Suggested serving size: 1 tbsp (15 mL)
Delicious on: A salad of spinach, arugula, sliced celery, grapefruit sections and toasted almonds

Caesar Dressing

Oil: 3 tbsp (45 mL) extra virgin olive oil
Acid: 2 tbsp + 2 tsp (40 mL) freshly squeezed lemon juice
Water/juice: 1 tbsp (15 mL) water
Add-ins: 1 tsp (5 mL) minced garlic, 1 tsp (5 mL) Worcestershire sauce, 1 tsp (5 mL) Dijon mustard, ½ tsp (2 mL) freshly ground black pepper
Yield: About ½ cup (125 mL)
Suggested serving size: 1 tbsp (15 mL)
Delicious on: Romaine lettuce with whole-grain croutons; whole wheat rotini pasta with freshly grated Parmesan cheese

Creamy Salad Dressings

You can create salad dressings that taste rich and creamy using low-fat plain yogurt as the base instead of mayonnaise or sour cream. Aside from having significantly less fat than regular mayo and sour cream, yogurt provides added protein and other nutrients. The method is similar to the one for vinaigrettes:

1. In a small bowl, stir together yogurt, sweetener and/or add-ins until well combined.

2. Cover and store in the refrigerator for up to 5 days (3 days if you've added garlic). Shake before using.

Here are some fantastic lower-fat creamy salad dressings:

Creamy Low-Calorie Herb Dressing

Yogurt: ¼ cup (60 mL) low-fat plain yogurt
Add-ins: ⅓ cup (75 mL) buttermilk, 2 chopped green onions, 2 tbsp (30 mL) chopped fresh dill or basil, ½ tsp (2 mL) dried oregano
Yield: About ¾ cup (175 mL)
Suggested serving size: 2 tbsp (30 mL)
Delicious on: Green salads or coleslaw

Creamy and Tangy Dressing

Yogurt: ¾ cup (175 mL) low-fat plain yogurt
Sweetener: 2 tsp (10 mL) liquid honey
Add-ins: ¼ cup (60 mL) chopped fresh dill, 1 tbsp (15 mL) freshly squeezed lemon juice, 2 tsp (10 mL) Dijon mustard

Yield: About 1 cup (250 mL)
Suggested serving size: 2 tbsp (30 mL)
Delicious on: Coleslaws with a variety of veggies, such as cabbage, carrot, broccoli stalks and fennel

Creamy Chili Lime Dressing

Yogurt: 6 tbsp (90 mL) low-fat plain yogurt
Sweetener: 1½ tsp (7 mL) granulated sugar
Add-ins: 3 tbsp (45 mL) freshly squeezed lime juice, 1 tsp (5 mL) chili powder
Yield: About ²/₃ cup (150 mL)
Suggested serving size: 2 tbsp (30 mL)
Delicious on: A salad of mixed greens, oranges, avocado, red onion and prawns or shrimp

✔ **Kid Approved**

Take advantage of the marvelous fresh, colorful and tasty berries available in many parts of Canada during the summer. This is an ideal breakfast treat, and is perfect for a light dessert as well.

Tips

This fantastic dressing can also be used as a dip for fruit, as a topping for cereal or as a light sauce for crêpes or pancakes. It works well with regular sour cream too.

You'll get two servings of Vegetables and Fruit from a serving of this pretty salad.

Serving Idea

Make a yogurt parfait by layering this fruit salad with Great Grains, Fruit and Nut Granola with Honey and Almond Butter (page 36) and Vanilla Maple Yogurt Dressing.

Nutrients per serving

Calories	104
Fat	1.5 g
Saturated fat	0.6 g
Sodium	26 mg (1% DV)
Carbohydrate	22 g
Fiber	6 g (24% DV)
Protein	3 g
Calcium	87 mg (8% DV)
Iron	0.8 mg (6% DV)

Very high in: Vitamin C

Diabetes Food Choice Values:
1   Carbohydrate
½   Fat

Canadian Summertime Fruit Salad with Vanilla Maple Yogurt Dressing

Mary Sue Waisman, Dietitian, Nova Scotia

1 cup	blueberries	250 mL
1 cup	raspberries	250 mL
1 cup	sliced strawberries	250 mL
1 cup	blackberries or Saskatoon berries	250 mL
¼ cup	toasted finely chopped hazelnuts (optional)	60 mL

Vanilla Maple Yogurt Dressing

¼ cup	low-fat vanilla yogurt	60 mL
¼ cup	light sour cream	60 mL
1 tbsp	pure maple syrup	15 mL
Pinch	ground cinnamon	Pinch

1. In a bowl, gently combine blueberries, raspberries, strawberries and blackberries.

2. *Dressing:* In a small bowl, combine yogurt, sour cream, maple syrup and cinnamon. Use immediately or cover and refrigerate for up to 3 days.

3. Place 1 cup (250 mL) berry mixture in each serving bowl. Top each with 2 tbsp (30 mL) dressing and 2 tsp (10 mL) hazelnuts (if using).

Warm Canadian Winter Fruit Salad

Mary Sue Waisman, Dietitian, Nova Scotia

✔ **Kid Approved**

Thanks to modern storage techniques, fresh apples and pears are available in Canada all year long. How lucky we are to be able to enjoy fresh fruit in the winter!

Variation

Add a sprinkling of dried fruit, such as raisins, cranberries, cherries or blueberries, or nuts, such as finely chopped hazelnuts or walnuts.

Serving Ideas

Serve topped with Vanilla Maple Yogurt Dressing (page 142).

Serve spooned over vanilla ice cream for an easy winter dessert.

1 tsp	butter or non-hydrogenated margarine	5 mL
1 tsp	pure maple syrup	5 mL
1	cooking apple, such as Granny Smith, peeled and cut into 8 wedges	1
1	pear, peeled and cut into 8 wedges	1

1. In a large nonstick skillet, melt butter over medium heat. Add maple syrup, swirling to coat pan. Add apple and pear wedges; cook for 2 to 3 minutes per side, turning to brown lightly on all sides.

Nutrients per serving

Calories	49
Fat	1.0 g
Saturated fat	0.6 g
Sodium	7 mg (0% DV)
Carbohydrate	11 g
Fiber	2 g (8% DV)
Protein	0 g
Calcium	6 mg (1% DV)
Iron	0.1 mg (1% DV)

Diabetes Food Choice Values:
½ Carbohydrate

✔ **Kid Approved**

The many varieties of canned fruits and imported fresh fruits available to us are particularly helpful during the winter months, when fresh fruit is hard to find or expensive.

Tip

Avoid buying canned fruits packed in light or heavy syrup, as they contain substantial amounts of added sugar.

Variation

Top with 2 tbsp (30 mL) toasted unsalted sunflower seeds or nuts, such as pecans, hazelnuts, walnuts or almonds.

Serving Idea

Serve topped with low-fat peach yogurt.

Cold Canadian Winter Fruit Salad

Adam Hudson, Dietitian, Ontario

1	can (14 oz/398 mL) unsweetened sliced peaches, drained	1
1	can (14 oz/398 mL) unsweetened sliced pears, drained	1
1	banana, cut into slices	1
1 cup	halved seedless red grapes	250 mL
2 tsp	orange juice	10 mL
2 tsp	lime juice	10 mL
1 tbsp	finely chopped candied ginger (optional)	15 mL

1. In a large bowl, combine peaches, pears, banana and grapes. Sprinkle orange and lime juice over fruit and stir gently to coat. Top with ginger (if using).

Nutrients per serving

Calories	56
Fat	0.1 g
Saturated fat	0.0 g
Sodium	3 mg (0% DV)
Carbohydrate	15 g
Fiber	1 g (4% DV)
Protein	1 g
Calcium	7 mg (1% DV)
Iron	0.3 mg (2% DV)

Diabetes Food Choice Values:

1   Carbohydrate

Pinto Bean Tortilla Soup (page 130)

Red Leaf Salad with Mango Chutney Dressing (page 149)

Citrus Fennel Slaw (page 153)

Nutty and Fruity Quinoa Salad
with Maple Vinaigrette (page 166)

Fruity Sautéed Chicken (page 175)

Greek Chicken (page 182)

Cranberry-Glazed
Turkey Breast Cutlets (page 185)

Mediterranean Roasted Beef and Veggies (page 196)

✔ **Kid Approved**

This salad is vibrant in color, crisp in texture and bursting with flavor — perfect for a hot summer day. At first glance, it looks like just a Greek salad with tomatoes, so the first time Brendine made it, her family cheered for the watermelon. Now, they request this version almost every time she asks, "What kind of salad would you like tonight?"

Tips

Kids can help by scooping the seeds from the cucumber and crumbling the feta cheese.

This salad becomes very liquidy if left overnight, but there likely won't be any leftovers to worry about!

Variation

For a twist, drizzle with 1 tbsp (15 mL) balsamic vinegar.

Nutrients per serving

Calories	69
Fat	3.9 g
Saturated fat	1.6 g
Sodium	106 mg (4% DV)
Carbohydrate	8 g
Fiber	1 g (4% DV)
Protein	2 g
Calcium	62 mg (6% DV)
Iron	0.4 mg (3% DV)

Diabetes Food Choice Values:

½ Carbohydrate
1   Fat

Cucumber Watermelon Salad

Brendine Partyka, Ontario

½	seedless watermelon, rind removed, flesh cut into 1-inch (2.5 cm) chunks (4 to 6 cups/1 to 1.5 L)	½
1	English cucumber, quartered lengthwise, seeds removed and cut into ¼-inch (0.5 cm) slices	1
1 tbsp	canola or extra virgin olive oil	15 mL
½ cup	finely chopped fresh basil	125 mL
½ cup	crumbled feta cheese	125 mL

1. In a large bowl, combine watermelon and cucumber. Drizzle with oil. Add basil and cheese; gently toss to combine.

> Try planting watermelon and cucumbers in your garden or community garden — it's a great way for kids to learn about food. You can also start a small herb garden in your kitchen, so your family can enjoy fresh herbs year-round. Kids can paint small terra cotta pots and choose their favorite herbs to plant.

This salad was created by Jennifer's husband's grandmother, and it is still a favorite at family gatherings. Jennifer's three-year-old son loves to stir the dressing and top the salad greens with the berries, cheese and nuts.

Tips

Use only fresh strawberries. Frozen ones would make this salad too soggy.

Toast the almonds for added flavor (see page 139).

Variation

Walnuts are a nice alternative to almonds.

Green Salad with Apple Balsamic Vinaigrette

Jennifer House, Dietitian, Alberta

6 cups	mixed salad greens	1.5 L
2 cups	sliced strawberries	500 mL
½ cup	crumbled feta cheese	125 mL
¼ cup	slivered almonds	60 mL
Dressing		
1	clove garlic, minced	1
1 tbsp	lightly packed brown sugar	15 mL
2 tbsp	unsweetened apple juice	30 mL
1 tbsp	balsamic vinegar	15 mL
½ tsp	honey Dijon mustard	2 mL
¼ cup	canola oil	60 mL

1. In a large bowl, combine greens, strawberries, cheese and almonds.

2. *Dressing:* In a small bowl, whisk together garlic, brown sugar, apple juice, vinegar and mustard. Gradually whisk in oil.

3. Pour dressing over salad and toss to coat.

Feta cheese can be made from cow's, sheep's or goat's milk. It is a fresh curd cheese that is preserved in brine. It's most often associated with Greek cuisine, but its salty taste and unique texture make it a delicious ingredient in many other dishes as well.

Nutrients per serving

Calories	181
Fat	14.4 g
Saturated fat	2.8 g
Sodium	162 mg (7% DV)
Carbohydrate	11 g
Fiber	3 g (12% DV)
Protein	4 g
Calcium	120 mg (11% DV)
Iron	1.0 mg (7% DV)

Very high in: Vitamin C and folate

High in: Magnesium

Diabetes Food Choice Values:
½ Carbohydrate
½ Meat & Alternatives
2½ Fats

Makes 8 servings

✔ **Kid Approved**

Jessica was inspired by a similar salad at one of her favorite restaurants and decided to try making it at home. She has a hit on her hands!

Tips

The vinaigrette makes 1 cup (250 mL), but you only need ⅓ cup (75 mL) for 8 servings. Place the remainder in a jar, cover and refrigerate for up to 1 week.

Jessica's original recipe called for a purchased low-fat poppy seed dressing; we created this fruit-based poppy seed dressing as a homemade alternative.

Serving Idea

Topped with slices of grilled chicken, this salad makes a terrific main course.

Nutrients per serving

Calories	97
Fat	5.0 g
Saturated fat	1.3 g
Sodium	63 mg (3% DV)
Carbohydrate	11 g
Fiber	2 g (8% DV)
Protein	3 g
Calcium	53 mg (5% DV)
Iron	1.2 mg (9% DV)

Very high in: Vitamin A and folate

High in: Vitamin C

Diabetes Food Choice Values:
½ Carbohydrate
1   Fat

Spinach and Goat Cheese Salad

Jessica Kelly, Dietitian, Ontario

● **Blender or food processor**

8 cups	baby spinach	2 L
1	can (10 oz/284 mL) juice-packed mandarin orange segments, drained	1
½	large red onion, finely diced	½
2 oz	goat cheese, crumbled	60 g
¼ cup	honey-roasted almonds	60 mL
¼ cup	dried cranberries	60 mL
Dressing		
¾ cup	thawed frozen raspberries	175 mL
2 tbsp	granulated sugar	30 mL
2 tbsp	canola oil	30 mL
4 tsp	raspberry-flavored vinegar	20 mL
1 tsp	poppy seeds	5 mL

1. In a large bowl, combine spinach, oranges, red onion, goat cheese, almonds and cranberries.

2. *Dressing:* In blender, combine raspberries, sugar, 3 tbsp (45 mL) water, oil and vinegar; blend until smooth. Pour into a small bowl and stir in poppy seeds.

3. Pour ⅓ cup (75 mL) of the dressing over the salad and toss to coat; reserve the remainder for another use.

> Ontario has some wonderful local goat cheeses; fruit-flavored goat cheeses like cranberry work really well in this recipe.

This salad offers a nice combination of flavors that even people who are not fans of blue cheese will enjoy. For a milder blue cheese flavor, try Cambozola cheese.

Tips

Rinse arugula well to remove all dirt and grit, and spin or pat it dry so the dressing will cling to it. Use kitchen scissors to cut the arugula leaves.

Caroline prefers to use a Canadian blue cheese for this salad.

Variation

Use pears instead of apples and toasted pine nuts or pecan halves instead of sunflower seeds.

Nutrients per serving

Calories	221
Fat	16.5 g
Saturated fat	4.8 g
Sodium	336 mg (14% DV)
Carbohydrate	13 g
Fiber	3 g (12% DV)
Protein	8 g
Calcium	177 mg (16% DV)
Iron	1.5 mg (11% DV)

Very high in: Magnesium and folate

High in: Thiamine

Diabetes Food Choice Values:

½ Carbohydrate
1 Meat & Alternatives
2 Fats

Arugula, Apple and Blue Cheese Salad

Caroline Dubeau, Dietitian, Ontario

4 cups	arugula, chopped	1 L
2	apples, diced	2
4 oz	blue cheese, crumbled	125 g
½ cup	toasted unsalted sunflower seeds (see page 139)	125 mL

Dressing

3 tbsp	light mayonnaise	45 mL
1 tbsp	canola oil	15 mL
1 tbsp	cider vinegar	15 mL
2 tsp	liquid honey	10 mL
1 tsp	Dijon mustard	5 mL
	Freshly ground black pepper	

1. In a large bowl, gently combine arugula, apples, blue cheese and sunflower seeds.

2. *Dressing:* In a small bowl, whisk together mayonnaise, oil, vinegar, 1 tbsp (15 mL) water, honey and mustard. Season to taste with pepper.

3. Pour dressing over salad and toss to coat.

Gala, Cortland and Jonagold apples are less likely to brown when cut.

✔ **Kid Approved**

This salad features attractive colors and textures, not to mention delicious flavor.

Tips

You could also whisk the dressing instead of using a food processor or blender. Shemina's young son gets a kick out of this task.

Much of the fat in this salad comes from the peanuts, which provide mostly unsaturated fat. If you want to reduce the total amount of fat, use ½ cup (125 mL) peanuts. The protein will also be reduced if you make this change.

Nutrients per serving

Calories	211
Fat	15.7 g
Saturated fat	1.9 g
Sodium	113 mg (5% DV)
Carbohydrate	15 g
Fiber	3 g (12% DV)
Protein	7 g
Calcium	43 mg (4% DV)
Iron	1.1 mg (8% DV)

Very high in: Vitamin A
High in: Magnesium, zinc, folate and niacin

Diabetes Food Choice Values:
½	Carbohydrate
1	Meat & Alternatives
2	Fats

Red Leaf Salad with Mango Chutney Dressing

Shemina Patni, Dietitian, British Columbia

● **Blender or food processor**

8 cups	torn red leaf lettuce	2 L
1	tart apple, coarsely chopped	1
½ cup	sliced green onions	125 mL
½ cup	halved seedless red grapes	125 mL
1 cup	unsalted roasted whole peanuts	250 mL

Dressing

1 tsp	curry powder	5 mL
½ tsp	granulated sugar	2 mL
⅛ tsp	ground turmeric	0.5 mL
Pinch	salt	Pinch
¼ cup	freshly squeezed lemon juice	60 mL
3 tbsp	mild or hot mango chutney	45 mL
2 tbsp	red wine vinegar	30 mL
¼ cup	canola oil	60 mL

1. In a large bowl, combine lettuce, apple, green onions and grapes.

2. *Dressing:* In blender, combine curry powder, sugar, turmeric, salt, ¼ cup (60 mL) water, lemon juice, chutney and vinegar; blend until smooth. With the motor running, through the feed tube, gradually add oil and process until blended.

3. Pour half the dressing over salad and toss to coat. Garnish with peanuts. Pass the remaining dressing at the table, if desired.

> Chutneys are sweet, spicy and tangy from the essential ingredients of sugar, spices and vinegar. They can be smooth or, more traditionally, quite lumpy. Purchased mango chutney is available mild or hot; either will work well in this dressing.

Makes 8 servings

✔ Kid Approved

Haloumi cheese holds its shape when heated and is a delightful complement to sweet pears.

Tips

Poke the pears with a fork to test doneness. The fork should encounter minimal resistance when it enters the center of the pear slices.

Ask your cheesemonger to recommend other Canadian cheeses suitable for grilling.

Variation

Substitute apples for the pears.

Serving Idea

This dish is a great start to either a Sunday brunch or an evening of entertaining.

Nutrients per serving

Calories	166
Fat	10.5 g
Saturated fat	5.2 g
Sodium	355 mg (15% DV)
Carbohydrate	13 g
Fiber	2 g (8% DV)
Protein	7 g
Calcium	180 mg (16% DV)
Iron	0.7 mg (5% DV)

High in: Vitamin A and folate

Diabetes Food Choice Values:

1	Carbohydrate
1	Meat & Alternatives
1	Fat

Pears with Grilled Haloumi Cheese

Claude Gamache, Dietitian, Quebec

2 tbsp	lightly packed brown sugar	30 mL
1 tsp	butter	5 mL
2	pears, peeled, cored and cut lengthwise into 8 slices each	2
1 tbsp	balsamic vinegar	15 mL
1	package (7 oz/210 g) Haloumi cheese, cut into 8 slices	1
4 cups	lightly packed spinach, trimmed	1 L
¼ cup	lightly toasted chopped walnuts (see page 139)	60 mL
2 tbsp	dried cranberries	30 mL

1. In a nonstick skillet, melt brown sugar and butter over medium heat. Sauté pears for about 5 minutes or until fork-tender. Add vinegar and stir well to coat pears. Transfer pears to a bowl and set aside.

2. Wipe skillet clean and return to medium heat. Add cheese slices and cook, turning once, for 1 to 2 minutes per side or until lightly browned. Transfer to a plate.

3. Divide spinach among 8 serving plates. Garnish each with 2 pear slices and 1 slice of cheese. Sprinkle evenly with walnuts and cranberries.

> Haloumi is a sheep's milk cheese often used in Greek and Middle Eastern cooking. It's perfect in this recipe, as it holds its shape during cooking.

✔ Kid Approved

Frozen grapes give extra coolness to this refreshing main course salad, perfect for a hot summer evening. If you omit the chicken, it's also a terrific starter.

Tips

Freeze the grapes for at least 1 hour before making this salad.

If you have leftover cooked chicken breasts, feel free to use them here.

The salad dressing makes 1 cup (250 mL), but you only need ½ cup (125 mL) for 6 servings. Place the remainder in a jar, cover and refrigerate for up to 3 days.

Nutrients per serving

Calories	295
Fat	15.8 g
Saturated fat	4.1 g
Sodium	242 mg (10% DV)
Carbohydrate	17 g
Fiber	2 g (8% DV)
Protein	22 g
Calcium	92 mg (8% DV)
Iron	1.2 mg (9% DV)

Very high in: Niacin

High in: Magnesium, vitamin A, vitamin B$_6$ and folate

Diabetes Food Choice Values:

1	Carbohydrate
3	Meat & Alternatives

Spring Greens with Chicken and Fruit

Lauren Coles, Ontario

● **Blender or food processor**

1 tbsp	canola oil, divided	15 mL
1 lb	boneless skinless chicken breasts, cut into thin strips	500 g
6 cups	mixed greens	1.5 L
12	frozen grapes, cut in half	12
4 oz	goat cheese, crumbled	125 g
¼ cup	dried cherries	60 mL
¼ cup	chopped dried apples	60 mL

Dressing

¼ cup	granulated sugar	60 mL
1 tbsp	finely chopped shallot	15 mL
1 tsp	dry mustard	5 mL
¼ tsp	salt	1 mL
½ cup	light mayonnaise	125 mL
¼ cup	canola oil	60 mL
¼ cup	white wine vinegar	60 mL
2 tbsp	unsweetened apple juice	30 mL
1 tbsp	poppy seeds	15 mL

1. Heat a wok or large skillet over medium heat. Add half the oil and swirl to coat. In batches, stir-fry chicken for 6 to 8 minutes or until golden brown and no longer pink inside, adding oil between batches as necessary. As each batch is completed, transfer to a plate and set aside.

2. *Dressing:* In blender, combine sugar, shallot, mustard, salt, mayonnaise, oil, vinegar and apple juice; blend until smooth. Transfer to a small bowl and stir in poppy seeds.

3. Divide mixed greens among six plates. Top with cooked chicken, grapes, goat cheese, cherries and apples. Using ½ cup (125 mL) of the dressing, drizzle evenly over the salads.

✔ Kid Approved

When Joanne and her colleague made this salad for their students, it got glowing reviews, even from people who don't usually like coleslaw! It's a terrific choice for a summertime barbecue.

Tips

Use a mandoline or a food processor with a cutting blade to shred the cabbage.

This dressing works for a variety of salads.

Variations

Replace the orange with sliced apple and use cider vinegar in place of the lemon juice.

Use peanuts, pecans, cashews or sunflower seeds instead of walnuts.

Add ½ cup (125 mL) crumbled blue cheese to the salad.

Nutrients per serving

Calories	155
Fat	12.0 g
Saturated fat	1.5 g
Sodium	223 mg (9% DV)
Carbohydrate	11 g
Fiber	3 g (12% DV)
Protein	3 g
Calcium	92 mg (8% DV)
Iron	1.0 mg (7% DV)

Very high in: Vitamin C and folate

Diabetes Food Choice Values:
½   Carbohydrate
2½   Fats

Fresh Slaw

Joanne Rankin, Dietitian, British Columbia

½	head cabbage, finely shredded	½
3	green onions, finely chopped	3
3	stalks celery, finely sliced	3
1	large orange	1
½ cup	toasted chopped walnuts (see page 139)	125 mL
½ cup	loosely packed chopped fresh parsley	125 mL

Dressing

½ cup	low-fat plain yogurt	125 mL
½ cup	light mayonnaise	125 mL
2 tbsp	Dijon mustard	30 mL
2 tbsp	freshly squeezed lemon juice	30 mL
1 tbsp	canola or olive oil	15 mL
Pinch	salt	Pinch
	Freshly ground black pepper	

1. In a large bowl, combine cabbage, green onions and celery.

2. Using a knife, peel orange, removing as much of the white pith as possible. Cut orange in half, then lengthwise into quarters. Cut each quarter crosswise into ¼-inch (0.5 cm) slices. Add to the cabbage mixture, along with any juice from the cutting board; toss to combine.

3. *Dressing:* In a small bowl, whisk together yogurt, mayonnaise, mustard, lemon juice, oil, salt and pepper to taste.

4. Pour dressing over salad and toss to coat. Cover and refrigerate for at least 30 minutes or for up to 8 hours before serving. Top with walnuts and parsley just before serving.

The fennel and citrus combination is a natural in this crunchy twist on coleslaw. Kids enjoy the citrus flavors.

Tips

To get thin, even slices, use a mandoline to cut the fennel bulb.

Instead of serving on top of greens on individual plates, you can also simply pass the slaw.

Variation

Substitute toasted unsalted sunflower seeds for the pine nuts.

Citrus Fennel Slaw

Jaclyn Pritchard, Dietitian, Ontario

1	large fennel bulb	1
¼	red onion, very thinly sliced	¼
	Grated zest and juice of 1 lemon	
	Grated zest of 1 orange	
2 tbsp	freshly squeezed orange juice	30 mL
1 tbsp	canola oil	15 mL
Pinch	salt	Pinch
	Freshly ground black pepper	
6 cups	mesclun mix	1.5 L
3 tbsp	toasted pine nuts (see page 139)	45 mL

1. Remove the stalks and tough outer leaves of the fennel bulb and discard. Cut bulb in half lengthwise and trim out core. Cut bulb crosswise into very thin slices.

2. Place fennel slices and red onion in a large bowl. Stir in lemon zest, lemon juice, orange zest and orange juice. Drizzle with oil and sprinkle with salt and pepper to taste.

3. Divide mesclun mix evenly among six small plates. Mound one-sixth of the fennel slaw on each plate and garnish with pine nuts.

> Fresh fennel is reasonably new to Canadian cuisine, though it's been used extensively in Mediterranean cooking for centuries. It has a mild licorice flavor. The bulb is delicious used in salads, soups and stews. The frond, though beautiful, is rarely used in cooking.

Nutrients per serving

Calories	85
Fat	5.4 g
Saturated fat	0.4 g
Sodium	88 mg (4% DV)
Carbohydrate	9 g
Fiber	3 g (12% DV)
Protein	2 g
Calcium	72 mg (7% DV)
Iron	1.1 mg (8% DV)

Very high in: Folate
High in: Vitamin C

Diabetes Food Choice Values:
1   Fat

Use all your homegrown herbs in this delightfully fresh salad, which you can double, triple or quadruple to serve up to four people.

Tips

To chop basil, place several leaves flat on top of each other. Roll tightly and then cut into thin strips (known as chiffonade).

It's best not to use dried herbs in this salad, as there is not enough time or moisture for them to soften and release their flavors.

Vary the amounts of the herbs to your liking.

Personal Garden Herb Salad

Judy Campbell-Gordon, Dietitian, Quebec

1	tomato, cut into 8 wedges	1
1 cup	baby arugula leaves	250 mL
⅓ cup	chopped cucumber	75 mL
2 tbsp	chopped fresh oregano	30 mL
2 tbsp	chopped fresh basil	30 mL
2 tbsp	chopped fresh mint	30 mL
1 tbsp	chopped fresh chives	15 mL
1 tbsp	balsamic vinegar	15 mL
2 tsp	extra virgin olive oil	10 mL
4	kalamata olives, pitted	4
1 tbsp	crumbled feta cheese	15 mL
¼ tsp	freshly ground black pepper	1 mL

1. In a medium bowl, combine tomato, arugula, cucumber, oregano, basil, mint and chives. Drizzle with vinegar and oil. Top with olives, cheese, pepper and salt.

Nutrients per serving

Calories	211
Fat	15.5 g
Saturated fat	3.3 g
Sodium	482 mg (20% DV)
Carbohydrate	16 g
Fiber	5 g (20% DV)
Protein	6 g
Calcium	241 mg (22% DV)
Iron	4.5 mg (32% DV)

Very high in: Magnesium, vitamin A, vitamin C and folate

Diabetes Food Choice Values:
3   Fats

Makes 8 servings

✔ **Kid Approved**

This salad is a perfect way to introduce kids to a variety of different vegetables on their own terms. They'll have fun experimenting, discovering for themselves how different combinations create different flavors.

Tips

The salad dressing makes 1 cup (250 mL), but you only need ½ cup (125 mL) for 8 servings. Place the remainder in a jar, cover and refrigerate and for up to 3 days.

Rather than combining the salad ingredients, you can also place each item in a separate bowl on the table and let children create their own salads.

Nutrients per serving

Calories	73
Fat	2.7 g
Saturated fat	0.9 g
Sodium	160 mg (7% DV)
Carbohydrate	8 g
Fiber	3 g (12% DV)
Protein	5 g
Calcium	116 mg (11% DV)
Iron	1.1 mg (8% DV)

Very high in: Vitamin A and folate

High in: Vitamin C

Diabetes Food Choice Values:
½ Meat & Alternatives

Kid-Friendly Garden Salad

Ella and Keira Russell, Manitoba

1	head romaine lettuce, torn into bite-size pieces	1
½	English cucumber, chopped	½
2 cups	grape tomatoes	500 mL
1 cup	shredded carrots	250 mL
1 cup	shredded light Cheddar cheese	250 mL
Peppered Ranch Dressing		
½ cup	buttermilk	125 mL
⅓ cup	low-fat plain yogurt	75 mL
¼ cup	light mayonnaise	60 mL
1 tbsp	white wine vinegar	15 mL
2	cloves garlic, minced	2
2 tbsp	finely grated fresh Parmesan cheese (optional)	30 mL
1 tbsp	finely chopped fresh parsley	15 mL
1 tsp	grated onion	5 mL
½ tsp	freshly ground black pepper	2 mL
Pinch	salt	Pinch

1. In a large bowl, combine lettuce, cucumber, tomatoes, carrots and Cheddar cheese.

2. *Dressing:* In a small bowl, whisk together buttermilk, yogurt, mayonnaise and vinegar. Stir in garlic, Parmesan (if using), parsley, onion, pepper and salt.

3. Place 1 tbsp (15 mL) salad dressing in each of eight small condiment bowls and set at individual place settings.

At Sarah's family get-togethers, creative salads are always on the menu. Here's one of her best, passed down from her mother, full of color, texture and flavor.

Tips

For a salad with a less salty flavor, omit the olives.

Radicchio is native to Italy but is now grown in Canada. Its leaves turn the characteristic red color as the temperature cools before harvest.

To reduce the fat and sodium, use less feta cheese and fewer olives.

Radicchio on Down Salad

Sarah Baker, Ontario

1	bunch fresh watercress, stems removed	1
1	small head radicchio, cut in half and coarsely chopped	1
1	green onion, finely chopped	1
½ cup	crumbled feta cheese	125 mL
½ cup	kalamata olives	125 mL
½ cup	toasted whole almonds (see page 139)	125 mL
½ cup	freshly grated Parmesan cheese	125 mL
	Freshly ground black pepper	

Dressing

½ tsp	granulated sugar	2 mL
¼ cup	olive oil	60 mL
2 tbsp	red wine vinegar	30 mL
1 tbsp	Dijon mustard	15 mL

1. In a large bowl, gently combine watercress, radicchio, green onion, feta, olives, almonds and Parmesan.

2. *Dressing:* In a small bowl, whisk together sugar, oil, vinegar and mustard.

3. Pour dressing over salad and toss to coat. Season to taste with pepper.

> In early 19th-century England, it was common for the working class to eat watercress sandwiches for breakfast. When money was scarce, they ate the watercress alone; thus, it came to be known as "poor man's bread."

Nutrients per serving

Calories	186
Fat	16.7 g
Saturated fat	4.0 g
Sodium	382 mg (16% DV)
Carbohydrate	4 g
Fiber	1 g (4% DV)
Protein	7 g
Calcium	161 mg (15% DV)
Iron	0.7 mg (5% DV)

High in: Vitamin B$_{12}$

Diabetes Food Choice Values:
1 Meat & Alternatives
2½ Fats

Nutrients per serving

Calories	308
Fat	13.9 g
Saturated fat	2.5 g
Sodium	391 mg (16% DV)
Carbohydrate	24 g
Fiber	6 g (24% DV)
Protein	23 g
Calcium	231 mg (21% DV)
Iron	2.9 mg (21% DV)

Very high in: Magnesium, vitamin D, folate, vitamin B$_{12}$, thiamine and niacin

High in: Zinc, vitamin A, vitamin C, vitamin B$_6$ and riboflavin

Diabetes Food Choice Values:

1	Carbohydrate
2	Meat & Alternatives
1	Fat

Niçoise Salad

Edie Shaw-Ewald, Dietitian, Nova Scotia

1	head Boston or romaine lettuce, leaves separated	1
2	cans (each 7½ oz/213 g) salmon, drained and flaked	2
1 cup	grape tomatoes	250 mL
8 oz	yellow beans, steamed until tender-crisp and cooled	250 g
8 oz	asparagus spears, trimmed, steamed until tender-crisp and cooled	250 g
20	tiny new potatoes, boiled, cooled and cut in half	20
3	hard-cooked eggs, quartered	3
¼ cup	niçoise olives	60 mL
Dressing		
2	cloves garlic, minced	2
1 tbsp	finely chopped shallots	15 mL
½ tsp	freshly ground black pepper	2 mL
Pinch	salt	Pinch
3 tbsp	extra virgin olive oil	45 mL
3 tbsp	freshly squeezed lemon juice	45 mL
1 tbsp	red wine vinegar	15 mL
1½ tsp	Dijon mustard	7 mL

1. Arrange lettuce leaves on a large platter and scatter salmon over top. Starting at one end, arrange on top, in order: tomatoes, beans, asparagus, potatoes and eggs.

2. *Dressing:* In a small bowl, whisk together garlic, shallots, pepper, salt, oil, lemon juice, 2 tbsp (30 mL) water, vinegar and mustard.

3. Pour dressing over salad and scatter olives on top.

> "À la Niçoise," meaning "in the style of Nice," is the correct term for this salad. Nice, France, is located between the Mediterranean Sea to the south and groves of olives, which produce niçoise olives, to the north. Traditional Niçoise salad also contains anchovies, but due to their high salt content, we've omitted them from this recipe.

✔ **Kid Approved**

The simplicity of this salad makes it very appealing. To top it off, it's pretty and delicious! Sarah's children love to crumble the feta and toss the nuts into the salad.

Tips

Choose beets that are uniform in size so they will all cook in the same time.

Peeling the beets after roasting, instead of before, saves time and is much easier.

Be sure to use white wine vinegar; red wine vinegar will add a pink tinge to the yellow beets and the feta.

Variation

Add 1 tbsp (15 mL) finely chopped red onion to the salad.

Serving Idea

Serve on individual plates on a bed of fresh arugula leaves.

Nutrients per serving

Calories	115
Fat	9.2 g
Saturated fat	1.6 g
Sodium	162 mg (7% DV)
Carbohydrate	7 g
Fiber	2 g (8% DV)
Protein	3 g
Calcium	45 mg (4% DV)
Iron	0.7 mg (5% DV)

High in: Folate

Diabetes Food Choice Values:
2   Fats

Golden Beet Salad

Sarah McKenna, Alberta

- **Preheat oven to 375°F (190°C)**

1 lb	golden beets (about 4)	500 g
¼ cup	crumbled feta cheese	60 mL
¼ cup	toasted chopped walnuts (see page 139)	60 mL
Dressing		
2 tbsp	canola oil	30 mL
2 tbsp	white wine vinegar	30 mL
Pinch	salt	Pinch
	Freshly ground black pepper	

1. Scrub beets and cut away tops and tails. Wrap in foil and place in a baking dish. Bake in preheated oven for about 45 minutes or until just tender. Unwrap and let cool. Peel under running water. Cut into thin slices and place in a large bowl.

2. *Dressing:* In a small bowl, whisk together oil, vinegar, 2 tbsp (30 mL) water, salt and pepper to taste.

3. Sprinkle cheese over beets and drizzle with dressing. Sprinkle with nuts.

Take this fresh, flavorful, healthy potato salad along to your next summertime barbecue and impress your neighbors. It's a great alternative to heavy, mayonnaise-based potato salad.

Tip

Grow your own herbs in pots on your patio or in your backyard. In the winter, you can bring them inside and keep them going on a sunny windowsill. That way, you'll always have fresh herbs at your fingertips.

Variation

Use orange juice instead of lemon juice.

Nutrients per serving

Calories	165
Fat	4.8 g
Saturated fat	0.4 g
Sodium	56 mg (2% DV)
Carbohydrate	28 g
Fiber	3 g (12% DV)
Protein	3 g
Calcium	28 mg (3% DV)
Iron	1.5 mg (11% DV)

High in: Magnesium, vitamin C and vitamin B_6

Diabetes Food Choice Values:

1½ Carbohydrates

1 Fat

Herbed Green Potato Salad

Adam Hudson, Dietitian, Ontario

2 lbs	tiny new potatoes (unpeeled)	1 kg
2 tbsp	white wine vinegar	30 mL
2	cloves garlic, minced	2
2 tbsp	finely chopped fresh parsley	30 mL
2 tbsp	finely snipped fresh chives	30 mL
2 tbsp	finely snipped fresh dill	30 mL
2 tbsp	finely minced fresh sage	30 mL
1 tsp	freshly ground black pepper	5 mL
Pinch	salt	Pinch
2 tbsp	canola or olive oil	30 mL
2 tbsp	freshly squeezed lemon juice	30 mL
½ cup	cooked green peas	125 mL

1. Place potatoes in a medium saucepan and add enough cold water to cover. Bring to a boil over medium-high heat; reduce heat and boil gently for 15 to 20 minutes or until just tender. Drain and let cool slightly. Cut potatoes in half and transfer to a bowl. Add vinegar, toss and set aside for 30 minutes.

2. In a small bowl, combine garlic, parsley, chives, dill, sage, pepper, salt, oil and lemon juice. Pour over potatoes and stir gently to coat. Stir in peas.

New potatoes are sometimes called baby potatoes or creamer potatoes. They are young, immature potatoes that are harvested before the rest of the potato crop. They come in a variety of colors, are waxy in texture and have a paper-thin skin that generally does not need to be removed.

This spicy chilled potato salad is a great alternative to traditional potato salad.

Variation

Use red wine vinegar instead of white.

Serving Idea

Serve with Maple-Glazed Pork Tenderloin (page 212) and steamed green beans.

Nutrients per serving

Calories	156
Fat	4.9 g
Saturated fat	0.4 g
Sodium	63 mg (3% DV)
Carbohydrate	26 g
Fiber	3 g (12% DV)
Protein	3 g
Calcium	16 mg (1% DV)
Iron	1.2 mg (9% DV)

High in: Vitamin C and vitamin B_6

Diabetes Food Choice Values:

1½ Carbohydrates
1   Fat

Fiery Red Potato Salad

Adam Hudson, Dietitian, Ontario

2 lbs	tiny new red-skinned potatoes (unpeeled)	1 kg
2 tbsp	white wine vinegar	30 mL
2	cloves garlic, minced	2
2 tsp	chili powder	10 mL
1 tsp	hot pepper flakes	5 mL
¼ tsp	smoked paprika	1 mL
¼ tsp	cayenne pepper	1 mL
Pinch	salt	Pinch
2 tbsp	canola or olive oil	30 mL
2 tbsp	freshly squeezed lemon juice	30 mL

1. Place potatoes in a medium saucepan and add enough cold water to cover. Bring to a boil over medium-high heat; reduce heat and boil gently for 15 to 20 minutes or until just tender. Drain and let cool slightly. Cut potatoes in half and transfer to a bowl. Add vinegar, toss and set aside for 30 minutes.

2. In a small bowl, combine garlic, chili powder, hot pepper flakes, paprika, cayenne, salt, oil and lemon juice. Pour over potatoes and stir gently to coat. Cover and refrigerate for at least 2 hours or for up to 8 hours before serving.

> Paprika is made from a dried sweet pimiento pepper, which is ground into a powder. It has a mild flavor and is often used as a garnish to add a pleasant red color. Smoked paprika, made from smoked peppers, has a strong smoky flavor, so use it sparingly.

Makes 6 servings

✔ **Kid Approved**

Homegrown tomatoes and fresh herbs will make this salad a summertime favorite.

Tip

This is a great way to use up leftover boiled potatoes.

Variations

Add 1/2 cup (125 mL) diced bocconcini cheese or 1 tbsp (15 mL) balsamic vinegar.

If using dried herbs, use about one-third as much and add all of them to the salad mixture. Cover and refrigerate for at least 2 hours or for up to 8 hours to allow the flavor of the herbs to infuse the salad.

Roasted Red Pepper, Tomato and Potato Salad

Sandra Gabriele, Dietitian, Ontario

2	medium to large tomatoes, each cut into 8 wedges	2
2	red-skinned potatoes, boiled until fork-tender, then coarsely chopped	2
2	roasted red bell peppers (see box, page 124), cut into thin strips	2
2	cloves garlic, minced	2
3 tbsp	finely minced fresh basil, divided	45 mL
1 tbsp	finely minced fresh oregano	15 mL
1/2 tsp	salt	2 mL
2 tbsp	canola oil	30 mL
	Hot pepper sauce (optional)	

1. In a large bowl, combine tomatoes, potatoes and roasted peppers. Add garlic, 1 tbsp (15 mL) of the basil, oregano, salt, oil and hot pepper sauce to taste (if using); stir to coat vegetables. Garnish with the remaining basil.

> Round red-skinned potatoes are ideal for potato salads, roasting and boiling. Russet, Idaho and Yukon gold potatoes are excellent for baking, mashing and frying.

Nutrients per serving

Calories	108
Fat	4.8 g
Saturated fat	0.4 g
Sodium	197 mg (8% DV)
Carbohydrate	16 g
Fiber	2 g (8% DV)
Protein	2 g
Calcium	19 mg (2% DV)
Iron	0.8 mg (6% DV)

Very high in: Vitamin C
High in: Vitamin B$_6$

Diabetes Food Choice Values:
1/2 Carbohydrate
1 Fat

Canned beans are a time saver and work very well in this dish.

Tip

Be sure to wash cilantro thoroughly, as it often contains a lot of grit.

Serving Idea

Add half an egg salad sandwich and a glass of milk for a satisfying lunch.

Best Bean Salad

Lucia Weiler, Dietitian, Ontario

2	large tomatoes, chopped	2
1	can (19 oz/540 mL) mixed bean medley, drained and rinsed	1
¼ cup	finely sliced red onion	60 mL
¼ cup	chopped fresh cilantro	60 mL
2 tbsp	chopped fresh basil	30 mL
Dressing		
1	clove garlic, minced	1
¼ tsp	hot pepper flakes	1 mL
¼ tsp	freshly ground black pepper	1 mL
Pinch	salt	Pinch
1½ tbsp	extra virgin olive oil	22 mL
2 tsp	balsamic vinegar	10 mL
1 tsp	freshly squeezed lemon juice	5 mL

1. In a medium bowl, combine tomatoes, bean medley, red onion, cilantro and basil.

2. *Dressing:* In a small bowl, whisk together garlic, hot pepper flakes, black pepper, salt, oil, vinegar and lemon juice.

3. Pour dressing over bean mixture and toss gently to coat. Cover and refrigerate for at least 1 hour, until chilled, or for up to 1 day.

Nutrients per serving

Calories	143
Fat	4.3 g
Saturated fat	0.7 g
Sodium	379 mg (16% DV)
Carbohydrate	21 g
Fiber	6 g (24% DV)
Protein	7 g
Calcium	43 mg (4% DV)
Iron	1.2 mg (9% DV)

High in: Vitamin A, vitamin C, folate

Diabetes Food Choice Values:

1	Carbohydrate
½	Meat & Alternatives
½	Fat

✔ **Kid Approved**

Teresa likes to serve one dish with a legume in it when she entertains guests, and this simple salad is always a hit. She believes food preparation is a family event, and her sons have learned how to make this salad, along with many other foods.

Tips

Keep a can of lentils in your pantry so you can make this easy salad when guests drop in.

Most of the sodium in this recipe comes from the purchased salad dressing. To reduce the sodium, use the dressing from Radicchio on Down Salad (page 156).

Variation

Add ¼ cup (60 mL) crumbled feta cheese or chopped black olives.

Nutrients per serving

Calories	96
Fat	0.6 g
Saturated fat	0.1 g
Sodium	473 mg (20% DV)
Carbohydrate	17 g
Fiber	4 g (16% DV)
Protein	7 g
Calcium	27 mg (2% DV)
Iron	2.6 mg (19% DV)

Very high in: Folate

Diabetes Food Choice Values:
1   Carbohydrate
½   Meat & Alternatives

3, 2, 1 Tomato Lentil Salad

Teresa Taillefer, Dietitian, Ontario

3	green onions, sliced	3
2	tomatoes, coarsely chopped	2
1	can (19 oz/540 mL) lentils, drained and rinsed	1
¼ cup	loosely packed, chopped fresh parsley	60 mL
½ cup	fat-free Italian salad dressing	125 mL

1. In a medium bowl, combine green onions, tomatoes, lentils and parsley. Pour dressing over salad and toss to coat.

Makes 6 servings

Rye berries are very inexpensive and are packed with good nutrition. Chwen involves school children in shopping for the ingredients, cutting up vegetables and stirring the salad.

Tip

The rye berries can be cooked 1 day in advance and kept in an airtight container in the refrigerator.

Variation

Substitute wheat berries for the rye berries.

Nutrients per serving

Calories	206
Fat	6.9 g
Saturated fat	1.2 g
Sodium	258 mg (11% DV)
Carbohydrate	32 g
Fiber	6 g (24% DV)
Protein	8 g
Calcium	53 mg (5% DV)
Iron	1.5 mg (11% DV)

Very high in: Magnesium

High in: Zinc, folate and thiamine

Diabetes Food Choice Values:

1½ Carbohydrates
1½ Fats

The Rye Salad

Chwen Johnson, Dietitian, Ontario

1 cup	rye berries	250 mL
2 cups	reduced-sodium chicken broth or water	500 mL
1	English cucumber, chopped	1
1 cup	grape or cherry tomatoes, cut in half	250 mL
½ cup	finely minced red onion	125 mL
½ cup	coarsely chopped fresh cilantro	125 mL
⅓ cup	dried cranberries	75 mL
2 tbsp	crumbled feta cheese	30 mL
2 tbsp	freshly squeezed lemon juice	30 mL
1 tbsp	sesame oil	30 mL
2 tsp	black bean sauce	10 mL
¼ cup	toasted unsalted sunflower seeds (see page 139)	60 mL

1. Place rye berries in a large bowl and add enough water to cover. Cover and let soak overnight.

2. Drain rye berries and transfer to a large saucepan. Add broth and bring to a boil over medium-high heat. Cover, reduce heat to low and simmer for 1 to 1½ hours or until berries are tender. Check occasionally to make sure the liquid has not evaporated; if it has, add more water as needed until berries are cooked. Drain and rinse under cold running water until cool.

3. Transfer rye berries to a large serving bowl. Add cucumber, tomatoes, red onion, cilantro, cranberries and feta; toss to combine.

4. In a small bowl, whisk together lemon juice, oil and black bean sauce. Pour over salad and toss to combine. Garnish with sunflower seeds.

> Rye berries (and wheat berries) are the entire kernel of the grain, with only the tough outer husk removed. As such, they contain all the vitamins and minerals found in the germ (the core of the kernel), along with the fiber found mostly in the bran, or outer layer, of the kernel.

Makes 6 to 8 servings

This colorful salad has Middle Eastern flare.

Tip

Cooking the vinegar, mustard and garlic along with the broth intensifies the flavor of the cooked bulgur.

Variations

Use freshly squeezed lemon juice instead of vinegar.

Add ½ cup (125 mL) mixed chopped fresh herbs, such as basil, oregano, tarragon and thyme.

For added protein and fiber, add 1 cup (250 mL) cooked chickpeas, lentils or black beans.

Nutrients per serving

Calories	94
Fat	2.9 g
Saturated fat	0.4 g
Sodium	153 mg (6% DV)
Carbohydrate	15 g
Fiber	3 g (12% DV)
Protein	3 g
Calcium	22 mg (2% DV)
Iron	0.7 mg (5% DV)

High in: Vitamin C

Diabetes Food Choice Values:
1   Carbohydrate
½   Fat

Bulgur Salad with Broccoli, Radishes and Celery

Pam Hatton, Dietitian, Ontario

- **Steamer basket**

1½ cups	broccoli florets	375 mL
1	clove garlic, minced	1
¾ cup	reduced-sodium chicken broth	175 mL
3 tbsp	red wine vinegar	45 mL
1½ tsp	Dijon mustard	7 mL
1 cup	bulgur	250 mL
⅓ cup	chopped radishes	75 mL
⅓ cup	chopped celery	75 mL
⅓ cup	chopped red bell pepper	75 mL
¼ cup	chopped green onions	60 mL
1½ tbsp	extra virgin olive oil	22 mL
½ tsp	freshly ground black pepper	2 mL
¼ tsp	salt	1 mL

1. In a large pot fitted with a steamer basket, steam broccoli for 4 to 5 minutes or until tender-crisp. Drain and set aside.

2. In a medium saucepan, combine garlic, broth, vinegar and mustard; bring to a boil over high heat. Remove from heat and stir in bulgur. Cover and let stand for 15 minutes. Fluff with a fork.

3. Add broccoli, radishes, celery, red pepper and green onions to bulgur mixture and stir to combine. Gently stir in oil, pepper and salt.

As we were testing this salad, we realized that a dressing from another recipe submitter might work well with it, so we paired the two for a winning combination. The salad has natural sweetness from the dried fruits, and the nuts give it crunch.

Tip

If you're making quinoa on the weekend, cook extra to make this salad during the week.

Serving Idea

Serve with Maple Mustard Pork Tenderloin with Sautéed Apples (page 214).

Nutrients per serving

Calories	233
Fat	8.3 g
Saturated fat	1.1 g
Sodium	29 mg (1% DV)
Carbohydrate	36 g
Fiber	4 g (16% DV)
Protein	6 g
Calcium	47 mg (4% DV)
Iron	3.1 mg (22% DV)

Very high in: Magnesium

Diabetes Food Choice Values:
2 Carbohydrates
1½ Fats

Nutty and Fruity Quinoa Salad with Maple Vinaigrette

Melinda Figliano-Lamarche, Dietitian, Ontario (Salad), and Kristi Rokosh, Dietitian, Alberta (Dressing)

1 cup	quinoa, rinsed	250 mL
½ cup	sliced almonds	125 mL
½ cup	coarsely chopped apple	125 mL
½ cup	coarsely chopped dried apricots	125 mL
¼ cup	toasted unsalted sunflower seeds (see page 139)	60 mL
¼ cup	dried cranberries	60 mL
¼ cup	raisins	60 mL
2 tbsp	finely chopped fresh mint	30 mL
½ cup	Maple Vinaigrette (see recipe, opposite)	125 mL

1. In a medium saucepan, combine quinoa and 2 cups (500 mL) water; bring to a boil over high heat. Reduce heat to low, cover and simmer for about 20 minutes or until liquid is absorbed and quinoa is tender. Let stand for 5 minutes. Fluff with a fork.

2. Transfer quinoa to a large bowl. Add almonds, apple, apricots, sunflower seeds, cranberries, raisins and mint; toss to combine. Pour in vinaigrette and toss gently to coat.

> Quinoa is an ancient grain from South America. Some brands need to be rinsed before cooking, to remove a bitter outer coating; others do not. Familiarize yourself with the quinoa brands available in your area to learn whether rinsing is required.

Maple Vinaigrette

⅓ cup	pure maple syrup	75 mL
¼ cup	cider vinegar	60 mL
¼ cup	honey mustard	60 mL
2 tbsp	canola oil	30 mL

1. In a jar, combine maple syrup, vinegar, mustard, oil and 2 tbsp (30 mL) water. Seal and shake until well blended.

2. Store in the refrigerator for up to 1 week, shaking well before use.

Makes 1 cup (250 mL)

Tip
You can also use reduced-sugar maple-flavored syrup in the dressing.

Chicken, Turkey and Duck

Everyone loves chicken! In fact, it's one of the most popular meats in Canada, in part because of its versatility: it can be cooked whole, in parts, chopped or ground, and even the bones can be used to make delicious stock. But chicken isn't the only bird in town! Try our delicious recipes for turkey and duck — you'll love the variety and flavor of these poultry products.

Not Just for Thanksgiving

Turkey is a favorite at Thanksgiving, but why not enjoy it at other times of the year? It's naturally low in sodium and is a great source of protein, as well as many other vitamins and minerals. As with chicken, the white meat has less fat than the dark meat. Roast a bird in the spring or summer to surprise your family — as a bonus, you'll have plenty left over for easy lunches and dinners.

Free-Range Poultry

While the term "free-range" (aka "free-roaming") is not legally defined in Canada, the generally accepted meaning is that animals are permitted to graze or forage outdoors. If you want to buy free-range poultry or other meat, ask for information from your butcher or at the farmers' market.

Don't Panic Over Poultry

Many people are extra-cautious when cooking chicken and turkey and sometimes overcook it for fear of salmonella poisoning. Salmonella is a bacteria that can cause an illness known as salmonellosis. Proper hygiene, safe food handling and safe preparation practices are the keys to preventing salmonellosis and other food-borne illnesses. The good news is that salmonella bacteria are destroyed when food is cooked to a safe internal temperature. So there's no need to overcook your poultry; just cook it to the temperature recommended in our recipes. If you're cooking smaller pieces of chicken, where it might be difficult to get an accurate reading from a meat thermometer, you can rely on other clues that your chicken is done: for breasts, no pink should remain inside; for legs and thighs, the juices should run clear when the chicken is pierced.

For more complete information on internal cooking temperatures and other helpful food safety information, visit the Canadian Food Inspection Agency's website: www.inspection.gc.ca.

Family Cooking Lesson

Roasting and Baking vs. Broiling

Roasting and baking are actually the same process, in which food is surrounded with dry heated air in a closed environment such as an oven. The term "roasting" is generally used with meats and poultry; "baking" is used for fish, grain dishes, casseroles and baked goods such as breads, cookies, cakes and pies. The food cooks as heat transfers to the surface and then penetrates to the center.

Generally speaking, when you're roasting a whole chicken or turkey or a larger cut of beef, pork, lamb or other meat, it's best to place the item on a rack so that air can circulate around it and the bottom does not sit directly on the hot pan, where it can overcook or burn.

Roasting temperatures vary depending on the desired result. For example, prime rib roast is often slow-roasted at a low temperature (250°F to 300°F/120°C to 150°C) to get the same degree of doneness throughout the roast. Higher temperatures produce a roast that is more well done at the ends and rarer in the center. Be sure to follow the recommended temperature and roasting time in your recipe for the best results.

Since there is no added moisture in this cooking method, the best cuts of meat for roasting are tender, well-marbled cuts from the loin, rib or leg. If you use a less tender cut, such as round or sirloin tip, slow-roasting is a good choice, as the lower temperature prevents the roast from drying out.

Broiling is a cooking method that uses heat (generally high heat) from above. Foods are placed on a preheated metal grate or heatproof platter, then placed under the broiler. Only tender cuts of meat, such as beef or pork tenderloin, chicken breasts or meats that have been tenderized through marinating, should be broiled. Fish can also be broiled. The broiler is also used to finish a product, as with caramelizing sugar on crème brûlée or melting cheese on top of a casserole.

Joanne says that if she takes the entire chicken to the table, it will all be eaten. But if she presents a dinner plate with the chicken already portioned, everyone eats less and the remaining chicken can be served at another meal.

Tip

Brining chicken in a mild salt solution produces delightfully tender meat. Do not brine the chicken for longer than 8 hours. Over-brining may adversely affect the texture of the cooked chicken.

Nutrients per serving

Calories	168
Fat	7.6 g
Saturated fat	1.8 g
Sodium	456 mg (19% DV)
Carbohydrate	1 g
Fiber	0 g (0% DV)
Protein	23 g
Calcium	12 mg (1% DV)
Iron	1.1 mg (8% DV)

Very high in: Niacin

High in: Zinc and vitamin B$_6$

Diabetes Food Choice Values:

3   Meat & Alternatives

Brined and Tender Lemon Roast Chicken

Joanne Rankin, Dietitian, British Columbia

● **Roasting pan**

1	whole roasting chicken (3 to 4 lbs/ 1.5 to 2 kg)	1
3 tbsp	kosher salt	45 mL
12 cups	water	3 L
1	lemon	1
2 tsp	canola or olive oil	10 mL
½ tsp	salt	2 mL

1. Trim excess fat from chicken. Rinse inside and out under cold running water.

2. In a large pot, combine kosher salt and water, stirring to dissolve salt. Add chicken, breast side down, making sure it is fully submerged. Cover and refrigerate for at least 4 hours or for up to 8 hours.

3. About 30 minutes before cooking, drain brine from chicken and discard. Rinse chicken under running water and pat dry. Place on a clean plate and let stand at room temperature.

4. Place oven rack in center of oven, place empty roasting pan on rack and preheat oven to 425°F (220°C).

5. Meanwhile, place whole lemon in a small saucepan and add water to cover. Bring to a boil over high heat. Reduce heat and simmer for 5 minutes. Remove from heat and leave lemon in hot water until ready to use.

6. Rub chicken all over with oil and sprinkle with ½ tsp (2 mL) salt. Remove the lemon from the hot water, discarding water. Poke several holes in the lemon and insert it into the cavity of the chicken.

7. Carefully remove the hot roasting pan from the oven, place chicken, breast side up, in pan, and roast for 30 minutes. Reduce heat to 400°F (200°C). Roast chicken for 60 minutes or until skin is dark golden and crispy, drumsticks wiggle when touched and a meat thermometer inserted in the thickest part of a thigh registers 185°F (85°C). Transfer chicken to a cutting board, tent with foil and let rest for 10 to 15 minutes before carving.

8. Using kitchen tongs, remove lemon from the chicken. Cut lemon in half and squeeze juice over hot chicken pieces.

Brining is an effective way to add flavor and moisture to meats. The light salt solution helps to loosen the meat muscle fibers, making them more tender. The salt also helps the meat retain some water from the brine, again helping to tenderize. Any flavors in the brine will also infuse into the meat, adding flavor to the final product. With the focus on reducing sodium intake, eat brined meats only occasionally and accompany them with lower-sodium options.

Tip

Tenting the chicken with foil and letting it rest before carving allows the juices to redistribute throughout the meat, creating a much moister chicken.

Variation

For added flavor, insert fresh or dried herbs, such as thyme, rosemary, savory or marjoram, into the cavity of the chicken along with the lemon.

Serving Idea

Place a baking dish of scrubbed, pierced small sweet potatoes in the oven next to the roasting pan during the final hour of cooking the chicken. Simply add a salad and dinner is done!

Makes 6 servings

✔ **Kid Approved**

Nothing could be simpler than a roast chicken for Sunday dinner. Use any delicious leftovers for chicken sandwiches or chicken salad for Monday's lunch.

Tip

Add only warm or cool broth to a roux (a fat and flour mixture). If you add cold broth, the fat in the roux could become more solid, creating lumps that are difficult to dissolve.

Variation

Add 2 sprigs of thyme to the cavity of the chicken along with the rosemary.

Serving Idea

Serve with mashed potatoes and steamed green beans for a traditional Sunday dinner.

Nutrients per serving

Calories	176
Fat	7.1 g
Saturated fat	1.7 g
Sodium	191 mg (8% DV)
Carbohydrate	2 g
Fiber	0 g (0% DV)
Protein	24 g
Calcium	13 mg (1% DV)
Iron	1.2 mg (9% DV)

Very high in: Vitamin B_6 and niacin

High in: Zinc and vitamin B_{12}

Diabetes Food Choice Values:

3   Meat & Alternatives

Roast Chicken Stuffed with Apples and Oranges

Judy Jenkins, Dietitian, Nova Scotia

- **Preheat oven to 350°F (180°C)**
- **Roasting pan with rack**

1	whole roasting chicken (3 to 4 lbs/ 1.5 to 2 kg)	1
2	cloves garlic, minced	2
1	small apple, cored and chopped	1
1	small orange, peeled and chopped	1
1	sprig fresh rosemary	1
2 tbsp	all-purpose flour	30 mL
1 cup	reduced-sodium chicken broth	250 mL

1. Trim excess fat from chicken. Rinse inside and out under cold running water and pat dry.

2. Stuff chicken cavity with garlic, apple, orange and rosemary. Place chicken, breast side down, on rack in roasting pan. Roast in preheated oven for 1 hour, basting with drippings halfway through.

3. Turn the chicken over so it is breast side up, baste with drippings and roast for $1\frac{1}{4}$ hours or until skin is dark golden and crispy, drumsticks wiggle when touched and a meat thermometer inserted in the thickest part of a thigh registers 185°F (85°C). Transfer chicken to a cutting board, tent with foil and let rest for 10 to 15 minutes before carving.

4. Skim off fat from the drippings and discard. You should have about 2 tbsp (30 mL) drippings. Place drippings in a small saucepan over medium-high heat. Sprinkle with flour and cook, whisking, for 1 minute. Gradually pour in broth, whisking constantly so no lumps form. Reduce heat to low and simmer, whisking often, for about 5 minutes or until slightly thickened.

5. Remove garlic, apple, orange and rosemary from cavity and discard. Carve the chicken and arrange on a platter. Pass the gravy to spoon over top.

Any leftovers from this flavorful recipe would be delicious for lunch the next day, in a wrap or pita or served over a salad.

Tip

Make the paste the night before and cut up the chicken. Wrap them separately and refrigerate until ready to bake.

Variations

Use 2½ lbs (1.25 kg) chicken breasts or thighs instead of a mixture.

Use the spice mixture on pork, beef or lamb.

Serving Idea

Serve with rice or flatbread and a side of tzatziki.

Nutrients per serving

Calories	193
Fat	9.6 g
Saturated fat	1.4 g
Sodium	197 mg (8% DV)
Carbohydrate	2 g
Fiber	1 g (4% DV)
Protein	24 g
Calcium	25 mg (2% DV)
Iron	1.7 mg (12% DV)

Very high in: Niacin
High in: Zinc and vitamin B$_6$

Diabetes Food Choice Values:
3   Meat & Alternatives

Indian Spiced Chicken

Compass Group Canada

● **13- by 9-inch (33 by 23 cm) glass baking dish**

¼ cup	canola oil	60 mL
1 tbsp	ground cumin	15 mL
2 tsp	ground coriander	10 mL
2 tsp	ground cinnamon	10 mL
2 tsp	paprika	10 mL
2 tsp	hot pepper flakes (or to taste)	10 mL
1 tsp	garlic powder	5 mL
1 tsp	ground ginger	5 mL
½ tsp	freshly ground black pepper	2 mL
½ tsp	salt	2 mL
1¼ lbs	boneless skinless chicken thighs	625 g
1¼ lbs	boneless skinless chicken breasts	625 g

1. In a small bowl, combine oil, cumin, coriander, cinnamon, paprika, hot pepper flakes, garlic powder, ginger, black pepper and salt to make a thick paste. Cover and let stand for 30 minutes.

2. Preheat oven to 350°F (180°C).

3. Cut chicken thighs and breasts into bite-size pieces and place in baking dish. Add spice paste and stir to coat chicken well. Bake for 40 minutes or until juices run clear when thighs are pierced and breasts are no longer pink inside.

> Herbs are the flavorful leaves of a plant, whereas spices are obtained from other parts of a plant, including bark (such as cinnamon) and seeds (such as coriander). In this recipe, letting the dry spices stand in the oil for at least 30 minutes allows them to soften and release their flavor. Although most of the spices in this dish are not produced in Canada, we are fortunate to have access to imports to add flavor and variety to meals.

Baked "Fried" Chicken

Hélène Dufour, Dietitian, British Columbia

This clever method creates tasty chicken that tastes like fried, but isn't!

Tips

It's very important to line the baking sheet with parchment paper for this dish. Without it, your baking sheet will likely end up with burned spots and the chicken will probably stick.

Be careful not to overcook the chicken or it may become dry.

This method will not work with chicken breasts, as they have insufficient fat and will end up much too dry.

Serving Idea

Serve with mashed sweet potatoes and fresh coleslaw to complete a traditional fried chicken meal.

- **Preheat oven to 450°F (230°C)**
- **Large rimmed baking sheet, lined with parchment paper**

½ cup	whole wheat flour	125 mL
3 tbsp	paprika	45 mL
1½ tbsp	dried dillweed	22 mL
1½ tbsp	onion powder	22 mL
½ tsp	celery salt	2 mL
½ tsp	freshly ground black pepper	2 mL
8	boneless skinless chicken thighs	8

1. In a shallow dish, stir together flour, paprika, dill, onion powder, celery salt and pepper.

2. Unfold chicken thighs and dry each piece with a paper towel. Dip each thigh in flour mixture, coating well and shaking off excess coating. Refold thighs loosely and lay on prepared baking sheet. Discard any excess flour mixture.

3. Bake in preheated oven for 30 minutes. Flip each piece over and bake for 20 to 25 minutes or until chicken is crispy and looks fried, juices run clear and a meat thermometer inserted in the thickest part of a thigh registers 165°F (74°C).

Fried chicken is traditionally made by coating chicken in a spiced breading mixture and then deep-frying it, yielding plenty of fat and calories. This method, which mimics the flavor and texture of fried chicken, yields substantially less fat and fewer calories. The natural fat of the chicken thigh is released at the high baking temperature and acts to "fry" the chicken without any added oil.

Nutrients per serving

Calories	225
Fat	6.9 g
Saturated fat	1.7 g
Sodium	253 mg (11% DV)
Carbohydrate	17 g
Fiber	4 g (16% DV)
Protein	25 g
Calcium	59 mg (5% DV)
Iron	3.6 mg (26% DV)

Very high in: Magnesium, zinc, vitamin A, vitamin B_6 and niacin

High in: Riboflavin

Diabetes Food Choice Values:

1	Carbohydrate
3	Meat & Alternatives

✔ **Kid Approved**

This dish uses the natural juices from fruit to lend a delicate flavor to the tender chicken. It's a great example of how to include more fruit in your diet throughout the day.

Variation

To add a rich red color to the sauce, add 2 tbsp (30 mL) dried cranberries with the other fruit.

Serving Idea

Serve over cooked whole wheat couscous or brown rice.

Nutrients per serving

Calories	280
Fat	8.4 g
Saturated fat	1.7 g
Sodium	460 mg (19% DV)
Carbohydrate	30 g
Fiber	4 g (16% DV)
Protein	23 g
Calcium	31 mg (3% DV)
Iron	1.7 mg (12% DV)

Very high in: Zinc and niacin

High in: Magnesium, vitamin C, vitamin B$_6$ and riboflavin

Diabetes Food Choice Values:

1½ Carbohydrates

3 Meat & Alternatives

Fruity Sautéed Chicken

Christine D. Lee, British Columbia

8	boneless skinless chicken thighs	8
	Salt and freshly ground black pepper	
2 tsp	canola oil, divided	10 mL
½ cup	orange juice	125 mL
2	large cooking apples, chopped	2
1	large pear, chopped	1
½ cup	halved seedless grapes	125 mL
3	thin slices gingerroot (optional)	3
1	4-inch (10 cm) cinnamon stick (optional)	1
2 tbsp	chopped fresh parsley	30 mL

1. Sprinkle chicken with a pinch each of salt and pepper. In a Dutch oven or large pot, heat 1 tsp (5 mL) oil over medium-high heat. Add half the chicken and cook, turning once, for 3 to 4 minutes per side or until lightly browned. Transfer to a bowl and set aside. Add the remaining oil to the pot and brown the remaining chicken. Transfer to bowl.

2. Add orange juice and deglaze the pot, scraping up any brown bits. Return chicken and any accumulated juices to the pot. Stir in apples, pear, grapes, ginger (if using), cinnamon stick (if using), ½ tsp (2 mL) salt and ½ tsp (2 mL) pepper; bring to a boil. Reduce heat to medium, cover and simmer for 15 minutes or until fruit is soft. Uncover and simmer for 5 minutes or until sauce is slightly thickened and juices run clear when chicken is pierced. Discard cinnamon stick and ginger. Serve garnished with parsley.

> Deglazing is a process whereby any flavorful browned and caramelized bits that have formed during the cooking process are scraped up from the pan. To deglaze, you add liquid to the pan, scrape up the brown bits and then stir to incorporate them into the liquid, capturing their flavor.

Mole is a traditional Mexican sauce made with plenty of chile peppers and other spices, as well as a bit of Mexican chocolate, which gives mole its distinctive flavor.

Tips

If you can't find Mexican chocolate, use 1½ oz (45 g) semisweet chocolate, ½ tsp (2 mL) ground cinnamon and 2 drops almond extract.

This dish can be made up to 2 days ahead. Let cool, cover and refrigerate until ready to use. Reheat in a pot over low heat, stirring often, until hot and bubbly.

Nutrients per serving

Calories	344
Fat	15.9 g
Saturated fat	3.1 g
Sodium	377 mg (16% DV)
Carbohydrate	19 g
Fiber	2 g (8% DV)
Protein	32 g
Calcium	67 mg (6% DV)
Iron	2.8 mg (20% DV)

Very high in: Magnesium, zinc, vitamin B_6 and niacin

High in: Vitamin C, vitamin B_{12} and riboflavin

Diabetes Food Choice Values:

1 Carbohydrate
4 Meat & Alternatives

Chicken Mole

Simone Demers-Collins, Alberta

● **Food processor**

2 lbs	boneless skinless chicken thighs	1 kg
Pinch	salt	Pinch
Pinch	freshly ground black pepper	Pinch
2 tbsp	canola oil, divided	30 mL
1 cup	chopped onion	250 mL
3	cloves garlic, minced	3
¼ cup	sliced almonds	60 mL
2 tbsp	chopped chipotle peppers in adobo sauce	30 mL
2 tsp	ground cumin	10 mL
1 tsp	ground coriander	10 mL
1½ cups	reduced-sodium chicken broth	375 mL
	Grated zest of 1 orange	
1 cup	orange juice	250 mL
2 tbsp	raisins	30 mL
1 tsp	dried oregano	5 mL
1½ oz	Mexican chocolate, chopped	45 g
¼ cup	chopped fresh cilantro	60 mL

1. Sprinkle chicken with salt and pepper. In a large, heavy Dutch oven or pot, heat 1 tbsp (15 mL) oil over medium-high heat. Add half the chicken and cook, turning once, for 3 to 4 minutes per side or until lightly browned. Transfer to a bowl and set aside. Add 1 tsp (5 mL) oil to the pot and brown the remaining chicken. Transfer chicken to bowl.

2. Reduce heat to medium and add the remaining oil to the pot. Sauté onion for 3 to 4 minutes or until golden brown. Add garlic, almonds, chipotles, cumin and coriander; sauté for 2 minutes or until garlic and nuts begin to brown. Stir in broth, orange zest, orange juice, raisins and oregano; bring to a boil. Return chicken to the pot, along with any accumulated juices. Reduce heat to medium-low, cover and simmer, stirring occasionally, for 30 minutes or until juices run clear when chicken is pierced.

3. Remove from heat. Using tongs, remove chicken from sauce, transfer to a bowl and cover to keep warm. Add chocolate to sauce and let stand for 15 minutes or until chocolate is melted and sauce is slightly cooled. Meanwhile, coarsely shred reserved chicken.

4. Transfer sauce to food processor in batches and purée to a uniform texture (some bits may remain). Return sauce to pot. Stir chicken into sauce to coat well. Serve garnished with cilantro.

Mexican chocolate is made from dark chocolate, often mixed with sugar and ground nuts, along with other spices, such as cinnamon. These additions give the solid cakes or disks a grainy texture. Chocolate has held a special place in Mexican culture for centuries, and was revered and coveted as a sacred food.

Variation
For a mole with a chunkier texture, omit the steps of puréeing the sauce and shredding the chicken.

Serving Idea
Serve over brown rice or with warmed whole wheat tortillas for dipping.

Makes 6 servings

✔ **Kid Approved**

A perfect pairing of lemon and garlic enhances the flavor of grilled chicken.

Variations

Instead of using the barbecue, you can broil the chicken. Preheat broiler. Remove chicken from marinade, discarding marinade. Place chicken in a lightly greased 9-inch (23 cm) square metal baking pan. Broil, turning once, for 5 to 6 minutes per side or until chicken is no longer pink inside and a meat thermometer inserted in the thickest part of a breast resisters 165°F (74°C).

Use pork loin steaks instead of chicken breasts.

Nutrients per serving

Calories	182
Fat	5.3 g
Saturated fat	0.8 g
Sodium	118 mg (5% DV)
Carbohydrate	1 g
Fiber	0 g (0% DV)
Protein	30 g
Calcium	9 mg (1% DV)
Iron	0.5 mg (4% DV)

Very high in: Vitamin B_6 and niacin

High in: Vitamin B_{12}

Diabetes Food Choice Values:

3   Meat & Alternatives

Grilled Lemon Garlic Chicken Breasts

Jessie Kear, Dietitian, Ontario

2	cloves garlic, minced	2
1/3 cup	dry white wine	75 mL
3 tbsp	canola oil	45 mL
1 tsp	dried tarragon	5 mL
1 tsp	freshly ground black pepper	5 mL
1/4 tsp	salt	1 mL
	Grated zest and juice of 1 lemon	
6	small boneless skinless chicken breasts (1 1/2 lbs/750 g total)	6

1. In a shallow dish, whisk together garlic, wine, oil, tarragon, pepper, salt, lemon zest and lemon juice. Add chicken and turn to coat. Cover and refrigerate, turning chicken occasionally, for at least 1 hour or for up to 6 hours.

2. Meanwhile, preheat barbecue grill to medium.

3. Remove chicken from marinade, discarding marinade. Place chicken on grill, cover and cook, turning once, for 8 to 10 minutes per side or until chicken is no longer pink inside and a meat thermometer inserted in the thickest part of a breast registers 165°F (74°C). Let stand for 5 minutes.

Chicken in Dill Sauce

Dianna Bihun, Dietitian, British Columbia

- **Preheat oven to 375°F (190°C)**
- **13- by 9-inch (33 by 23 cm) glass baking dish, greased**

4	large boneless skinless chicken breasts (each about 8 oz/250 g)	4
½ tsp	salt	2 mL
½ tsp	freshly ground black pepper	2 mL
1½ cups	chopped carrots	375 mL
1 cup	chopped celery	250 mL
1 cup	chopped onion	250 mL
2 cups	reduced-sodium chicken broth	500 mL
1 cup	frozen green peas, thawed	250 mL
2½ tbsp	all-purpose flour	37 mL
½ cup	2% evaporated milk	125 mL
1 tbsp	finely chopped fresh dill	15 mL

1. Place 1 chicken breast flat on a cutting board. Place one hand on top of the chicken and, using a sharp knife and slicing parallel with the board, cut through the chicken to obtain 2 thin cutlets. Repeat with the remaining breasts.

2. Place chicken cutlets in prepared baking dish, overlapping as necessary. Sprinkle with salt and pepper. Cover with carrots, celery and onion. Pour broth over top. Cover with foil.

3. Bake in preheated oven for about 30 minutes or until vegetables are soft. Remove dish from oven and stir in peas. Replace foil and bake for 10 minutes or until chicken is no longer pink inside.

4. Ladle 1 cup (250 mL) of the cooking liquid into a small bowl. While whisking, sprinkle flour over the hot liquid and whisk until there are no lumps and liquid is smooth. Gradually whisk in evaporated milk and dill. Pour sauce evenly over chicken and vegetables in baking dish. Bake, uncovered, for 5 minutes or until sauce is hot.

✔ **Kid Approved**

This easy-to-prepare one-dish recipe is both sweet and spicy.

Tip

You'll be able to cut more evenly sliced cutlets if you start cutting at the thicker end of the breast.

Variation

Choose a salsa that suits your tolerance for heat.

Serving Idea

Serve over a bed of brown or wild rice or, for a homemade burrito, roll each chicken breast into a warm whole wheat tortilla with shredded lettuce and cheese.

Nutrients per serving

Calories	183
Fat	2.0 g
Saturated fat	0.5 g
Sodium	404 mg (17% DV)
Carbohydrate	15 g
Fiber	1 g (4% DV)
Protein	27 g
Calcium	19 mg (2% DV)
Iron	0.8 mg (6% DV)

Very high in: Vitamin B$_6$ and niacin

Diabetes Food Choice Values:

1   Carbohydrate
3   Meat & Alternatives

Sweet and Spicy Salsa Chicken

Debbie Houle, Dietitian, British Columbia

- **Preheat oven to 400°F (200°C)**
- **13- by 9-inch (33 by 23 cm) glass baking dish, greased**

4	boneless skinless chicken breasts (each about 8 oz/250 g)	4
¾ cup	salsa	175 mL
½ cup	ketchup	125 mL
¼ cup	liquid honey	60 mL
1 tbsp	Dijon mustard	15 mL
1 tsp	chili powder	5 mL
½ tsp	ground cumin	2 mL

1. Place 1 chicken breast flat on a cutting board. Place one hand on top of the chicken and, using a sharp knife and slicing parallel with the board, cut through the chicken to obtain 2 thin cutlets. Repeat with the remaining breasts.

2. Arrange chicken cutlets in prepared baking dish, overlapping as necessary. Bake in preheated oven for 30 minutes.

3. Meanwhile, in a small saucepan, combine salsa, ketchup, honey, mustard, chili powder and cumin. Cook over medium heat, stirring often, for 5 minutes or until sauce is heated through.

4. Remove chicken from oven; drain off and discard any liquid that has accumulated in dish. Pour sauce over chicken, turning each piece to coat with sauce. Bake for 10 minutes or until chicken is no longer pink inside.

> Honey has a long, rich history. In ancient times, it was used as a preservative. It is part of many cultural ceremonies, including religious christenings, marriages and burial rites. Its historical medicinal uses have included treatments for coughs, colds, fever and skin conditions, to name a few. The flavor of honey varies depending on the flowers the bees have been feeding on.

Makes 8 servings

Chicken chili is the perfect supper on one of Canada's many cool nights.

Tips

Cut up all the vegetables, measure out all the spices and open up the cans before you start to make the chili; that way, cooking is a snap.

Much of the sodium in this recipe comes from the canned beans and tomatoes. If you want to reduce the sodium, use 2 cups (500 mL) cooked rehydrated dried kidney beans and 2 cups (500 mL) cooked rehydrated dried chickpeas. Look for no-salt-added diced tomatoes.

Nutrients per serving

Calories	251
Fat	4.2 g
Saturated fat	0.6 g
Sodium	662 mg (28% DV)
Carbohydrate	34 g
Fiber	9 g (36% DV)
Protein	21 g
Calcium	99 mg (9% DV)
Iron	3.6 mg (26% DV)

Very high in: Magnesium, vitamin A, vitamin C, vitamin B$_6$, folate and niacin

High in: Zinc and thiamine

Diabetes Food Choice Values:

1 Carbohydrate
2 Meat & Alternatives

Light and Easy Chicken Chili

Phyllis Quarrie, Alberta

1 tbsp	canola oil	15 mL
2 cups	chopped onions	500 mL
1 cup	chopped carrots	250 mL
1 cup	chopped celery	250 mL
1 cup	chopped red bell pepper	250 mL
2	cloves garlic, minced	2
1 lb	boneless skinless chicken breasts, cut into 1-inch (2.5 cm) cubes	500 g
2 to 3 tbsp	chili powder	30 to 45 mL
2 tsp	ground cumin	10 mL
1 tsp	dried oregano	5 mL
1/2 tsp	salt	2 mL
1/4 tsp	hot pepper flakes	1 mL
1	can (19 oz/540 mL) red kidney beans, drained and rinsed	1
1	can (19 oz/540 mL) chickpeas, drained and rinsed	1
1	can (28 oz/796 mL) diced tomatoes, with juice	1
1/4 cup	chopped fresh parsley	60 mL

1. In a large pot, heat oil over medium-high heat. Sauté onions, carrots, celery and red pepper for 4 to 5 minutes or until softened. Add garlic and sauté for 30 seconds.

2. Add chicken and cook, stirring occasionally, for 7 to 8 minutes or until starting to brown. Add chili powder, cumin, oregano, salt and hot pepper flakes; sauté for 1 to 2 minutes or until fragrant.

3. Stir in kidney beans, chickpeas and tomatoes; bring to a boil, stirring. Reduce heat and simmer, stirring occasionally, for 30 minutes or until sauce is slightly thickened and chicken is no longer pink inside. Serve garnished with parsley.

Cumin is a spice of Egyptian descent. It is available as seeds and in ground form. The seeds are sometimes toasted whole and then ground, particularly for curry dishes.

This one-pan dish is great way to prepare a quick, flavor-filled Greek meal.

Tips

Cut the chicken into uniform pieces to ensure it cooks evenly.

Remove the seeds from the tomatoes if you wish.

Variation

Add a sprig of rosemary and a few hot pepper flakes to the chicken mixture before baking. Remove the rosemary before serving.

Serving Idea

Serve over brown rice or with whole wheat pita chips for dipping.

Nutrients per serving

Calories	300
Fat	13.0 g
Saturated fat	4.1 g
Sodium	484 mg (20% DV)
Carbohydrate	12 g
Fiber	2 g (8% DV)
Protein	35 g
Calcium	150 mg (14% DV)
Iron	1.8 mg (13% DV)

Very high in: Vitamin C, vitamin B_6, vitamin B_{12} and niacin

High in: Magnesium, zinc, vitamin A and riboflavin

Diabetes Food Choice Values:

4   Meat & Alternatives

Greek Chicken

Laura Bennett, British Columbia

- Preheat oven to 375°F (190°C)
- 13- by 9-inch (33 by 23 cm) glass baking dish

1½ lbs	boneless skinless chicken breasts, cut into 1-inch (2.5 cm) cubes	750 g
6	cloves garlic, minced	6
5	plum (Roma) tomatoes, chopped	5
1 cup	chopped onion	250 mL
1 cup	chopped red bell pepper	250 mL
¾ cup	crumbled feta cheese	175 mL
½ cup	freshly squeezed lemon juice, divided	125 mL
1½ tbsp	dried oregano	22 mL
1½ tbsp	dried basil	22 mL
2 tbsp	canola oil	30 mL
½ cup	pitted kalamata olives	125 mL
¼ cup	chopped fresh basil	60 mL

1. In a large bowl, combine chicken, garlic, tomatoes, onion, red pepper, cheese, ⅓ cup (75 mL) of the lemon juice, oregano, basil and oil, stirring well to coat chicken. Spread in prepared baking dish and cover with foil.

2. Bake in preheated oven for 30 minutes. Stir and replace foil. Bake for 20 to 30 minutes or until chicken is no longer pink inside. Stir in the remaining lemon juice, olives and basil.

> Many of the herbs used in traditional Greek cuisine are grown in abundance here in Canada and are easy to grow at home, either on the windowsill in your kitchen or in outdoor herb gardens. Basil, oregano, thyme and rosemary are commonly used in dishes such as souvlaki, tzatziki and roasted potatoes. Pair these herbs with readily available imported lemons and olives, and you are well on your way to creating a number of Greek-inspired meals.

Apples and raisins provide a sweet contrast to the spicy curry powder in this dish. Serve with a dollop of low-fat plain yogurt on top.

Tips

Turmeric can stain hands, counters and utensils, so use care and wipe up spills quickly.

Add only warm or cool broth to a roux (a fat and flour mixture). If you add cold broth, the fat in the roux could become more solid, creating lumps that are difficult to dissolve.

Variation

Replace the raisins with chopped dried dates or apricots.

Serving Idea

Serve with traditional naan bread.

Nutrients per serving

Calories	293
Fat	9.1 g
Saturated fat	1.0 g
Sodium	521 mg (22% DV)
Carbohydrate	25 g
Fiber	2 g (8% DV)
Protein	28 g
Calcium	37 mg (3% DV)
Iron	1.7 mg (12% DV)

Very high in: Vitamin B_6 and niacin

High in: Magnesium

Diabetes Food Choice Values:

1	Carbohydrate
3	Meat & Alternatives
1	Fat

Chicken Curry

Anne Wall, Alberta

1 lb	boneless skinless chicken breasts, cut into 1-inch (2.5 cm) cubes	500 g
	Salt and freshly ground black pepper	
2 tbsp	canola oil, divided	30 mL
1 cup	chopped onion	250 mL
2 tbsp	all-purpose flour	30 mL
1 tbsp	curry powder	15 mL
1 tsp	garam masala	5 mL
1/4 tsp	ground turmeric	1 mL
1 1/4 cups	reduced-sodium chicken broth	300 mL
2 tbsp	cherry jam	30 mL
1 tbsp	mango chutney	15 mL
3/4 cup	chopped apple	175 mL
2 tbsp	raisins	30 mL

1. Season chicken with 1/4 tsp (1 mL) salt and 1/4 tsp (1 mL) pepper. In a large skillet, heat 1 tbsp (15 mL) oil over medium heat. Add half the chicken and sauté for 3 to 4 minutes or until lightly browned on all sides. Transfer to a bowl and set aside. Brown the remaining chicken and transfer to bowl.

2. Add the remaining oil to the skillet. Sauté onion for 3 to 4 minutes or until softened. Add flour, curry powder, garam masala and turmeric; sauté for 30 seconds. Gradually pour in broth, stirring to prevent lumps, and bring to a boil. Reduce heat and simmer, stirring often, for 3 minutes.

3. Stir in jam, chutney, 1/4 tsp (1 mL) pepper and a pinch of salt. Return chicken to the pot, along with any accumulated juices. Reduce heat to low, cover and simmer, stirring occasionally, for 10 minutes.

4. Stir in apple and raisins; cover and simmer for 5 minutes or until apples are soft and chicken is no longer pink inside.

> Authentic Indian curries rarely use commercially prepared curry powder. Rather, cooks use individual spices, including cayenne pepper, cinnamon, coriander, cloves, cumin, fennel, fenugreek, ground mustard and black pepper, to create a unique, intense curry flavor.

Leftover chicken takes on a new life in this delicious pasta sauce.

Tips

Cold chicken shredded by hand into irregular, bite-size pieces is more visually appealing and creates more surface area for the flavorful sauce to cling to than cubes cut with a knife.

For the best texture, be careful not to boil the chicken in the sauce.

If your family is just starting to eat whole wheat pasta, mix it half and half with regular pasta at first. Gradually increase the percentage of whole wheat until the whole dish is whole-grain.

Variation

Use leftover turkey or meatballs instead of chicken.

Nutrients per serving

Calories	347
Fat	9.5 g
Saturated fat	2.3 g
Sodium	476 mg (20% DV)
Carbohydrate	49 g
Fiber	6 g (24% DV)
Protein	20 g
Calcium	140 mg (13% DV)
Iron	2.9 mg (21% DV)

Very high in: Magnesium, zinc, vitamin C, folate and niacin

High in: Vitamin B_6 and thiamine

Diabetes Food Choice Values:

2½ Carbohydrates
2 Meat & Alternatives

Pasta with Chicken and Vegetable Sauce

Joanne Rankin, Dietitian, British Columbia

1 lb	whole wheat penne or rotini pasta	500 g
2 tbsp	canola or olive oil	30 mL
1 cup	chopped onion	250 mL
3	cloves garlic, minced	3
½ tsp	hot pepper flakes (optional)	2 mL
4 cups	bite-size broccoli florets (about 1 large head)	1 L
1 cup	canned diced tomatoes with juice	250 mL
1½ cups	shredded cooked chicken	375 mL
2 tbsp	basil pesto	30 mL
½ cup	coarsely chopped fresh parsley	125 mL
¼ tsp	salt	1 mL
	Freshly ground black pepper	
½ cup	freshly grated Parmesan cheese	125 mL

1. In a large pot of boiling salted water, cook pasta according to package directions until al dente. Drain, reserving ½ cup (125 mL) of the cooking water. Transfer pasta to a large serving bowl.

2. Meanwhile, in a large skillet, heat oil over medium-high heat. Sauté onion for about 3 minutes or until softened and edges are lightly browned. Add garlic and hot pepper flakes (if using); sauté for 30 seconds. Add broccoli and cook, stirring occasionally, for about 5 minutes or until bright green.

3. Stir in tomatoes and bring to a boil. Stir in chicken, pesto and reserved pasta water. Reduce heat and simmer, stirring often, for about 3 minutes or until chicken is heated through. Remove from heat and stir in parsley, salt and pepper to taste.

4. Pour sauce over pasta and stir to combine. Sprinkle with Parmesan.

Makes 4 servings

This meal tastes like Thanksgiving dinner, but with only one pan!

Tips

Either ask your butcher to cut turkey breast into cutlets of the proper thickness or, if you can only find thicker cutlets, gently pound them with a meat mallet to the desired thickness.

To reduce the carbohydrate in this recipe, use only 1/4 cup (60 mL) brown sugar.

Nutrients per serving

Calories	363
Fat	6.9 g
Saturated fat	1.0 g
Sodium	375 mg (16% DV)
Carbohydrate	48 g
Fiber	3 g (12% DV)
Protein	27 g
Calcium	57 mg (5% DV)
Iron	2.6 mg (19% DV)

Very high in: Vitamin B₆ and niacin

High in: Magnesium, zinc, vitamin C, vitamin D, folate, vitamin B₁₂ and thiamine

Diabetes Food Choice Values:

3 Carbohydrates

3 Meat & Alternatives

Cranberry-Glazed Turkey Breast Cutlets

Joan Rew, Dietitian, Manitoba

1/3 cup	all-purpose flour	75 mL
1/2 tsp	salt	2 mL
1/2 tsp	freshly ground white pepper	2 mL
4	turkey breast cutlets, cut 1/2 inch (1 cm) thick (about 1 lb/500 g total)	4
4 tsp	canola oil, divided	20 mL
1 cup	orange juice	250 mL
1 1/2 cups	fresh or frozen cranberries	375 mL
1/2 cup	firmly packed brown sugar	125 mL
1 tbsp	all-purpose flour	15 mL
1 tsp	ground cinnamon	5 mL
1/4 tsp	ground cloves	1 mL
1/4 tsp	ground allspice	1 mL
1 1/2 tbsp	red wine vinegar	22 mL

1. In a small shallow bowl, combine 1/3 cup (75 mL) flour, salt and pepper. Dip each turkey cutlet in flour mixture, coating evenly and shaking off excess. Set aside on a plate. Discard any excess flour mixture.

2. In a large nonstick skillet, heat 2 tsp (10 mL) oil over medium heat. Brown 2 cutlets, turning once, for about 2 minutes per side or until lightly browned on the outside but still pink inside. Remove and set aside on a clean plate. Repeat with the remaining oil and cutlets.

3. Add orange juice and deglaze the skillet, scraping up any brown bits. Add cranberries and brown sugar; cook, stirring often, for about 5 minutes or until cranberries pop open.

4. Meanwhile, in a small bowl, whisk together 1 tbsp (15 mL) flour, cinnamon, cloves, allspice and vinegar to form a paste. Stir into cranberry mixture and simmer, stirring constantly, for about 2 minutes or until thickened.

5. Return turkey to the skillet, turning to coat with sauce. Reduce heat to low, cover with a tight-fitting lid and simmer for 6 to 8 minutes or until turkey is no longer pink inside.

Cranberries are very tart and often need some type of sweetener to be palatable. Here, the sweet orange juice, brown sugar and spices work together to create a delicious sauce.

BBQ Tarragon Mustard Turkey

Jessie Kear, Dietitian, Ontario

● **Preheat greased barbecue grill to medium**

2	cloves garlic, finely minced	2
2 tsp	dried tarragon	10 mL
½ tsp	salt (optional)	2 mL
½ tsp	freshly ground black pepper	2 mL
2 tbsp	Dijon mustard	30 mL
2 tbsp	chicken broth	30 mL
1 tbsp	canola oil, divided	15 mL
1	bone-in skin-on turkey breast (about 2 lbs/1 kg)	1

1. In a small bowl, combine garlic, tarragon, salt (if using), pepper, mustard, broth and 2 tsp (10 mL) of the oil.

2. Gently loosen and raise the skin of the turkey breast, but do not remove it. Spread the garlic mixture evenly on the meat under the skin and replace the skin. Spread the remaining oil over the skin.

3. Place turkey, skin side down, on preheated grill. Close lid and grill for 10 minutes. Turn breast over so skin side is up, close lid and grill for 40 to 45 minutes or until no longer pink inside and a meat thermometer inserted in the thickest part registers 170°F (77°C). Transfer to a cutting board, tent with foil and let rest for 10 minutes before slicing.

Nutrients per serving

Calories	122
Fat	3.8 g
Saturated fat	0.9 g
Sodium	107 mg (4% DV)
Carbohydrate	1 g
Fiber	0 g (0% DV)
Protein	20 g
Calcium	21 mg (2% DV)
Iron	1.1 mg (8% DV)

Very high in: Niacin

High in: Zinc and vitamin B_6

Diabetes Food Choice Values:
2½ Meat & Alternatives

Jambalaya is a dish native to New Orleans, developed from the traditional Spanish dish paella.

Tips

Themed dinners are a great way to explore new cuisines. Consider making this jambalaya the centerpiece of a Cajun-themed dinner.

Much of the sodium in this recipe comes from the sausages and the canned beans. If you want to reduce the sodium, look for reduced-sodium sausages and use cooked rehydrated dried kidney beans.

Variation

Jambalaya was designed to use up leftovers, so instead of cooking fresh sausage, you could add cooked sausage or chicken to the rice mixture.

Nutrients per serving

Calories	315
Fat	7.4 g
Saturated fat	1.5 g
Sodium	619 mg (26% DV)
Carbohydrate	45 g
Fiber	8 g (32% DV)
Protein	18 g
Calcium	86 mg (8% DV)
Iron	3.1 mg (22% DV)

Very high in: Magnesium, zinc, vitamin C, vitamin B$_6$, vitamin B$_{12}$ and niacin

High in: Vitamin A, folate, thiamine and riboflavin

Diabetes Food Choice Values:

2   Carbohydrates

2   Meat & Alternatives

Spicy Brown Rice Jambalaya

Giovanna Pizzin, Dietitian, British Columbia

2 tsp	canola oil	10 mL
1 lb	lean hot turkey sausages, cut into 1-inch (2.5 cm) pieces	500 g
1	jalapeño pepper, seeded and finely chopped	1
1 cup	chopped red onion	250 mL
1 cup	chopped green bell pepper	250 mL
1 cup	chopped red bell pepper	250 mL
1 cup	chopped celery	250 mL
4	cloves garlic, minced	4
2	bay leaves	2
1 tbsp	Cajun seasoning	15 mL
1 tsp	dried oregano	5 mL
2 tbsp	tomato paste	30 mL
1	can (19 oz/540 mL) kidney beans, drained and rinsed	1
1	can (14 oz/398 mL) diced tomatoes, with juice	1
1½ cups	long-grain brown rice	375 mL
½ cup	coarsely chopped fresh parsley	125 mL

1. In a large, heavy pot, heat oil over medium heat. Sauté sausage for 4 to 5 minutes or until browned on all sides. Transfer to a plate and set aside.

2. Drain off and discard all but 2 tsp (10 mL) fat from pot. Add jalapeño, red onion, green pepper, red pepper and celery; sauté for 5 to 7 minutes or until softened. Add garlic and sauté for 30 seconds. Add bay leaves, Cajun seasoning, oregano and tomato paste; cook, stirring, for 2 minutes.

3. Return sausage to the pot and stir in beans, tomatoes, rice and 3½ cups (875 mL) water; bring to a boil. Reduce heat and simmer, stirring occasionally, for 1¼ hours or until liquid is absorbed and rice is tender. Add more water if rice is chewy. Serve garnished with parsley.

Fusion Pasta

Marie Rainey, Nova Scotia

✔ **Kid Approved**

Turkey sausage and penne start to sing when you add curry, feta and lemon! Marie cooks her creation once every two weeks, and it's enjoyed by children and guests alike.

Tip

If you're feeling adventurous, you can add up to 2 tbsp (30 mL) more curry powder.

Variations

Use pork sausage instead of turkey sausage.

Use peas or carrots instead of broccoli.

Use boneless skinless chicken breast, cut into bite-size pieces, instead of sausage and sauté in step 1 until no longer pink inside.

Nutrients per serving

Calories	362
Fat	10.4 g
Saturated fat	3.0 g
Sodium	557 mg (23% DV)
Carbohydrate	47 g
Fiber	4 g (16% DV)
Protein	20 g
Calcium	85 mg (8% DV)
Iron	3.3 mg (24% DV)

Very high in: Zinc, folate, vitamin B_{12}, thiamine and niacin

High in: Magnesium, vitamin B_6 and riboflavin

Diabetes Food Choice Values:

3	Carbohydrates
1½	Meat & Alternatives
½	Fat

1 tbsp	canola or olive oil	30 mL
1 lb	lean turkey sausage, removed from casings and crumbled	500 g
1 lb	penne or rotini pasta	500 g
1 cup	chopped onion	250 mL
1	clove garlic, finely minced	1
2 cups	chopped broccoli florets	500 mL
1 tbsp	curry powder	15 mL
2 tbsp	freshly squeezed lemon juice	30 mL
½ cup	crumbled feta cheese	125 mL

1. In a large skillet, heat oil over medium-high heat. Cook sausage, breaking it up with the back of a spoon, for about 8 minutes or until no longer pink. Using a slotted spoon, transfer sausage to a bowl and set aside. Drain off all but 2 tsp (10 mL) fat from the pan.

2. Meanwhile, in a large pot of boiling salted water, cook pasta according to package directions until al dente. Drain and transfer to a large serving bowl.

3. Reduce heat under skillet to medium. Sauté onion for 3 to 4 minutes or until softened. Add garlic and sauté for 30 seconds. Stir in broccoli, curry powder and ¼ cup (60 mL) water; simmer, stirring often, for 3 to 4 minutes or until broccoli is tender-crisp. Stir in reserved sausage and lemon juice; cook, stirring, for 2 to 3 minutes or until heated through.

4. Pour sausage mixture over pasta and stir to combine. Sprinkle with feta.

> Pasta should be cooked until al dente, which literally means "to the tooth." It should be tender, with a hint of firmness. Depending on the shape of the pasta, allow 5 to 12 minutes for dry pasta and 1 to 4 minutes for fresh. When in doubt, use the package directions as a guideline.

These meatballs are delicate in flavor and tender in texture.

Tip

Be very gentle when mixing and forming the meatballs. Overmixing will produce a compact, tough texture.

Variations

Replace the turkey with ground beef, pork or veal, or a mixture of all three meats.

If you prefer a stronger garlic flavor, use 3 cloves minced raw garlic in this recipe.

Serving Idea

Serve with fresh vegetables and dip, along with a glass of milk, for a delicious lunch for your children.

Nutrients per serving

Calories	291
Fat	17.4 g
Saturated fat	4.3 g
Sodium	437 mg (18% DV)
Carbohydrate	8 g
Fiber	2 g (8% DV)
Protein	26 g
Calcium	117 mg (11% DV)
Iron	2.5 mg (18% DV)

Very high in: Zinc, vitamin D, vitamin B$_{12}$ and niacin

High in: Magnesium, vitamin B$_6$ and riboflavin

Diabetes Food Choice Values:
½ Carbohydrate
3½ Meat & Alternatives

Super-Moist Turkey Meatballs

Kristin Wiens, Dietitian, Alberta

1	slice whole wheat bread	1
2 tbsp	2% milk	30 mL
1	egg, beaten	1
1 lb	lean ground turkey	500 g
¼ cup	chopped fresh parsley	60 mL
3 tbsp	freshly grated Parmesan cheese	45 mL
2 tbsp	roasted garlic (see box, below), minced	30 mL
2 tbsp	chopped fresh chives	30 mL
2 tbsp	ground flax seeds (flaxseed meal)	30 mL
1 tbsp	chopped fresh rosemary	15 mL
¼ tsp	salt	1 mL
½ tsp	freshly ground black pepper	2 mL
1 tbsp	canola oil	15 mL
⅓ cup	reduced-sodium chicken broth	75 mL

1. Tear bread into small pieces and place in a large bowl. Cover with milk and let soak for 2 minutes. Add egg, turkey, parsley, cheese, garlic, chives, flax seeds, rosemary, salt and pepper. Using clean hands, gently mix together until evenly incorporated. Form into 1½-tbsp (22 mL) meatballs.

2. In a large nonstick skillet, heat oil over medium-high heat. Add half the meatballs and cook, turning occasionally, for 8 to 10 minutes or until evenly browned on all sides. Transfer to a bowl. Brown the remaining meatballs.

3. Add broth and deglaze the pan, scraping up any brown bits. Return meatballs to the pan, reduce heat to medium-low, cover with a tight-fitting lid and simmer for 5 to 6 minutes or until broth is reduced, leaving minimal liquid, and meatballs are no longer pink inside.

How to Roast Garlic

Cut off the top of the head, exposing the cloves but not separating them. Place the head on a large square of foil and drizzle with 1 to 2 tsp (5 to 10 mL) oil. Enclose garlic in the foil and roast in a 400°F (200°C) oven for 25 to 30 minutes or until cloves are soft and lightly browned. Let cool. Squeeze garlic cloves out of their papery shells.

This classic dish would make a beautiful entrée for a special dinner party.

Tip

Farm-raised (domesticated) duck has a lot more fat than wild duck. If you use farm-raised duck, there will be a significant amount of fat in the pan after roasting. Be very careful when removing the duck from the pan, to prevent fat burns. Be careful, too, to skim off all the fat from the drippings before making the sauce.

Nutrients per serving

Calories	318
Fat	14.7 g
Saturated fat	5.5 g
Sodium	159 mg (7% DV)
Carbohydrate	14 g
Fiber	1 g (4% DV)
Protein	31 g
Calcium	34 mg (3% DV)
Iron	3.8 mg (27% DV)

Very high in: Zinc, vitamin C, vitamin B_{12}, thiamine, riboflavin and niacin

High in: Vitamin B_6 and folate

Diabetes Food Choice Values:

1 Carbohydrate

4 Meat & Alternatives

Canard à l'Orange

Lise Arsenault, Dietitian, New Brunswick

- **Preheat oven to 425°F (220°C)**
- **Roasting pan with rack**

1	whole duck (about 5 lbs/2.2 kg), giblets removed	1
Pinch	salt	Pinch
Pinch	freshly ground black pepper	Pinch
2	oranges	2
2	apples, peeled and chopped	2
1 tsp	curry powder	5 mL
1 cup	orange juice	250 mL
½ cup	unsweetened apple juice or dry white wine	125 mL
2 tsp	cognac (optional)	10 mL
1 tbsp	cornstarch	15 mL
2 tbsp	cold water	30 mL

1. Trim excess fat from duck. Rinse inside and out under cold running water and pat dry. Prick skin with a fork. Season the cavity with salt and pepper.

2. Grate zest from oranges and cut oranges into thin slices. In a small bowl, combine apples, curry powder and half the orange zest. Loosely stuff the cavity with the apple mixture. Place the duck, breast side up, on rack in roasting pan. Scatter orange slices in bottom of pan. Pour in ½ cup (125 mL) water.

3. Roast in preheated oven for 20 minutes. Reduce heat to 350°F (180°C) and roast for 1¾ to 2 hours, basting with roasting liquid twice, until skin is dark golden and crispy, drumsticks wiggle when touched and a meat thermometer inserted in the thickest part of a thigh registers 185°F (85°C). Transfer duck to a cutting board, tent with foil and let rest for 10 to 15 minutes before carving.

4. Skim off fat from the drippings and discard. Place drippings in a small saucepan over medium-high heat. Stir in the remaining orange zest, orange juice, apple juice and cognac (if using); bring to a boil.

5. In a small bowl, whisk together cornstarch and cold water to make a slurry. Gradually whisk into the sauce and cook, whisking, for about 2 minutes or until thickened.

6. Remove apple mixture from cavity and discard. Carve the duck and arrange on a platter. Pass the sauce to spoon over top.

Duck and goose are popular holiday fare in Canada. Cooking methods for these birds are usually designed to render (remove) as much fat as possible, and rarely is the fatty skin eaten. It is common to serve duck and goose with a citrus or cherry sauce to counter the fatty taste of the meat.

Tip
Tenting the duck with foil and letting it rest before carving allows the juices to redistribute throughout the meat, creating a much moister duck.

Serving Idea
Serve with Scalloped Potatoes (page 308) and steamed Brussels sprouts.

Nutrients per serving

Calories	304
Fat	7.6 g
Saturated fat	2.8 g
Sodium	318 mg (13% DV)
Carbohydrate	38 g
Fiber	0 g (0% DV)
Protein	17 g
Calcium	39 mg (4% DV)
Iron	2.4 mg (17% DV)

Very high in: Niacin

High in: Zinc and riboflavin

Diabetes Food Choice Values:

2½ Carbohydrates
2   Meat & Alternatives

Roast Duck Breast with Pomegranate Sauce

Lucia Weiler, Dietitian, Ontario

- **Preheat oven to 400°F (200°C)**
- **13- by 9-inch (33 by 23 cm) metal baking pan**

⅓ cup	granulated sugar	75 mL
2 cups	unsweetened pomegranate juice	500 mL
2 cups	reduced-sodium chicken broth	500 mL
1½ tsp	hot chili and garlic sauce	7 mL
1½ tsp	balsamic vinegar	7 mL
¼ tsp	ground cumin	1 mL
1 tbsp	cornstarch	15 ml
2 tbsp	cold water	30 mL
	Salt and freshly ground black pepper	
6	skin-on boneless duck breasts (each 5 oz/150 g)	6
½ tsp	ground coriander	2 mL
¼ cup	pomegranate seeds	60 mL

1. In a large saucepan, combine sugar, pomegranate juice, broth and chili sauce. Bring to a boil over medium heat, stirring to dissolve sugar. Reduce heat and simmer for 20 to 25 minutes or until sauce is reduced by about two-thirds. Whisk in vinegar and cumin. Remove from heat.

2. In a small bowl, whisk together cornstarch and cold water to make a slurry. Gradually whisk into the sauce and cook, whisking, for about 2 minutes or until thickened. Stir in a pinch each of salt and pepper. Set aside.

3. Meanwhile, score duck skin with five cuts in one direction. Repeat in the opposite direction, making a diamond pattern. Season with ¼ tsp (1 mL) pepper and rub with coriander.

4. Heat a large, heavy skillet over medium-high heat. Add 2 duck breasts, skin side down, reduce heat to medium and cook for about 7 minutes or until skin is crisp and deep brown. Flip over and cook for 1 minute. Transfer to baking pan, skin side up. Repeat until all duck breasts are browned.

5. Roast in preheated oven for about 5 minutes or until slightly pink inside for medium-rare. Transfer duck to a cutting board, tent with foil and let rest for 5 minutes.

6. Thinly slice each breast crosswise on a slight diagonal. Arrange on plates and spoon sauce over top. Sprinkle with pomegranate seeds.

How to Remove the Seeds from a Pomegranate

Forget about poking each seed out with the tip of a knife or banging half a pomegranate on the counter, splattering the juice everywhere — there's a better, cleaner way to get those tasty little seeds out! Simply cut off the ends of the pomegranate, then make 4 to 6 slits along the length of the skin. Submerge the pomegranate in a large bowl of cold water and break it apart, then gently knead each section to extract the seeds. The seeds will fall to the bottom, and the flesh will float to the top. Remove the flesh, then strain out the seeds.

Tips
The skin on duck breast is very thick and fatty. The nutrient analysis assumes the skin is not eaten.

Note that the recommended internal temperature of cooked poultry pieces, including duck, is 165°F (74°C).

Serving Idea
Serve with a brown and wild rice pilaf and sautéed snow peas with water chestnuts.

Beef, Pork, Lamb and Game

Beef, pork, lamb and game provide a variety of essential nutrients, including protein, iron, B vitamins and zinc. Your body needs protein to maintain and repair itself. Iron helps to carry oxygen to all body parts, to make energy and to prevent infection and anemia. B vitamins, such as thiamin, riboflavin and B_{12}, help your body make red blood cells and use the energy from food. Zinc is necessary for proper growth and helps you fight infection. For best nutrition, choose lean meats prepared with little or no fat, trim visible fat from meat where possible and use healthy cooking techniques such as roasting, grilling, broiling, stewing and braising, shying away from deep-frying.

Grilling 101

Grilling is a dry-heat cooking method in which the heat source is below the food. The terms "grilling" and "barbecuing" are often used interchangeably. It's best to grill only tender cuts of meat, such as beef grilling or marinating steaks or pork tenderloin, or ground meat patties, such as hamburgers. Fatty fish, such as salmon, trout and char, and some seafood, including shrimp, prawns, scallops and lobster, can also be grilled.

Lean Towards Lean

Ground meats are labeled according to the maximum fat content allowed by law. All ground meats, whether beef, pork, chicken, turkey or other, are allowed the same maximum fat content. Extra-lean ground meat has a maximum of 10% fat, lean meat, 17%; medium meat, 23%; and regular meat, 30%. All ground meats are nutrient-rich, convenient and delicious. To reduce your saturated fat intake, choose lean or extra-lean more often.

What's on Your Plate?

One easy way to check if you're eating in a healthful way is to look at your plate. If it's mostly filled with colorful vegetables, along with some whole grains and a meat or alternative, you're on your way to healthy eating. Specifically, take a plate and divide it in half. Fill one half with colorful vegetables of your choice. Divide the other half into two more halves. Fill one with your whole grain or starch choice, such as barley pilaf or wild rice, and the other half with your meat or alternative. Pay close attention to portion size! You can get better acquainted with portion sizes by checking out Eating Well with Canada's Food Guide at www.healthcanada.gc.ca/foodguide.

Family Cooking Lesson

How to Braise and Stew Meat

Braising and stewing use a combination of dry-heat and moist-heat cooking methods. In braising, the cut of meat used is generally larger, such as a beef shank; stewing is usually done with small, even cubes of meat. In both techniques, the meat is first browned in a small amount of fat at a high temperature (the dry-heat component). Then vegetables and liquid ingredients such as wine or broth are added, along with seasonings. The pot is covered and the meat is braised or stewed in the oven or on the stove over low heat for several hours (the moist-heat component). Less tender cuts of meat are suitable for braising and stewing, as the added liquid and the long cooking time tenderize the meat by breaking down the connective tissue.

This colorful, nutrient-rich dinner cooks all at once, for minimal fuss. Serve with cooked couscous, quinoa, rice or pasta.

Tip

Set aside 2 cups (500 mL) each of the roasted veggies and slivered thinly sliced roasted beef to make the next day's main course salad or sandwich.

Nutrients per serving

Calories	204
Fat	7.1 g
Saturated fat	2.3 g
Sodium	130 mg (5% DV)
Carbohydrate	7 g
Fiber	2 g (8% DV)
Protein	26 g
Calcium	27 mg (2% DV)
Iron	3.1 mg (22% DV)

Very high in: Zinc, vitamin C, vitamin B$_{12}$ and niacin

High in: Vitamin B$_6$ and riboflavin

Diabetes Food Choice Values:

3   Meat & Alternatives

Mediterranean Roasted Beef and Veggies

Beef Information Centre (www.beefinfo.org)

- **Preheat oven to 275°F (140°C)**
- **Rimmed baking sheet, lined with foil, foil greased**
- **Heavy ovenproof sauté pan or skillet with rack**

	Vegetable cooking spray	
6	cloves garlic, peeled	6
3	plum (Roma) tomatoes, cored and quartered	3
1	small Spanish onion, cut into 12 wedges	1
1	baby eggplant, cut into chunks	1
1	red bell pepper, cut into chunks	1
1	yellow bell pepper, cut into chunks	1
8 oz	zucchini (about 2 small), cut crosswise into $\frac{1}{2}$-inch (1 cm) slices	250 g
4 oz	mushrooms, quartered	125 g
4 tbsp	basil pesto, divided	60 mL
2 tsp	olive oil	10 mL
3 lb	boneless beef sirloin tip or inside round oven roast	1.5 kg
Pinch	each salt and freshly ground black pepper	Pinch
1 tbsp	balsamic vinegar	15 mL
1 tsp	liquid honey	5 mL

1. Lightly spray prepared baking sheet with cooking spray. In a large bowl, combine garlic, tomatoes, onion, eggplant, red pepper, yellow pepper, zucchini, mushrooms and 3 tbsp (45 mL) of the pesto; toss to coat. Spread evenly on prepared baking sheet; set aside.

2. In ovenproof sauté pan, heat oil over medium-high heat. Season beef with salt and pepper. Cook beef, turning with tongs, for about 10 minutes or until browned all over. Spread the remaining pesto over roast. Place on rack in the same sauté pan.

3. Roast beef and vegetables in preheated oven for about 1$\frac{1}{2}$ hours or until a meat thermometer inserted in the thickest part of the roast registers 140°F (60°C) for medium-rare, or until desired doneness. Transfer roast to a cutting board, tent with foil and let stand for 10 to 15 minutes.

4. Using a rubber spatula, scrape vegetables into a large bowl. Add vinegar and honey; toss to coat.

5. Carve roast across the grain into thin slices. Serve with vegetables.

Makes 4 to
6 servings

Cutting strip loin steaks across the grain into slices makes for an attractive presentation.

Tips

You can use red wine instead of white, but the sour cream sauce will take on a pink tinge.

The key here is portion size. Note that the two steaks serve up to six people.

Variations

Use sliced baby portobello or cremini mushrooms instead of white mushrooms.

Add 2 tbsp (30 mL) drained green peppercorns with the shallots and mushrooms.

Nutrients per serving

Calories	144
Fat	6.1 g
Saturated fat	2.1 g
Sodium	140 mg (6% DV)
Carbohydrate	3 g
Fiber	1 g (4% DV)
Protein	17 g
Calcium	19 mg (2% DV)
Iron	1.9 mg (14% DV)

Very high in: Zinc, vitamin B$_{12}$ and niacin

Diabetes Food Choice Values:

2   Meat & Alternatives

Strip Loin Steak with Mushroom Sauce

Mary Sue Waisman, Dietitian, Nova Scotia

● **Preheat barbecue grill to medium-high**

2	boneless beef strip loin grilling steaks (each 8 oz/250 g)	2
	Freshly ground black pepper	
2 tsp	canola oil	10 mL
2 cups	sliced mushrooms	500 mL
2 tbsp	minced shallots	30 mL
2	cloves garlic, minced	2
1 tsp	dried tarragon	5 mL
1/4 cup	dry white wine	60 mL
1 tsp	Worcestershire sauce	5 mL
1/4 cup	light sour cream	60 mL
1/4 tsp	salt	1 mL

1. Season steaks with 1/4 tsp (1 mL) pepper. Place on preheated grill, cover and grill for 3 to 4 minutes per side for medium-rare or until desired doneness. Transfer to a cutting board, tent with foil and let rest for 5 to 10 minutes to allow juices to redistribute.

2. Meanwhile, in a large skillet, heat oil over medium heat. Sauté mushrooms and shallots for 3 to 4 minutes or until mushrooms are soft but not browned. Add garlic and sauté for 30 seconds. Stir in tarragon, wine and Worcestershire sauce; bring to a boil, scraping up any brown bits. Boil, stirring often, for 2 to 3 minutes or until wine is slightly reduced. Remove from heat and stir in sour cream, salt and pepper to taste.

3. Trim fat from outer edge of steaks and discard. Cut steaks across the grain into 1/4-inch (0.5 cm) thick slices. Serve mushroom sauce over sliced steak.

Sweet apricot jam and fresh rosemary add subtle sweetness to flank steak.

Tips

Silverskin is the tough, shiny connective tissue sheath sometimes found on meats such as pork tenderloin, flank steak and other meats. It must be trimmed off before cooking. Ask the butcher to remove it or, to remove it yourself, slip the tip of a knife under one end of the silverskin, then run the knife between the meat and the skin, gripping the silverskin with a paper towel to pull it off.

Be sure to let the marinade cool completely before adding the meat.

Variation

Use chopped shallots instead of onion.

Nutrients per serving

Calories	227
Fat	8.8 g
Saturated fat	3.1 g
Sodium	97 mg (4% DV)
Carbohydrate	12 g
Fiber	0 g (0% DV)
Protein	24 g
Calcium	9 mg (1% DV)
Iron	2.1 mg (15% DV)

Very high in: Zinc, vitamin B$_{12}$ and niacin

Diabetes Food Choice Values:

1   Carbohydrate
3   Meat & Alternatives

Apricot and Rosemary Flank Steak

Mary Sue Waisman, Dietitian, Nova Scotia

2 tbsp	canola oil	30 mL
1/2 cup	chopped onion	125 mL
3	cloves garlic, minced	3
1/2 cup	dry red wine	125 mL
1/2 cup	apricot jam	125 mL
2 tbsp	liquid honey	30 mL
1 tbsp	reduced-sodium soy sauce	15 mL
4	sprigs fresh rosemary	4
1	flank marinating steak (1 1/2 lbs/750 g), trimmed	1

1. In a skillet, heat oil over medium heat. Sauté onion for 3 to 4 minutes or until softened. Add garlic and sauté for 30 seconds. Stir in wine, jam, honey, soy sauce and rosemary. Cook for 2 to 3 minutes or until jam melts. Remove from heat and let cool completely.

2. Transfer marinade to a glass or ceramic bowl or a sealable plastic bag. Pierce steak all over with a fork. Add to bowl or bag, turning to coat well. Cover tightly or seal and refrigerate for 24 hours, turning twice.

3. Preheat barbecue grill to medium. Remove steak from marinade, discarding marinade, and scrape off any bits of onion or rosemary stuck to steak.

4. Place steak on grill, close the lid and grill for 6 minutes. Rotate steak 90 degrees, cover and grill for 3 minutes. Flip steak over, cover and grill for 4 minutes or until a meat thermometer placed sideways into the center of the steak registers 130°F (54°C). Transfer to a cutting board, tent with foil and let rest for 10 to 15 minutes to allow juices to redistribute and steak to reach an internal temperature of 135°F (57°C). Cut across the grain, on the diagonal, into 1/4-inch (0.5 cm) thick slices.

> Flank steak is a less tender cut of meat. With careful cooking, however, it becomes flavorful and tender. It is best cooked by marinating and quick grilling to medium-rare. It's also important to slice it thinly across the grain.

A meld of Asian
seasonings produce a
flavorful flank steak.

Tips

Sesame oil has a strong flavor,
so a little goes a long way.
You could use an additional
teaspoon (5 mL), but any more
will create an overpowering
sesame flavor.

Chinese five-spice powder,
a blend of finely ground
cinnamon, cloves, fennel
seeds, star anise and
Szechwan peppercorns, adds
a unique, subtly sweet flavor
to many Asian dishes.

Variation

Add 1 star anise pod to the
marinade. Be sure to remove it
before grilling the steak.

Nutrients per serving

Calories	209
Fat	10.3 g
Saturated fat	3.2 g
Sodium	142 mg (6% DV)
Carbohydrate	4 g
Fiber	0 g (0% DV)
Protein	24 g
Calcium	9 mg (1% DV)
Iron	2.1 mg (15% DV)

Very high in: Zinc, vitamin B_{12}
and niacin

Diabetes Food Choice Values:

3   Meat & Alternatives

Asian Five-Spice Flank Steak

Mary Sue Waisman, Dietitian, Nova Scotia

4	cloves garlic, minced	4
1 tsp	Chinese five-spice powder	5 mL
1 tsp	hot pepper flakes	5 mL
½ tsp	ground cloves	2 mL
3 tbsp	canola oil	45 mL
2 tbsp	liquid honey	30 mL
1 tbsp	reduced-sodium soy sauce	15 mL
1 tsp	sesame oil	5 mL
1	flank marinating steak (1½ lbs/750 g), trimmed	1

1. In a shallow dish or sealable plastic bag, combine garlic, five-spice powder, hot pepper flakes, cloves, canola oil, honey, soy sauce and sesame oil. Add steak and turn to coat well. Cover tightly or seal and refrigerate for 24 hours, turning twice.

2. Preheat barbecue grill to medium. Remove steak from marinade, discarding marinade.

3. Place steak on grill, close the lid and grill for 6 minutes. Rotate steak 90 degrees, cover and grill for 3 minutes. Flip steak over, cover and grill for 4 minutes or until a meat thermometer placed sideways into the center of the steak registers 130°F (54°C). Transfer to a cutting board, tent with foil and let rest for 10 to 15 minutes to allow juices to redistribute and steak to reach an internal temperature of 135°F (57°C). Cut across the grain, on the diagonal, into ¼-inch (0.5 cm) thick slices.

This recipe uses ingredients that are full of flavor, such as hoisin sauce and Chinese five-spice.

Szechwan Beef

Beef Information Centre (www.beefinfo.org)

- **Preheat barbecue grill to medium-high**
- **Preheat broiler**
- **Large rimmed baking sheet, lined with foil**

3	green onions	3
2	red bell peppers, cut into chunks	2
2 cups	sugar snap peas, trimmed	500 mL
2 tbsp	hoisin sauce	30 mL
2 tsp	rice vinegar	10 mL
2 tsp	minced gingerroot	10 mL
2 tsp	minced garlic	10 mL
1 lb	boneless beef top sirloin grilling steak (about ¾ inch/2 cm thick)	500 g
½ tsp	Chinese five-spice powder	2 mL
½ cup	unsalted roasted peanuts, chopped	125 mL

Sesame Noodles

12 oz	whole wheat linguine pasta	375 g
½ tsp	hot pepper flakes	2 mL
1 tsp	sesame oil	5 mL

1. Cut green onion tops into thin slices; set aside. Cut the remaining onion sections into 2-inch (5 cm) lengths and place on prepared baking sheet. Add red peppers, peas, hoisin sauce, vinegar, ginger and garlic; toss to coat. Set aside.

2. Rub beef all over with five-spice powder. Place on preheated grill, cover and grill for 3 to 4 minutes per side for medium-rare or until desired doneness. Transfer to a cutting board, tent with foil and let rest for 10 minutes.

3. *Noodles:* Meanwhile, in a large pot of boiling salted water, cook pasta according to package directions. Drain and toss with the reserved sliced green onion tops, hot pepper flakes and sesame oil.

4. Meanwhile, broil vegetables, stirring occasionally, for 5 to 8 minutes or until lightly charred.

5. Cut steak across the grain into thin slices. Mound noodles on serving plates and top with vegetables and beef. Sprinkle with peanuts.

Nutrients per serving

Calories	396
Fat	10.5 g
Saturated fat	2.4 g
Sodium	283 mg (12% DV)
Carbohydrate	52 g
Fiber	7 g (28% DV)
Protein	28 g
Calcium	59 mg (5% DV)
Iron	4.0 mg (29% DV)

Very high in: Magnesium, zinc, vitamin C, vitamin B$_6$, vitamin B$_{12}$, thiamine and niacin

High in: Vitamin A, folate and riboflavin

Diabetes Food Choice Values:

3   Carbohydrates
2½   Meat & Alternatives

Ginger, garlic and orange are a winning combination in this beef stir-fry.

Tip

Be sure not to crowd the beef while sautéing it, or it will steam instead of browning. You may need to brown it in three batches if you have a smaller skillet.

Variation

Use trimmed snow peas instead of mushrooms.

Nutrients per serving

Calories	269
Fat	11.8 g
Saturated fat	2.5 g
Sodium	138 mg (6% DV)
Carbohydrate	12 g
Fiber	1 g (4% DV)
Protein	28 g
Calcium	24 mg (2% DV)
Iron	2.2 mg (16% DV)

Very high in: Zinc, vitamin B_{12} and niacin

High in: Magnesium, vitamin C, vitamin B_6, thiamine and riboflavin

Diabetes Food Choice Values:
½   Carbohydrate
3   Meat & Alternatives
1   Fat

Orange Ginger Beef

Jennifer Garus, Dietitian, Nova Scotia

2 tbsp	minced gingerroot	30 mL
1 tbsp	minced garlic	15 mL
1 tsp	freshly ground black pepper	5 mL
2 tbsp	canola oil, divided	30 mL
1 tbsp	hoisin sauce	15 mL
1 lb	beef eye of round marinating steak, cut into 3- by ½-inch (7.5 by 1 cm) strips	500 g
1 tbsp	cornstarch	15 mL
1 tbsp	grated orange zest	15 mL
¾ cup	orange juice	175 mL
2 cups	quartered mushrooms	500 mL
2 tbsp	chopped fresh cilantro	30 mL

1. In a shallow bowl, combine ginger, garlic, pepper, 1 tbsp (15 mL) of the oil and hoisin sauce. Add beef and stir to coat well. Cover and refrigerate for at least 4 hours or up to 12 hours.

2. Drain marinade from beef, discarding marinade. Pat beef strips dry with paper towels. Heat a large nonstick skillet over medium heat. Add half the beef and sauté for 3 to 4 minutes or until lightly browned. Transfer to a bowl and set aside. Repeat with the remaining beef.

3. In a small bowl, whisk together cornstarch and orange juice.

4. Add the remaining oil to skillet and sauté mushrooms for 3 to 4 minutes or until lightly browned. Return beef and accumulated juices to skillet. Stir in cornstarch mixture and cook, stirring, for about 3 minutes or until sauce is thickened. Serve garnished with orange zest and cilantro.

> Eye of round is a lean cut of beef. Marinating it before cooking maximizes its tenderness.

Nutrients per serving

Calories	282
Fat	17.3 g
Saturated fat	3.5 g
Sodium	231 mg (10% DV)
Carbohydrate	11 g
Fiber	3 g (12% DV)
Protein	22 g
Calcium	32 mg (3% DV)
Iron	2.5 mg (18% DV)

Very high in: Zinc, vitamin C, vitamin B$_{12}$ and niacin

High in: Magnesium and vitamin B$_6$

Diabetes Food Choice Values:

3   Meat & Alternatives
1   Fat

Beef Kebabs with Peanut Sauce

Caroline Dubeau, Dietitian, Ontario (Kebabs), and Crystal Conrad, Quebec (Peanut Sauce)

- **6 metal or bamboo skewers, at least 10 inches (25 cm) long, soaked if bamboo**

1 tsp	ground cumin	5 mL
1 tsp	ground coriander	5 mL
1 tsp	ground cinnamon	5 mL
1 tsp	hot pepper flakes (or to taste)	5 mL
½ tsp	garlic powder	2 mL
½ tsp	ground ginger	2 mL
3 tbsp	canola oil	45 mL
2 tbsp	rice vinegar	30 mL
1½ lbs	boneless beef top sirloin or strip loin grilling steak, cut into 1-inch (2.5 cm) cubes	750 g
1	red onion, cut into 1-inch (2.5 cm) square pieces	1
1	yellow bell pepper, cut into 1-inch (2.5 cm) square pieces	1
1	green bell pepper, cut into 1-inch (2.5 cm) square pieces	1

Peanut Sauce

1	clove garlic, minced	1
1 tsp	granulated sugar	5 mL
½ cup	crunchy peanut butter	125 mL
½ cup	reduced-sodium chicken broth	125 mL
1 tbsp	reduced-sodium soy sauce	15 mL
2 tsp	freshly squeezed lemon juice	10 mL
1 tsp	garlic-chili sauce	5 mL
¼ cup	light coconut milk	60 mL

1. In a large bowl, combine cumin, coriander, cinnamon, hot pepper flakes, garlic powder and ginger. Stir in oil and vinegar. Add beef and stir to coat well. Cover and refrigerate for at least 30 minutes or up to 12 hours.

2. *Sauce:* In a medium saucepan, combine garlic, sugar, peanut butter, broth, soy sauce, lemon juice and garlic-chili sauce; bring to a boil over medium-high heat, stirring often. Reduce heat and simmer, stirring, for about 1 minute or until sauce thickens slightly. Stir in coconut milk and cook, stirring, until heated through. Remove from heat and keep warm.

3. Preheat barbecue grill to medium.

4. Thread red onion, yellow pepper, green pepper and beef onto skewers. Place on preheated grill and grill, turning once, for about 5 minutes per side for medium-rare or until desired doneness. Serve skewers with peanut sauce for dipping.

There are three basic varieties of rice vinegar (sometimes called Chinese vinegar): white (sometimes seasoned with salt and sugar), red and black. White rice vinegar is the most common, and the most widely used in North America.

Tip

You may be able to purchase precut beef cubes; otherwise, buy 1-inch (2.5 cm) thick steaks and cut them into 1-inch (2.5 cm) cubes.

Serving Idea

Serve over Couscous Primavera (page 314).

Makes 8 servings

Pot pie is a wonderful way to use up leftover roast beef. Kids of all ages love the biscuit topping! Sharon's young children help cut the margarine into the topping and help her choose which vegetables to use in the pie.

Tips

You can use leftover cooked potatoes and carrots instead of cooking them in step 1.

Add only warm or cool broth to a roux (a fat and flour mixture). If you add cold broth, the fat in the roux could become more solid, creating lumps that are difficult to dissolve.

Nutrients per serving

Calories	349
Fat	14.8 g
Saturated fat	2.8 g
Sodium	452 mg (19% DV)
Carbohydrate	37 g
Fiber	3 g (12% DV)
Protein	17 g
Calcium	120 mg (11% DV)
Iron	2.9 mg (21% DV)

Very high in: Zinc, vitamin A, vitamin D, folate, vitamin B$_{12}$, thiamine and niacin

High in: Vitamin B$_6$ and riboflavin

Diabetes Food Choice Values:

2	Carbohydrates
1½	Meat & Alternatives
2	Fats

Beef Pot Pie

Sharon Deters Dusyk, Alberta

* **Preheat oven to 450°F (230°C)**
* **12-cup (3 L) casserole dish, lightly greased**

2 cups	cubed peeled potatoes (½-inch/ 1 cm cubes)	500 mL
1 cup	cubed carrots (½-inch/1 cm cubes)	250 mL
3 tbsp	non-hydrogenated margarine or canola oil	45 mL
1 cup	sliced mushrooms	250 mL
½ cup	chopped onion	125 mL
2	cloves garlic, minced	2
⅓ cup	all-purpose flour	75 mL
½ tsp	salt	2 mL
½ tsp	freshly ground black pepper	2 mL
2 cups	reduced-sodium beef broth	500 mL
¾ cup	1% milk	175 mL
1 tsp	fresh thyme leaves	5 mL
2 cups	cubed leftover cooked roast beef (½- to ¾-inch/1 to 2 cm cubes)	500 mL
½ cup	frozen green peas	125 mL

Biscuit Topping

1½ cups	all-purpose flour	375 mL
2 tsp	baking powder	10 mL
½ tsp	salt	2 mL
⅓ cup	cold non-hydrogenated margarine	75 mL
1 tbsp	finely snipped fresh chives (optional)	15 mL
¾ cup	1% milk	175 mL

1. Place potatoes and carrots in a pot and add enough cold water to cover. Bring to a boil over medium-high heat; reduce heat and simmer for 6 to 8 minutes or until vegetables are fork-tender. Drain and set aside.

2. Meanwhile, in a large nonstick skillet, melt margarine over medium-high heat. Sauté mushrooms and onion for 3 to 4 minutes or until onion is softened. Add garlic and sauté for 30 seconds. Stir in flour, salt and pepper; cook, stirring, for 1 minute.

3. Gradually stir in broth, milk and thyme; bring to a boil, stirring often. Reduce heat and simmer, stirring occasionally, for 3 to 4 minutes or until sauce is thickened.

4. Stir in cooked potatoes and carrots, beef and peas; bring to a boil. Reduce heat and simmer, stirring often, for about 5 minutes or until heated through. Pour into prepared casserole dish.

5. *Topping:* In a large bowl, combine flour, baking powder and salt. Using a pastry blender or two knives, cut in margarine until mixture resembles coarse crumbs. Stir in chives (if using). Add milk and stir with a fork until just combined. Drop 12 biscuits on top of beef mixture.

6. Bake in preheated oven for 20 minutes or until biscuits are golden and sauce is bubbling.

How to Clean and Store Mushrooms

Clean mushrooms with a damp cloth. Do not immerse them in water — they soak it up like a sponge. Store fresh mushrooms in the refrigerator for up to 1 week in a paper bag, rather than in plastic, where they are too moist and become slimy.

Variation
Use sweet potatoes instead of white potatoes, and frozen corn instead of peas.

Serving Idea
Serve with Green Salad with Apple Balsamic Vinaigrette (page 146).

Sunny Day Shepherd's Pie

Jennifer Lactin, British Columbia

- **Preheat oven to 350°F (180°C)**
- **8-inch (20 cm) square glass baking dish**

1 lb	extra-lean ground beef	500 g
½ cup	chopped onion	125 mL
½ cup	chopped carrot	125 mL
½ cup	chopped celery	125 mL
½ tsp	freshly ground black pepper	2 mL
¼ tsp	salt	1 mL
¼ tsp	ground nutmeg	1 mL
1	clove garlic, minced	1
1½ tbsp	all-purpose flour	22 mL
1¼ cups	reduced-sodium beef broth	300 mL
½ cup	drained no-salt-added canned corn	125 mL
2 cups	mashed sweet potatoes (about 2 medium)	500 mL

1. In a large skillet, over medium-high heat, cook beef, breaking it up with the back of a spoon, for about 8 minutes or until no longer pink. Using a slotted spoon, transfer beef to a bowl and set aside. Drain off all but 2 tsp (10 mL) fat from the pan.

2. Reduce heat to medium. Add onion, carrot, celery, pepper, salt and nutmeg to the skillet and sauté for 4 to 5 minutes or until vegetables are softened. Add garlic and sauté for 30 seconds. Sprinkle with flour and cook, stirring, for 1 minute. Gradually stir in broth and bring to a boil; boil, stirring, until thickened. Return beef and accumulated juices to the pan and stir to coat.

3. Pour beef mixture into baking dish. Sprinkle corn evenly over top. Spread sweet potatoes evenly over corn.

4. Bake in preheated oven for 35 to 40 minutes or until a knife inserted in the center comes out hot.

> Traditionally, shepherd's pie was eaten to use up leftover cooked lamb or mutton, gravy and vegetables.

Nutrients per serving

Calories	241
Fat	6.6 g
Saturated fat	2.7 g
Sodium	312 mg (13% DV)
Carbohydrate	26 g
Fiber	4 g (16% DV)
Protein	19 g
Calcium	50 mg (5% DV)
Iron	2.6 mg (19% DV)

Very high in: Zinc, vitamin A, vitamin B_{12} and niacin

High in: Magnesium, vitamin B_6 and riboflavin

Diabetes Food Choice Values:

1½ Carbohydrates

2 Meat & Alternatives

The heat from the cayenne is nicely offset by the creamy melted blue cheese in this modern take on a classic.

Tips

Make sure the cayenne pepper is evenly distributed throughout the meat mixture.

This meatloaf makes great sandwiches for lunch. Keep your sandwich safe by packing it with a freezer pack in an insulated lunch box.

Variations

Use extra-lean ground pork instead of beef.

If you're feeling adventurous, try using up to 4 tsp (20 mL) cayenne pepper.

Nutrients per serving

Calories	255
Fat	11.0 g
Saturated fat	4.8 g
Sodium	420 mg (18% DV)
Carbohydrate	19 g
Fiber	5 g (20% DV)
Protein	24 g
Calcium	70 mg (6% DV)
Iron	3.3 mg (24% DV)

Very high in: Magnesium, zinc, vitamin B_{12} and niacin

High in: Vitamin B_6 and riboflavin

Diabetes Food Choice Values:

1   Carbohydrate

3   Meat & Alternatives

Blue Cheese-Stuffed Sweet and Spicy Meatloaf

Katherine Ng, Dietitian, Alberta

- **Preheat oven to 350°F (180°C)**
- **9- by 5-inch (23 by 12.5 cm) metal loaf pan**

1 lb	extra-lean ground beef	500 g
1	egg, beaten	1
¾ cup	natural bran	175 mL
⅓ cup	finely chopped dried cranberries	75 mL
⅓ cup	finely chopped dried apricots	75 mL
2 tsp	cayenne pepper	10 mL
1 tsp	freshly ground black pepper	5 mL
½ tsp	salt	2 mL
1½ oz	blue cheese, cut into 6 pieces	45 g

1. In a large bowl, gently combine beef, egg, bran, cranberries, apricots, cayenne, black pepper and salt.

2. Lightly pack three-quarters of the beef mixture into the loaf pan. Make a valley 1 inch (2.5 cm) wide by ½ inch (1 cm) deep in the middle of the loaf. Arrange blue cheese pieces evenly along the valley and cover with the remaining beef mixture, encasing the blue cheese.

3. Bake in preheated oven for 25 to 30 minutes or until an instant-read thermometer inserted in the center of the meat (not touching the cheese layer) registers 160°F (71°C). Let stand for 10 minutes before cutting into slices.

Quinoa-Stuffed Peppers

Lisa Diamond, Dietitian, British Columbia

✔ **Kid Approved**

Lisa's kids love these colorful peppers — they resemble lasagna in a pepper!

Tip

Don't overstuff the peppers; the quinoa mixture should divide evenly among them.

- **Preheat oven to 375°F (190°C)**
- **Rimmed baking sheet, greased**

12	small to medium red, yellow or orange bell peppers	12
2 cups	2% cottage cheese, drained	500 mL
1/3 cup	freshly grated Parmesan cheese	75 mL
1 cup	quinoa, rinsed	250 mL
2 tsp	canola oil	10 mL
1 lb	extra-lean ground beef	500 g
1 cup	chopped onion	250 mL
1 cup	chopped mushrooms	250 mL
2	cloves garlic, minced	2
1 1/2 cups	tomato sauce	375 mL
1/2 cup	chopped drained canned water chestnuts	125 mL
1/2 tsp	dried oregano	2 mL
1/2 tsp	dried basil	2 mL
	Freshly ground black pepper	
1/2 cup	shredded Cheddar cheese	125 mL

1. Remove the stem and seeds from peppers. Make an opening at the top of each pepper large enough to allow you to fill the pepper. If peppers won't sit upright, remove a small slice from the bottom, being sure not to create an opening. Set peppers aside.

2. In a small bowl, combine cottage cheese and Parmesan; set aside.

3. In a medium saucepan with a tight-fitting lid, combine quinoa and 2 cups (500 mL) water; bring to a boil over high heat. Reduce heat to low, cover and simmer for 15 minutes or until liquid is absorbed. Remove cover and let cool for 5 minutes. Fluff with a fork. Set aside.

4. Meanwhile, in a large nonstick skillet, heat oil over medium-high heat. Cook beef, breaking it up with the back of a spoon, for about 8 minutes or until no longer pink. Using a slotted spoon, transfer beef to a bowl and set aside. Drain off all but 2 tsp (10 mL) fat from the pan.

Nutrients per serving

Calories	238
Fat	8.1 g
Saturated fat	3.4 g
Sodium	412 mg (17% DV)
Carbohydrate	23 g
Fiber	3 g (12% DV)
Protein	19 g
Calcium	121 mg (11% DV)
Iron	3.2 mg (23% DV)

Very high in: Magnesium, zinc, vitamin A, vitamin C, vitamin B_{12} and niacin

High in: Vitamin B_6, folate and riboflavin

Diabetes Food Choice Values:

1/2 Carbohydrate
2 Meat & Alternatives

5. Reduce heat to medium. Add onion and mushrooms to the skillet and sauté for 4 to 5 minutes or until onion is softened. Add garlic and sauté for 30 seconds. Return beef and accumulated juices to the pan. Stir in tomato sauce, water chestnuts, oregano, basil and pepper to taste; bring to a boil. Reduce heat and simmer, stirring occasionally, for 10 minutes. Stir in quinoa and remove from heat.

6. Spoon quinoa mixture into peppers, filling them just less than halfway. Divide cottage cheese mixture evenly on top, then fill peppers to the top with quinoa mixture and sprinkle with Cheddar cheese. Place on prepared baking sheet.

7. Bake in preheated oven for about 20 minutes or until a knife inserted in the filling comes out hot.

> Red bell peppers contain about 10 times as much beta carotene as green or yellow bell peppers.

Variation
Use ground chicken or pork, or leftover shredded cooked beef, chicken or pork, instead of ground beef.

Serving Idea
Serve with sliced tomatoes, bocconcini and fresh basil drizzled with extra virgin olive oil and balsamic vinegar.

Nutrients per serving

Calories	299
Fat	11.1 g
Saturated fat	2.6 g
Sodium	307 mg (13% DV)
Carbohydrate	28 g
Fiber	3 g (12% DV)
Protein	21 g
Calcium	130 mg (12% DV)
Iron	4.0 mg (29% DV)

Very high in: Zinc, vitamin A, folate, vitamin B$_{12}$ and niacin

High in: Magnesium, vitamin D, vitamin B$_6$, thiamine and riboflavin

Diabetes Food Choice Values:

1½   Carbohydrates

2   Meat & Alternatives

Meaty Cannelloni à la Florentine

Caroline Dubeau, Dietitian, Ontario

- **Preheat oven to 350°F (180°C)**
- **13- by 9-inch (33 by 23 cm) glass baking dish**

1 tsp	canola oil	5 mL
1 lb	lean ground veal	500 g
3	shallots, chopped, divided	3
1	clove garlic, minced	1
1	package (10 oz/300 g) frozen chopped spinach, thawed and drained	1
¼ tsp	ground nutmeg	1 mL
	Freshly ground black pepper	
2 tbsp	canola oil	30 mL
2 tbsp	all-purpose flour	30 mL
2 cups	reduced-sodium chicken broth	500 mL
1	can (28 oz/796 mL) no-salt-added diced tomatoes, drained	1
1 tbsp	dried basil	15 mL
	Salt	
18	oven-ready cannelloni noodles	18

1. In a skillet, heat 1 tsp (5 mL) oil over medium heat. Cook veal, two-thirds of the shallots and garlic, breaking veal up with the back of a spoon, for 8 to 10 minutes or until veal is no longer pink. Stir in spinach, nutmeg and ¼ tsp (1 mL) pepper. Set aside.

2. Meanwhile, in a medium saucepan, heat 2 tbsp (30 mL) oil over medium heat. Sauté flour and the remaining shallots for 1 minute. Gradually stir in broth and bring to a boil, stirring often. Reduce heat and boil gently, stirring often, for about 5 minutes or until slightly thickened. Stir in tomatoes and basil. Season to taste with salt and pepper.

3. Stuff cannelloni with meat mixture. Pour ½ cup (125 mL) water into baking dish and arrange stuffed cannelloni in dish. Pour sauce over cannelloni and cover with foil. Bake in preheated oven for 1 hour or until pasta is tender.

This elegant entrée is a wonderful choice when you have dinner guests.

Tips

Cortland, Jonagold or Empire apples work well in this recipe.

If you have no stale bread, toast bread slices to medium brown.

Serving Idea

Serve with Quick and Delicious Maple Squash (page 305) and steamed snow peas.

Nutrients per serving

Calories	193
Fat	4.5 g
Saturated fat	1.5 g
Sodium	183 mg (8% DV)
Carbohydrate	6 g
Fiber	1 g (4% DV)
Protein	31 g
Calcium	18 mg (2% DV)
Iron	1.0 mg (7% DV)

Very high in: Vitamin B$_6$, vitamin B$_{12}$, thiamine and niacin
High in: Zinc

Diabetes Food Choice Values:
3   Meat & Alternatives

Pork Loin Roast with Fennel and Apple Stuffing

Heather McColl, Dietitian, British Columbia

- Preheat oven to 375°F (190°C)
- Large roasting pan with rack

2 tsp	canola oil	10 mL
1 cup	finely chopped fennel bulb	250 mL
1 cup	finely chopped onion	250 mL
2	cloves garlic, minced	2
1	apple, peeled and chopped	1
½ cup	torn stale bread	125 mL
⅓ cup	unsweetened apple cider or apple juice	75 mL
2 tsp	chopped fresh thyme	10 mL
½ tsp	salt	2 mL
½ tsp	freshly ground black pepper	2 mL
1	3- to 4-lb (1.5 to 1.75 kg) centre-cut boneless pork loin roast	1

1. In a large skillet, heat oil over medium heat. Sauté fennel and onion for 3 to 4 minutes or until onion is softened. Add garlic and sauté for 30 seconds. Add apple and sauté for 4 minutes or until starting to soften. Stir in bread, apple cider, thyme, salt and pepper; cook, stirring, until liquid is absorbed. Remove from heat and let cool to room temperature.

2. Trim excess fat from roast. Cut loin in half lengthwise to open like a book. Spread cooled stuffing over one side of loin. Place the other half evenly on top and truss with kitchen string or skewers. Place on rack in roasting pan.

3. Roast for 1¼ to 1½ hours or until a meat thermometer inserted in the center of the roast registers 155°F (68°C). Transfer to a cutting board, tent with foil and let rest for 10 to 15 minutes to allow juices to redistribute and pork to reach an internal temperature of 160°F (71°C).

In cooking, the term "truss" is most often used with poultry, where it means to tie or skewer the legs and wings to the body to hold them in place. But it can also be used as a way to describe tying or skewering meat to hold stuffing inside it, as in this butterflied pork roast.

A sweet glaze with a hint of mustard makes this tenderloin a winner.

Tips

Silverskin is the tough, shiny connective tissue sheath found on pork tenderloin and other meats, and it must be trimmed off before cooking. To remove it, slip the tip of a knife under one end of the silverskin, then run the knife between the meat and the skin.

A well-seasoned cast-iron skillet works best in this recipe.

Nutrients per serving

Calories	175
Fat	4.0 g
Saturated fat	0.9 g
Sodium	285 mg (12% DV)
Carbohydrate	8 g
Fiber	0 g (0% DV)
Protein	26 g
Calcium	20 mg (2% DV)
Iron	1.5 mg (11% DV)

Very high in: Zinc, vitamin B_{12}, thiamine, riboflavin and niacin

High in: Vitamin B_6

Diabetes Food Choice Values:

½   Carbohydrate

3   Meat & Alternatives

Maple-Glazed Pork Tenderloin

Diane Kermay Nielsen, Dietitian, Alberta

- **Preheat oven to 375°F (190°C)**
- **Large ovenproof skillet**

2 tbsp	minced shallot	30 mL
3 tbsp	pure maple syrup	45 mL
4 tsp	Dijon mustard	20 mL
2 tsp	cider vinegar	10 mL
2 tsp	reduced-sodium soy sauce	10 mL
2	pork tenderloins (each about 12 oz/375 g), trimmed	2
¼ tsp	salt	1 mL
¼ tsp	freshly ground black pepper	1 mL
1 tbsp	canola oil	15 mL
¼ cup	reduced-sodium chicken broth	60 mL

1. In a small bowl, whisk together shallot, maple syrup, mustard, vinegar and soy sauce; set aside.

2. Sprinkle pork with salt and pepper. In ovenproof skillet, heat oil over medium-high heat. Add pork and cook for about 1 minute per side or until browned on all sides. Generously brush top and sides with some of the maple syrup mixture. Pour in broth, increase heat and bring to a boil.

3. Transfer skillet to preheated oven and roast for 20 to 25 minutes, brushing generously with maple syrup mixture three times, until a meat thermometer inserted in the thickest part of the tenderloin registers 155°F (68°C). Transfer pork to a cutting board, tent with foil and let rest for 5 to 10 minutes to allow juices to redistribute and pork to reach an internal temperature of 160°F (71°C).

4. Meanwhile, bring pan juices to a boil over high heat. Add the remaining maple syrup mixture. Boil, stirring occasionally, for 3 minutes or until slightly thickened.

5. Cut pork crosswise into thin slices and serve drizzled with sauce.

A few simple ingredients and a hot grill make for a delicious dinner.

Tip

Vary the type of honey you use, for unique flavors.

Serving Idea

Serve with Flowering Sweet Potatoes (page 306) and Citrus Fennel Slaw (page 153) for a summertime barbecue.

Honey and Dill Pork Tenderloin

Kara McDonald, Dietitian, Ontario

● **Preheat barbecue to medium**

¼ cup	liquid honey	60 mL
¼ cup	Dijon mustard	60 mL
1 tbsp	snipped fresh dill	15 mL
3	pork tenderloins (each about 1 lb/500 g), trimmed	3

1. In a small bowl, combine honey, mustard and dill; set aside.

2. Place pork on preheated grill, close the lid and grill, turning once, for 20 to 25 minutes or until a meat thermometer inserted in the thickest part of the tenderloins registers 150°F (66°C). Brush one side of tenderloins with a small amount of sauce and grill for 2 minutes. Turn tenderloins over and brush with sauce. Grill until thermometer registers 155°F (68°C). Transfer to a cutting board, tent with foil and let rest for 5 to 10 minutes to allow juices to redistribute and pork to reach an internal temperature of 160°F (71°C).

3. Cut pork crosswise into thin slices and serve drizzled with the remaining sauce.

> Dijon mustard gets its name from the Dijon region of France, where it was first made. To create its distinctive flavor, the mustard seeds are combined with salt, white vinegar, white wine and spices.

Nutrients per serving

Calories	183
Fat	3.0 g
Saturated fat	1.2 g
Sodium	142 mg (6% DV)
Carbohydrate	7 g
Fiber	0 g (0% DV)
Protein	30 g
Calcium	15 mg (1% DV)
Iron	1.5 mg (11% DV)

Very high in: Zinc, vitamin B_6, vitamin B_{12}, thiamine, riboflavin and niacin

Diabetes Food Choice Values:
½ Carbohydrate
3½ Meat & Alternatives

Pork pairs well with many fruits; here, cooked apples take center stage in this pleasing pairing.

Tip

Cortland, Empire and Honeycrisp apples will work well in this recipe, as they retain their shape during cooking.

Variation

Add ¼ cup (60 mL) chopped dried cranberries to the apples with the syrup.

Nutrients per serving

Calories	212
Fat	3.6 g
Saturated fat	0.9 g
Sodium	356 mg (15% DV)
Carbohydrate	18 g
Fiber	1 g (4% DV)
Protein	26 g
Calcium	34 mg (3% DV)
Iron	1.9 mg (14% DV)

Very high in: Zinc, vitamin B$_{12}$, thiamine, riboflavin and niacin

High in: Magnesium and vitamin B$_6$

Diabetes Food Choice Values:

1 Carbohydrate
3 Meat & Alternatives

Maple Mustard Pork Tenderloin with Sautéed Apples

Compass Group Canada

- **Preheat oven to 375°F (190°C)**
- **Roasting pan, greased**

2	pork tenderloins (each about 12 oz/375 g), trimmed	2
5 tbsp	pure maple syrup, divided	75 mL
3 tbsp	Dijon mustard	45 mL
1 tsp	chopped fresh rosemary	5 mL
½ tsp	salt	2 mL
½ tsp	freshly ground black pepper	2 mL
2 tsp	canola oil	10 mL
3 cups	sliced peeled apples	750 mL
¼ cup	water or unsweetened apple juice	60 mL
2 tbsp	finely chopped fresh parsley	30 mL

1. Place pork in prepared roasting pan. In a small bowl, combine 2 tbsp (30 mL) of the maple syrup, mustard, rosemary, salt and pepper. Brush over pork. Roast in preheated oven for 25 minutes or until a meat thermometer inserted in the thickest part of the tenderloin registers 155°F (68°C). Transfer to a cutting board, tent with foil and let rest for 5 to 10 minutes to allow juices to redistribute and pork to reach an internal temperature of 160°F (71°C).

2. Meanwhile, in a large skillet, heat oil over medium heat. Add apples and sauté for 10 minutes or until apples are lightly browned. Reduce heat to low and add the remaining maple syrup. Simmer, stirring occasionally, for 5 minutes or until apples are tender.

3. Add water to the roasting pan and deglaze the pan, scraping up any brown bits. Strain liquid into the apple mixture and stir to combine.

4. Cut pork crosswise into thin slices. Top each serving with apples and garnish with parsley.

Makes 8 to 10 servings

This sweet and tangy fruit chutney makes a pleasant pairing with the tender pork.

Tips

The chutney can be prepared up to 3 days in advance.

The chutney can also be served with roasted or grilled chicken. Or try it as an appetizer, served with cream cheese atop crudités, or as part of cheese tray — it's yummy with soft cheese, such as Brie or Camembert.

You can also grill the tenderloins on the barbecue over medium heat, covered, for 25 to 30 minutes, turning them over halfway through. Tent with foil and let rest as directed.

Nutrients per serving

Calories	208
Fat	3.1 g
Saturated fat	1.3 g
Sodium	201 mg (8% DV)
Carbohydrate	14 g
Fiber	1 g (4% DV)
Protein	31 g
Calcium	22 mg (2% DV)
Iron	1.7 mg (12% DV)

Very high in: Zinc, vitamin B$_6$, vitamin B$_{12}$, thiamine, riboflavin and niacin

High in: Magnesium

Diabetes Food Choice Values:
½   Carbohydrate
3½   Meat & Alternatives

Pork Tenderloin with Blueberry Chutney

Heather McColl, Dietitian, British Columbia

- Preheat oven to 375°F (190°C)
- 13- by 9-inch (33 by 23 cm) metal baking pan, greased

Blueberry Chutney

2	shallots, finely chopped	2
2	cloves garlic, minced	2
2 cups	fresh or frozen blueberries	500 mL
1 tbsp	grated gingerroot	15 mL
¼ cup	cider vinegar	60 mL
3 tbsp	liquid honey	45 mL

Pork

2 tbsp	packed brown sugar	30 mL
½ tsp	freshly ground black pepper	2 mL
¼ tsp	salt	1 mL
¼ cup	grainy mustard	60 mL
3	pork tenderloins (each about 1 lb/500 g), trimmed	3

1. *Chutney:* In a medium saucepan, combine shallots, garlic, blueberries, ginger, vinegar and honey. Bring to a boil over medium heat. Reduce heat and simmer, stirring frequently, for about 20 minutes or until chutney is thickened. Transfer to a bowl and let cool.

2. *Pork:* Meanwhile, in a small bowl, combine brown sugar, pepper, salt and mustard. Rub all over tenderloins. Place pork in prepared baking pan. Roast in preheated oven for 25 to 30 minutes or until a meat thermometer inserted in the thickest part of the tenderloins registers 155°F (68°C). Transfer to a cutting board, tent with foil and let rest for 5 to 10 minutes to allow juices to redistribute and pork to reach an internal temperature of 160°F (71°C).

3. Cut pork crosswise into thin slices and serve with chutney.

Pork Tenderloin with Rhubarb Chutney

Jennifer Miller, Dietitian, Saskatchewan

- **Preheat oven to 375°F (190°C)**
- **Small roasting pan, greased**

Rhubarb Chutney

¾ cup	granulated sugar	175 mL
2 tbsp	minced gingerroot	30 mL
2 tbsp	minced garlic (about 6 cloves)	30 mL
2 tsp	ground cumin	10 mL
1 tsp	ground cinnamon	5 mL
1 tsp	ground cloves	5 mL
½ tsp	hot pepper flakes	2 mL
⅓ cup	white wine vinegar	75 mL
½	red onion, chopped	½
4 cups	chopped rhubarb	1 L
⅓ cup	raisins	75 mL

Pork

1 tbsp	ground cumin	15 mL
1 tsp	garlic powder	5 mL
½ tsp	freshly ground black pepper	2 mL
2	pork tenderloins (each about 12 oz/375 g), trimmed	2

1. *Chutney:* In a large saucepan, combine sugar, ginger, garlic, cumin, cinnamon, cloves, hot pepper flakes and vinegar. Bring to a simmer over medium heat, stirring occasionally until sugar dissolves. Stir in red onion, rhubarb and raisins; bring to a boil, stirring often. Reduce heat and simmer, stirring occasionally, for about 20 minutes or until rhubarb is tender and mixture thickens and becomes syrupy.

2. *Pork:* Meanwhile, in a small bowl, combine cumin, garlic powder and pepper. Rub all over tenderloin. Place pork in prepared roasting pan. Roast in preheated oven for 20 minutes. Spread half the chutney over pork. Roast for 5 to 10 minutes or until a meat thermometer inserted in the thickest part of the tenderloin registers 155°F (68°C). Transfer to a cutting board, tent with foil and let rest for 5 to 10 minutes to allow juices to redistribute and pork to reach an internal temperature of 160°F (71°C).

3. Cut tenderloin crosswise into thin slices and serve with the remaining chutney.

Tarragon adds a subtle licorice flavor to the delightful topping for these chops.

Tip

Trim all visible fat from the pork chops to reduce the amount of fat in your dish and to minimize spatter when cooking.

Serving Idea

Serve with Scalloped Potatoes (page 308) and Radicchio on Down Salad (page 156).

Nutrients per serving

Calories	234
Fat	10.6 g
Saturated fat	4.1 g
Sodium	545 mg (23% DV)
Carbohydrate	6 g
Fiber	1 g (4% DV)
Protein	27 g
Calcium	124 mg (11% DV)
Iron	1.5 mg (11% DV)

Very high in: Vitamin B_{12}, thiamine and niacin

High in: Zinc, vitamin B_6 and riboflavin

Diabetes Food Choice Values:
½ Carbohydrate
3½ Meat & Alternatives

Broiled Pork Chops with a Mustard Parmesan Crust

Helen Ann Dillon, Dietitian, Ontario

- Preheat broiler
- Broiler rack

4	¾-inch (2 cm) thick bone-in pork loin chops (each about 6 oz/175 g)	4
¼ cup	fine dry bread crumbs	60 mL
¼ cup	finely grated Parmesan cheese	60 mL
2 tsp	dried tarragon	10 mL
¼ tsp	salt	1 mL
¼ cup	Dijon mustard	60 mL

1. Place pork chops on broiler rack and broil, turning once, for about 8 minutes per side or until just a hint of pink remains inside.

2. Meanwhile, in a small bowl, combine bread crumbs, cheese, tarragon, salt and mustard.

3. Spread a thick layer of the mustard mixture on each pork chop. Broil for 2 to 3 minutes or until cheese melts, tops are golden brown and a meat thermometer inserted in the center of the chops registers 160°F (71°C). Let rest for 5 minutes before serving.

Sweet-and-Sour Pork

Anne Taylor, Dietitian, Ontario

● **Dutch oven**

✔ **Kid Approved**

The combination of sweet and sour flavors, often featured in Asian dishes, is a perennial kids' favorite that's popular with grown-ups too!

Tips

Trim as much fat and silverskin as you can from the pork.

When browning the pork, be sure it lifts easily before you turn it, to avoid sticking.

Variation

For a leaner version, use medallions of pork tenderloin instead of pork shoulder; reduce the simmering time to 10 minutes.

3 tbsp	all-purpose flour	45 mL
½ tsp	freshly ground black pepper	2 mL
2 lbs	boneless pork shoulder, trimmed of fat and cut into 1-inch (2.5 cm) pieces	1 kg
2 tbsp	canola oil, divided	30 mL
2	cloves garlic, minced	2
2 cups	diced celery	500 mL
2 cups	reduced-sodium chicken broth, divided	500 mL
1	can (14 oz/398 mL) pineapple chunks, with juice	1
1	red bell pepper, cut into thin strips	1
3 tbsp	cornstarch	45 mL
¼ cup	granulated sugar	60 mL
½ cup	white vinegar	125 mL
1 tbsp	reduced-sodium soy sauce	15 mL

1. In a large, shallow bowl, combine flour and pepper. Dredge pork in seasoned flour, shaking off excess, and place on a clean plate. Discard any excess flour mixture.

2. In a Dutch oven, heat 1 tbsp (15 mL) oil over medium-high heat. Add half the pork and cook for 3 to 4 minutes or until well browned on all sides. Transfer pork to a clean plate. Repeat with the remaining oil and pork.

3. Return all pork and accumulated juices to pot. Add garlic and celery; sauté for 1 minute. Pour in 1 cup (250 mL) of the broth and deglaze the pot, scraping up any browned bits. Stir in pineapple with juice and bring to a boil. Reduce heat to low, cover with a tight-fitting lid and simmer, stirring occasionally, for 20 minutes. Stir in red pepper, cover and simmer for 10 minutes or until pork is tender.

4. Meanwhile, in a medium bowl, whisk cornstarch into the remaining broth. Whisk in sugar, vinegar and soy sauce, whisking until sugar is dissolved. Stir into pot and simmer, stirring, for about 5 minutes or until sauce is thick.

Nutrients per serving

Calories	244
Fat	7.5 g
Saturated fat	1.8 g
Sodium	316 mg (13% DV)
Carbohydrate	23 g
Fiber	1 g (4% DV)
Protein	21 g
Calcium	31 mg (3% DV)
Iron	1.8 mg (13% DV)

Very high in: Zinc, vitamin C, vitamin B_{12}, thiamine and niacin

High in: Magnesium, vitamin B_6 and riboflavin

Diabetes Food Choice Values:

1   Carbohydrate
3   Meat & Alternatives

A Dutch oven is a large, heavy pot with a tight-fitting lid. It is most often used to prepare stews. Here, it works well to brown the meat and provides ample room for the added ingredients.

Here's a quick, simple and delicious way to prepare succulent lamb chops.

Tip

Trim all visible fat from the lamb chops to reduce the amount of fat in your dish and to minimize spatter when cooking.

Variation

Use 4 bone-in pork loin chops instead of the lamb chops.

Serving Idea

Serve with Personal Garden Herb Salad (page 154) and Squash Casserole (page 304).

Grilled Dijon Lamb Chops

June Martin, Dietitian, Ontario

- **Preheat greased barbecue grill to medium-high**

2	cloves garlic, minced	2
1 tbsp	dried thyme	15 mL
1 tsp	freshly ground black pepper	5 mL
2 tbsp	Dijon mustard	30 mL
1 tsp	canola oil	5 mL
8	lamb chops (each about 4 oz/125 g)	8

1. In a small bowl, combine garlic, thyme, pepper, mustard and oil. Rub evenly over both sides of lamb chops.

2. Place lamb chops on preheated grill, close the lid and grill, turning once, for 4 to 5 minutes per side for medium or to desired doneness.

> Lamb is the meat of sheep that are under one year of age. It is usually quite tender and works well with most cooking methods. Mutton, on the other hand, is sheep slaughtered after two years of age. It often has a strong aroma during cooking.

Nutrients per serving

Calories	182
Fat	8.3 g
Saturated fat	3.1 g
Sodium	146 mg (6% DV)
Carbohydrate	2 g
Fiber	1 g (4% DV)
Protein	24 g
Calcium	46 mg (4% DV)
Iron	3.1 mg (22% DV)

Very high in: Zinc, vitamin B_{12} and niacin

High in: Riboflavin

Diabetes Food Choice Values:

3 Meat & Alternatives

George loves to hunt, so deer meat is often on the menu at his house.

Tips

Venison is very lean and tends to be tough, but long, slow cooking produces succulent, tender results.

This recipe works with most cuts of deer meat, including round, blade and shoulder roasts. Chops are too tender for this cooking method; they work best grilled.

Nutrients per serving

Calories	243
Fat	7.8 g
Saturated fat	3.6 g
Sodium	375 mg (16% DV)
Carbohydrate	18 g
Fiber	1 g (4% DV)
Protein	24 g
Calcium	33 mg (3% DV)
Iron	3.8 mg (27% DV)

Very high in: Zinc, vitamin A, vitamin B$_{12}$, thiamine and niacin

High in: Vitamin B$_6$ and riboflavin

Diabetes Food Choice Values:

1   Carbohydrate
3   Meat & Alternatives

Slow-Roasted Venison

George Petrie, Nova Scotia

- **Minimum 4-quart slow cooker**

2 lb	boneless venison (deer) roast (see tip, at left)	1 kg
Pinch	salt	Pinch
1/2 tsp	freshly ground black pepper	2 mL
1	large onion	1
2	cloves garlic, minced	2
2 tbsp	lightly packed brown sugar	30 mL
1/2 tsp	dried thyme	2 mL
1 cup	lager beer or water	250 mL
1/2 cup	chicken-and-rib-style barbecue sauce	125 mL
1 tbsp	prepared yellow mustard	15 mL
1 tsp	reduced-sodium soy sauce	5 mL
5 to 6	baby potatoes	5 to 6
1 cup	thickly sliced carrots	250 mL

1. Trim off silverskin and any visible fat from venison. Sprinkle with salt and pepper.

2. Cut one-quarter of the onion into rings and set aside. Coarsely chop the remaining onion. Scatter 1/2 cup (125 mL) of the chopped onion in bottom of slow cooker. Place meat on top.

3. In a small bowl, combine the remaining chopped onion, garlic, brown sugar, thyme, beer, barbecue sauce, mustard and soy sauce. Pour over meat and onions. Arrange onion rings on top.

4. Cover and cook on High for 4 hours or on Low for 6 hours. One hour before meat is cooked, add potatoes and carrots to slow cooker and cover with sauce.

✔ **Kid Approved**

These delightful little loaves are a wonderful way to introduce children of all ages to game meat. Andrea and her family like them best when they're made with elk meat.

Tips

Stir mixture gently, just to combine, to avoid a compact, tough meat mixture.

If you prefer, you can use 1% or 2% milk instead of skim milk.

Low-fat Cheddar cheese can be used in place of regular cheese in this recipe.

Variation

Substitute ground beef for the venison.

Nutrients per serving

Calories	226
Fat	10.0 g
Saturated fat	4.9 g
Sodium	457 mg (19% DV)
Carbohydrate	11 g
Fiber	1 g (4% DV)
Protein	22 g
Calcium	115 mg (10% DV)
Iron	2.8 mg (20% DV)

Very high in: Zinc, vitamin B_{12} and niacin

High in: Magnesium, thiamine and riboflavin

Diabetes Food Choice Values:

½   Carbohydrate
3   Meat & Alternatives

Little Cheddar Venison Meatloaves

Andrea Toogood, Dietitian, Saskatchewan

- **Preheat oven to 350°F (180°C)**
- **12-cup muffin pan, lightly greased**

1 lb	ground elk, moose or deer meat	500 g
1	egg	1
½ cup	shredded Cheddar cheese	125 mL
½ cup	quick-cooking rolled oats	125 mL
¼ cup	chopped onion	60 mL
½ tsp	salt	2 mL
¼ tsp	garlic powder	1 mL
½ cup	skim milk	125 mL
2 tsp	lightly packed brown sugar	10 mL
¼ cup	ketchup	60 mL
2 tsp	prepared yellow mustard	10 mL

1. In a large bowl, gently combine elk, egg, cheese, oats, onion, salt, garlic powder and milk. Divide evenly among prepared muffin cups.

2. In a small bowl, combine brown sugar, ketchup and mustard. Spread evenly over each mini loaf. Bake in preheated oven for 25 to 30 minutes or until a meat thermometer inserted in the center of a loaf registers 160°F (71°C).

Wild game meats are very lean and often need to be cooked using a method that will tenderize the meat, such as stewing or braising. Here, the addition of traditional meatloaf ingredients produces a tender product, but you will see very little, if any, residual fat in the pan.

Fish and Seafood

Fish and seafood are delicious, healthy options from the Meat and Alternatives food group. There are a variety of fresh, frozen and canned products available to meet every budget. *Canada's Food Guide* recommends that Canadians eat at least two servings of fish a week. As always, be conscious of portion size: a portion of fresh or frozen fish or seafood is 2½ oz (75 g); a portion of canned fish is ½ cup (125 mL). Enjoy fish using healthier cooking methods such as baking, broiling, grilling or steaming and shy away from deep-frying.

Omega What?

Hardly a day goes by that you don't see a commercial or read something on the Internet about omega-3 fats. So just what are they? Omega-3 simply refers to the chemical composition of particular types of fats. There are three different types of omega-3 fats: ALA, EPA and DHA.

ALA is found in plant-based foods such as flax and canola oil. ALA is called an essential fat because our bodies can't make it but require it to function normally. This means that we need to get ALA from the foods we eat. EPA and DHA are found in fatty fish like salmon, sardines and mackerel. EPA and DHA are not considered essential fats because our bodies can convert ALA into

EPA and DHA, but only to a limited extent.

Research shows that EPA and DHA are important for heart health and the development of the brain, nerves and eyes in infants. To get the benefits of EPA and DHA from food, eat fish twice a week. To ensure that you get enough essential ALA to maintain a healthy diet, choose flax seeds, flax oil, canola oil, walnuts, walnut oil, wheat germ or soy.

Note that just because a product label says it contains omega-3 fats, that doesn't make it a healthy choice. For example, some cookies, ice cream and chips have added omega-3s, but they have few other important nutrients. As always, look at the Nutrition Facts table to choose foods with the biggest nutritional punch.

Seafood and You

Fatty fish, with their healthy omega-3s, get all the media attention these days, but there are many other seafood options that can be part of a tasty and healthy diet.

- **Crustaceans** (shellfish that have their skeleton on the outside) include shrimp, crab and lobster. Shrimp contain a fair dose of cholesterol and so should be eaten in moderation. Crab and lobster are sought-after delicacies in the culinary world. Thanks to their mild, sweet flavor, only simple steaming is required to make them feast-worthy. Both contain relatively high amounts of naturally occurring sodium, so be mindful of portion size.

- **Mollusks** (soft invertebrates) include scallops, oysters, mussels and clams. All are delicious protein sources that are best cooked with just a few flavor-enhancing ingredients and simple cooking methods such as steaming or sautéing. Clams are likely the richest food source of vitamin B_{12}, followed by oysters and mussels. Clams are also one of the best sources of iron, while oysters and mussels provide less but still important amounts. Scallops can't boast of a similar nutrient profile, but like their fellow mollusks, they provide high-quality protein and very little fat.

While most seafood is naturally low in fat, the cooking method often cranks up the fat and calories; just look at deep-fried clams and shrimp, or scallops, crab or lobster laden with drawn butter. Instead, check out the many flavorful, healthful ways we prepare fish and seafood in this chapter.

Family Cooking Lesson

Cooking Fish So It's Delish!

Nearly all types of fish can be baked, grilled or broiled. Oily fish, such as salmon, trout and swordfish, are better grilled or baked, while filets of lean fish, such as flounder and sole, are better broiled.

It's important not to overcook fish. Overcooked fish is dry and can taste strong and "fishy." A general rule of thumb is to cook fish for about 10 minutes for every inch (2.5 cm) of thickness. Very thin fillets of sole will cook in under 5 minutes, while a thicker piece of salmon steak might take 10 to 15 minutes.

So how do you know when fish is done? A simple test is to insert a fork into the thickest part of the fish and twist it gently. If the fish flakes easily and is opaque, it is done. If it still appears wet, it needs more cooking time.

Family Cooking Lesson

Fish in Parchment (en Papillote)

One of the most delicious, healthy and foolproof ways to cook fish is "en papillote": wrapped in parchment. Aromatic herbs, vegetables and/or spices, along with a steaming liquid such as wine or broth, are added to the parchment pouch with the fish, and the packets are cooked in a hot oven or on a barbecue grill. The presentation is lovely, as individual pouches can be placed on serving plates; the guest opens the pouch at the table, releasing a lovely aroma. Recipes for fish en papillote appear on pages 230 and 231.

Sustainable Fish

SeaChoice is a Canadian sustainable seafood program. To learn more about choosing sustainable seafood, visit their website at www.seachoice.org.

✔ **Kid Approved**

Sunflower seeds add crunch and a delightful nutty flavor to the haddock in this recipe. Jaclyn's kids help by breading the fish. Be sure they have clean hands and wash up well afterwards.

Tip

If you don't have a mortar and pestle, place seeds on a cutting board and press with the bottom of clean can or non-breakable mug to crush.

Variation

You can also use tilapia or any other white fish.

Nutrients per serving

Calories	366
Fat	18.8 g
Saturated fat	2.2 g
Sodium	263 mg (11% DV)
Carbohydrate	20 g
Fiber	4 g (16% DV)
Protein	30 g
Calcium	102 mg (9% DV)
Iron	4.0 mg (29% DV)

Very high in: Magnesium, vitamin B$_6$, folate, vitamin B$_{12}$, thiamine and niacin

High in: Zinc

Diabetes Food Choice Values:

1	Carbohydrate
4	Meat & Alternatives

Sunflower-Crusted Haddock

Jaclyn Pritchard, Dietitian, Ontario

1 tsp	fennel seeds	5 mL
1 tsp	cumin seeds	5 mL
½ cup	unsalted raw sunflower seeds	125 mL
½ cup	fine dry whole wheat bread crumbs	125 mL
¼ tsp	freshly ground black pepper	1 mL
Pinch	salt	Pinch
¼ cup	all-purpose flour	60 mL
1	egg	1
4	skinless haddock fillets (about 1 lb/ 500 g total)	4
2 tbsp	canola oil, divided	30 mL

1. In a dry skillet, over medium heat, toast fennel and cumin seeds, stirring constantly, for 1 to 2 minutes or until golden and fragrant. Immediately transfer to a mortar and pestle, add sunflower seeds and crush slightly. Transfer to a shallow bowl and stir in bread crumbs, pepper and salt.

2. Place flour in another shallow bowl. Place egg in a small bowl and whisk lightly with a fork. Dip each haddock fillet first in flour, then in egg and finally in seed mixture. Discard any excess flour, egg and seed mixture.

3. In a skillet, heat 1 tbsp (15 mL) oil over medium-high heat until hot but not smoking. Add 2 fillets and fry for about 5 minutes or until evenly browned, adjusting heat as necessary so fish does not burn. Flip fillets over and fry for 5 minutes or until fish is opaque and flakes easily when tested with a fork. Transfer to a plate and keep warm. Repeat with the remaining oil and fish.

> The higher fat in this recipe comes mostly from the sunflower seeds, a source of polyunsaturated fatty acids. If you want to lower the fat, you can reduce the sunflower seeds to ¼ to ⅓ cup (60 to 75 mL). You can also reduce the oil to 1 tbsp (15 mL), but the fish will not be as crispy.

You won't be tempted by deep-fried battered fish once you taste this simple, healthy version.

Tips

For the fish fillets, try tilapia, sole or haddock.

If you cannot find seasoned bread crumbs for fish in your supermarket, create your own by combining regular dry bread crumbs with a little salt, lemon pepper and dried parsley.

Serving Idea

Serve with Citrus Fennel Slaw (page 153) and Roasted Lemon Asparagus (page 297).

Nutrients per serving

Calories	275
Fat	5.8 g
Saturated fat	1.9 g
Sodium	308 mg (13% DV)
Carbohydrate	19 g
Fiber	1 g (4% DV)
Protein	37 g
Calcium	73 mg (7% DV)
Iron	2.2 mg (16% DV)

Very high in: Vitamin D, vitamin B_{12} and niacin

High in: Magnesium, folate, thiamine and riboflavin

Diabetes Food Choice Values:

1	Carbohydrate
4	Meat & Alternatives

Oven-Fried Fish

Eileen Campbell, Ontario

- **Preheat oven to 350°F (180°C)**
- **Baking sheet, greased**

1	egg	1
½ cup	milk	125 mL
½ cup	all-purpose flour	125 mL
1	pouch (2 oz/57 g) seasoned bread crumbs for fish (see tip, at left)	1
4	thin white fish fillets (about 1½ lbs/ 750 g total)	4
	Vegetable cooking spray	

1. In a shallow bowl, whisk egg and milk. Place flour on one plate and bread crumbs on another.

2. Dip both sides of fish in flour, then in egg mixture. Coat well with crumbs. Place on prepared baking sheet and spray top lightly with vegetable cooking spray. Discard any excess flour, egg and crumb mixtures.

3. Bake in preheated oven for 10 minutes or until fish is opaque and flakes easily with a fork.

✔ **Kid Approved**

This is a great way to use up leftover cooked salmon and mashed potatoes, but it's just as good made with canned salmon.

Tip

Use plain puréed or mashed potato, without milk or butter added.

Variation

Vary the flavor by using 6 oz (175 g) cooked haddock, crab or diced shrimp instead of salmon. Change the herbs and veggies depending on the fish or seafood you choose.

Serving Idea

Serve with Red Leaf Salad with Mango Chutney Dressing (page 149). Enjoy Apples with Maple Custard Sauce (page 363) for dessert.

Nutrients per serving

Calories	149
Fat	5.1 g
Saturated fat	1.2 g
Sodium	179 mg (7% DV)
Carbohydrate	12 g
Fiber	1 g (4% DV)
Protein	13 g
Calcium	125 mg (11% DV)
Iron	0.8 mg (6% DV)

Very high in: Vitamin D, vitamin B$_{12}$ and niacin
High in: Vitamin C

Diabetes Food Choice Values:
$\frac{1}{2}$ Carbohydrate
2   Meat & Alternatives

Tasty Fish Cakes

Eileen Campbell, Ontario

1	can (7$\frac{1}{2}$ oz/213 g) salmon, drained, skin and large bones removed (or 6 oz/ 175 g leftover cooked salmon)	1
1 cup	puréed or mashed potatoes	250 mL
$\frac{1}{4}$ cup	finely chopped green onion	60 mL
$\frac{1}{4}$ cup	finely chopped red bell pepper	60 mL
3 tbsp	chopped fresh dill	45 mL
3 tbsp	milk	45 mL
	Salt and freshly ground black pepper	
1	egg, beaten	1
	Vegetable cooking spray	

1. In a medium bowl, combine salmon, potatoes, green onion, red pepper, dill and milk. Season to taste with salt and pepper. Gently stir in egg. Form mixture into four $\frac{3}{4}$-inch (2 cm) thick cakes. Cover and refrigerate for at least 30 minutes or overnight to let flavor develop.

2. Heat a large nonstick skillet over medium heat. Spray with vegetable cooking spray. Add fish cakes and cook for about 2 minutes per side, or until browned on both sides and hot in the center.

Three simple ingredients meld to create a delicious sauce for fish.

Tips

Do not boil the sauce or it may curdle. Curdling is not harmful, but the look is less appealing.

Extra sauce may be cooled, covered and refrigerated for up to 3 days and reheated to serve over hot cooked pasta or cooked chicken.

This sauce also works well with cooked tilapia or cod.

Nutrients per serving

Calories	176
Fat	5.7 g
Saturated fat	1.8 g
Sodium	166 mg (7% DV)
Carbohydrate	3 g
Fiber	0 g (0% DV)
Protein	27 g
Calcium	130 mg (12% DV)
Iron	1.2 mg (9% DV)

Very high in: Magnesium, vitamin D, vitamin B_{12} and niacin

High in: Vitamin B_6

Diabetes Food Choice Values:
$3\frac{1}{2}$ Meat & Alternatives

Halibut with Sun-Dried Tomato and Chèvre Sauce

Mary Sue Waisman, Dietitian, Nova Scotia

- **Double boiler**
- **Food processor or blender**

9	oil-packed sun-dried tomatoes, drained and patted dry	9
1½ cups	2% evaporated milk	375 mL
4 oz	goat cheese, crumbled	125 g
6	halibut steaks (about 1½ lbs/750 g total)	6
½ tsp	freshly ground black pepper	2 mL
Pinch	salt	Pinch
1 tbsp	canola oil, divided	15 mL

1. In the top of a double boiler, over medium-high heat, combine tomatoes and milk. Simmer for 10 minutes or until tomatoes begin to soften. Remove from heat and transfer to food processor. Process until puréed (some tomato bits may remain). Add goat cheese and process until smooth. Set aside.

2. Meanwhile, season halibut with pepper and salt. In a large nonstick skillet, heat 1½ tsp (7 mL) oil over medium heat. Place 3 steaks in pan and fry for 4 to 5 minutes or until lightly brown on the bottom. Flip steaks over and fry, adjusting heat as necessary so that fillets brown but do not burn, for 3 to 4 minutes or until fish is opaque and flakes easily when tested with a fork. Transfer to a serving dish and keep warm. Repeat with the remaining fish.

3. Place each steak on a plate and top with 2 tbsp (30 mL) sauce. Reserve the remaining sauce for another use.

> Chèvre is the French name for cheese made from goat's milk. It is a soft cheese but, unlike other soft cheeses, is more crumbly than smooth. It has a distinctive tart flavor.

Isla first made this dish using fresh grouper while on vacation in the Caribbean. Back in Ontario, she uses a firm white fish, such as halibut.

Tip

The cooking time will vary depending on the thickness of the fish. The general rule of thumb for fish is 10 minutes per inch (2.5 cm) of thickness.

Variation

Use pimiento-stuffed green olives instead of black olives.

Serving Idea

Serve with cooked quinoa or brown rice and steamed asparagus.

Nutrients per serving

Calories	289
Fat	15.2 g
Saturated fat	4.4 g
Sodium	406 mg (17% DV)
Carbohydrate	8 g
Fiber	2 g (8% DV)
Protein	27 g
Calcium	189 mg (17% DV)
Iron	2.2 mg (16% DV)

Very high in: Magnesium, vitamin D, vitamin B_6, vitamin B_{12} and niacin

High in: Riboflavin

Diabetes Food Choice Values:
3½ Meat & Alternatives
1 Fat

White Fish with Mediterranean Flavors

Isla Horvath, Ontario

2 tsp	dried basil	10 mL
1 tsp	dried oregano	5 mL
2 tbsp	olive oil, divided	30 mL
	Juice of 1 lemon	
4	skinless halibut steaks (about 1 lb/ 500 g total)	4
¾ cup	finely chopped onion	175 mL
2	cloves garlic, minced	2
¾ cup	chopped plum (Roma) tomatoes	175 mL
½ cup	sliced black olives	125 mL
½ cup	dry white wine	125 mL
½ cup	crumbled feta cheese	125 mL
	Lemon wedges	

1. In a medium shallow dish, combine basil, oregano, 1 tbsp (15 mL) oil and lemon juice. Add halibut, turning to coat both sides. Marinate at room temperature for 5 to 10 minutes.

2. Heat a large nonstick skillet over medium heat. Add halibut and fry for 3 to 4 minutes per side or until browned on both sides. Transfer to a plate and keep warm.

3. Wipe out skillet, add the remaining oil and sauté onion for 3 to 4 minutes or until softened. Add garlic and sauté for 30 seconds. Add tomatoes, olives and wine; boil, stirring, until wine is slightly reduced. Return fish to skillet and spoon sauce over top; reduce heat and simmer for 1 to 2 minutes or until fish is opaque and flakes easily when tested with a fork.

4. Place each steak on a plate and drizzle sauce evenly over top. Sprinkle evenly with feta cheese and garnish with lemon wedges.

En papillote means to cook individual portions in little parcels. Here, the flavors of Tuscany are captured in the packets of fish.

Tips

Opening the packets at the table makes a dramatic presentation, as guests are enchanted by the aromas.

You can also use frozen fish fillets. Increase the baking time to 15 to 18 minutes.

Nutrients per serving

Calories	274
Fat	18.2 g
Saturated fat	3.3 g
Sodium	121 mg (5% DV)
Carbohydrate	3 g
Fiber	1 g (4% DV)
Protein	23 g
Calcium	32 mg (3% DV)
Iron	1.0 mg (7% DV)

Very high in: Vitamin D, vitamin B$_6$, vitamin B$_{12}$, thiamine and niacin

High in: Magnesium and folate

Diabetes Food Choice Values:

3   Meat & Alternatives

Tuscan Fish en Papillote

Christina Blais, Dietitian, Quebec

- **Preheat oven to 425°F (220°C)**
- **4 sheets parchment paper, each about 16 by 12 inches (40 by 30 cm)**

4	pieces skinless salmon fillet or white fish fillets (about 1 lb/500 g total)	4
1	clove garlic, thinly sliced	1
1/2 tsp	fresh thyme leaves	2 mL
2 tbsp	dry white wine	30 mL
1 1/2 tbsp	extra virgin olive oil, divided	22 mL
4	ripe black olives, sliced	4
3	oil-packed sun-dried tomatoes, drained, patted dry and julienned	3
3/4 cup	julienned fennel bulb	175 mL
3 to 4	fresh basil leaves, cut into thin strips	3 to 4
1	lemon, cut into 4 wedges	1

1. Place 1 piece of fish on each sheet of parchment paper. Fold all four sides of the paper to form creases about 4 inches (10 cm) from the edge, but do not close. (This will prevent liquids from spilling off the paper).

2. In a small bowl, combine garlic, thyme, wine and 1 tbsp (15 mL) oil. Drizzle evenly over fish. Divide olives, tomatoes and fennel evenly on top of fish. Bring the two long sides of the parchment paper together on top of the fish and fold over repeatedly to close the center, then fold the sides together, tucking the ends under the packet to hold them in place.

3. Place packets on a baking sheet. Bake in preheated oven for 10 to 12 minutes or until fish flakes easily when tested with a fork.

4. Transfer packets to serving plates. Cut paper open with a sharp knife or scissors and add basil, a lemon wedge and a drizzle of the remaining oil to each packet.

> Sun-dried tomatoes have been dehydrated by the sun's heat. They are sold either dry or packed in oil. The oil-packed variety has more fat and calories, but also more flavor. The tomatoes can be drained and dried with paper towels to remove some of the oil before cooking.

Aromatic Thai ingredients add hot, sweet, salty and tangy flavors as the fish steams in individual parcels.

Tips

Mature green mangos have a flavor and texture similar to those of a crisp, tart green apple. Choose one that has an unblemished skin and firm flesh.

Opening the packets at the table makes a dramatic presentation, as guests are enchanted by the aromas.

You can also use frozen fish fillets. Increase the baking time to 15 to 18 minutes.

Nutrients per serving

Calories	269
Fat	13.5 g
Saturated fat	3.3 g
Sodium	310 mg (13% DV)
Carbohydrate	13 g
Fiber	2 g (8% DV)
Protein	23 g
Calcium	27 mg (2% DV)
Iron	0.7 mg (5% DV)

Very high in: Vitamin C, vitamin D, vitamin B$_6$, vitamin B$_{12}$, thiamine and niacin

High in: Magnesium, vitamin A and folate

Diabetes Food Choice Values:

½ Carbohydrate
3 Meat & Alternatives

Thai Fish en Papillote

Christina Blais, Dietitian, Quebec

- **Preheat oven to 425°F (220°C)**
- **4 sheets parchment paper, each about 16 by 12 inches (40 by 30 cm)**

4	pieces skinless salmon fillet or white fish fillets (about 1 lb/500 g total)	4
1 tbsp	grated gingerroot	15 mL
¼ cup	light coconut milk	60 mL
2 tsp	fish sauce	10 mL
1 tsp	hot chili and garlic sauce	5 mL
	Grated zest and juice of 1 lime	
1	red bell pepper, julienned	1
1	green mango (see tip, at left), julienned	1
2 tbsp	fresh cilantro leaves	30 mL
1	lime, cut into 4 wedges	1

1. Place 1 piece of fish on each sheet of parchment paper. Fold all four sides of the paper to form creases about 4 inches (10 cm) from the edge, but do not close. (This will prevent liquids from spilling off the paper).

2. In a small bowl, combine ginger, coconut milk, fish sauce, chili and garlic sauce, lime zest and lime juice. Drizzle evenly over fish. Divide red pepper and green mango evenly on top of fish. Bring the two long sides of the parchment paper together on top of the fish and fold over repeatedly to close the center, then fold the sides together, tucking the ends under the packet to hold them in place.

3. Place packets on a baking sheet. Bake in preheated oven for 10 to 12 minutes or until fish flakes easily when tested with a fork.

4. Transfer packets to serving plates. Cut paper open with a sharp knife or scissors and add cilantro and a lime wedge to each packet.

Although botanically a fruit, coconut contains ample amounts of saturated fat and should be used in moderation. Compare the labels of regular and light versions of coconut milk; many light versions contain significantly less fat than the regular milk.

Salmon Wraps

Judy Reynolds, Saskatchewan

- **Preheat oven to 375°F (190°C)**
- **Baking sheet, lightly greased**

6	8-inch (20 cm) rice paper rounds	6
6	sprigs fresh dill, stems removed	6
6	pieces skinless salmon fillet (about 1½ lbs/750 g total)	6
1	lemon, cut in half	1
Pinch	salt	Pinch

1. Fill a shallow dish with warm water. Lay out a clean, lint-free towel. Working with 1 round at a time, place rice paper in warm water for about 1 minute to soften. Carefully lift out of water and place on towel. Place 1 sprig fresh dill in the center of the round. Place 1 salmon fillet on top of dill. Sprinkle with a squeeze of lemon juice and a few grains of salt. Fold bottom half of rice paper up over salmon, fold in sides, then fold top down to enclose the salmon. Turn parcels over and place seam side down on prepared baking sheet. Repeat to make 6 parcels.

2. Bake in preheated oven for 10 to 12 minutes or until fish flakes easily when tested with a fork.

Orange Walnut Baked Salmon

Dale Mayerson, Dietitian, Ontario

- **Preheat oven to 350°F (180°C)**
- **11- by 7-inch (28 by 18 cm) glass baking dish, greased**

4	pieces skinless salmon fillet (about 1 lb/500 g total)	4
¼ cup	thawed frozen orange juice concentrate	60 mL
½ cup	finely chopped walnuts	125 mL
2 tsp	canola oil	10 mL

1. Place salmon fillets in prepared baking dish. Drizzle evenly with orange juice concentrate and sprinkle with walnuts. Drizzle with oil.

2. Bake in preheated oven for about 15 minutes or until fish is opaque and flakes easily when tested with a fork.

> The salmon and the walnuts contribute equally to the higher fat in this recipe. Both are sources of omega-3 fatty acids. Walnuts provide ALA (a plant-based omega-3 fatty acid that our bodies require), and salmon supplies EPA and DHA, which are important for heart health and the development of the brain, nerves and eyes in infants. If you want to lower the total fat, reduce the walnuts to ¼ cup (60 mL).

This show-stopping salad has bright color, varying textures and delicious flavor.

Tip

To avoid cross contamination, use separate brushes to baste the onions and salmon.

Variation

Use a combination of blueberries, blackberries and raspberries in the salad.

Nutrients per serving

Calories	348
Fat	17.2 g
Saturated fat	2.5 g
Sodium	98 mg (4% DV)
Carbohydrate	30 g
Fiber	5 g (20% DV)
Protein	20 g
Calcium	95 mg (9% DV)
Iron	2.2 mg (16% DV)

Very high in: Magnesium, vitamin A, vitamin C, vitamin D, vitamin B$_6$, folate, vitamin B$_{12}$, thiamine and niacin

High in: Riboflavin

Diabetes Food Choice Values:

1	Carbohydrate
3	Meat & Alternatives
1	Fat

Grilled Salmon, Mango and Raspberry Spinach Salad

Heather McColl, Dietitian, British Columbia

- Preheat barbecue grill to medium
- Blender or food processor
- Two 12-inch (30 cm) bamboo skewers, soaked

Raspberry Vinaigrette

⅔ cup	fresh or frozen raspberries (thawed and drained if frozen)	150 mL
3 tbsp	balsamic vinegar	45 mL
1 tbsp	liquid honey	15 mL
2 tbsp	water	30 mL
½ tsp	Dijon mustard	2 mL
¼ tsp	freshly ground black pepper	1 mL
2 tbsp	canola or olive oil	30 mL
1 tbsp	finely chopped shallots	15 mL

Salad

1	red onion, cut into 8 wedges	1
4	salmon steaks (about 1 lb/500 g total)	4
6 cups	lightly packed baby spinach	1.5 L
1	ripe mango, thinly sliced	1
1 cup	fresh raspberries	250 mL

1. *Vinaigrette:* Purée raspberries in blender. Press through a sieve to remove seeds.

2. In a small bowl, whisk together puréed raspberries, vinegar, honey, 2 tbsp (30 mL) water, mustard and pepper. Gradually whisk in oil until blended. Stir in shallots. Divide vinaigrette in half. Set half aside for end and use half for grilling.

3. *Salad:* Thread 4 onion wedges onto each skewer and brush with some of the vinaigrette for grilling. Brush salmon on both sides with vinaigrette. Place skewers and salmon on preheated grill, close lid and grill, basting frequently with vinaigrette and turning once, for 10 minutes or until fish is opaque and flakes easily when tested with a fork.

4. Remove onions from skewers and place in a salad bowl. Add spinach, mango, raspberries and reserved vinaigrette; toss to coat. Divide salad among four plates and top each with grilled salmon.

There are hundreds of varieties of mangos grown in tropical climates, but only a few of these make their way to North America. Ripe mangos have a mild, sweet flavor, similar to a ripe peach, but with a denser texture. Some mangos are intended to be eaten under-ripe, or green, while others should be eaten ripe.

Serving Idea

This is an ideal main course salad. Simply add whole-grain bread sticks for crunch and enjoy Broiled Strawberries with Cool Vanilla Yogurt (page 362) for dessert.

A few simple ingredients and a hot barbecue make for a fine fish dinner. It's the perfect entrée for a hot summer night.

Tips

Do not cover the fish with foil.

Instead of one large piece of foil, you can use six smaller pieces and place one fillet on each piece.

The cooking time will vary depending on the thickness of the fish. The general rule of thumb for fish is 10 minutes per inch (2.5 cm) of thickness.

Variation

Sprinkle uncooked fish with salt-free fish seasoning before adding the mayo-mustard spread.

Salmon à la West Coast

Debbie Houle, Dietitian, British Columbia

● **Preheat barbecue grill to medium**

6	pieces salmon fillet (about 1½ lbs/750 g total)	6
¼ cup	light mayonnaise	60 mL
¼ cup	Dijon mustard	60 mL
1 tbsp	lightly packed brown sugar	15 mL

1. Place salmon fillets, skin side down, on a large piece of foil. Fold foil to form a lip around the edges.

2. In a small bowl, combine mayonnaise and mustard. Spread evenly over fillets. Sprinkle evenly with brown sugar.

3. Place foil on preheated grill, close lid and grill for 10 to 12 minutes or until fish is opaque and flakes easily when tested with a fork.

Nutrients per serving

Calories	212
Fat	13.6 g
Saturated fat	2.6 g
Sodium	250 mg (10% DV)
Carbohydrate	4 g
Fiber	0 g (0% DV)
Protein	18 g
Calcium	27 mg (2% DV)
Iron	0.5 mg (4% DV)

Very high in: Vitamin D, vitamin B_6, vitamin B_{12} and niacin

High in: Thiamine

Diabetes Food Choice Values:
2½ Meat & Alternatives
½ Fat

Makes 4 servings

✔ Kid Approved

This is a family favorite at the Bamford house. It has held a rarified position on their menu two to four times per month for over 10 years now, and they still look forward to it. So will you!

Tips

Visit www.seachoice.org to learn about sustainable fish choices.

Use no more than one garlic clove, even if you're a garlic lover; more than that will overpower the other flavors.

Variation

Use rainbow trout instead of salmon.

Nutrients per serving

Calories	298
Fat	14.4 g
Saturated fat	2.5 g
Sodium	206 mg (9% DV)
Carbohydrate	14 g
Fiber	0 g (0% DV)
Protein	20 g
Calcium	29 mg (3% DV)
Iron	0.5 mg (4% DV)

Very high in: Vitamin D, vitamin B_6, vitamin B_{12} and niacin

High in: Thiamine and riboflavin

Diabetes Food Choice Values:

1	Carbohydrate
3	Meat & Alternatives

Scotch Salmon

Mary Bamford, Dietitian, Ontario

- **Preheat broiler, with rack placed 4 inches (10 cm) from the heat source**
- **Rimmed baking sheet, greased**

4	pieces skinless salmon fillet (about 1 lb/500 g total)	4
1	clove garlic, minced	1
1 tsp	grated gingerroot (optional)	5 mL
1/3 cup	Scotch whisky	75 mL
1/4 cup	pure maple syrup	60 mL
1 tbsp	canola or olive oil	15 mL
1 tbsp	reduced-sodium soy sauce	15 mL

1. Place salmon fillets in a shallow glass or ceramic dish. In a small bowl, combine garlic, ginger (if using), Scotch, maple syrup, oil and soy sauce. Pour marinade over fish and let stand at room temperature for at least 15 minutes but no longer than 30 minutes. Pour marinade into a small saucepan.

2. Place salmon on prepared baking sheet. Broil for 7 to 10 minutes or until fish is opaque and flakes easily when tested with a fork.

3. Meanwhile, bring the reserved marinade to a boil over high heat. Reduce heat and simmer for 3 to 4 minutes or until slightly thickened.

4. Serve salmon topped with sauce.

Makes 4 servings

This dish is simple enough for a weeknight meal and fancy enough for entertaining.

Tip

The baking time will vary depending on the thickness of the fish. The general rule of thumb for fish is 10 minutes per inch (2.5 cm) of thickness.

Variation

Add 1 tsp (5 mL) finely minced garlic and 1 tsp (5 mL) finely minced gingerroot to the maple syrup mixture.

Baked Salmon with Maple Syrup

Sue Mah, Dietitian, Ontario

- Preheat oven to 375°F (190°C)
- Rimmed baking sheet, lined with parchment paper or lightly greased

2 tbsp	packed brown sugar	30 mL
2 tbsp	pure maple syrup	30 mL
1 tbsp	reduced-sodium soy sauce	15 mL
4	pieces skinless salmon fillet (about 1 lb/500 g total)	4
2 tsp	toasted sliced almonds (see page 139)	10 mL

1. In a small bowl, combine brown sugar, maple syrup and soy sauce.

2. Place salmon fillets on prepared baking sheet and bake in preheated oven for 10 minutes. Remove from oven and drizzle evenly with maple syrup sauce. Bake for 2 to 3 minutes or until fish is opaque and flakes easily when tested with a fork. Serve sprinkled with almonds.

> Maple syrup is made by boiling down the sap tapped from maple trees. Tapping involves inserting a metal spigot into the bark and placing a pail underneath to catch the sap as it "runs" in the springtime. Early in maple syrup season, the syrup is generally clear and the taste slightly sweet; as the season progresses, the syrup becomes darker and more caramelized, with a richer, deeper flavor. Most of Canada's maple syrup is produced in Quebec.

Nutrients per serving

Calories	242
Fat	11.4 g
Saturated fat	2.3 g
Sodium	208 mg (9% DV)
Carbohydrate	14 g
Fiber	0 g (0% DV)
Protein	20 g
Calcium	29 mg (3% DV)
Iron	0.7 mg (5% DV)

Very high in: Vitamin D, vitamin B_6, vitamin B_{12} and niacin

High in: Thiamine

Diabetes Food Choice Values:

1 Carbohydrate
3 Meat & Alternatives

Asian Salmon

Sarah Cormier, Dietitian, Nova Scotia

Sarah Cormier, Dietitian, Nova Scotia

Makes 4 servings

✔ Kid Approved

This sweet and spicy salmon is sure to please the whole family.

Tips

Hoisin sauce, an extremely flavorful sauce made with soybeans, garlic and other spices, contains a lot of sodium, so use it sparingly.

You can substitute red or white wine vinegar if you don't have rice vinegar.

Use any leftover salmon to make salmon cakes or salmon salad.

This marinade also works well for chicken, pork, shrimp or scallops and makes a great stir-fry sauce for noodle or rice dishes.

- **Preheat oven to 375°F (190°C)**
- **Rimmed baking sheet, lined with foil, then parchment paper**

1	garlic clove, finely minced	1
2 tsp	finely minced gingerroot	10 mL
Pinch	hot pepper flakes	Pinch
¼ cup	hoisin sauce	60 mL
1 tbsp	rice vinegar	15 mL
1 tbsp	liquid honey	15 mL
2 tsp	reduced-sodium soy sauce	10 mL
1 tsp	sesame oil	5 mL
4	pieces skinless salmon fillet (about 1 lb/500 g total)	4

1. In a small bowl, stir together garlic, ginger, hot pepper flakes, hoisin sauce, vinegar, honey, soy sauce and oil. Transfer all but 2 tbsp (30 mL) marinade to a sealable plastic bag. Add salmon fillets and distribute marinade to coat salmon. Seal bag and let stand at room temperature for 10 minutes or refrigerate for up to 2 hours.

2. Remove salmon from marinade and place on prepared baking sheet. Discard marinade from bag.

3. Bake in preheated oven, basting once with the reserved marinade, for 10 to 12 minutes or until fish is opaque and flakes easily when tested with a fork.

Nutrients per serving

Calories	231
Fat	12.2 g
Saturated fat	2.4 g
Sodium	309 mg (13% DV)
Carbohydrate	9 g
Fiber	0 g (0% DV)
Protein	20 g
Calcium	19 mg (2% DV)
Iron	0.5 mg (4% DV)

Very high in: Vitamin D, vitamin B_6, vitamin B_{12} and niacin

High in: Folate and thiamine

Diabetes Food Choice Values:

½   Carbohydrate
3   Meat & Alternatives

This dish is cooked entirely in the microwave. Sole has a delicate, neutral flavor and very tender flesh.

Tip

Cooking times vary depending on the power of your microwave. These times are based on a 1,500-watt microwave; adjust them as necessary.

Variation

Use salmon instead of sole and herb-and-garlic-flavored cream cheese instead of plain.

Nutrients per serving

Calories	228
Fat	9.8 g
Saturated fat	5.5 g
Sodium	331 mg (14% DV)
Carbohydrate	7 g
Fiber	2 g (8% DV)
Protein	27 g
Calcium	136 mg (12% DV)
Iron	1.9 mg (14% DV)

Very high in: Magnesium, vitamin A, vitamin D, folate, vitamin B$_{12}$ and niacin

High in: Vitamin B$_6$ and riboflavin

Diabetes Food Choice Values:

3½ Meat & Alternatives

Sole and Cream Cheese Rolls

Kelly Light, Dietetics Student, Quebec

- **9-inch (23 cm) square microwave-safe baking dish**

1	package (10 oz/300 g) frozen chopped spinach	1
4	skinless sole fillets (about 1 lb/500 g total)	4
4 oz	light cream cheese, divided	125 g
½ cup	julienned carrots	125 mL
1 tbsp	butter	15 mL
1 tbsp	all-purpose flour	15 mL
½ cup	reduced-sodium chicken broth	125 mL

1. Place spinach in baking dish, cover with plastic wrap, leaving one corner open for a vent, and microwave on High for 4 minutes. Using a fork, separate spinach as much as possible. Cover and microwave on High for 3 minutes. Drain in a colander, discarding liquid. Spread spinach evenly over bottom of dish.

2. On a clean work surface, pat sole fillets dry with paper towels. Spread 1 tbsp (15 mL) of the cream cheese over each fillet, then roll up as you would a jelly roll, enclosing the cheese; secure with a toothpick, if necessary.

3. Place rolls evenly on top of spinach. Scatter carrots around fish. Cover and microwave on High for 6 minutes. Set aside.

4. In a small microwave-safe bowl, melt butter on Medium (50%) for 15 to 20 seconds. Whisk in flour, then gradually whisk in broth. Microwave on High for 2 minutes. Whisk in the remaining cream cheese. Microwave on High for 2 minutes or until cheese is melted. Stir sauce and pour over fish. Cover and microwave on High for 2 minutes or until fish flakes easily when tested with a fork. Let stand, covered, for 2 minutes. Remove toothpicks before serving.

Orange Ginger Beef (page 201)

Maple-Glazed Pork Tenderloin (page 212)

Grilled Dijon Lamb Chops (page 219)

Halibut with Sun-Dried Tomato and Chèvre Sauce (page 228)

Thai Fish en Papillote (page 231)

Prawn Bouillabaisse (page 248)

Butternut Squash,
Spinach and Feta Frittata (page 258)

Moroccan Vegetable Curry
(page 272)

There's nothing like fresh rainbow trout! This simple recipe cooks up hot and tasty with lots of freshly ground black pepper.

Tips

Keep your kitchen fan on to quickly remove any excess smoke that may be generated from searing the fish at a high heat.

This seems like a lot of pepper, but it yields a delicious, spicy flavor.

Variation

Use salmon or arctic char instead of trout and increase the cooking time in step 3 as necessary.

Nutrients per serving

Calories	217
Fat	9.2 g
Saturated fat	1.9 g
Sodium	131 mg (5% DV)
Carbohydrate	6 g
Fiber	2 g (8% DV)
Protein	22 g
Calcium	101 mg (9% DV)
Iron	2.2 mg (16% DV)

Very high in: Vitamin D, vitamin B$_6$, vitamin B$_{12}$ and niacin

High in: Magnesium and thiamine

Diabetes Food Choice Values:

3   Meat & Alternatives

Pepper-Crusted Rainbow Trout

Michelle Gelok, Dietitian, United Arab Emirates

4 tbsp	coarsely ground black pepper	60 mL
¼ tsp	coarse sea salt	1 mL
4	rainbow trout fillets (about 1 lb/500 g total)	4
1 tbsp	canola oil	15 mL
1 cup	dry white wine	250 mL
¼ cup	freshly squeezed lemon juice	60 mL

1. In a large shallow dish, combine pepper and salt; spread out over bottom of dish. Firmly press trout fillets, flesh side down, into pepper mixture, coating flesh completely (do not coat the skin side). Shake off excess and set aside on a clean plate. Discard any excess pepper mixture.

2. In a large skillet, heat oil over medium-high heat until hot but not smoking. In batches as necessary, place fillets, flesh side down, in skillet. Cover and cook for 1 to 2 minutes or until fish is brown and crispy. Transfer fish to a plate. Repeat with the remaining fillets.

3. Return trout to pan, flesh side up. Reduce heat to medium-low and add wine and lemon juice to the skillet. Cover and cook for 8 to 10 minutes or until fish is opaque and flakes easily when tested with a fork. If pan begins to dry out, add 1 to 2 tbsp (15 to 30 mL) water.

Whether you're lucky enough to catch it yourself or you pick up fresh fillets from your local fishmonger, rainbow trout is a tasty way to stock up on health-promoting omega-3 fats. Rainbow trout is also sometimes called silver trout or steelhead. It is stocked in the Great Lakes and caught off the Pacific shore. It is a freshwater fish that can adapt to salt water.

The delicate flavor of peaches and their pleasant orange color complement trout beautifully.

Tip

The blanching time of the peaches will vary depending on their ripeness.

Variations

Use nectarines or plums, adjusting the blanching time to suit the ripeness of the fruit.

Use salmon or arctic char instead of trout and increase the cooking time as necessary.

Nutrients per serving

Calories	203
Fat	6.4 g
Saturated fat	1.8 g
Sodium	176 mg (7% DV)
Carbohydrate	11 g
Fiber	1 g (4% DV)
Protein	25 g
Calcium	89 mg (8% DV)
Iron	0.7 mg (5% DV)

Very high in: Vitamin D, vitamin B_6, vitamin B_{12} and niacin

High in: Magnesium and thiamine

Diabetes Food Choice Values:

½ Carbohydrate
3 Meat & Alternatives

Peachy Glazed Trout

Compass Group Canada

- **Preheat oven to 400°F (200°C)**
- **13- by 9-inch (33 by 23 cm) glass baking dish, greased**

3	peaches	3
1	clove garlic, minced	1
2 tsp	grated gingerroot	10 mL
2 tbsp	lightly packed brown sugar	30 mL
½ tsp	freshly ground black pepper	2 mL
⅓ cup	unsweetened orange juice	75 mL
1 tbsp	reduced-sodium soy sauce	15 mL
1 tbsp	Dijon mustard	15 mL
6	skinless trout fillets (about 1½ lbs/750 g total)	6

1. Using a paring knife, make a small X at the bottom of each peach. In a medium saucepan of simmering water, blanch peaches for 2 to 3 minutes or until skins begin to peel back. Using a slotted spoon, transfer peaches to ice water to stop the cooking process. Let cool for 5 minutes or until cool enough to handle. Peel off and discard skin. Chop peaches.

2. In a medium bowl, combine peaches, garlic, ginger, brown sugar, pepper, orange juice, soy sauce and mustard.

3. Pat trout fillets dry with paper towels. Place in prepared baking dish and pour sauce evenly over fish.

4. Bake in preheated oven, basting occasionally with sauce, for 12 to 15 minutes or until fish is opaque and flakes easily when tested with a fork.

> Peaches are one of the four most popular fruits in North America (the others being banana, apple and orange). Freestone peaches are the best choice when the flesh needs to be quickly removed from the stone, as in canning or pie making. Clingstone peaches, as the name implies, have flesh that is more difficult to remove from the stone. They are useful in recipes where the shape of the whole fruit must be retained, such as the classic dish peach Melba.

Makes 4 servings

An attractive presentation and delicious flavor make this dish a perfect choice for entertaining.

Tips

Be sure to buy a skinless fillet; otherwise, when you try to cut the spanakopita into portions, the skin and bottom crust will be left behind.

This recipe works best with a large, thick trout fillet, such as steelhead.

Variation

Use salmon or arctic char instead of trout.

Nutrients per serving

Calories	323
Fat	15.6 g
Saturated fat	4.0 g
Sodium	279 mg (12% DV)
Carbohydrate	17 g
Fiber	1 g (4% DV)
Protein	28 g
Calcium	163 mg (15% DV)
Iron	2.1 mg (15% DV)

Very high in: Magnesium, vitamin A, vitamin D, vitamin B$_6$, folate, vitamin B$_{12}$, thiamine and niacin

High in: Riboflavin

Diabetes Food Choice Values:

1   Carbohydrate
3½ Meat & Alternatives
1   Fat

Trout Spanakopita

Kristy Lalonde, Nutrition Student, Ontario

- **Preheat oven to 400°F (200°C)**
- **Rimmed baking sheet, greased**

4 tsp	canola or olive oil, divided	20 mL
½ cup	finely chopped onion	125 mL
2	cloves garlic, minced	2
½ tsp	freshly ground black pepper	2 mL
3 cups	lightly packed roughly chopped fresh spinach	750 mL
¼ cup	crumbled feta cheese	60 mL
1	skinless trout fillet (about 1 lb/500 g total)	1
	Vegetable cooking spray	
4	sheets frozen phyllo pastry, thawed	4

1. In a large skillet, heat 1 tsp (5 mL) oil over medium heat. Sauté onion for 3 to 4 minutes or until softened. Add garlic and pepper; sauté for 30 seconds. Add spinach, one handful at a time, stirring until wilted before adding the next handful. Add up to ¼ cup (60 mL) water to help the wilting, if necessary. Once all of the spinach is wilted, remove pan from heat and stir in cheese. Transfer to a medium bowl and set aside.

2. Wipe out skillet, place over medium-high heat and add the remaining oil. Sear trout fillet, turning once, for about 1 minute per side (do not cook all the way through). Remove from heat.

3. Spray a work surface lightly with cooking spray. Lay 1 sheet of phyllo on greased surface and spray pastry evenly with cooking spray. Carefully cover with a second sheet of pastry and spray with cooking spray. Repeat with the remaining 2 phyllo sheets. Place seared trout in center of phyllo and top evenly with spinach mixture. Carefully fold bottom edge of phyllo over fish, fold in sides, then fold down top to form a loose package. Place seam side down on prepared baking sheet and spray top with cooking spray.

4. Bake in preheated oven for 15 to 20 minutes or until pastry is golden and fish flakes easily when tested with a fork.

Dig in and enjoy these savory morsels, using whole-grain buns or crusty bread to sop up the tasty sauce.

Tips

Scrub and rinse mussels in two to three changes of cold water to get rid of any grit. Use a hard brush to scrub off any beards on the outer shell. Discard mussels with broken shells and any that do not snap shut when tapped. After cooking, discard mussels that do not open, as they may not be safe to eat.

Reduce the hot pepper flakes if you prefer a less spicy sauce.

Nutrients per serving

Calories	153
Fat	3.8 g
Saturated fat	0.6 g
Sodium	380 mg (16% DV)
Carbohydrate	12 g
Fiber	2 g (8% DV)
Protein	12 g
Calcium	86 mg (8% DV)
Iron	5.3 mg (38% DV)

Very high in: Vitamin B$_{12}$

High in: Magnesium, zinc, vitamin C, folate, thiamine and niacin

Diabetes Food Choice Values:

1½   Meat & Alternatives

Mussels in Spicy Tomato Sauce

Mary Sue Waisman, Dietitian, Nova Scotia

2 tsp	canola oil	10 mL
1 cup	finely chopped onion	250 mL
4	cloves garlic, minced	4
1	can (19 oz/540 mL) tomatoes, coarsely chopped	1
1 tbsp	dried oregano	15 mL
1 tbsp	dried basil	15 mL
1 tsp	hot pepper flakes	5 mL
1 tsp	freshly ground black pepper	5 mL
1 cup	dry white wine	250 mL
4 lbs	mussels, scrubbed and debearded (see tip, at left)	2 kg

1. In a large pot, heat oil over medium heat. Sauté onion for 3 to 4 minutes or until softened. Add garlic and sauté for 30 seconds. Stir in tomatoes, oregano, basil, hot pepper flakes, black pepper and wine; bring to a boil. Reduce heat and simmer, stirring occasionally, for 8 to 10 minutes or until liquid is reduced by about one-quarter.

2. Add mussels, pressing to immerse in liquid, cover and simmer for 6 to 8 minutes or until mussels open. Discard any mussels that do not open.

Mussels in Curry

Barbara Jaques, Ontario

Makes 6 servings

Prepared curry pastes can be very high in sodium, but this homemade curry sauce helps keep sodium in check.

Tip

When you're sweating the green onions and red pepper in step 1, check occasionally to make sure they're not browning and reduce the heat if they are.

Variation

Remove the mussels from the shells and return them to the sauce. Serve as a soup.

Serving Idea

Serve in wide soup plates with crusty whole wheat sourdough bread and a fresh green salad on the side.

2 tsp	canola oil	10 mL
3	green onions, finely sliced	3
½	large red bell pepper, finely diced	½
1½ tsp	curry powder	7 mL
1 tsp	ground cumin	5 mL
½ tsp	hot pepper flakes	2 mL
2 tbsp	grated gingerroot	30 mL
2 tbsp	coarsely chopped fresh cilantro	30 mL
1	can (14 oz/398 mL) light coconut milk	1
1 cup	reduced-sodium chicken broth	250 mL
4 lbs	mussels, scrubbed and debearded (see tip, page 244)	2 kg

1. In a large pot, heat oil over medium heat. Stir in green onions and red pepper; cover and sweat for 3 to 4 minutes or until softened. Stir in curry, cumin and hot pepper flakes; sauté for 30 seconds or until fragrant. Stir in ginger, cilantro, coconut milk and broth; bring to a boil. Reduce heat and simmer for 10 minutes.

2. Add mussels, pressing to immerse in liquid, cover and simmer for 6 to 8 minutes or until mussels open. Discard any mussels that do not open.

> In Canada, mussels are plentiful along the Atlantic coastline. Together with their shellfish counterparts clams and oysters, mussels are one of the best sources of vitamin B_{12}.

Nutrients per serving

Calories	157
Fat	8.3 g
Saturated fat	3.9 g
Sodium	374 mg (16% DV)
Carbohydrate	7 g
Fiber	1 g (4% DV)
Protein	12 g
Calcium	39 mg (4% DV)
Iron	4.2 mg (30% DV)

Very high in: Vitamin B_{12}

High in: Magnesium, zinc, vitamin C, folate and niacin

Diabetes Food Choice Values:

1½   Meat & Alternatives

1   Fat

The delicate flavor of scallops works beautifully with the creamy risotto in this elegant recipe.

Tips

If you use the small bay scallops, they do not need to be cut into smaller pieces. Sea scallops, however, are much larger, up to 2 inches (5 cm) in diameter, and should be cut into smaller pieces for this recipe. Be sure to trim off the tough muscle from the sides of scallops before cutting.

Pancetta, often known as Italian bacon, is high in fat, so use it sparingly.

The scallops are cooked separately so they don't overcook.

Nutrients per serving

Calories	199
Fat	6.2 g
Saturated fat	2.5 g
Sodium	458 mg (19% DV)
Carbohydrate	23 g
Fiber	1 g (4% DV)
Protein	10 g
Calcium	112 mg (10% DV)
Iron	0.5 mg (4% DV)

High in: Vitamin B_{12}

Diabetes Food Choice Values:

1½ Carbohydrates
1 Meat & Alternatives

Scallop Risotto

Summer-Lee Clark, Ontario

Risotto

3 cups	reduced-sodium chicken broth	750 mL
1 tsp	olive oil	5 mL
1 tsp	butter	5 mL
¼ cup	finely diced shallots	60 mL
2	cloves garlic, minced	2
1 cup	Arborio rice	250 mL
1 cup	dry white wine	250 mL
⅔ cup	freshly grated Parmesan cheese	150 mL
Pinch	salt	Pinch
	Freshly ground white pepper	
1 tbsp	chopped fresh thyme (optional)	15 mL

Scallops

2 tsp	olive oil	10 mL
¼ cup	finely chopped shallots	60 mL
2	cloves garlic, minced	2
¼ cup	finely diced pancetta	60 mL
1 cup	sea scallops, trimmed and cut into ¾-inch (2 cm) pieces (see tip, at left)	250 mL

1. In a saucepan, combine broth and 3 cups (750 mL) water; bring to a simmer over high heat. Reduce heat to low and keep warm.

2. *Risotto:* In a medium saucepan, heat oil and butter over medium heat. Sauté shallots for 1 to 2 minutes or until softened but not browned. Add garlic and sauté for 30 seconds. Stir in rice until coated. Add wine and bring to a simmer. Simmer, stirring, until liquid is reduced. Stir in 1 cup (250 mL) broth; simmer, stirring often, until liquid is almost absorbed and the starch from the rice begins to release. Continue to add broth, 1 cup (250 mL) at a time, stirring often, until only 1 cup (250 mL) of broth remains. Make sure broth never completely absorbs into rice between additions.

3. *Scallops:* Meanwhile, in a nonstick skillet, heat oil over medium heat. Sauté shallots for 1 to 2 minutes or until softened but not browned. Add garlic and sauté for 30 seconds. Add pancetta and sauté for 5 minutes or until some of the fat is released. Add scallops and sauté for 2 to 3 minutes or until almost firm and opaque. Transfer scallop mixture to a plate and keep warm.

4. Check the consistency of the rice. If al dente, continue to step 5. If not yet al dente, stir in the remaining broth and cook, stirring, until al dente.

5. Stir in scallop mixture, cheese and salt. Season to taste with pepper. Serve garnished with thyme, if using.

Arborio rice is a short-grain rice that is high in starch, making it ideal for risotto. Carnaroli, another short-grain rice, also works for risotto. Rice for risotto should not be rinsed before use, as the starch in the outer coating helps make the risotto creamy.

Variation
Use small shrimp (size 36 to 45) instead of chopped scallops.

Serving Ideas
If serving this dish as an entrée, simply add some steamed asparagus and carrots to complete the meal.

To serve as an appetizer, place in attractive scallop shells that have been transformed into dishes.

Orange zest and fennel make a bright and flavorful combination in this hearty bouillabaisse, a seafood stew with origins in the Provence area of France.

Tips

If you can't find spot prawns, use medium shrimp (size 31 to 35).

To thaw prawns, place the frozen package in a bowl in the refrigerator overnight.

Have everything prepped before you start cooking, as the ingredients need to be added to the pot quickly in this dish.

Leeks can harbor a lot of dirt and sand between the layers, so be sure to wash them well.

Nutrients per serving

Calories	160
Fat	4.4 g
Saturated fat	1.2 g
Sodium	374 mg (16% DV)
Carbohydrate	9 g
Fiber	2 g (8% DV)
Protein	19 g
Calcium	91 mg (8% DV)
Iron	2.6 mg (19% DV)

Very high in: Magnesium, vitamin B_{12} and niacin

High in: Vitamin B_6

Diabetes Food Choice Values:

2   Meat & Alternatives

Prawn Bouillabaisse

Heather McColl, Dietitian, British Columbia

1 tbsp	canola oil	15 mL
1 tbsp	butter	15 mL
1 tsp	fennel seeds, crushed	5 mL
1	leek, white part only, thinly sliced	1
1	fennel bulb, finely chopped	1
1 cup	chopped onion	250 mL
2	cloves garlic, minced	2
2 tbsp	tomato paste	30 mL
½ tsp	dried thyme	2 mL
1 cup	dry white wine	250 mL
4	plum (Roma) tomatoes, diced	4
2	cans (each 14 oz/398 mL) clam juice	2
¼ cup	coarsely chopped fresh parsley	60 mL
Pinch	saffron threads	Pinch
	Grated zest of 1 small orange	
1 lb	skinless white fish fillets (such as haddock, cod or halibut), cut into cubes	500 g
1	package (12 oz/340 g) wild British Columbia spot prawns, peeled and deveined	1
Pinch	salt	Pinch
	Freshly ground black pepper	

1. In a large pot, heat oil and butter over medium heat. Sauté fennel seeds for about 30 seconds or until fragrant. Add leek, fennel bulb and onion; sauté for 5 minutes or until softened. Add garlic and sauté for 30 seconds. Stir in tomato paste and thyme; sauté for 2 minutes.

2. Add wine and deglaze the pan, scraping up any brown bits. Stir in tomatoes, clam juice, parsley, saffron and orange zest; cover and bring to a boil. Stir in fish and boil for 2 minutes. Stir in prawns and boil for 2 minutes or until fish is opaque and flakes easily when tested with a fork and prawns are pink and opaque. Stir in salt and pepper to taste.

> Spot prawns are a shrimp variety found in the waters off Canada's west coast. The body is usually reddish brown or tan, with white horizontal bars and distinctive white spots on the shell. They have a sweet, delicate flavor and a firm texture.

Carrots peeled into ribbons give this dish an elegant appearance and an interesting texture. Serve atop fluffy brown rice.

Tip

Test your peeling skills on a carrot *before* making this for guests.

Serving Idea

Serve over brown rice, with steamed asparagus as an attractive color contrast.

Nutrients per serving

Calories	172
Fat	7.0 g
Saturated fat	3.0 g
Sodium	167 mg (7% DV)
Carbohydrate	8 g
Fiber	2 g (8% DV)
Protein	18 g
Calcium	75 mg (7% DV)
Iron	2.9 mg (21% DV)

Very high in: Vitamin A, vitamin B$_{12}$ and niacin

High in: Magnesium

Diabetes Food Choice Values:

2½ Meat & Alternatives

Curry Shrimp and Shaved Carrots

Candace Ivanco-Boutot, British Columbia

2 lbs	large shrimp, peeled and deveined	1 kg
6	cloves garlic, minced	6
3 tbsp	curry powder	45 mL
1 tbsp	canola oil	15 mL
6	carrots	6
1	can (14 oz/398 mL) light coconut milk	1
	Juice of ½ lime	
¼ cup	finely chopped fresh cilantro	60 mL

1. In a large bowl, combine shrimp, garlic, curry powder and oil, making sure shrimp are well coated. Marinate at room temperature for 30 minutes.

2. Meanwhile, peel outer layer from carrots. Using the vegetable peeler, press firmly against one side of a carrot to cut large ribbons. Turn carrot and continue to cut ribbons. Discard the inner core of the carrot if it seems tough. Repeat with the remaining carrots. You should have about 6 cups (1.5 L) of loosely packed carrot curls.

3. Heat a large skillet over medium-high heat. Add half the shrimp and cook for 1 to 2 minutes or until shrimp turn pink. Turn shrimp over and cook for 1 to 2 minutes or until almost firm. Transfer to a plate and keep warm. Repeat with the remaining shrimp.

4. Return all shrimp to the skillet and add carrot ribbons and coconut milk; bring to a boil. Reduce heat and simmer for 2 minutes or until carrots are tender and shrimp are opaque. Sprinkle with lime juice and serve garnished with cilantro.

> Shrimp are packaged and sold according to size. The number on the package indicates the number of shrimp per lb (454 g). For example, a bag labeled "21 to 25" has 21 to 25 shrimp per lb (454 g), and these will be fairly large. In a bag of shrimp labeled "51 to 60," the shrimp will be much smaller.

This recipe is a tasty adventure with a unique green!

Tips

Do not inhale the fumes while cooking the hot pepper flakes.

Use whole wheat or tri-colored pasta instead of white.

Nutrients per serving

Calories	251
Fat	6.7 g
Saturated fat	1.5 g
Sodium	264 mg (11% DV)
Carbohydrate	31 g
Fiber	4 g (16% DV)
Protein	17 g
Calcium	173 mg (16% DV)
Iron	3.6 mg (26% DV)

Very high in: Folate, vitamin B_{12} and niacin

High in: Magnesium, zinc, vitamin A and thiamine

Diabetes Food Choice Values:

1½ Carbohydrates

1½ Meat & Alternatives

Karen's Rapini and Shrimp Pasta

Karen Benevento, Ontario

3 cups	penne or rotini pasta	750 mL
1	bunch rapini (about 1 lb/500 g), trimmed and coarsely chopped	1
2 tbsp	canola oil, divided	30 mL
3	cloves garlic, minced	3
1 tsp	hot pepper flakes	5 mL
1 tsp	dried basil	5 mL
1 lb	large shrimp, peeled and deveined	500 g
1	large red onion, very thinly sliced	1
1½ cups	sliced mushrooms (¼-inch/0.5 cm thick slices)	375 mL
½ cup	freshly grated Parmesan cheese	125 mL

1. In a large pot of boiling salted water, cook pasta according to package directions until al dente. Drain and transfer to a large serving bowl.

2. Meanwhile, in a saucepan, bring 3 cups (750 mL) water to a boil over high heat. Add rapini, reduce heat to medium-high, cover and boil for 3 to 4 minutes or until just tender. Drain and rinse under cold running water; set aside.

3. In a large skillet, heat 1 tbsp (15 mL) oil over medium heat. Sauté garlic, hot pepper flakes and basil for 1 minute or until garlic starts to soften but does not brown. Add shrimp and sauté for 2 to 3 minutes or until starting to turn pink. Reduce heat to low, cover and cook for 2 minutes, until shrimp are pink and opaque. Transfer shrimp to a bowl and set aside.

4. Wipe out skillet. Increase heat to medium-high and add the remaining oil. Sauté onions and mushrooms for 3 to 4 minutes or until onions are softened. Add rapini and shrimp and sauté for 2 to 3 minutes or until heated through.

5. Pour shrimp mixture over pasta and stir to combine. Sprinkle with Parmesan.

Rapini, also known as broccoli rabe, is a bitter green prized for its assertive flavor. Before use, trim off the stems below the point where the leaves begin.

Light, refreshing flavors complement whole wheat linguine perfectly in this delightful seafood pasta dish.

Tips

If you can't find spot prawns, use medium shrimp (size 31 to 35).

Cooking the asparagus with the pasta saves a pot.

Variation

Use 2 cups (500 mL) chopped broccoli instead of asparagus.

Nutrients per serving

Calories	280
Fat	6.1 g
Saturated fat	1.8 g
Sodium	416 mg (17% DV)
Carbohydrate	33 g
Fiber	4 g (16% DV)
Protein	21 g
Calcium	163 mg (15% DV)
Iron	3.1 mg (22% DV)

Very high in: Magnesium, folate, vitamin B_{12} and niacin
High in: Zinc and thiamine

Diabetes Food Choice Values:
2   Carbohydrates
2   Meat & Alternatives

Asparagus, Lemon and Dill Shrimp Linguine

Heather McColl, Dietitian, British Columbia

8 oz	whole wheat linguine	250 g
8 oz	asparagus spears, trimmed and cut into 2-inch (5 cm) pieces	250 g
1 tbsp	canola oil	15 mL
3	shallots, sliced	3
3	cloves garlic, minced	3
1 cup	dry white wine	250 mL
	Grated zest and juice of 1 lemon	
1	package (12 oz/340 g) wild British Columbia spot prawns, peeled and deveined	1
½ cup	freshly grated Parmesan cheese	125 mL
¼ cup	chopped fresh dill	60 mL

1. In a large pot of boiling salted water, cook pasta according to package directions until al dente, adding asparagus for the last 3 minutes of cooking time. Drain and transfer to a large serving bowl.

2. Meanwhile, in a large skillet, heat oil over medium heat. Sauté shallots for 3 to 4 minutes or until softened. Add garlic and sauté for 30 seconds. Add wine, lemon zest and lemon juice; bring to a boil, stirring. Stir in prawns and simmer for 2 to 3 minutes or until pink and opaque.

3. Pour prawn mixture over pasta mixture and stir to combine. Sprinkle with Parmesan and dill.

Makes 6 servings

This easy, versatile sauce is loaded with flavor. It's delicious over spaghetti squash, as in this recipe, but also works well over whole wheat pasta.

Tips

Canned tomatoes can vary in their acidity. Taste the sauce and adjust the seasoning with extra sugar to counteract the acidity, if required.

Depending on the size of the squash, you may need less sauce. Refrigerate extras for up to 2 days for another meal.

Nutrients per serving

Calories	175
Fat	3.1 g
Saturated fat	0.6 g
Sodium	210 mg (9% DV)
Carbohydrate	30 g
Fiber	6 g (24% DV)
Protein	10 g
Calcium	110 mg (10% DV)
Iron	7.5 mg (54% DV)

Very high in: Vitamin A, vitamin C and vitamin B$_{12}$

High in: Magnesium, vitamin B$_6$, folate and niacin

Diabetes Food Choice Values:

1   Carbohydrate
1   Meat & Alternatives

Red Clam Sauce over Spaghetti Squash

Brigitte Lamoureux, Dietitian, Manitoba

- • **Preheat oven to 350°F (180°C)**
- • **13- by 9-inch (33 by 23 cm) glass baking dish**

1	spaghetti squash	1
2	cans (each 5 oz/142 g) baby clams, with juice	2
1 tsp	canola or olive oil	5 mL
1 cup	finely chopped onion	250 mL
1	clove garlic, minced	1
1	can (28 oz/796 mL) no-salt-added diced tomatoes, with juice	1
1	can (5½ oz/156 mL) tomato paste	1
¼ cup	finely chopped fresh parsley	60 mL
¼ cup	finely chopped fresh basil	60 mL
2 tbsp	freshly grated Parmesan cheese	30 mL
1 tbsp	granulated sugar	15 mL
1 tsp	garlic powder	5 mL
½ tsp	freshly ground black pepper	2 mL
Pinch	salt	Pinch
¼ cup	dry red wine	60 mL

1. Trim off both ends of squash and cut squash in half lengthwise. Place squash, flesh side up, in baking dish. Pour in ½ inch (1 cm) water and cover dish with foil. Bake in preheated oven for 45 minutes or until tender. Transfer squash to a wire rack and let cool.

2. Drain juice from clams, reserving half the juice. Set clams and juice aside.

3. Meanwhile, in a medium saucepan, heat oil over medium heat. Sauté onion for 3 to 4 minutes or until softened. Add garlic and sauté for 30 seconds. Reduce heat to medium-low and sauté for about 5 minutes or until onions begin to caramelize.

4. Stir in clams with reserved juice, tomatoes with juice, tomato paste, parsley, basil, cheese, sugar, garlic powder, pepper, salt and wine; bring to a boil, stirring often. Reduce heat to low, cover and simmer for 30 minutes.

5. When squash is cool enough to handle, scrape out seeds. Using a fork, scrape squash into strands and place in a large serving bowl. Discard skins. Pour sauce over squash.

Makes 4 servings

Freshly cooked lobster meat is best, but thawed frozen canned lobster also works well in this traditional Maritime dish.

Tips

This is the traditional way to make lobster rolls. But for added nutrition, use whole wheat hot dog buns or whole-grain crusty buns and add shredded lettuce and other chopped vegetables.

Stir the salad gently to avoid overmixing.

Lobster Rolls

Mary Sue Waisman, Dietitian, Nova Scotia

2 cups	torn or chopped cooked lobster meat	500 mL
¼ cup	finely diced onion	60 mL
¼ cup	finely diced celery	60 mL
2 tbsp	light mayonnaise	30 mL
1 tbsp	freshly squeezed lemon juice	15 mL
¼ tsp	freshly ground black pepper	1 mL
4	soft white hot dog buns, split	4

1. In a medium bowl, gently combine lobster, onion, celery, mayonnaise, lemon juice and pepper. Divide mixture evenly among buns.

Nutrients per serving

Calories	231
Fat	5.0 g
Saturated fat	1.0 g
Sodium	548 mg (23% DV)
Carbohydrate	26 g
Fiber	1 g (4% DV)
Protein	19 g
Calcium	114 mg (10% DV)
Iron	1.9 mg (14% DV)

Very high in: Zinc, folate, vitamin B_{12} and niacin

High in: Magnesium and thiamine

Diabetes Food Choice Values:

1½ Carbohydrates

2   Meat & Alternatives

Vegetarian Main Courses

The recipes in this chapter are great examples of how we can use Canadian-produced foods to make vegetarian and vegan dishes with international flare, thanks to the ready availability of imported spices and specialty products from other countries. A well-planned vegetarian diet can provide all the nutrients your body needs, though you must pay special attention to getting enough vitamin B_{12}, calcium, iron and other nutrients. But the payoff could be great: some evidence shows that a vegan diet may have potential health benefits, including lower rates of obesity, type 2 diabetes, high blood pressure, heart disease and certain types of cancer.

Types of Vegetarian Eating

Although any meal plan that excludes meat can be considered a vegetarian diet, some vegetarians are stricter than others in what else they exclude:

- **Lacto-vegetarians** exclude all sources of animal protein except for dairy products.
- **Ovo-vegetarians** exclude all sources of animal protein except for eggs and egg products.
- **Lacto-ovo-vegetarians** exclude all sources of animal protein except for dairy and egg products.
- **Vegans** exclude all animal products, including honey, and foods that contain animal products, such as gelatin and casein.

Do Vegans Get Enough Nutrients?

The vegan eating pattern can take some extra planning. Vegans must pay particular attention to getting enough of certain nutrients, including protein, iron, zinc, calcium, vitamins D and B_{12} and omega-3 fats. A well-planned vegan diet can meet all these needs. It is safe and healthy for pregnant and breastfeeding women, babies, children, teens and seniors. A variety of plant foods eaten throughout the day can provide enough protein to promote and maintain good health.

Pick Those Pulses

Pulses, the dried seeds of legumes, include peas, beans, chickpeas and lentils. They provide protein and dietary fiber and are low in fat. Most are also high in iron and contain many other vitamins and minerals.

Canada grows plenty of pulses! They're an inexpensive source of delicious nutrition, so try to use pulses every day. Here are some practical ideas:

- Purée cooked beans and add them to tomato-based pasta sauces.
- Add lentils to soup — they will help thicken it without the need for rich cream.
- Use cooked brown lentils instead of ground beef in dishes such as lasagna or shepherd's pie.
- Sprinkle cooked lentils or chickpeas on pizza, along with other toppings.
- Add cooked red kidney beans to rice pilaf for extra color and fiber.
- Add cooked chickpeas to salads.

Family Cooking Lesson

Making Vegetable Stock

Flavorful, versatile vegetable stock is easy to make, and you decide which vegetables to use. Plus, you can control the amount of added salt — this recipe doesn't use any salt, and it's still delicious.

Vegetable stock can be used in most recipes that call for meat stock. Just be aware that vegetable stock is thin, rather than gelatinous, when it's cold, because it contains no gelatin (a by-product of cooking stock from animal bones).

The best bet with vegetable stock is to keep it simple, using only a few types of vegetables. When preparing the recipe below, add the tomato if you plan to use the stock in recipes with other tomato products; omit it if you're going to make light-colored soups, such as mushroom or cauliflower. Add the turnip if you plan to use the stock in recipes with other root vegetables.

This recipe makes 8 cups (2 L) of vegetable stock.

Sachet

8	parsley stems	8
4	fresh thyme sprigs	4
1	dried bay leaf	1
¼ tsp	freshly crushed black peppercorns	1 mL

Stock

2 tbsp	canola oil	30 mL
3	cloves garlic, peeled and smashed	3
1	onion, chopped	1
1	leek, white and green parts, chopped	1
1	large carrot, chopped	1
1	stalk celery, chopped	1
1	tomato, chopped (optional)	1
½ cup	diced turnip or fennel (optional)	125 mL

1. *Sachet:* Lay a square of cheesecloth out flat and fold it in half. Place parsley, thyme, bay leaf and peppercorns in center of cheesecloth. Fold up sides of cheesecloth and cinch together; secure with kitchen twine. Cut away excess cheesecloth.

2. *Stock:* In a large stockpot, heat oil over medium heat. Add garlic, onion, leek, carrot, celery, tomato (if using) and turnip (if using). Cover and sweat vegetables for 8 to 10 minutes or until some of the juices release, reducing heat if necessary to prevent browning.

3. Add 8 cups (2 L) water and sachet. Increase heat to high and bring to a boil. Reduce heat to low and simmer, uncovered, for 35 to 40 minutes or until stock is flavorful. Strain and discard vegetables and sachet. Use immediately or let cool completely, transfer to airtight containers and refrigerate for up to 5 days.

Family Cooking Lesson

How to Cook Dried Beans

Cooked legumes, such as kidney beans and chickpeas, can be purchased in cans for convenience. However, they are often high in sodium. Rinsing the beans can remove up to half of the sodium, but if you have the time, cooking dried beans and/or peas yourself can be more economical, and you'll know there's no added sodium. Here's what to do:

Soaking

Dried beans and peas (except for lentils and split peas) must be soaked before they are cooked to replace the water lost in drying. A general rule is to use 3 cups (750 mL) of water for every 1 cup (250 mL) beans. After soaking, discard the soaking water and rinse the beans (this helps cut down on the substance that causes gas). Here are three soaking options:

- **Overnight soak:** Let beans and water stand overnight in a bowl. Drain. (**Note:** Whole peas need only be soaked for 1 to 2 hours; chickpeas and beans are best when soaked for 8 hours or overnight.)
- **Quick soak:** In a large saucepan, bring water and beans to a boil; cover and boil for 2 minutes. Remove from heat and let stand for 1 hour. Drain.
- **Microwave soak:** In a microwave-safe casserole dish, combine hot water and beans. Cover and microwave on High for 15 minutes or until boiling. Let stand for 1 hour. Drain.

Cooking

To cook soaked beans, use 3 cups (750 mL) water for every 1 cup (250 mL) soaked beans and follow one of the methods below. The longer you store the soaked beans, the more they dry out and the longer you need to cook them.

- **Stovetop cooking:** In a large saucepan, combine water and soaked beans. Cover and bring to a full rolling boil. Reduce heat and simmer for 45 to 60 minutes or until fork-tender. Lentils will require less cooking time (20 to 30 minutes).
- **Microwave cooking:** In a microwave-safe casserole dish, combine water and soaked beans. Cover and microwave on High for 10 to 15 minutes or until boiling. Stir and microwave on Medium (50%) for 15 minutes. Stir again and microwave on Medium (50%) for 10 to 20 minute or until fork-tender.

These are guidelines only; when in doubt, check the package directions.

Lindsay buys free-range eggs from her co-worker and has found a new appreciation for fresh eggs in this colorful frittata.

Tip

Butternut squash can be difficult to peel. To make the task easier, first cut the squash in half crosswise, to create two flat surfaces. Place each squash half on its flat surface and use a sharp utility knife to remove the tough peel.

Serving Idea

Serve with a green salad or a steamed green vegetable such as peas, beans or edamame. To boost the protein in this meal, sprinkle the salad or vegetable with toasted nuts or seeds.

Nutrients per serving

Calories	151
Fat	8.0 g
Saturated fat	4.1 g
Sodium	192 mg (8% DV)
Carbohydrate	12 g
Fiber	2 g (8% DV)
Protein	9 g
Calcium	177 mg (16% DV)
Iron	1.2 mg (9% DV)

Very high in: Vitamin A and vitamin B_{12}

High in: Magnesium, folate and riboflavin

Diabetes Food Choice Values:

½   Carbohydrate
1   Meat & Alternatives
1   Fat

Butternut Squash, Spinach and Feta Frittata

Lindsay Mandryk, Dietitian, British Columbia

- **Preheat oven to 400°F (200°C)**
- **13- by 9-inch (33 by 23 cm) glass baking dish, lightly greased**

1	butternut squash, peeled and cubed (4 to 5 cups/1 to 1.25 L)	1
1	package (10 oz/300 g) frozen chopped spinach, thawed and drained	1
1½ cups	cubed peeled potatoes	375 mL
¾ cup	thinly sliced red onion	175 mL
8	eggs	8
½ cup	1% milk	125 mL
	Freshly ground black pepper	
1 cup	shredded Cheddar cheese	250 mL
½ cup	crumbled feta cheese	125 mL

1. Place squash in a large microwave-safe bowl and cover with plastic wrap, leaving a corner open to vent. Microwave on High for about 5 minutes or until fork-tender. Drain off excess liquid. Gently stir in spinach, potatoes and red onion. Spread in prepared baking dish.

2. In a bowl, whisk together eggs and milk. Season to taste with pepper. Pour over vegetables and stir gently to distribute. Sprinkle evenly with Cheddar and feta.

3. Bake in preheated oven for 35 to 40 minutes or until eggs are set.

> In a frittata, the ingredients are mixed in with the eggs; in an omelet they are folded inside cooked eggs.

Makes 6 servings

The delicate vegetable flavors in this quiche are enhanced by the smokiness of the cheese.

Tip

It's important to parboil the potatoes to soften them and keep them from turning brown, but make sure not to overcook them in step 1, or they will break apart.

Variations

For some heat, add 1/4 tsp (1 mL) cayenne pepper or 1/2 tsp (2 mL) hot pepper sauce to the vegetables.

For a slightly different flavor, add 1/2 tsp (2 mL) ground cumin to the vegetables.

Nutrients per serving

Calories	203
Fat	10.8 g
Saturated fat	5.3 g
Sodium	181 mg (8% DV)
Carbohydrate	16 g
Fiber	2 g (8% DV)
Protein	11 g
Calcium	197 mg (18% DV)
Iron	1.2 mg (9% DV)

Very high in: Vitamin A and vitamin B$_{12}$
High in: Vitamin B$_6$, folate and riboflavin

Diabetes Food Choice Values:
1/2 Carbohydrate
1 Meat & Alternatives
1 Fat

Potato-Crusted Zucchini, Carrot and Smoked Cheddar Quiche

Heather McColl, Dietitian, British Columbia

- **Preheat oven to 350°F (180°C)**
- **9-inch (23 cm) glass pie plate, greased**

12 oz	russet potatoes, cut into 1/8-inch (3 mm) slices	375 g
1 tsp	canola oil	5 mL
2 cups	chopped zucchini	500 mL
1 cup	thinly sliced carrot coins	250 mL
1/3 cup	finely chopped onion	75 mL
1	clove garlic, minced	1
1/2 tsp	freshly ground black pepper	2 mL
Pinch	ground nutmeg	Pinch
4	eggs	4
1 cup	shredded applewood-smoked Cheddar cheese	250 mL
1/2 cup	2% milk	125 mL

1. Bring a medium saucepan of water to a boil over high heat. Add potatoes, reduce heat and simmer for 7 minutes or until fork-tender. Drain. Line bottom of prepared pie plate with enough slices to cover, overlapping slightly (you may not need all of the potato slices).

2. Meanwhile, in a skillet, heat oil over medium heat. Sauté zucchini, carrots and onion for 4 to 5 minutes or until softened. Add garlic, pepper and nutmeg; sauté for 30 seconds. Spoon vegetables over potatoes.

3. In a medium bowl, whisk eggs until blended. Stir in cheese and milk. Pour evenly over vegetable mixture.

4. Bake in preheated oven for 30 minutes or until set in the center. Let cool for 10 to 15 minutes. Cut into 6 wedges.

> Smoked cheese derives its flavor from light smoking using wood from a fruitwood tree, such as apple or cherry. Applewood smoking lends Cheddar cheese a sweet, subtle smoky flavor.

Makes 6 patties

Serving size: 1 patty

✔ **Kid Approved**

Our recipe testers served these veggie burgers to university students for lunch one day, and they all raved about them — now there's a compliment!

Tips

Make sure the mushrooms, onion and pepper are finely chopped so that patties stick together.

Choose mild, medium or hot salsa, depending on how much heat you like.

To reduce the sodium, choose buns with the lowest % DV for sodium.

Nutrients per serving

Calories	409
Fat	13.0 g
Saturated fat	6.8 g
Sodium	705 mg (29% DV)
Carbohydrate	54 g
Fiber	9 g (36% DV)
Protein	19 g
Calcium	352 mg (32% DV)
Iron	2.8 mg (20% DV)

Very high in: Magnesium, zinc, vitamin A, folate, thiamine and niacin

High in: Vitamin C, vitamin B_6 and riboflavin

Diabetes Food Choice Values:

3 Carbohydrates
1 Meat & Alternatives
1½ Fats

Legume and Veggie Burgers

Heather McColl, Dietitian, British Columbia

1	can (14 oz/398 mL) red kidney beans, rinsed and drained	1
2	cloves garlic, minced	2
1	carrot, grated	1
½ cup	finely chopped mushrooms	125 mL
½ cup	finely chopped onion	125 mL
½ cup	finely chopped red bell pepper	125 mL
½ cup	quick-cooking rolled oats	125 mL
2 tbsp	salsa	30 mL
¼ tsp	freshly ground black pepper	1 mL
	Vegetable cooking spray	
6	slices (each 1 oz/30 g) Monterey Jack cheese or vegan alternative	6
6	whole-grain buns, split	6

1. In a large bowl, using a fork, mash beans to a coarse texture. Add garlic, carrot, mushrooms, onion, red pepper, oats, salsa and pepper; mix well to combine. Shape into six ½-inch (1 cm) thick patties. Place on a large plate and refrigerate for 30 minutes.

2. Spray a nonstick skillet with cooking spray and preheat over medium heat. In batches as necessary, fry patties for 5 to 6 minutes or until bottom is golden. Flip over and fry for 5 to 6 minutes or until bottom is golden and patties are heated through.

3. Top patties with cheese and serve on buns.

> Rinsing canned beans well under cold water before use both reduces the sodium and, as a bonus, reduces the chance that you will experience uncomfortable and potentially embarrassing gas.

Alternative Cooking Techniques

1. **Grill:** Be sure your grill is clean and well oiled, or use a cookie sheet sprayed with vegetable cooking spray on the barbecue. Grill over medium heat for 4 to 5 minutes per side.

2. **Stovetop and grill:** Partially cook the burgers on the stovetop and grill on the barbecue for the last few minutes.

3. **Broiler:** Preheat broiler, with the rack placed 4 to 6 inches (10 to 15 cm) from the heat source. Place patties on a broiler pan and broil for 5 to 6 minutes per side.

Tip

Freeze the cooked patties individually for a quick meal at a later date. They keep in the freezer for up to 3 months. To reheat, remove from freezer and let thaw in refrigerator. Place on a baking sheet and reheat in a 325°F (160°C) oven or toaster oven until warmed through.

Variation

Use white beans instead of red and these will look like chicken burgers.

Serving Ideas

Serve on whole wheat buns, with your favorite burger toppings. Other tasty toppings include red onion slices, goat cheese, sautéed mushrooms or mango salsa.

Skip the bun and serve each patty over a green salad.

Pecan Patties

Melinda Heidebrecht, Dietitian, Ontario

Looking at these
ingredients, it's hard to
believe that the end result
resembles a hamburger,
but it does — and it's
delicious!

Tip

Don't be concerned that the
pecan mixture is too thin.
When you drop it into the pan,
it firms up nicely into patties.

Serving Idea

Serve on whole-grain buns,
with your favorite hamburger
toppings. Serve Nutty and
Fruity Quinoa Salad with
Maple Vinaigrette (page 166)
on the side to perk up the
protein in the meal.

4	eggs	4
½ cup	finely chopped pecans	125 mL
½ cup	finely chopped onion	125 mL
⅓ cup	shredded Cheddar cheese	75 mL
½ cup	fine dry bread crumbs	125 mL
¼ tsp	salt	1 mL
¼ tsp	freshly ground black pepper	1 mL
2 tsp	canola oil, divided	10 mL

1. In a small bowl, whisk eggs for 20 to 30 seconds. In
another bowl, combine pecans, onion, cheese, bread
crumbs, salt and pepper. Stir in eggs until evenly
blended. Let batter rest for 10 minutes.

2. In a nonstick skillet, heat 1 tsp (5 mL) oil over
medium heat. For each patty, drop ⅓ cup (75 mL)
pecan mixture into the pan. Fry 3 patties at a time
for 2 to 3 minutes or until browned. Flip patties over
and fry for 2 to 3 minutes or until patties feel firm
and no liquid oozes from the sides. Repeat with the
remaining oil and patties.

Nutrients per serving

Calories	191
Fat	13.9 g
Saturated fat	3.2 g
Sodium	241 mg (10% DV)
Carbohydrate	9 g
Fiber	2 g (8% DV)
Protein	8 g
Calcium	88 mg (8% DV)
Iron	1.1 mg (8% DV)

High in: Vitamin B_{12}

Diabetes Food Choice Values:

½   Carbohydrate

1   Meat & Alternatives

2   Fats

Makes 4 servings

Lynn created this recipe one night when her girls were teenagers. To encourage them to try new foods, she held Experimental Food Night once a week, with the only stipulation that everyone had to try the dish. If they didn't like it, they could prepare a sandwich for themselves. Years later, both of her girls enjoy all kinds of foods and are always on the lookout for new things.

Tips

Adding the chopped mushroom stems improves the texture of the cheese mixture.

The cheese mixture also makes a great veggie dip.

Nutrients per serving

Calories	278
Fat	6.9 g
Saturated fat	2.3 g
Sodium	663 mg (28% DV)
Carbohydrate	39 g
Fiber	6 g (24% DV)
Protein	19 g
Calcium	148 mg (13% DV)
Iron	2.9 mg (21% DV)

Very high in: Magnesium, folate, riboflavin and niacin

High in: Zinc, vitamin A, vitamin B_6, vitamin B_{12} and thiamine

Diabetes Food Choice Values:

2 Carbohydrates

1½ Meat & Alternatives

Portobello Mushroom Burgers with Cheese Filling

Lynn Dowling, Ontario

- **Preheat barbecue grill to medium**
- **Food processor**

4	large portobello mushrooms	4
2 tsp	olive oil	10 mL
2	cloves garlic, minced	2
2 cups	tightly packed fresh spinach leaves	500 mL
2 tbsp	chopped fresh basil	30 mL
1 cup	2% cottage cheese	250 mL
¼ cup	freshly grated Parmesan cheese	60 mL
4	4-inch (10 cm) whole wheat pitas, split open	4
	Roasted red pepper slices (optional)	

1. Wipe mushroom caps with a damp paper towel and gently twist off stems. Coarsely chop stems and set aside. Using the edge of a spoon, gently scrape off and discard the dark gills from the caps.

2. Brush both sides of mushroom caps with oil and place on preheated grill. Grill, turning once, for 2 to 3 minutes per side or until lightly browned on both sides. Set aside.

3. In food processor, combine mushroom stems, garlic, spinach, basil, cottage cheese and Parmesan; process until uniformly smooth but not puréed.

4. Place 1 grilled mushroom cap, rounded side down, on a pita half and fill with one-quarter of the cheese mixture. Top with the other pita half. Garnish with roasted peppers (if using).

> Most of the sodium in this recipe comes from the pitas. Read the Nutrition Facts table and choose pitas with the lowest amount of sodium per serving.

Open-face stuffed marinated mushrooms offer a delicious lunch or brunch alternative. Frances's whole family enjoys this delicious vegetarian entrée. Her firefighter hubby says, "You don't even miss the meat!"

Tip

The gills are generally removed from portobello mushrooms, as their brown-black color darkens other foods, which is undesirable when you're making a dish you want to stay light in color, such as a cream soup. In this recipe, it's optional to remove them.

Nutrients per serving

Calories	185
Fat	9.9 g
Saturated fat	4.9 g
Sodium	305 mg (13% DV)
Carbohydrate	16 g
Fiber	2 g (8% DV)
Protein	9 g
Calcium	160 mg (15% DV)
Iron	1.5 mg (11% DV)

Very high in: Riboflavin
High in: Vitamin B$_{12}$ and niacin

Diabetes Food Choice Values:

$^{1}/_{2}$	Carbohydrate
1	Meat & Alternatives
1	Fat

Portobello Perfection

Frances Russell, Dietitian, Alberta

- **13- by 9-inch (33 by 23 cm) glass or ceramic baking dish, greased**

4	large portobello mushrooms	4
2 to 3	plum (Roma) tomatoes, sliced	2 to 3
$^{1}/_{3}$ cup	freshly grated Parmesan cheese	75 mL
Marinade		
2 tsp	minced garlic	10 mL
1 tbsp	lightly packed brown sugar	15 mL
$^{1}/_{2}$ tsp	freshly ground black pepper	2 mL
$^{1}/_{3}$ cup	balsamic vinegar	75 mL
$^{1}/_{3}$ cup	vegetable broth or water	75 mL
Cream Cheese Filling		
2 tsp	canola oil	10 mL
$^{1}/_{2}$ cup	finely chopped onion	125 mL
2 tsp	minced garlic	10 mL
1 tbsp	minced fresh thyme	15 mL
2 tbsp	vegetable broth or water	30 mL
$^{1}/_{2}$ cup	light cream cheese	125 mL

1. Wipe mushroom caps with a damp paper towel. Gently twist off stems and discard or save for another use. If desired, use the edge of a spoon to gently scrape off and discard the dark gills from the caps. Place mushroom caps, rounded side down, in prepared baking dish.

2. *Marinade:* In a small bowl, combine garlic, brown sugar, pepper, vinegar and broth.

3. Spoon marinade evenly over the center of each mushroom. Cover and refrigerate for at least 4 hours or overnight.

4. Remove mushrooms from refrigerator and let stand at room temperature for 30 minutes. Meanwhile, preheat oven to 400°F (200°C).

5. Uncover dish and bake mushrooms for 10 minutes.

6. *Filling:* Meanwhile, in a small skillet, heat oil over medium-high heat. Sauté onion for 3 to 4 minutes or until softened. Add garlic and thyme; sauté for 30 seconds. Add broth and deglaze the pan, scraping up any brown bits. Add cream cheese and stir until melted and smooth.

7. Fill the center of each mushroom with one-quarter of the filling. Top with tomatoes and sprinkle with Parmesan. Bake for 10 minutes or until filling is heated through. Broil for 2 minutes or until cheese is browned.

Portobello mushrooms are large cremini mushrooms. They are a darker brown than their smaller, less mature siblings. Select firm, plump, fresh-looking portobellos; avoid those that look limp, shriveled or dried on the tops or edges. To store, remove them from packaging and place on a clean plate, making sure they don't overlap, for good air circulation. Cover with a dry absorbent towel and refrigerate for up to 5 days. Before use, brush off any debris with a damp paper towel or rinse the mushrooms quickly under cool water and dry them; do not soak them in water.

Variation

Use a flavored cream cheese, such as herb and garlic.

Serving Idea

Serve with Tofu Vegetable Pilaf (page 291) and Steamed Tarragon Carrots (page 299) for a sumptuous vegetarian feast.

Vegetarian Main Courses   **265**

The bright green veggies that adorn this pizza give it its name.

Tip

If you're in a rush, use a purchased parbaked pizza shell instead of fresh dough. Chances are good, however, that the sodium will be much higher in the store-bought crust. Look for one with the lowest % DV in sodium.

Variations

Replace half the ricotta with feta cheese.

Use half radicchio and half arugula.

Nutrients per serving

Calories	233
Fat	5.8 g
Saturated fat	1.9 g
Sodium	345 mg (14% DV)
Carbohydrate	36 g
Fiber	6 g (24% DV)
Protein	12 g
Calcium	189 mg (17% DV)
Iron	2.6 mg (19% DV)

Very high in: Magnesium, vitamin A and folate

High in: Iron, zinc, vitamin C, thiamine, riboflavin and niacin

Diabetes Food Choice Values:

1½ Carbohydrates

1 Meat & Alternatives

Emerald Summer Pizza

Honey Bloomberg, Dietitian, Ontario

- **Preheat oven to 400°F (200°C)**
- **12-inch (30 cm) pizza pan, lightly greased**

½	recipe Big-Batch Whole Wheat Pizza Dough (see recipe, opposite)	½
3 tbsp	basil pesto	45 mL
2 cups	chopped kale	500 mL
½ cup	cooked fresh or drained thawed frozen green peas	125 mL
1 cup	light ricotta cheese	250 mL
¾ cup	thinly sliced onion	175 mL
½ tsp	freshly ground black pepper	2 mL
1 cup	torn arugula leaves	250 mL

1. Roll out dough to a 12-inch (30 cm) diameter and fit into prepared pan. Spread pesto evenly over crust to within ½ inch (1 cm) of edge. Arrange kale and peas evenly over pesto. Drop ricotta by spoonfuls over top and spread slightly. Sprinkle with onion and pepper.

2. Bake in preheated oven for 14 to 16 minutes or until cheese has spread slightly, onions are lightly browned and crust is golden and crisp. Remove from oven and arrange arugula over pizza.

> Kale looks like long leaves of curly cabbage and is, indeed, a member of the cabbage family. This dark green vegetable is wonderful in salads and as a pizza topping.

Big-Batch Whole Wheat Pizza Dough

Eileen Campbell, Ontario

- **Electric mixer with dough hook**

2	packages (each ¼ oz/7 g) instant yeast	2
2 cups	whole wheat flour	500 mL
1 cup	all-purpose flour	250 mL
1 tsp	salt	5 mL
½ tsp	granulated sugar	2 mL
1½ cups	lukewarm water	375 mL
½ tsp	olive oil	2 mL

1. In the mixer bowl, combine yeast, whole wheat flour, all-purpose flour, salt and sugar. Attach dough hook and mixer bowl to mixer. With mixer running on low speed, gradually add water; knead until dough is smooth and elastic, about 10 minutes. Turn mixer off and pour oil down side of bowl. Set to low speed for 15 seconds to coat inside of bowl and cover dough lightly with oil. Remove mixer bowl and cover loosely with plastic wrap.

2. Let rise in a warm, draft-free place until doubled in bulk, about 2 hours.

3. Punch down dough and cut in half to make two balls. Place each ball in an airtight freezer bag and store for up to 3 months, or roll out for immediate usage.

4. To roll out, place dough ball on a floured work surface and form into a circle. Roll out until dough reaches a 12- to 15-inch (30 to 38 cm) diameter. Pierce dough with a fork before adding toppings.

Makes enough dough for two 12- to 15-inch (30 to 38 cm) pizza crusts

Serving size: ⅙ pizza crust

A homemade crust, when you have time to prepare it, will make a huge difference to the taste of your pizza and provides added nutrition.

Tip

If you do not have an electric mixer with a dough hook, you can use a food processor.

Nutrients per serving

Calories	129
Fat	0.8 g
Saturated fat	0.1 g
Sodium	194 mg (8% DV)
Carbohydrate	27 g
Fiber	4 g (16% DV)
Protein	5 g
Calcium	12 mg (1% DV)
Iron	1.7 mg (12% DV)

Very high in: Folate
High in: Magnesium, thiamine and niacin

Diabetes Food Choice Values:
1½ Carbohydrates

Some of Amanda's meat-loving friends have made this dish their go-to taco recipe, as it's faster and cheaper and has easier cleanup than meat tacos.

Tips

This dish is a breeze to prepare if one person gets the lentil mixture ready and sets the table while another chops the veggies and shreds the cheese.

You can use 1 can (19 oz/ 540 mL) lentils, drained and rinsed, instead of cooked lentils.

Variation

To make a taco salad, spoon the lentil filling on top of a bed of lettuce and tomato, then sprinkle with cheese and garnish with baked tortilla chips.

Quick and Easy Lentil Tacos

Amanda Beales, Dietitian, Ontario

1½ cups	cooked green lentils (see page 257)	375 mL
2 tbsp	finely minced red onion	30 mL
2 tbsp	finely minced red bell pepper	30 mL
¼ cup	salsa	60 mL
4	taco shells	4
¾ cup	finely shredded romaine or iceberg lettuce	175 mL
¾ cup	finely diced plum (Roma) tomatoes	175 mL
½ cup	shredded Cheddar or light Cheddar cheese	125 mL
½ cup	light sour cream (optional)	125 mL
1	avocado, cubed (optional)	1
½ cup	sliced black olives (optional)	125 mL

1. In a medium saucepan, over medium heat, combine lentils, onion, red pepper and salsa; cook, stirring often, for 3 to 4 minutes or until bubbling and hot.

2. Fill each taco shell with one-fourth of the lentil mixture, lettuce, tomatoes and cheese. If desired, top with sour cream, avocado and olives.

Nutrients per serving

Calories	219
Fat	8.0 g
Saturated fat	3.5 g
Sodium	238 mg (10% DV)
Carbohydrate	27 g
Fiber	5 g (20% DV)
Protein	12 g
Calcium	149 mg (14% DV)
Iron	3.2 mg (23% DV)

Very high in: Folate
High in: Magnesium, zinc, vitamin A and thiamine

Diabetes Food Choice Values:

1	Carbohydrate
1	Meat & Alternatives
½	Fat

Makes 8 servings

Enchiladas are traditionally made with chicken, but this meatless option is just as tasty and has more fiber. The rich, creamy sauce will make these a favorite.

Tip

The bulk of the sodium in this recipe comes from the tortillas, which vary considerably in sodium content. Look for those with the lowest % DV for sodium per serving.

Variations

Use canned pinto or kidney beans instead of black beans.

Add 1 finely chopped jalapeño pepper while sautéing the red peppers and onion.

Use flavored whole wheat tortillas, such as sun-dried tomato or pesto.

Nutrients per serving

Calories	289
Fat	11.4 g
Saturated fat	4.2 g
Sodium	706 mg (29% DV)
Carbohydrate	36 g
Fiber	7 g (28% DV)
Protein	12 g
Calcium	180 mg (16% DV)
Iron	2.2 mg (16% DV)

Very high in: Vitamin C and folate

High in: Magnesium, zinc, vitamin A, thiamine and niacin

Diabetes Food Choice Values:
1½ Carbohydrates
1 Meat & Alternatives
1 Fat

Black Bean and Corn Enchiladas

Heather Church, Dietitian, Nova Scotia

- Preheat oven to 400°F (200°C)
- 13- by 9-inch (33 by 23 cm) glass baking dish, greased

1 tsp	canola oil	5 mL
1½ cups	chopped red bell peppers	375 mL
1 cup	chopped onion	250 mL
2	cloves garlic, minced	2
2	plum (Roma) tomatoes, coarsely chopped	2
1	can (19 oz/540 mL) black beans, drained and rinsed	1
½ cup	thawed frozen corn kernels	125 mL
1 tsp	chili powder	5 mL
¼ tsp	freshly ground black pepper	1 mL
8	8-inch (20 cm) whole wheat flour tortillas	8
2 tbsp	non-hydrogenated margarine	30 mL
2 tbsp	all-purpose flour	30 mL
1 cup	vegetable broth	250 mL
½ cup	light sour cream	125 mL
1	can (4½ oz/128 mL) chopped mild green chiles	1
1 cup	shredded Monterey Jack or Cheddar cheese	250 mL

1. In a nonstick skillet, heat oil over medium heat. Sauté red peppers and onion for 4 to 5 minutes or until softened. Add garlic and sauté for 30 seconds. Stir in tomatoes, beans, corn, chili powder and pepper.

2. Divide bean mixture evenly among tortillas. Roll up burrito-style and place seam side down in prepared baking dish. Set aside.

3. In a small saucepan, melt margarine over medium heat. Whisk in flour and sauté for 30 seconds. Gradually whisk in broth and bring to a boil, whisking. Boil, whisking often, for 2 to 3 minutes or until thick. Remove from heat and stir in sour cream and chiles. Pour sauce over tortillas and sprinkle with cheese.

4. Bake in preheated oven for 20 minutes or until cheese is melted and sauce is bubbling.

Three Sisters Succotash

Dean Simmons, Dietitian, British Columbia

Dean Simmons, Dietitian, British Columbia

Makes 6 to 8 servings

✔ **Kid Approved**

This recipe is based on the "three sisters" — squash, corn and beans — which were important agricultural crops among the First Nations people living around the Great Lakes. It's a great fall dish that can serve as a vegetarian entrée.

Tips

Use 2 cups (500 mL) thawed frozen lima beans instead of canned.

Ask young kids to scoop the seeds out of the squash with a spoon. Older children can help by shredding the cheese and toasting the sunflower seeds in a toaster oven or dry skillet.

2 tbsp	canola or olive oil	30 mL
½	onion, finely chopped	½
3	cloves garlic, minced	3
1	can (19 oz/540 mL) baby lima beans, drained and rinsed	1
2 cups	cubed butternut or other winter squash (½-inch/1 cm cubes)	500 mL
2 cups	frozen corn kernels, thawed	500 mL
1 cup	vegetable broth	250 mL
1 tsp	dried oregano	5 mL
1 tsp	dried basil	5 mL
½ tsp	paprika	2 mL
½ tsp	salt	2 mL
½ tsp	freshly ground black pepper	2 mL
1 cup	shredded Cheddar cheese	250 mL
¾ cup	toasted sunflower seeds (see page 139)	175 mL

1. In a large skillet, heat oil over medium heat. Sauté onion for 3 to 4 minutes or until softened. Add garlic and sauté for 30 seconds.

2. Stir in lima beans, squash, corn, broth, oregano, basil, paprika, salt and pepper; bring to a boil. Reduce heat to low, cover with a tight-fitting lid and simmer for 10 to 15 minutes, stirring occasionally, or until squash is tender. If liquid remains, remove lid and boil until liquid is evaporated.

3. Sprinkle with cheese and sunflower seeds. Let stand for about 5 minutes or until cheese starts to melt.

Nutrients per serving

Calories	255
Fat	15.3 g
Saturated fat	4.0 g
Sodium	455 mg (19% DV)
Carbohydrate	23 g
Fiber	5 g (20% DV)
Protein	10 g
Calcium	158 mg (14% DV)
Iron	2.5 mg (18% DV)

Very high in: Magnesium, vitamin A, folate and thiamine

High in: Zinc, vitamin B_6 and niacin

Diabetes Food Choice Values:

1	Carbohydrate
1	Meat & Alternatives
2	Fats

Plenty of pleasant flavors are found in this delicious curry. Serve over brown basmati rice.

Tips

Prepare this dish on the weekend, transfer to airtight containers and let cool. Cover and refrigerate for up to 3 days and reheat for meals during the week.

You can use 1 can (19 oz/ 540 mL) chickpeas, drained and rinsed, instead of cooked chickpeas.

Use 1 cup (250 mL) drained thawed frozen chopped mango instead of fresh.

Nutrients per serving

Calories	209
Fat	4.9 g
Saturated fat	2.1 g
Sodium	295 mg (12% DV)
Carbohydrate	34 g
Fiber	5 g (20% DV)
Protein	9 g
Calcium	177 mg (16% DV)
Iron	2.6 mg (19% DV)

Very high in: Vitamin A, vitamin C and folate

High in: Magnesium, zinc and vitamin B_6

Diabetes Food Choice Values:
1½ Carbohydrates
1   Fat

Sweet Potato and Chickpea Curry

Heather McColl, Dietitian, British Columbia

1½ tsp	canola oil	7 mL
1 to 2	jalapeño peppers, seeded and minced	1 to 2
1½ cups	chopped red bell peppers	375 mL
1 cup	chopped onion	250 mL
4	cloves garlic, minced	4
1 tbsp	minced gingerroot	15 mL
1	can (19 oz/540 mL) whole tomatoes, with juice	1
2½ cups	cooked chickpeas (see page 257)	625 mL
2 cups	cubed peeled sweet potatoes (½-inch/1 cm cubes)	500 mL
1 tsp	ground cumin	5 mL
1 tsp	garam masala	5 mL
½ tsp	ground coriander	2 mL
½ tsp	salt	2 mL
1	mango, finely chopped	1
1 cup	light coconut milk	250 mL
	Freshly ground black pepper	
2 cups	low-fat plain yogurt	500 mL
¼ cup	finely chopped fresh cilantro	60 mL

1. In a large pot, heat oil over medium heat. Sauté jalapeño(s) to taste, red peppers and onion for 4 to 5 minutes or until softened. Add garlic and ginger; sauté for 30 seconds.

2. Stir in tomatoes with juice, chickpeas, sweet potatoes, cumin, garam masala, coriander and salt; increase heat to high and bring to a boil, stirring occasionally. Reduce heat and simmer, stirring occasionally, for about 20 minutes or until sweet potatoes are fork-tender.

3. Gently stir in mango and coconut milk; simmer for 5 to 10 minutes or until thickened. Season to taste with pepper. Serve topped with yogurt and sprinkled with cilantro.

> Chickpeas are popular in many world cuisines, including Italian, Spanish, Indian, Moroccan, Turkish and, of course, Canadian.

A rainbow of colors provides a variety of nutrients in this flavorful vegan dish.

Tip

Chop all the vegetables (except the eggplant) the night before you make this dish to make prep time easier. Store chopped vegetables in the refrigerator.

Nutrients per serving

Calories	299
Fat	5.3 g
Saturated fat	0.5 g
Sodium	202 mg (8% DV)
Carbohydrate	57 g
Fiber	8 g (32% DV)
Protein	9 g
Calcium	102 mg (9% DV)
Iron	2.8 mg (20% DV)

Very high in: Magnesium, vitamin A, vitamin C, vitamin B$_6$ and folate

High in: Thiamine and niacin

Diabetes Food Choice Values:

3   Carbohydrates

1   Fat

Moroccan Vegetable Curry

Jennifer Miller, Dietitian, Saskatchewan

2 tbsp	canola oil	30 mL
1½ cups	chopped onions	375 mL
4	cloves garlic, minced	4
2 tbsp	curry powder	30 mL
2 tsp	ground cinnamon	10 mL
1 tsp	ground turmeric	5 mL
1 tsp	cayenne pepper	5 mL
½ cup	vegetable broth or water (approx.)	125 mL
1	eggplant, peeled and cut into ¾-inch (2 cm) cubes (6 to 8 cups/1.5 to 2 L)	1
2 cups	cubed peeled sweet potatoes (½-inch/1 cm cubes)	500 mL
2 cups	chopped carrots	500 mL
1½ cups	chopped yellow bell peppers	375 mL
1½ cups	chopped red bell peppers	375 mL
1	can (19 oz/ 540 mL) chickpeas, drained and rinsed	1
2 cups	diced zucchini	500 mL
¼ cup	raisins	60 mL
1 cup	unsweetened orange juice	250 mL
1	package (10 oz/300 g) frozen chopped spinach, thawed and drained	1
2 cups	couscous	500 mL
2 cups	boiling water	500 mL
¼ cup	sliced almonds	60 mL
	Grated zest and juice of ½ lemon	

1. In a large Dutch oven, heat oil over medium heat. Sauté onions for 3 to 4 minutes or until softened. Add garlic, curry powder, cinnamon, turmeric and cayenne; sauté for 1 minute or until spices are fragrant.

2. Add broth and deglaze the pan, scraping up any brown bits. Add eggplant, sweet potatoes, carrots, yellow peppers and red peppers; sauté for 5 minutes. If vegetables begin to stick to the pan, add more broth.

3. Stir in chickpeas, zucchini, raisins and orange juice; bring to a boil. Reduce heat to low, cover and simmer for about 20 minutes or until sweet potatoes are fork-tender. Stir in spinach, cover and simmer for 5 minutes or until heated through

4. Meanwhile, place couscous in a large, shallow bowl. Stir in boiling water. Cover and let stand for 5 minutes or until liquid is absorbed. Fluff with a fork.

5. Spoon vegetable mixture over couscous and garnish with almonds, lemon zest and lemon juice.

> Couscous, a pasta-like product made from semolina flour, looks like tiny, irregularly shaped yellow pearls. It requires no cooking, but needs only to be rehydrated with an equal amount of water. (Israeli couscous, which is much larger than traditional couscous, does require cooking.)

Variations

Replace the chickpeas with black beans or kidney beans.

Use green bell peppers instead of red or yellow.

✔ **Kid Approved**

Donna's entire family
enjoys this dish,
whether she serves it
hot, lukewarm or cold.
Donna's husband likes
it with salsa.

Tip

Serve any leftovers for
breakfast the next day,
warmed up and topped with
a poached egg.

Gluten-Free Potato Kugel

Donna Ellah, Quebec

- **Preheat oven to 375°F (190°C)**
- **13- by 9-inch (33 by 23 cm) glass baking dish**

6	large Yukon gold potatoes, shredded (about 8 cups/2 L)	6
2	large carrots, shredded (about 2 cups/500 mL)	2
1	large onion, shredded	1
2	cloves garlic, minced	2
1/4 cup	rice bread crumbs	60 mL
1 tsp	salt	5 mL
1 tsp	freshly ground black pepper	5 mL
2	eggs, lightly beaten	2
1/4 cup	canola oil	60 mL
2 cups	shredded Cheddar cheese	500 mL

1. Place potatoes, carrots and onion in a colander and squeeze to drain off excess water. Place in a large bowl and stir to evenly combine.

2. In a small bowl, combine garlic, bread crumbs, salt, pepper, eggs and oil. Pour over vegetables and stir to combine. Pour into prepared pan (do not pat down).

3. Cover with foil and bake in preheated oven for 45 minutes or until vegetables are soft and a tester inserted in the center comes out hot. Uncover, sprinkle with cheese and bake for 3 to 4 minutes or until cheese is melted and bubbly.

Nutrients per serving

Calories	270
Fat	14.1 g
Saturated fat	5.5 g
Sodium	400 mg (17% DV)
Carbohydrate	27 g
Fiber	3 g (12% DV)
Protein	10 g
Calcium	190 mg (17% DV)
Iron	1.4 mg (10% DV)

Very high in: Vitamin A

High in: Magnesium, vitamin B$_6$, vitamin B$_{12}$ and niacin

Diabetes Food Choice Values:

1½ Carbohydrates

1 Meat & Alternatives

2 Fats

Makes 8 servings

This loaf is made from grains, nuts and seeds, yet its texture resembles that of meatloaf.

Serving Idea

Serve topped with your favorite tomato sauce, along with Steamed Tarragon Carrots (page 299) and sautéed snow peas.

Nutrients per serving

Calories	279
Fat	16.7 g
Saturated fat	7.2 g
Sodium	355 mg (15% DV)
Carbohydrate	19 g
Fiber	5 g (20% DV)
Protein	15 g
Calcium	243 mg (22% DV)
Iron	2.1 mg (15% DV)

Very high in: Magnesium, zinc and thiamine

High in: Vitamin A, folate, vitamin B$_{12}$, riboflavin and niacin

Diabetes Food Choice Values:

1	Carbohydrate
1½	Meat & Alternatives
2	Fats

Barley Terrine

Danielle Lamontagne, Dietitian, Québec

- **Preheat oven to 350°F (180°C)**
- **9- by 5-inch (23 by 12.5 cm) metal loaf pan, greased**

⅔ cup	pot barley	150 mL
3	eggs, lightly beaten	3
2 cups	shredded Cheddar cheese	500 mL
1 cup	chopped onion	250 mL
⅔ cup	finely diced celery	150 mL
½ cup	wheat germ	125 mL
⅓ cup	ground sunflower seeds	75 mL
¼ cup	finely chopped walnuts	60 mL
¼ cup	chopped fresh parsley	60 mL
½ tsp	dried thyme	2 mL
½ tsp	salt	2 mL
½ tsp	freshly ground black pepper	2 mL

1. In a medium saucepan, bring 1¾ cups (425 mL) water to a boil over high heat. Stir in barley. Reduce heat to low, cover and simmer for 1 hour or until tender. Drain and discard any excess water. Transfer barley to a large bowl and let cool slightly.

2. Add eggs, cheese, onion, celery, wheat germ, sunflower seeds, walnuts, parsley, thyme, salt and pepper to barley and stir to form a uniform mixture. Press gently into prepared loaf pan.

3. Bake in preheated oven for 50 minutes or until firm to the touch. Remove and let stand for 10 minutes. Unmold onto a cutting board and cut into 8 slices.

> Pot barley (also called Scotch barley) has only the outermost hull and bran removed during processing, while pearl barley also has the endosperm removed. Both are widely available for cooking. Pot barley takes about an hour to cook; pearl barley takes about 35 minutes. You can use pearl barley in this recipe if you adjust the cooking time in step 1 accordingly.

Makes 10 servings

This delicious one-pot meal simmers away in the slow cooker while you go on with your day.

Tip

Butternut squash can be difficult to peel. To make the task easier, first cut the squash in half crosswise, to create two flat surfaces. Place each squash half on its flat surface and use a sharp utility knife to remove the tough peel.

Variations

Add a 4-inch (10 cm) cinnamon stick to the squash mixture in step 1. Discard before serving.

Use dried cranberries or chopped dates instead of raisins.

Serving Idea

Serve with a crisp green salad and a glass of milk for a complete meal.

Nutrients per serving

Calories	230
Fat	3.8 g
Saturated fat	0.5 g
Sodium	346 mg (14% DV)
Carbohydrate	44 g
Fiber	5 g (20% DV)
Protein	8 g
Calcium	65 mg (6% DV)
Iron	2.4 mg (17% DV)

Very high in: Vitamin A and folate

High in: Magnesium

Diabetes Food Choice Values:

2   Carbohydrates
½   Meat & Alternatives
½   Fat

Slow Cooker Squash Couscous

Cheryl Fisher, Dietitian, Alberta

● **Minimum 5-quart slow cooker**

1	butternut squash (about 1½ lbs/750 g)	1
3 cups	cooked or rinsed drained canned chickpeas	750 mL
2 cups	chopped yellow summer squash or zucchini	500 mL
½ cup	thinly sliced onion	125 mL
½ cup	raisins	125 mL
2 tbsp	granulated sugar	30 mL
2 tsp	ground ginger	10 mL
½ tsp	ground turmeric	2 mL
½ tsp	freshly ground black pepper	2 mL
4 cups	reduced-sodium vegetable broth	1 L
2 tbsp	non-hydrogenated margarine	30 mL
1 cup	couscous	250 mL
¼ cup	coarsely chopped fresh parsley	60 mL

1. Peel butternut squash and cut the flesh into 1-inch (2.5 cm) cubes; you should have 4 to 5 cups (1 to 1.25 L) cubed squash.

2. In slow cooker stoneware, combine butternut squash, chickpeas, summer squash, onion, raisins, sugar, ginger, turmeric, pepper, broth and margarine. Cover and cook on Low for 4 to 5 hours or until vegetables are tender.

3. Uncover, increase heat to High and cook for 15 minutes or until liquid is reduced slightly. Using a slotted spoon, remove vegetable mixture to a large bowl. Cover and keep warm.

4. Place couscous in a large bowl and pour in 1 cup (250 mL) of the hot broth from the slow cooker. Cover with plastic wrap and let stand for 5 to 10 minutes or until couscous is plumped. Fluff with a fork.

5. Spoon vegetable mixture over couscous and ladle the remaining broth over top. Sprinkle with parsley.

Makes 6 servings

✔ **Kid Approved**

Kids love the taste and texture of this yummy stir-fry.

Tips

Stir-fries cook quickly, so be sure to have all your ingredients ready before starting.

This recipe works fine without the sesame oil or hoisin sauce, but they do add a nice flavor punch.

Variations

Substitute other vegetables, such as snow peas, bell peppers or green beans, adjusting the cooking time accordingly.

To increase the protein, add sautéed tofu or 2 to 3 beaten eggs in step 3. Or, if you're not a strict vegetarian, add shredded leftover chicken, turkey or beef.

Nutrients per serving

Calories	150
Fat	8.9 g
Saturated fat	1.1 g
Sodium	301 mg (13% DV)
Carbohydrate	16 g
Fiber	3 g (12% DV)
Protein	4 g
Calcium	33 mg (3% DV)
Iron	1.6 mg (11% DV)

Very high in: Vitamin C
High in: Folate

Diabetes Food Choice Values:
½ Carbohydrate
2 Fats

Chock Full of Veggies Chow Mein

Jennifer Lactin, British Columbia

1 tbsp	canola oil, divided	15 mL
2 tsp	sesame oil, divided	10 mL
2 cups	bite-size broccoli florets	500 mL
2 cups	bite-size cauliflower florets	500 mL
2 cups	sliced mushrooms	500 mL
1 cup	thinly sliced celery	250 mL
½ cup	thinly sliced onion	125 mL
2 tbsp	thinly sliced gingerroot	30 mL
1 tbsp	hoisin sauce	15 mL
1 tbsp	reduced-sodium soy sauce	15 mL
2 cups	fried chow mein noodles	500 mL
½ cup	reduced-sodium vegetable broth	125 mL
½ tsp	freshly ground black pepper	2 mL
2 to 3	drops hot pepper sauce (or to taste)	2 to 3

1. Heat a wok or large skillet over medium-high heat. Add 2 tsp (10 mL) canola oil and 1 tsp (5 mL) sesame oil, swirl to coat the surface and heat until hot but not smoking. Stir-fry broccoli and cauliflower for 7 to 8 minutes or until cauliflower is partly caramelized and broccoli is softened. Transfer to a large bowl.

2. Add the remaining canola oil and sesame oil to the wok and swirl to coat the surface; heat until hot but not smoking. Add mushrooms, celery, onion and ginger; stir-fry for 3 to 4 minutes or until softened. Return broccoli and cauliflower to the wok and stir in hoisin sauce and soy sauce.

3. Stir in noodles, broth, black pepper and hot pepper sauce; cover and boil, stirring once, for 2 to 3 minutes or until liquid is absorbed.

Makes 12 cups (3 L)

Serving size: ½ cup (125 mL)

✔ Kid Approved

This Italian master sauce makes a great base for many dishes. There are several recipes in this book that call for tomato sauce. You could buy a commercial product, but think how much more satisfying it is to have your own special sauce, right there in the freezer.

Tips

If you prefer a thicker sauce, purée it slightly.

Make a batch on the weekend. Transfer to airtight containers and keep some in the fridge for use during the week. Freeze the rest in 2-cup (500 mL) or 3-cup (750 mL) portions for later use.

Nutrients per serving

Calories	46
Fat	1.9 g
Saturated fat	0.3 g
Sodium	268 mg (11% DV)
Carbohydrate	7 g
Fiber	1 g (4% DV)
Protein	1 g
Calcium	48 mg (4% DV)
Iron	1.4 mg (10% DV)

High in: Vitamin C

Diabetes Food Choice Values:
½   Fat

Big-Batch Italian Tomato Master Sauce

Eileen Campbell, Ontario

● **Large (minimum 6-quart) slow cooker**

3 tbsp	olive oil	45 mL
6	cloves garlic, minced	6
1	large Spanish onion, finely diced	1
1 tsp	salt, divided	5 mL
4	cans (each 28 oz/796 mL) plum tomatoes, with juice, chopped	4
4	sprigs fresh basil, divided	4
1 tsp	dried oregano	5 mL
½ tsp	freshly ground black pepper	2 mL
	Granulated sugar (optional)	

1. In a large skillet, heat oil over medium-high heat. Add garlic and onion and season lightly with some of the salt. Sauté for 5 minutes or until lightly browned.

2. Transfer sautéed vegetables to slow cooker stoneware. Stir in tomatoes with juice, 3 of the basil sprigs, oregano, pepper and the remaining salt. Cover and cook on Low for 8 hours or until flavor is developed. If sauce is thin, near the end of the cooking time increase to High and keep lid slightly open until sauce thickens. Discard basil sprigs.

3. Remove leaves from remaining basil sprig, discarding stems; chop leaves and stir into sauce. Season with additional salt and pepper, if desired. Add sugar to taste if sauce is too tart.

Stovetop Method

If you don't have a slow cooker, you can still make this sauce by adjusting the method slightly. Sauté the onions and garlic in a large pot, then add all of the other ingredients and bring to a boil. Reduce heat to low, cover and simmer, stirring occasionally, for 4 hours until flavor is developed.

Makes 8 cups (2 L)

Serving size: 1 cup (250 mL)

This chunky sauce works best over shell, penne, rigatoni or other tubular pasta. Add a pinch of hot pepper flakes and some grated Parmesan cheese on top.

Tips

If the eggplant starts to stick when cooking in step 1, stir in 1 to 2 tbsp (15 to 30 mL) water, vegetable broth or wine.

This sauce freezes well. Transfer to airtight containers, let cool, cover and freeze for up to 3 months. Let thaw in the refrigerator or defrost in the microwave before reheating.

Nutrients per serving

Calories	125
Fat	6.0 g
Saturated fat	0.5 g
Sodium	269 mg (11% DV)
Carbohydrate	17 g
Fiber	4 g (16% DV)
Protein	3 g
Calcium	86 mg (8% DV)
Iron	2.5 mg (18% DV)

Very high in: Vitamin C

High in: Magnesium and vitamin B_6

Diabetes Food Choice Values:

½ Carbohydrate

1 Fat

Eggplant Sauce

Francy Pillo-Blocka, Dietitian, Ontario

3 tbsp	canola oil, divided	45 mL
1	eggplant, peeled and cut into 1-inch (2.5 cm) cubes (about 6 cups/1.5 L)	1
1 cup	chopped onion	250 mL
6	cloves garlic, minced	6
1 cup	dry white wine	250 mL
2	cans (each 28 oz/796 mL) whole tomatoes, with juice	2
8	oil-packed sun-dried tomato slices, drained, rinsed, patted dry and chopped	8
2 tsp	dried basil	10 mL
½ cup	coarsely chopped fresh basil	125 mL
	Freshly ground black pepper	

1. In a large saucepan, heat 2 tbsp (30 mL) oil over medium-high heat. Add eggplant, cover and cook, stirring occasionally, for 5 to 7 minutes or until thoroughly softened. Using a slotted spoon, transfer eggplant to a medium bowl.

2. Return pan to medium heat and add the remaining oil. Sauté onion for 3 to 4 minutes or until softened. Add garlic and sauté for 30 seconds. Add wine and deglaze the pan, scraping up any brown bits. Add eggplant, whole tomatoes with juice, sun-dried tomatoes and dried basil; bring to a boil, stirring occasionally. Reduce heat and simmer, stirring occasionally, for 50 minutes or until slightly thickened. Stir in fresh basil and simmer for 10 minutes. Season to taste with pepper.

Roasting vegetables brings out deep, rich color and flavor. Add the nutty taste of whole wheat pasta, the sweetness of fresh basil and a hint of salt from the Parmesan, and this recipe will please your whole palate.

Tips

Cutting all the vegetables to the same size ensures that they will cook evenly.

Serve with grilled vegetarian sausage to add protein to this meal.

Nutrients per serving

Calories	313
Fat	9.2 g
Saturated fat	1.8 g
Sodium	249 mg (10% DV)
Carbohydrate	52 g
Fiber	7 g (28% DV)
Protein	11 g
Calcium	126 mg (11% DV)
Iron	2.6 mg (19% DV)

Very high in: Magnesium, vitamin A, vitamin C and folate

High in: Zinc, vitamin B_6, thiamine and niacin

Diabetes Food Choice Values:

2½ Carbohydrates
2 Fats

Roasted Vegetable Pasta

Heather McColl, Dietitian, British Columbia

- **Preheat oven to 425°F (220°C)**
- **Rimmed baking sheet, lightly greased**

6	cloves garlic, unpeeled	6
4 tbsp	extra virgin olive oil, divided	60 mL
3 tbsp	balsamic vinegar	45 mL
½ tsp	freshly ground black pepper	2 mL
Pinch	salt	Pinch
1	red bell pepper, cut into ½-inch (1 cm) pieces	1
1	yellow bell pepper, cut into ½-inch (1 cm) pieces	1
1	onion, cut into ½-inch (1 cm) pieces	1
3 cups	cubed butternut squash (½-inch/1 cm cubes)	750 mL
2 cups	eggplant (unpeeled), cut into ½-inch (1 cm) pieces	500 mL
2 cups	chopped asparagus (½-inch/1 cm pieces)	500 mL
12 oz	whole wheat penne pasta	375 g
4	tomatoes, seeded and diced	4
¾ cup	lightly packed coarsely chopped fresh basil	175 mL
⅓ cup	freshly grated Parmesan cheese	75 mL

1. Cut the tip off the top of the garlic cloves. Place on a small piece of foil and drizzle with ½ tsp (2 mL) oil. Scrunch to enclose garlic in foil. Roast in preheated oven for 20 minutes or until soft. Remove from oven, leaving oven on, and let cool slightly. Squeeze garlic from skins, discarding skins; coarsely chop garlic and place in a small bowl. Whisk in vinegar, 2½ tbsp (37 mL) oil, pepper and salt; set aside.

2. In a large bowl, toss red pepper, yellow pepper, onion, squash and eggplant with 1 tbsp (15 mL) oil. Spread vegetables on prepared baking sheet. Roast on upper rack of oven, stirring occasionally, for 15 to 20 minutes or until almost tender.

3. In a small bowl, toss asparagus with the remaining oil. Add asparagus to baking sheet and bake for about 10 minutes or until vegetables are tender and lightly browned.

4. Meanwhile, in a large pot of boiling salted water, cook pasta according to package directions until al dente. Drain, reserving $\frac{1}{4}$ cup (60 mL) of the cooking liquid.

5. Transfer drained pasta to a large serving bowl and toss with the reserved cooking liquid. Add roasted vegetables, tomatoes, basil and roasted garlic mixture; toss well to combine. Sprinkle with Parmesan. Serve hot or cover and refrigerate for up to 24 hours (let stand at room temperature for 1 hour before serving).

Eggplants are botanically a fruit, but are most often used as a vegetable. There are dozens of varieties, ranging in size, shape and color. You can remove the peel or leave it on; it darkens during cooking and often falls off, so many cooks opt to remove it. It is also common practice to salt eggplant and let it set in a colander to remove some bitterness; this is no longer necessary, thanks to improvements in growing methods. Eggplants do have a spongy texture, though, and therefore absorb a lot of fat; salting before use may help to reduce the amount of oil absorbed.

Variations

Use zucchini instead of butternut squash.

If you like heat, add 1 tbsp (15 mL) chopped jalapeño pepper to the roasted vegetables in step 2, or add 1 tsp (5 mL) hot pepper flakes with the roasted garlic mixture in step 5.

Replace half the basil with coarsely chopped fresh oregano.

✔ **Kid Approved**

In this recipe, cashew cream replaces the whipping cream often used in cream sauces, retaining the rich texture and adding a nutty flavor that goes perfectly with whole wheat pasta.

Tips

Once the cream starts to thicken in step 3, it thickens quickly. Be sure to stir while it's simmering so the mixture does not burn.

This is a delicious way to introduce nuts other than peanuts to young children. They love the sound of the nuts whirling in the food processor!

Variation

Toss in cooked vegetables with the pasta and cheese.

Nutrients per serving

Calories	325
Fat	10.8 g
Saturated fat	2.6 g
Sodium	334 mg (14% DV)
Carbohydrate	48 g
Fiber	5 g (20% DV)
Protein	14 g
Calcium	106 mg (10% DV)
Iron	2.8 mg (20% DV)

Very high in: Magnesium and zinc

High in: Thiamine and niacin

Diabetes Food Choice Values:
3 Carbohydrates
½ Meat & Alternatives
1½ Fats

Fettuccini with Cashew Cream

Rory Hornstein, Dietitian, Alberta

● **Food processor**

8 oz	whole wheat fettuccine	250 g
½ cup	unsalted roasted cashews	125 mL
	Vegetable cooking spray	
3	cloves garlic, minced	3
¼ cup	freshly grated Parmesan cheese	60 mL
¼ tsp	freshly ground black pepper	1 mL
Pinch	salt	Pinch

1. In a large pot of boiling salted water, cook fettuccine according to package directions until al dente. Drain and set aside.

2. Meanwhile, in food processor, process cashews for about 2 minutes, scraping bowl once, until nuts turn to paste. With the motor running, through the feed tube, gradually add 1¼ cups (300 mL) water and process until smooth, scraping bowl once.

3. Transfer cashew cream to a small saucepan and bring to a boil over medium-high heat, stirring occasionally. Reduce heat and simmer, stirring, for 1 minute or until cream is thick (if it becomes too thick to stir easily, add 1 to 2 tbsp/15 to 30 mL water).

4. Meanwhile, spray a large nonstick skillet with cooking spray and heat over medium-high heat. Sauté garlic for 30 seconds. Stir in cashew cream, pasta, Parmesan, pepper and salt; cook, stirring, until heated through and pasta is coated with sauce.

✔ Kid Approved

Pasta e fagioli is Italian for "pasta and beans." This simple dish is a hearty, soup-like pasta meal that's perfect for Friday night supper.

Tips

Ditali pasta is the perfect size and shape for this dish. You can find it at most grocery stores, but if you strike out, try small shells or elbow macaroni.

Cooking the pasta in the broth adds terrific flavor to the finished product.

Serving Idea

Serve with a simple salad of sliced tomatoes and chopped fresh herbs, dressed with a drizzle of extra virgin olive oil and balsamic vinegar.

Nutrients per serving

Calories	291
Fat	3.4 g
Saturated fat	0.5 g
Sodium	587 mg (24% DV)
Carbohydrate	53 g
Fiber	8 g (32% DV)
Protein	12 g
Calcium	50 mg (5% DV)
Iron	2.9 mg (21% DV)

Very high in: Folate

High in: Magnesium, zinc, vitamin B_6, thiamine and niacin

Diabetes Food Choice Values:

3 Carbohydrates
½ Meat & Alternatives

Pasta e Fagioli

Francy Pillo-Blocka, Dietitian, Ontario

1 tbsp	olive oil	15 mL
6	cloves garlic, minced	6
1	large tomato, chopped	1
1	can (19 oz/540 mL) white kidney beans, drained and rinsed, divided	1
1	can (19 oz/540 mL) chickpeas, drained and rinsed, divided	1
3 cups	vegetable broth	750 mL
1 cup	dry white wine	250 mL
3 cups	ditali pasta	750 mL
2 tbsp	chopped fresh parsley	30 mL

1. In a large pot, heat oil over medium heat. Sauté garlic for 1 to 2 minutes or until softened but not browned. Add tomato and sauté for 1 to 2 minutes or until starting to soften. Add half each of the white kidney beans and chickpeas; mash with a potato masher and stir to combine.

2. Stir in broth, wine and the remaining kidney beans and chickpeas; bring to a boil. Stir in pasta and return to a boil. Reduce heat and boil gently for 8 to 10 minutes or until pasta is al dente. Stir in parsley.

While in college, Sarah
developed this delicious
one-pot meal as a
student project to create
a vegetarian recipe. She
tested it six times, and
each time made small
improvements! We made
only minor changes to
streamline the cooking
process. Nice job, Sarah!

Tips

Leftovers are delicious placed
in individual casseroles or
ramekins, topped with cheese
and broiled.

This recipe can easily be cut
in half.

Kids love to "taste test"
cooking pasta for doneness.

Nutrients per serving

Calories	280
Fat	3.9 g
Saturated fat	1.1 g
Sodium	470 mg (20% DV)
Carbohydrate	53 g
Fiber	9 g (36% DV)
Protein	14 g
Calcium	176 mg (16% DV)
Iron	4.7 mg (34% DV)

Very high in: Magnesium,
vitamin A, vitamin C and folate

High in: Zinc, vitamin B_6,
thiamine, riboflavin and niacin

Diabetes Food Choice Values:

2½ Carbohydrates

1 Meat & Alternatives

Spinach and Black Bean Pasta

Sarah Reid, Ontario

1 lb	whole wheat rotini or penne pasta	500 g
1 tbsp	canola oil	15 mL
1 cup	chopped onion	250 mL
1	clove garlic, minced	1
1 tsp	dried oregano	5 mL
1 tsp	ground cumin	5 mL
½ tsp	freshly ground black pepper	2 mL
¼ tsp	cayenne pepper	1 mL
1	can (28 oz/796 mL) diced tomatoes, with juice	1
1	can (5½ oz/156 mL) tomato paste	1
1	can (19 oz/540 mL) black beans, drained and rinsed	1
1	bag (10 oz/300 g) fresh spinach, trimmed and torn into bite-size pieces	1
2 cups	chopped broccoli	500 mL
1¼ cups	vegetable broth	300 mL
½ cup	freshly grated Parmesan cheese	125 mL

1. In a large pot of boiling water, cook pasta for 6 to
8 minutes or until almost al dente. Drain and set aside.

2. Meanwhile, in a large skillet, heat oil over medium heat.
Sauté onion for 3 to 4 minutes or until softened. Add
garlic, oregano, cumin, black pepper and cayenne; sauté
for 1 minute. Stir in tomatoes with juice, tomato paste,
beans, spinach, broccoli, broth and 1 cup (250 mL)
water; bring to a boil. Reduce heat to low and simmer,
stirring occasionally, for 7 to 8 minutes or until broccoli
is tender.

3. Gently stir in pasta and Parmesan; simmer for 5 minutes
or until pasta is al dente.

Spinach Spaghetti Pie

Jennie Cowan, Dietitian, Manitoba

Leftover spaghetti makes this microwave entrée a quick fix on a busy night. Serve with tzatziki on the side.

Tip

To make assembly a snap at the dinner hour, place the spinach in the refrigerator to thaw the night before you plan to prepare this.

Variation

Add ½ tsp (2 mL) hot pepper flakes to the spinach mixture.

● **9-inch (23 cm) microwave-safe pie plate**

2 cups	cold cooked whole wheat spaghetti	500 mL
6	eggs	6
1	package (10 oz/300 g) frozen chopped spinach, thawed, drained and squeezed dry	1
1 cup	shredded Asiago cheese	250 mL
½ cup	freshly grated Parmesan cheese	125 mL
1 tsp	dried basil	5 mL
1 tsp	dried oregano	5 mL
½ tsp	freshly ground black pepper	2 mL

1. Arrange cooked spaghetti evenly in bottom of pie plate.

2. In a large bowl, beat eggs until blended. Stir in spinach, Asiago, Parmesan, basil, oregano and pepper. Pour evenly over spaghetti.

3. Microwave on High for 12 to 14 minutes or until eggs are set.

How to Store and Reheat Cooked Pasta

While the pasta is still warm, toss it with 1 to 3 tsp (5 to 15 mL) vegetable oil. (This ensures that the pieces won't stick together when they cool.) Place pasta in a sealable food storage bag, let cool at room temperature for 15 minutes, then set it, unsealed, in the refrigerator. Once the pasta is cool, seal the bag and lightly turn the contents around to make sure the pasta is not sticking together. Store in the refrigerator for up to 3 days.

Use the pasta cold if the recipe calls for that (as here). Otherwise, reheat it by dropping the pasta into a pot of rapidly boiling water for 30 to 60 seconds, just until hot. Don't leave it in the water for longer than 1 minute, or it will become mushy.

Nutrients per serving

Calories	239
Fat	12.8 g
Saturated fat	5.8 g
Sodium	412 mg (17% DV)
Carbohydrate	15 g
Fiber	3 g (12% DV)
Protein	17 g
Calcium	302 mg (27% DV)
Iron	1.9 mg (14% DV)

Very high in: Vitamin A, folate and vitamin B$_{12}$

High in: Magnesium, riboflavin and niacin

Diabetes Food Choice Values:

1	Carbohydrate
2	Meat & Alternatives
1	Fat

✔ **Kid Approved**

Your children will be asking for this cheesy pasta on a regular basis. The carrot gives it the deep orange color of a classic macaroni and cheese.

Tip

Add only warm or cool liquid to a roux (a fat and flour mixture). If you add cold liquid, the fat could become more solid, creating lumps that are difficult to dissolve.

Variations

Use green peas or green beans instead of broccoli.

Season the cheese sauce with herbs of your choice, such as dried tarragon, basil, oregano or thyme.

Nutrients per serving

Calories	341
Fat	16.8 g
Saturated fat	6.5 g
Sodium	256 mg (11% DV)
Carbohydrate	36 g
Fiber	4 g (16% DV)
Protein	15 g
Calcium	313 mg (28% DV)
Iron	1.5 mg (11% DV)

Very high in: Vitamin A

High in: Magnesium, zinc, vitamin D, folate, riboflavin and niacin

Diabetes Food Choice Values:

2	Carbohydrates
1	Meat & Alternatives
2	Fats

Cheesy Vegetable Pasta Casserole

Sylvie Leblanc, Dietetic Student, New Brunswick

- **Preheat oven to 350°F (180°C)**
- **8-inch (20 cm) square glass baking dish, lightly greased**

2 cups	whole wheat rotini or penne pasta	500 mL
2½ tbsp	canola oil, divided	37 mL
1 cup	chopped onion	250 mL
3	cloves garlic, minced	3
1 cup	grated carrot	250 mL
2 tbsp	all-purpose flour	30 mL
2 cups	2% milk	500 mL
1 cup	shredded Cheddar cheese, divided	250 mL
1 cup	chopped broccoli	250 mL

1. In a large pot of boiling salted water, cook pasta according to package directions until al dente. Drain and set aside.

2. Meanwhile, in a large saucepan, heat 2 tsp (10 mL) oil over medium heat. Sauté onion for 3 to 4 minutes or until softened. Add garlic and sauté for 30 seconds. Add carrot and sauté for 3 to 4 minutes or until tender. Transfer vegetable mixture to a plate.

3. In the same pan, heat the remaining oil over medium heat. Sprinkle with flour and cook, stirring, for 30 seconds. Gradually add milk, whisking to ensure flour is distributed and no lumps remain. Bring to a boil, whisking, then immediately remove from heat. Add ¾ cup (175 mL) of the cheese and stir until melted. Stir in broccoli, reserved carrot mixture and pasta until well coated.

4. Transfer to prepared baking dish and sprinkle with the remaining cheese. Cover with foil and bake in preheated oven for 30 minutes or until hot and bubbly.

Makes 4 servings

This vegetarian entrée features a surprising filling that will delight your family.

Tips

If you cannot get 9 slices from the eggplant, cut larger slices in half lengthwise to obtain the desired number.

If you are trying to get picky eaters to eat more vegetables, use half lasagna sheets and half eggplant slices, then slowly add more eggplant over time.

The hummus mixture also makes a delicious dip.

Variation

Use 3 cooked whole wheat lasagna sheets instead of the eggplant.

Nutrients per serving

Calories	210
Fat	9.3 g
Saturated fat	2.4 g
Sodium	695 mg (29% DV)
Carbohydrate	21 g
Fiber	5 g (20% DV)
Protein	13 g
Calcium	140 mg (13% DV)
Iron	2.2 mg (16% DV)

Very high in: Vitamin A and folate

High in: Magnesium and niacin

Diabetes Food Choice Values:
½ Carbohydrate
1½ Meat & Alternatives
1 Fat

Eggplant Lasagna

Lorna Salgado, Ontario

- **Preheat oven to 400°F (200°C)**
- **Baking sheet, lightly greased**
- **9-inch (23 cm) square glass baking dish, lightly greased**

1	eggplant (about 1 lb/500 g)	1
½ tsp	freshly ground black pepper	2 mL
¼ tsp	salt	1 mL
1 cup	drained thawed chopped frozen spinach	250 mL
1 cup	tomato sauce	250 mL
1 cup	2% cottage cheese	250 mL
½ cup	spicy red pepper hummus (homemade or store-bought)	125 mL
2 tbsp	freshly grated Parmesan cheese	30 mL

1. Peel eggplant and cut lengthwise into 9 thin slices. Season both sides with pepper and salt. Place on prepared baking sheet and roast in preheated oven, turning once, for 15 minutes or until lightly browned. Set aside.

2. Meanwhile, in a small bowl, combine spinach and tomato sauce.

3. In another small bowl, combine cottage cheese and hummus.

4. Spread ¼ cup (60 mL) of the tomato sauce mixture over bottom of prepared baking dish. Arrange 3 eggplant slices on top. Spread with one-third of the cottage cheese mixture. Add 2 more layers of sauce, eggplant and cheese. Pour the remaining sauce over top and sprinkle with Parmesan.

5. Bake in preheated oven for 20 minutes or until cheese is golden and lasagna is heated through. Let stand for 10 minutes before cutting.

Makes 6 servings

✔ Kid Approved

Shortcuts, including purchased pasta sauce and oven-ready lasagna noodles, simplify the preparation of this recipe. It is a nice way to introduce tofu to your menu.

Tips

To thaw spinach quickly, heat a skillet over medium heat and add frozen spinach block. Heat, turning often, until thawed. Transfer to a colander and drain off excess water.

Leftovers of this lasagna freeze well. Wrap cooled lasagna in plastic wrap and place in an airtight container or freezer bag.

Nutrients per serving

Calories	381
Fat	13.7 g
Saturated fat	5.1 g
Sodium	491 mg (20% DV)
Carbohydrate	46 g
Fiber	5 g (20% DV)
Protein	18 g
Calcium	291 mg (26% DV)
Iron	4.3 mg (31% DV)

Very high in: Magnesium, vitamin A, folate, thiamine and niacin

High in: Zinc and riboflavin

Diabetes Food Choice Values:

2½	Carbohydrates
1½	Meat & Alternatives
1	Fat

Tofu and Spinach Lasagna

Caroline Dubeau, Dietitian, Ontario

- **Preheat oven to 350°F (180°C)**
- **13- by 9-inch (33 by 23 cm) baking dish**

1 tbsp	canola oil	15 mL
1	small onion, finely chopped	1
1	carrot, finely diced	1
1	package (18 oz/540 g) soft tofu, drained	1
1	package (10 oz/300 g) frozen chopped spinach, thawed and drained	1
1	egg, lightly beaten	1
⅓ cup	fine dry bread crumbs	75 mL
1	jar (22 oz/650 mL) tomato and basil pasta sauce	1
12	oven-ready lasagna noodles	12
1 cup	shredded Cheddar cheese	250 mL

1. In a large nonstick skillet, heat oil over medium-high heat. Sauté onion and carrot for 4 to 5 minutes or until softened.

2. Meanwhile, in a large bowl, mash tofu with a fork. Stir in onion mixture and spinach. Add egg and bread crumbs; mix well.

3. Pour ⅓ cup (75 mL) water into the baking dish, along with one-third of the pasta sauce. Mix together and spread over bottom of dish. Add another ⅓ cup (75 mL) water to the pasta sauce remaining in the jar and mix well.

4. Arrange 3 lasagna noodles on top of sauce in dish. Spread half the tofu mixture over noodles. Top with 3 lasagna noodles and pour half the remaining pasta sauce evenly over noodles. Top with 3 noodles and spread with the remaining tofu mixture. Top with the remaining 3 noodles and pour the remaining sauce over top. Sprinkle with cheese and cover with foil.

5. Bake in preheated oven for 45 to 50 minutes or until sauce is bubbling. Remove foil and bake for 10 minutes or until noodles are tender and top is browned. Let stand for 10 minutes before cutting.

> Many purchased pasta sauces are high in sodium. Look for ones that are labeled "lower in salt," "lower in sodium" or "no salt added" and select one that contains the least amount of sodium per serving. Or try our Big-Batch Italian Master Tomato Sauce (page 278).

Variations

When bell peppers are in season, replace the carrot with 1 finely chopped red or orange bell pepper.

Try using herb-and-garlic-flavored tofu.

Look for oven-ready whole wheat lasagna noodles to use instead of white.

Serving Idea

Serve with steamed asparagus.

Makes 8 servings

An Italian-flavored ground meat alternative gives delicious texture and flavor to this lasagna. It's a delicious way to introduce your family to meat alternatives.

Tip

Check the Nutrition Facts table when purchasing pasta sauce and look for one that is lower in sodium. Or make our Big-Batch Italian Master Tomato Sauce (page 278)!

Variation

When we first tested this, we accidentally used Asian-flavored vegetarian ground beef replacement, and it turned out to be a delicious alternative — give it a try!

Nutrients per serving

Calories	418
Fat	14.6 g
Saturated fat	5.7 g
Sodium	538 mg (22% DV)
Carbohydrate	47 g
Fiber	7 g (28% DV)
Protein	28 g
Calcium	392 mg (36% DV)
Iron	3.9 mg (28% DV)

Very high in: Zinc, vitamin B_6, vitamin B_{12}, thiamine, riboflavin and niacin

High in: Magnesium

Diabetes Food Choice Values:

2	Carbohydrates
2½	Meat & Alternatives

Tangy Meatless Lasagna

Anne Holtzman, Dietitian, British Columbia

● **13- by 9-inch (33 by 23 cm) glass baking dish**

12	whole wheat lasagna noodles	12
2 tbsp	canola or olive oil	30 mL
1 cup	finely chopped onion	250 mL
1	clove garlic, minced	1
1½ cups	reduced-sodium tomato pasta sauce	375 mL
1	package (12 oz/340 g) Italian-seasoned vegetarian ground beef replacement	1
1	egg	1
1 cup	light sour cream	250 mL
1 cup	light ricotta cheese	250 mL
2 cups	shredded part-skim mozzarella cheese	500 mL

1. In a large pot of boiling salted water, cook lasagna noodles according to package directions until almost tender but still firm (they will finish cooking in the oven). Drain and rinse under cold running water. Drain and lay flat on a plate; set aside.

2. In a large saucepan, heat oil over medium heat. Sauté onion for 3 to 4 minutes or until softened. Add garlic and sauté for 30 seconds. Stir in pasta sauce and bring to a boil. Reduce heat and simmer, stirring occasionally, for 10 minutes. Remove from heat and stir in ground beef replacement. Set aside.

3. In a small bowl, whisk egg until blended. Stir in sour cream, ricotta and ½ cup (125 mL) of the mozzarella.

4. Spread about 2 tbsp (30 mL) sauce over bottom of baking dish. Arrange 3 lasagna noodles on top and spread with half the remaining sauce. Top with 3 noodles and spread with sour cream mixture. Top with 3 noodles and spread with the remaining sauce. Arrange the remaining 3 noodles on top and sprinkle with the remaining mozzarella.

5. Bake in preheated oven for 30 minutes or until bubbling and golden. Let stand for 15 minutes before serving.

Tofu Vegetable Pilaf

Shefali Raja, Dietitian, British Columbia

Fluffy basmati rice forms the base of this Indian-inspired tofu and vegetable pilaf, a favorite in Shefali's home.

Tips

Be sure to remove the cinnamon sticks and cardamom pods before serving. The cardamom pods can become camouflaged by the peas, so look carefully.

The carbohydrate in this recipe may seem high, but remember that both vegetables and grains are provided in this one dish.

Serving Idea

Serve topped with chopped fresh cilantro and chopped roasted peanuts, with plain yogurt on the side.

2 tbsp	canola oil	30 mL
2	4-inch (10 cm) cinnamon sticks	2
4	cardamom pods	4
1 tsp	cumin seeds	5 mL
1½ cups	finely chopped onions	375 mL
1½ cups	diced potatoes	375 mL
1 cup	fresh or frozen green peas (thawed and drained if frozen)	250 mL
1 cup	diced carrots	250 mL
1 cup	cubed firm tofu	250 mL
3 tbsp	grated gingerroot	45 mL
½ tsp	ground turmeric	2 mL
1 cup	basmati rice	250 mL
½ tsp	salt	2 mL

1. In a large pot, heat oil over medium heat. Sauté cinnamon sticks, cardamom pods and cumin seeds for 1 minute or until fragrant. Add onions, potatoes, peas, carrots, tofu, ginger and turmeric; sauté for 3 to 4 minutes or until onions are softened.

2. Add rice, salt and 3 cups (750 mL) water; bring to a boil. Reduce heat to low, cover and simmer, stirring occasionally, for 15 minutes or until rice is tender and fluffy. (If rice starts to stick, stir in 1 to 2 tbsp/15 to 30 mL more water.) Discard cinnamon sticks and cardamom pods. Fluff rice with a fork.

> Cardamom is a tropical spice from the ginger family that is popular in both Indian and Scandinavian cuisine. In the latter case, it is particularly enjoyed in cardamom-spiced cookies.

Nutrients per serving

Calories	426
Fat	12.2 g
Saturated fat	1.2 g
Sodium	323 mg (13% DV)
Carbohydrate	64 g
Fiber	6 g (24% DV)
Protein	16 g
Calcium	154 mg (14% DV)
Iron	2.6 mg (19% DV)

Very high in: Magnesium, vitamin A, vitamin B_6, folate and niacin

High in: Zinc and thiamine

Diabetes Food Choice Values:

3½ Carbohydrates
1 Meat & Alternatives
1½ Fats

Side Dishes

Vegetables from asparagus to zucchini grow well in Canada, providing us with a host of vitamins, minerals, dietary fiber, antioxidants and phytonutrients. There are many ways to incorporate vegetables into your meal plan, and they are featured in every chapter in this book; here, they are highlighted in a variety of colorful, flavorful vegetable side dishes. You'll also find delectable recipes for grains. Whole grains, such as pot barley and quinoa, provide a rich array of nutrients and offer unique texture as side dishes.

Antioxidants

Vitamins C and E and beta carotene (the plant form of vitamin A) are examples of nutrients that act as antioxidants in the body. Antioxidants help counter the effects of free radicals, which are formed when cells oxidize. Free radicals can damage cells and are believed to play a role in the development of heart disease, cancer and cataracts and some deterioration associated with aging. This continues to be an area of active research.

Phyto-what?

Phytonutrients (meaning "plant nutrients") is the name for hundreds of beneficial chemicals that occur naturally in plant foods. Since new phytonutrients are being discovered all the time, it's best to eat a wide variety of fruits, vegetables and grains.

Simply Fabulous Veggies

Stuck for ideas on how to cook your favorite vegetables? Try these easy recipes for good nutrition and delicious flavor.

Vegetable	Cooking Method	Flavor Enhancers
Acorn squash	**Roast:** Cut 2 acorn squash in half lengthwise. Scoop out seeds and discard. Place squash, flesh side down, on a rimmed baking sheet. Roast in a 350°F (180°C) oven for 30 to 35 minutes or until a fork easily pierces the flesh.	Scoop cooked flesh into a large bowl. In a small microwave-safe bowl, combine 1/2 tsp (2 mL) ground allspice, 1/4 tsp (1 mL) ground cloves, 1 tbsp (15 mL) frozen orange juice concentrate and 1 tbsp (15 mL) pure maple syrup. Microwave on High for 30 seconds or until warm. Stir into cooked squash.
Asparagus	**Sauté:** For each lb (500 g) asparagus, trim off tough ends. In a skillet, melt 2 tsp (10 mL) non-hydrogenated margarine or butter over medium-high heat. Sauté asparagus for 5 minutes, shaking pan often. Add 1 minced garlic clove and sauté for 30 seconds.	Sprinkle cooked asparagus with 1 tbsp (15 mL) freshly grated Parmesan cheese and freshly ground black pepper or 1 tbsp (15 mL) grated orange zest.
Beets	**Roast:** Wash 2 lbs (1 kg) beets and cut away tops and tails. Wrap in foil, place on a baking sheet and roast in a 375°F (190°C) oven for about 45 minutes or until tender. Unwrap and rinse under cold water to cool. Peel and cut into chunks.	Sprinkle roasted beets with 1/4 cup (60 mL) chopped toasted walnuts, 1 to 2 tbsp (15 to 30 mL) balsamic vinegar and freshly ground black pepper.
Bok choy and other Asian greens	**Stir-fry:** In a wok or large skillet, heat 1 tbsp (15 mL) canola oil over medium heat. Stir-fry 4 cups (1 L) chopped bok choy for 2 minutes. Add 2 minced garlic cloves and stir-fry for 30 seconds.	Drizzle cooked bok choy with 1 tsp (5 mL) sesame oil and sprinkle with 1 tbsp (15 mL) white and/or black sesame seeds.
Broccoli	**Steam:** Steam 2 cups (500 mL) broccoli florets (see page 295) for 4 to 5 minutes or until tender. Drain.	Top cooked broccoli with 1/2 cup (125 mL) shredded Cheddar cheese and place under broiler for 1 minute or until bubbly.
Brussels sprouts	**Steam:** Steam 2 cups (500 mL) halved trimmed Brussels sprouts (see page 295) for 4 to 5 minutes or until tender. Drain.	Grate nutmeg over cooked Brussels sprouts.
Carrots	**Steam:** Steam 2 cups (500 mL) carrot coins (see page 295) for 4 to 5 minutes or until fork-tender. Drain.	Meanwhile, sauté 1 tbsp (15 mL) shallots in 1 tsp (5 mL) olive oil. Stir in 2 tsp (10 mL) liquid honey and 1 tsp (5 mL) each chopped fresh dill and tarragon. Pour over cooked carrots.

Vegetable	Cooking Method	Flavor Enhancers
Cauliflower	**Steam:** Steam 2 cups (500 mL) cauliflower florets (see page 295) for 4 to 5 minutes or until tender. Drain.	Mash cooked cauliflower and stir in 2 tbsp (30 mL) chopped roasted red bell peppers and 1 tsp (5 mL) dried parsley. Season with salt and freshly ground black pepper.
Celery root	**Roast:** Peel 1 large celery root and cut into $1/2$-inch (1 cm) sticks. In a small bowl, combine 1 tsp (5 mL) ground cumin, 1 tbsp (15 mL) orange juice and 2 tsp (10 mL) canola oil; toss with celery root. Roast in a 425°F (220°C) oven, shaking occasionally, for 30 minutes or until tender and browned.	Sprinkle cooked celery root with $1/4$ cup (60 mL) chopped fresh parsley.
Corn on the cob	**Boil:** Shuck corn and remove all silk. Cut in half. Cook in a large pot of boiling water for 5 minutes or until tender.	Serve each cob with 1 tsp (5 mL) basil-lime compound butter: Soften $1/4$ cup (60mL) butter. Stir in 1 tbsp (15 mL) finely chopped basil and 1 tsp (5 mL) grated lime zest. Transfer to a small bowl and refrigerate until firm.
Green beans	**Steam:** Steam 2 cups (500 mL) trimmed green beans (see page 295) for 5 to 6 minutes or until fork-tender. Drain.	Sprinkle cooked green beans with 2 tsp (10 mL) walnut oil and $1/4$ cup (60 mL) toasted chopped walnuts.
Kale	**Stir-fry:** In a wok or large skillet, heat 2 tsp (10 mL) canola oil and 1 tsp (5 mL) sesame oil over high heat. Add 4 cups (1 L) chopped kale and $1/2$ cup (125 mL) sliced onions. Stir-fry for 3 to 5 minutes or until limp.	Combine 1 tbsp (15 mL) tahini, 2 tsp (10 mL) hot pepper sauce and 2 tsp (10 mL) reduced-sodium soy sauce. Pour over cooked kale.
Mushrooms	**Roast:** Spread 2 cups (500 mL) button mushrooms and 1 cup (250 mL) shiitake mushroom caps on a lightly greased baking sheet. Drizzle with 1 tbsp (15 mL) canola oil. Roast in a 400°F (200°C) oven for 15 to 18 minutes or until golden but not shriveled.	Sprinkle roasted mushrooms with 1 tbsp (15 mL) balsamic vinegar, 2 tsp (10 mL) chopped fresh thyme and $1/2$ tsp (2 mL) freshly ground black pepper; stir to combine.
Parsnips	**Roast:** Cut 2 lbs (1 kg) parsnips into 1-inch (2.5 cm) thick diagonal slices. Place on a rimmed baking sheet, drizzle with 2 tsp (10 mL) canola oil and sprinkle with $1/2$ tsp (2 mL) ground cinnamon and $1/4$ tsp (1 mL) ground nutmeg. Roast in a 425°F (220°C) oven for 30 minutes or until tender.	During the last 10 minutes of roasting, stir parsnips and drizzle with 1 tbsp (15 mL) pure maple syrup.
Zucchini	**Sauté:** Using a vegetable peeler, cut 2 large unpeeled zucchini into ribbons. In a large skillet, heat 2 tsp (10 mL) canola oil over medium heat. Sauté 2 tbsp (30 mL) minced shallots and 3 minced garlic cloves for 1 to 2 minutes or until softened. Add zucchini and sauté for 3 to 4 minutes or until tender.	Sprinkle cooked zucchini ribbons with $1/4$ cup (60 mL) freshly grated Parmesan cheese and $1/2$ tsp (2 mL) freshly ground black pepper.

Family Cooking Lesson

Steamed Vegetables

Steaming is one of the best ways to cook vegetables while retaining their nutrients, color and flavor. The method is simple.

What You Need

A steamer basket and a pot with a cover *or* a double boiler with a cover and perforated upper pan
Vegetables of your choice
Water (plain or with added herbs or aromatic vegetables), broth or wine

How to Steam Vegetables

1. Wash vegetables and peel if necessary. Cut vegetables to a uniform shape and size to make sure all pieces cook evenly. Place in a single layer in the steamer basket (or the top of the double boiler).

2. Pour about 1 inch (2.5 cm) of the liquid of your choice (see options, above) into the pot (or the bottom of the double boiler); bring to a boil over high heat.

3. Place steamer basket (or top of double boiler) over the boiling liquid and reduce heat to medium-high. Cover and cook to the desired doneness — for most vegetables this will be tender-crisp.

Gorgeous Grains!

There's a whole world of grains waiting to be explored! Here are some of our favorites, which offer unique flavor and texture and great nutrition.

- **Amaranth leaves**, which have a slightly sweet flavor, are widely used in Asian cuisine. When milled, amaranth seeds yield a flour that is used in baking.

- **Barley** is famous for its use in soups and is also delicious as a base in pilafs.

- **Kamut**, an ancient grain dating back to 4000 BC, is the ancestor of modern strains of wheat. Its kernels are two to three times the size of modern wheat and have a delicious nutty flavor. Kamut flour is often used to make pasta, cereals and crackers. We use it to make Ancient Grains Chocolate Chip Cookies (page 336).

- **Millet**. Some people associate millet with bird food, but in some parts of the world, millet is a staple human food, used in dishes such as hot cereal or pilafs. When ground, millet flour can be used to make puddings, breads and cakes.

- **Quinoa**, a tiny, bead-shaped grain with a mild flavor, dates back to the time of the ancient Incas and is often called the "mother grain." It is a source of complete, high-quality protein and is often heralded as a high-protein grain that can substitute for meat products. However, it should be noted that it provides just 2.5 g of protein per $\frac{1}{2}$ cup (125 mL) cooked quinoa — substantially less than the 6 to 7 g of protein found in 1 egg or 1 oz (30 g) of meat.

- **Spelt** is an ancient grain originally harvested in Asia and Southern Europe over 9,000 years ago. In baking, it can be substituted for all-purpose flour.

Family Cooking Lesson

Cooking Common Grains

The amount of time and the amount of liquid required to cook grains varies depending on the type and size of the grain, as does the yield of the cooked grain. The table below is a guideline only. When in doubt, check the package directions.

Grain (1 cup/250 mL)	Water or broth	Cooking time	Yield
Brown rice	2 cups (500 mL)	45 minutes	3 cups (750 mL)
Wild rice	3 cups (750 mL)	60 minutes	4 cups (1 L)
Millet	3 cups (750 mL)	25 minutes	3½ cups (875 mL)
Pearl barley	3 cups (750 mL)	35 minutes	3½ cups (875 mL)
Pot barley	3 cups (750 mL)	60 minutes plus	3½ cups (875 mL)
Quinoa	2 cups (500 mL)	15 minutes	2½ cups (625 mL)
Kamut or wheat kernels	2 cups (500 mL)	60 minutes	3 cups (750 mL)

To cook, combine grain and liquid in a large pot with a tight-fitting lid; bring to a boil. Reduce heat and simmer, covered, for the suggested cooking time or until liquid is absorbed. Fluff with a fork.

This was the first dish Honey prepared in her own kitchen after getting married. It has loads of tang from the fresh lemon juice and zest, so pucker up!

Tips

The baking time will vary depending on the width of the asparagus spears. Check occasionally for doneness.

For an extra flourish, sprinkle the cooked asparagus with 2 tbsp (30 mL) freshly grated Parmesan cheese.

You can also grill the asparagus, either on the baking sheet or in a grill basket on a barbecue grill preheated to medium-high.

Roasted Lemon Asparagus

Honey Bloomberg, Dietitian, Ontario

- **Preheat oven to 350°F (180°C)**
- **Rimmed baking sheet, lined with foil**

1	bunch asparagus (about 1 lb/500 g), ends trimmed	1
1	lemon	1
2	cloves garlic, minced	2
2 tbsp	olive oil	30 mL
1/4 tsp	salt	1 mL
1/4 tsp	freshly ground black pepper	1 mL

1. Spread asparagus on prepared baking sheet. Grate zest and squeeze juice from 1/2 lemon into a small bowl. Stir in garlic, oil, salt and pepper. Pour over asparagus and shake pan to ensure each spear is coated.

2. Cut the remaining lemon half into slices and place among asparagus spears.

3. Bake in preheated oven, turning once, for 10 to 12 minutes or until lightly browned and tender-crisp.

> References to asparagus go as far back as Egyptian hieroglyphics. There are many varieties, including wild, purple, variegated, green and white asparagus. White asparagus is grown under mounds of soil, so the plant gets no sunlight, blocking its ability to produce chlorophyll. Cook asparagus soon after you purchase it or the natural sugars will quickly turn to starch and the texture will be woody.

Nutrients per serving

Calories	83
Fat	6.9 g
Saturated fat	1.0 g
Sodium	155 mg (6% DV)
Carbohydrate	5 g
Fiber	2 g (8% DV)
Protein	2 g
Calcium	23 mg (2% DV)
Iron	0.8 mg (6% DV)

Very high in: Folate

Diabetes Food Choice Values:
1½ Fats

Braised Red Cabbage

Corinne Eisenbraun, Dietitian, Manitoba

A lovely German woman once said that braised red cabbage should only have seven ingredients: butter, apple, onion, cabbage, brown sugar, cider vinegar and spice. And when Corinne prepares this recipe, from her mom, that's exactly what she uses. But she does usually add some salt: "I guess that's cheating, as it makes eight ingredients." This flavor and aroma is so evocative, it takes Corinne right back to her childhood home.

Tip

Corinne prefers to refrigerate the cooked cabbage for 24 hours, then reheat it in a pot over medium-low heat, stirring often, until heated through. She finds that this technique produces the most flavorful dish.

Variation

Use ground allspice instead of ground cloves.

2 tsp	butter or canola oil	10 mL
1 cup	chopped onion	250 mL
1	apple, peeled and chopped	1
8 cups	shredded red cabbage (1 small to medium head)	2 L
¾ cup	packed brown sugar	175 mL
1 tsp	ground cloves	5 mL
½ tsp	salt	2 mL
½ tsp	freshly ground black pepper	2 mL
½ cup	cider vinegar	125 mL

1. In a Dutch oven with a tight-fitting lid, melt butter over medium heat. Sauté onion for 3 to 4 minutes or until softened. Add apple and sauté for 1 minute or until softened.

2. Stir in cabbage, brown sugar, cloves, salt, pepper and vinegar; increase heat to medium-high and bring to a boil. Reduce heat to low, cover and simmer, stirring occasionally, for about 30 minutes or until cabbage is soft. Serve warm or transfer to a bowl and refrigerate until chilled.

Nutrients per serving

Calories	125
Fat	1.1 g
Saturated fat	0.7 g
Sodium	165 mg (7% DV)
Carbohydrate	30 g
Fiber	2 g (8% DV)
Protein	1 g
Calcium	55 mg (5% DV)
Iron	1.0 mg (7% DV)

Diabetes Food Choice Values:

1½   Carbohydrate

Steamed Tarragon Carrots

Shelley Wilcox, Nova Scotia

- **9-inch (23 cm) microwave-safe baking dish with lid**

3	large carrots, julienned (about 2 cups/ 500 mL sticks)	3
1 tsp	butter or non-hydrogenated margarine	5 mL
½ tsp	dried tarragon	2 mL

1. Place carrots in baking dish. Drop butter in small pieces over carrots and sprinkle with tarragon. Cover loosely with lid.

2. Microwave on High for 2 minutes. Stir, cover and microwave on High for about 1 minute or until fork-tender.

> Vegetables cook evenly when they're cut to the same size and shape. A sharp knife is a must for julienne-cut vegetables, which are generally 2 by ⅛ by ⅛ inch (5 cm by 3 mm by 3 mm). If you cannot cut them this thin, be sure to cut them all the same size and shape and adjust the cooking time accordingly.

Nutrients per serving

Calories	33
Fat	1.1 g
Saturated fat	0.6 g
Sodium	47 mg (2% DV)
Carbohydrate	6 g
Fiber	2 g (8% DV)
Protein	1 g
Calcium	22 mg (2% DV)
Iron	0.3 mg (2% DV)

Very high in: Vitamin A

Diabetes Food Choice Values:
1   Extra

Indian-Spiced Cauliflower, Potatoes and Chickpeas

Judy Coveney, Dietitian, Ontario

Makes 8 servings

✔ **Kid Approved**

Roasting the vegetables and chickpeas adds a deep, delicious flavor to this exotic dish.

- **Preheat oven to 475°F (240°C)**
- **2 large rimmed baking sheets**

1	can (19 oz/540 mL) chickpeas, drained and rinsed	1
1 lb	Yukon gold potatoes, peeled and cut into 1/2-inch (1 cm) cubes	500 g
4 cups	cauliflower florets (about 1 medium cauliflower)	1 L
1/4 cup	canola or olive oil, divided	60 mL
1/2 tsp	cumin seeds	2 mL
1/8 tsp	salt	0.5 mL
3	cloves garlic, minced	3
1 cup	finely chopped onion	250 mL
2 tsp	minced fresh jalapeño pepper, including seeds	10 mL
2 tsp	minced gingerroot	10 mL
1 tsp	ground cumin	5 mL
1 tsp	ground coriander	5 mL
1/4 tsp	ground turmeric	1 mL
1/4 tsp	cayenne pepper	1 mL
1/4 cup	chopped fresh cilantro or parsley (optional)	60 mL

1. Place baking sheets in preheated oven for 5 minutes to heat.

2. In a large bowl, toss together chickpeas, potatoes, cauliflower, 2 tbsp (30 mL) oil, cumin seeds and salt. Remove baking sheets from oven. Divide mixture evenly among baking sheets and spread out in a single layer. Roast, stirring occasionally, for 25 minutes or until potatoes are tender.

Nutrients per serving

Calories	190
Fat	7.9 g
Saturated fat	0.7 g
Sodium	192 mg (8% DV)
Carbohydrate	26 g
Fiber	5 g (20% DV)
Protein	5 g
Calcium	39 mg (4% DV)
Iron	1.4 mg (10% DV)

Very high in: Vitamin B$_6$ and folate

High in: Vitamin C

Diabetes Food Choice Values:

1 Carbohydrate
1 1/2 Fats

3. Meanwhile, in a Dutch oven, heat the remaining oil over medium heat. Sauté garlic, onion, jalapeño and ginger for 5 to 6 minutes or until onion is soft and starting to turn golden. Stir in ground cumin, coriander, turmeric and cayenne. Add $\frac{1}{4}$ cup (60 mL) water, scraping up all the bits from the bottom of the pan.

4. Stir in roasted vegetables. Cover and boil, stirring occasionally, for 5 minutes or until flavors are combined and most of the water is absorbed. Serve garnished with cilantro (if using).

> Cauliflower means "cabbage flower"; this is a fitting name, since cauliflower is a variety of cabbage — hence the strong cabbage-like aroma when it's cooked.

Tips

For less heat, remove the seeds from the jalapeño.

This recipe is ideal for a potluck. Transfer hot vegetables to a slow cooker set on Warm.

Serving Idea

Serve as an accompaniment to Brined and Tender Lemon Roast Chicken (page 170).

✔ **Kid Approved**

Here's a quick, easy, clever way to use fresh Canadian corn — and it's so delicious! Most recipes for creamed corn use whipping cream, but Leslie wanted to make a lower-fat version.

Tip

The easiest way to remove corn from the cob is to break the cob in half so you have a flat end. Stand the cob on the flat end and, using a sharp serrated knife, slice the corn off each half.

Variation

Add a pinch of ground nutmeg instead of cayenne pepper.

Homemade Creamed Corn

Leslie Gareau, Dietitian, Alberta

3 to 4	cobs corn	3 to 4
1 cup	whole milk	250 mL
1 tbsp	butter or non-hydrogenated margarine	15 mL
$\frac{1}{4}$ tsp	salt	1 mL
$\frac{1}{2}$ tsp	freshly ground black pepper	2 mL
Pinch	cayenne pepper (optional)	Pinch

1. Using a serrated knife, cut kernels from corn cobs. You should have $3\frac{1}{2}$ to 4 cups (875 mL to 1 L) kernels.

2. In a medium saucepan, bring corn and milk to a boil over medium-high heat. Reduce heat to medium and boil gently, stirring occasionally, for 10 minutes or until most, but not all, of the liquid is absorbed. Stir in butter, salt, black pepper and cayenne (if using).

Nutrients per serving

Calories	218
Fat	6.7 g
Saturated fat	3.2 g
Sodium	213 mg (9% DV)
Carbohydrate	39 g
Fiber	4 g (16% DV)
Protein	7 g
Calcium	74 mg (7% DV)
Iron	1.0 mg (7% DV)

Very high in: Folate and thiamine

High in: Magnesium and niacin

Diabetes Food Choice Values:

2 Carbohydrates

$1\frac{1}{2}$ Fats

Makes 4 servings

✔ **Kid Approved**

Spinach, kale or Swiss chard — it's all "spinach" to Danielle's children. They like to rinse and spin the greens in the salad spinner, singing Popeye's song as they do: "I'm strong to the finish, 'cause I eat my spinach, I'm Popeye the sailor man!"

Variation

Use a medium bunch of kale or Swiss chard instead of spinach. Fold the leaves in half and cut away the tough central stem, then shred the leaves into bite-size pieces. Kale takes a few minutes longer to steam than spinach.

Popeye's Spinach

Danielle Aldous, Dietitian, Ontario

1 tbsp	canola or olive oil	15 mL
2	cloves garlic, minced	2
1	bag (10 oz /300 g) spinach, trimmed	1
Pinch	freshly ground black pepper	Pinch
¼	lemon	¼

1. In a large skillet, heat oil over medium heat. Sauté garlic for about 30 seconds or until fragrant. Add spinach and sauté, adding 1 to 2 tbsp (15 to 30 mL) water as necessary to moisten, until leaves start to wilt. Cover and steam for 2 to 3 minutes or until spinach is wilted and bright green. Remove from heat and sprinkle with pepper and squeeze lemon over top.

Nutrients per serving

Calories	48
Fat	3.6 g
Saturated fat	0.3 g
Sodium	48 mg (2% DV)
Carbohydrate	3 g
Fiber	2 g (8% DV)
Protein	2 g
Calcium	96 mg (9% DV)
Iron	2.5 mg (18% DV)

Very high in: Vitamin A and folate

High in: Magnesium

Diabetes Food Choice Values:
½ Fat

Makes 8 servings

✔ **Kid Approved**

Walnuts and cranberries add color and texture to mashed squash.

Tip

Grate toast on the coarse side of a box grater.

Variation

Use pecans instead of walnuts and Oka cheese instead of Cheddar.

Squash Casserole

Lindsay Manley, Dietitian, Ontario

- **Preheat oven to 350°F (180°C)**
- **Microwave-safe bowl**
- **8-inch (20 cm) square glass baking dish, greased**

1	large buttercup squash, peeled, seeded and chopped	1
½ cup	frozen cranberries, thawed and cut in half	125 mL
1 tsp	ground nutmeg	5 mL
½ tsp	ground cinnamon	2 mL
1	egg, lightly beaten	1
2 tbsp	light sour cream	30 mL
3	slices whole-grain toast, crusts removed, grated into coarse crumbs	3
¼ cup	chopped walnuts	60 mL
1 cup	shredded Cheddar cheese	250 mL

1. Place squash in microwave-safe bowl, cover with plastic wrap, leaving one corner open for a vent, and microwave on High for 4 to 5 minutes or until soft. Drain off and discard excess liquid. Using a potato masher, mash squash until smooth. You should have about 4 cups (1 L) mashed squash. Stir in cranberries, nutmeg, cinnamon, egg and sour cream.

2. In a small bowl, combine toast crumbs, walnuts and cheese.

3. Spread squash in prepared baking dish and sprinkle with nut mixture.

4. Cover with foil and bake in preheated oven for 30 minutes or until hot in the center. Uncover and bake for 5 minutes or until topping is browned.

Nutrients per serving

Calories	168
Fat	8.6 g
Saturated fat	3.7 g
Sodium	164 mg (7% DV)
Carbohydrate	18 g
Fiber	3 g (12% DV)
Protein	7 g
Calcium	159 mg (14% DV)
Iron	1.4 mg (10% DV)

High in: Magnesium and folate

Diabetes Food Choice Values:
½ Carbohydrate
½ Meat & Alternatives
1 Fat

Erin dislikes peeling and chopping squash, so she developed a method that requires neither!

Tip

Microwave ovens vary in their capacity and power. Use a baking dish that fits easily inside. Cut the squash into smaller pieces, if necessary, or cook it one half at a time. Check the squash occasionally for doneness.

Variation

Use 1 large buttercup or 2 medium acorn squash.

Quick and Delicious Maple Squash

Erin Nelson, New Brunswick

● **Large microwave-safe dish**

1	butternut squash	1
2 tbsp	pure maple syrup	30 mL
2 tsp	non-hydrogenated margarine	10 mL
½ tsp	freshly ground black pepper	2 mL
¼ tsp	salt	1 mL

1. Cut squash in half lengthwise. Scoop out and discard seeds and stringy pulp. Place squash, skin side down, in microwave-safe dish. Place 1 tbsp (15 mL) maple syrup and 1 tsp (5 mL) margarine in the hollow of each half.

2. Cover dish with plastic wrap, leaving one corner open for a vent, and microwave on High for 8 to 10 minutes or until fork-tender. Scoop squash out of skins into a serving dish. Sprinkle with pepper and salt.

Butternut squash is one of the varieties classified as a winter squash (others include acorn and Hubbard). Winter squash are harvested in the late fall and can take as long as 3 months to ripen. They have tough outer skins that help them store well over the winter months.

Nutrients per serving

Calories	97
Fat	1.4 g
Saturated fat	0.2 g
Sodium	120 mg (5% DV)
Carbohydrate	22 g
Fiber	3 g (12% DV)
Protein	2 g
Calcium	76 mg (7% DV)
Iron	1.2 mg (9% DV)

Very high in: Vitamin A

High in: Magnesium, vitamin C and folate

Diabetes Food Choice Values:
1½ Carbohydrate

✔ Kid Approved

Sweet potato "flowers" are easy to make, pretty and fun! Kids can spread the margarine and sprinkle the brown sugar after you cut the "petals." At the table, let them peel the potato from the skin to eat with their fingers.

Tips

Shorter sweet potatoes make the most attractive flowers.

If cooking 1 potato, cook for 3 minutes, flip, then cook for another 3 minutes. Add 2 minutes for each additional potato.

Variations

Sprinkle with ground cinnamon or nutmeg instead of brown sugar.

Place a mini marshmallow in the middle of each potato to form the stigma of the flower.

Nutrients per serving

Calories	109
Fat	3.0 g
Saturated fat	0.4 g
Sodium	70 mg (3% DV)
Carbohydrate	20 g
Fiber	3 g (12% DV)
Protein	2 g
Calcium	35 mg (3% DV)
Iron	0.5 mg (4% DV)

Very high in: Vitamin A

Diabetes Food Choice Values:
1   Carbohydrate
½   Fat

Flowering Sweet Potatoes

Hilary Gnus, Dietitian, Ontario

● **Microwave-safe dish or plate**

2	sweet potatoes	2
1 tbsp	non-hydrogenated margarine	15 mL
1 to 2 tsp	packed brown sugar	5 to 10 mL

1. Pierce each sweet potato several times with a fork. Place potatoes on microwave-safe dish. Microwave on High for 4 minutes. Turn potatoes over and microwave on High for 4 minutes or until tender. Let cool for 2 to 3 minutes.

2. Cut potatoes in half crosswise. Stand the potato on end, cut side up, and slice each half into quarters without cutting all the way through. With your fingers, push up the end of the potato so it fans out like a flower. Spread a small amount of margarine on each "petal" and sprinkle with brown sugar to taste.

Makes 8 servings

✔ **Kid Approved**

Oven-baking sweet potato fries lowers the fat and calories while maintaining all the flavor. The curry mayo was a real hit with our taste testers.

Tips

Cut the potatoes to a uniform size and shape to facilitate even cooking.

Kids can get involved by making the curry mayo.

If you serve these fries without the curry mayo, you'll reduce the fat content per serving by a third.

Variation

Use 1 tsp (5 mL) paprika and 1 tsp (5 mL) chili powder in place of cumin. Or use 1 tsp (5 mL) ground cinnamon and 2 tbsp (30 mL) chopped fresh rosemary.

Nutrients per serving

Calories	146
Fat	9.5 g
Saturated fat	0.9 g
Sodium	71 mg (3% DV)
Carbohydrate	15 g
Fiber	2 g (8% DV)
Protein	1 g
Calcium	25 mg (2% DV)
Iron	0.8 mg (6% DV)

Very high in: Vitamin A

Diabetes Food Choice Values:

1	Carbohydrate
2	Fats

Oven-Baked Sweet Potato Fries with Curry Mayo

Jessica Kelly, Dietitian, Ontario

- **Preheat oven to 425°F (220°C)**
- **Baking sheet, lined with foil**

Sweet Potato Fries

1½ lbs	sweet potatoes, peeled and cut into ½-inch (1 cm) thick spears	750 g
¼ cup	canola or olive oil	60 mL
1 tsp	ground cumin	5 mL
½ tsp	sea salt (optional)	2 mL

Curry Mayo

¼ cup	light mayonnaise	60 mL
1 tsp	curry powder	5 mL
1 tsp	liquid honey	5 mL

1. *Fries:* In a large bowl, combine sweet potatoes, oil and cumin, tossing until fries are well coated. Spread in a single layer on prepared baking sheet. Bake in preheated oven for 15 minutes. Flip potatoes over and bake for 15 minutes or until browned and tender. Transfer potatoes to a plate lined with paper towels and sprinkle with sea salt (if using).

2. *Mayo:* Meanwhile, in a small bowl, combine mayonnaise, curry powder and honey. Cover and refrigerate until ready to use.

3. Serve fries with curry mayo for dipping.

Using chicken broth instead of milk or cream helps keep the fat content in check in this traditionally higher-fat side dish.

Tip

Leftovers are good mixed with chopped ham and reheated.

Serving Idea

Serve as an accompaniment to the Strip Loin Steak with Mushroom Sauce (page 197).

Scalloped Potatoes

Anne Wall, Alberta

- **Preheat oven to 325°F (160°C)**
- **10-cup (2.5 L) casserole dish, greased**

5	large Yukon gold potatoes (about 1¾ lbs/875 g), peeled and cut crosswise into ¼-inch (0.5 cm) slices	5
¾ cup	chopped onion	175 mL
3 tbsp	non-hydrogenated margarine	45 mL
¼ cup	all-purpose flour	60 mL
1¾ cups	reduced-sodium chicken broth	425 mL
2 tbsp	light mayonnaise	30 mL
½ tsp	freshly ground black pepper	2 mL
¼ tsp	salt	1 mL
Pinch	paprika	Pinch

1. Layer potatoes and onion in prepared baking dish; set aside.

2. In a medium saucepan, melt margarine over medium heat. Stir in flour until smooth; cook, stirring, for 30 seconds. Gradually whisk in broth to form a smooth sauce. Stir in mayonnaise, pepper and salt; cook, stirring, for 2 minutes or until thick and bubbling. Pour evenly over potatoes. Sprinkle with paprika.

3. Cover and bake in preheated oven for 1 hour or until potatoes are fork-tender. Let stand for 10 minutes before serving.

There are two basic types of potatoes: baking and boiling. Baking potatoes have thick skin and a high starch content, and are ideal for baking, mashing and frying. Russet (also known as Idaho) is a common variety of baking potato. Boiling potatoes, sometimes called waxy potatoes, have thin skin; they are higher in moisture but have a low starch content. They are best suited to soups, casseroles and potato salad, as they hold their shape. Some potatoes, such as Yukon gold, fall in the middle and are all-purpose potatoes.

Nutrients per serving

Calories	172
Fat	5.7 g
Saturated fat	0.8 g
Sodium	289 mg (12% DV)
Carbohydrate	28 g
Fiber	2 g (8% DV)
Protein	3 g
Calcium	18 mg (2% DV)
Iron	0.5 mg (4% DV)

High in: Vitamin B$_6$

Diabetes Food Choice Values:

1½ Carbohydrates
1 Fat

✔ **Kid Approved**

Gillian loves potato salad, but not the heavy mayonnaise type. She also loves green beans, so she combined beans and potatoes into a simple salad. It's a delicious way to get children to eat green veggies!

Tips

Save time by cleaning and trimming the green beans and sautéing the onions and garlic while the potatoes are steaming.

This recipe can easily be doubled.

Variation

Add 2 to 3 strips of crumbled cooked bacon.

Nutrients per serving

Calories	160
Fat	7.0 g
Saturated fat	1.0 g
Sodium	151 mg (6% DV)
Carbohydrate	22 g
Fiber	3 g (12% DV)
Protein	3 g
Calcium	29 mg (3% DV)
Iron	1.1 mg (8% DV)

High in: Vitamin C

Diabetes Food Choice Values:
1   Carbohydrate
1½   Fats

Green Bean and Potato Nugget Salad

Gillian Kelly, Dietitian, British Columbia

● **Steamer basket**

1 lb	baby red potatoes (nuggets)	500 g
5 oz	green beans, trimmed and cut in half	150 g
2 tbsp	olive oil, divided	30 mL
½	small onion, chopped	½
1	clove garlic, minced	1
¼ tsp	salt	1 mL
¼ tsp	freshly ground black pepper	1 mL

1. Place potatoes in a steamer basket set in a pot of boiling water over medium-high heat. Cover and steam for 15 minutes or until fork-tender. Transfer potatoes to a plate and let cool. Cut into quarters and transfer to a large bowl.

2. Meanwhile, return basket to pot and ensure there is still about 1 inch (2.5 cm) of water in the pot. Add beans, cover and steam for 6 minutes or until fork-tender. Remove basket and rinse beans under cool water to stop the cooking process. Drain well and add to potatoes.

3. In a small skillet, heat 1 tbsp (15 mL) oil over medium heat. Sauté onion for 3 to 4 minutes or until softened. Add garlic and sauté for 30 seconds.

4. Add onion mixture to potato mixture, along with the remaining oil, salt and pepper, and stir gently to combine. Serve hot or let cool, cover and refrigerate until ready to serve, for up to 24 hours.

✔ **Kid Approved**

Use multicolored veggie pasta to make this a really pretty dish.

Tip

Have all your vegetables chopped before you start to cook, so they're ready to add at the right time.

Veggie Bow Tie Pasta

Carolyn Petrie, Nova Scotia

2 cups	bow tie pasta	500 mL
1½ tbsp	olive oil	22 mL
1 cup	chopped onion	250 mL
½ tsp	freshly ground black pepper	2 mL
¼ tsp	salt	1 mL
4	cloves garlic, minced	4
½	large red bell pepper, thinly sliced	½
2 cups	quartered mushrooms	500 mL
1 cup	chopped zucchini	250 mL
2 tbsp	dry red wine	30 mL
1	large plum (Roma) tomato, chopped	1
2 cups	lightly packed baby spinach	500 mL
⅓ cup	freshly grated Parmesan cheese	75 mL

1. In a large pot of boiling salted water, cook pasta according to package directions until al dente. Drain and transfer to a large serving bowl.

2. Meanwhile, in a large nonstick skillet, heat oil over medium heat. Sauté onions for 3 to 4 minutes or until softened. Sprinkle with pepper and salt. Add garlic and sauté for 30 seconds. Add red pepper, mushrooms and zucchini; reduce heat to medium-low and sauté for 6 to 8 minutes or until softened.

3. Increase heat to medium-high. Add wine and deglaze the pan, scraping up any brown bits. Boil, stirring, until most of the wine is evaporated. Stir in tomato and spinach; cover and cook for 2 to 3 minutes or until spinach is wilted.

4. Pour vegetable mixture over pasta. Sprinkle with Parmesan.

Nutrients per serving

Calories	185
Fat	5.1 g
Saturated fat	1.4 g
Sodium	258 mg (11% DV)
Carbohydrate	23 g
Fiber	1 g (4% DV)
Protein	7 g
Calcium	104 mg (9% DV)
Iron	1.4 mg (10% DV)

High in: Magnesium, vitamin A, vitamin C and niacin

Diabetes Food Choice Values:

1½ Carbohydrates
1 Fat

✔ **Kid Approved**

This time-saving side dish
is made entirely in the
microwave oven. You'll be
surprised at its simplicity
and how well it mimics
true risotto.

Tip

To achieve the desired
"risotto" results, be sure to
use a short-grain rice that is
high in starch, such as Arborio
or Carnaroli. The starch helps
to make the risotto creamy.

Variation

Mix ¼ cup (60 mL) freshly
grated Parmesan cheese
with the Cheddar.

Nutrients per serving

Calories	191
Fat	7.8 g
Saturated fat	4.9 g
Sodium	258 mg (11% DV)
Carbohydrate	23 g
Fiber	1 g (4% DV)
Protein	7 g
Calcium	114 mg (10% DV)
Iron	0.7 mg (5% DV)

High in: Zinc, vitamin D,
vitamin B$_6$, thiamine, riboflavin

Diabetes Food Choice Values:
1½ Carbohydrates
½   Meat & Alternatives
1   Fat

Mushroom and Cheese Risotto

Adapted from Dairy Farmers of Canada
(www.dairygoodness.ca)

● **9-inch (23 cm) microwave-safe square baking dish**

2 tbsp	butter	30 mL
3 cups	sliced mushrooms	750 mL
⅔ cup	chopped onion	150 mL
1	large clove garlic, minced	1
1 cup	Arborio or other Italian-style rice	250 mL
2 cups	reduced-sodium chicken broth	500 mL
½ cup	dry white wine or additional broth	125 mL
1 cup	shredded Cheddar cheese	250 mL
2 tbsp	finely chopped fresh parsley	30 mL

1. Place butter in baking dish and microwave on High for
   about 30 seconds or until melted. Stir in mushrooms,
   onion and garlic until coated. Microwave on High for
   5 minutes.

2. Stir in rice, broth and wine. Microwave on High for
   20 to 30 minutes, stirring halfway through, until rice is
   tender. If rice isn't moist enough, add more broth toward
   the end. Stir in cheese and let stand for 5 minutes.
   Sprinkle with parsley.

✔ **Kid Approved**

Caramelized onions and two mushroom varieties add deep, rich flavor to this dish.

Tips

Pearl barley is more processed than pot barley and requires less cooking time. If you want to use pot barley, use the same amount of water and increase the cooking time to close to 1 hour.

Do not let the onions scorch in step 2. If they start to get dark spots, add a little water.

Nutrients per serving

Calories	115
Fat	1.8 g
Saturated fat	0.5 g
Sodium	55 mg (2% DV)
Carbohydrate	23 g
Fiber	3 g (12% DV)
Protein	3 g
Calcium	17 mg (2% DV)
Iron	1.1 mg (8% DV)

High in: Niacin

Diabetes Food Choice Values:

1   Carbohydrate
½   Fat

Barley with Mushrooms and Caramelized Onions

Compass Group Canada

⅔ cup	pearl barley, rinsed	150 mL
1 tsp	canola or olive oil	5 mL
1 cup	chopped onion	250 mL
1 tsp	butter or non-hydrogenated margarine	5 mL
2 cups	sliced mushrooms	500 mL
1½ cups	shiitake mushroom caps (about 3 oz/90 g)	375 mL
2 tsp	minced garlic	10 mL
1½ tsp	reduced-sodium soy sauce	7 mL
¼ tsp	freshly ground black pepper	1 mL
1½ tsp	minced fresh thyme	7 mL

1. In a medium saucepan with a tight-fitting lid, bring 1½ cups (375 mL) water to a boil over high heat. Stir in barley. Cover and return to a boil. Reduce heat to low and simmer, stirring occasionally, for 30 to 35 minutes or until barley is tender. Remove from heat and drain off any excess liquid.

2. In a large skillet, heat oil over medium heat. Add onion and stir to coat with oil. Cook, stirring frequently, for 10 minutes or until golden brown. Transfer to a bowl and set aside.

3. Return skillet to medium heat and melt butter. Sauté mushrooms, shiitake mushrooms and garlic for 4 to 5 minutes or until tender. Return onions to pan. Stir in cooked barley, soy sauce, pepper and thyme.

> Shiitake mushrooms are commonly used in Asian cuisines, and are now widely available in Canada.

Makes 6 servings

Mediterranean-style quinoa makes a great addition to a summertime family meal.

Tip

Store a batch of this multi-purpose dressing in the refrigerator so it's ready when you need it. It can be stored for up to 5 days.

Variation

Add chopped roasted mushrooms to the salad.

Nutrients per serving

Calories	238
Fat	9.4 g
Saturated fat	0.9 g
Sodium	375 mg (16% DV)
Carbohydrate	33 g
Fiber	6 g (24% DV)
Protein	7 g
Calcium	59 mg (5% DV)
Iron	3.8 mg (27% DV)

Very high in: Magnesium, vitamin C and folate

High in: Zinc, vitamin A and vitamin B_6

Diabetes Food Choice Values:

1½ Carbohydrates
2 Fats

Quinoa à la Med

Lisa Diamond, Dietitian, British Columbia

1 cup	quinoa, rinsed	250 mL
2 cups	bite-size broccoli florets, blanched and drained	500 mL
1 cup	diced tomatoes	250 mL
⅔ cup	drained diced oil-marinated artichoke hearts, patted dry	150 mL
⅔ cup	diced roasted red bell peppers (see box, page 124)	150 mL
¼ cup	finely chopped kalamata olives	60 mL
1 cup	drained rinsed canned chickpeas	250 mL
Dressing		
2 tbsp	Dijon mustard	30 mL
2 tbsp	red wine vinegar	30 mL
1 tbsp	freshly squeezed lemon juice	30 mL
2 tbsp	canola oil	30 mL
¾ tsp	freshly ground black pepper	3 mL
¼ tsp	salt	1 mL

1. In a medium saucepan, combine quinoa and 2 cups (500 mL) water; bring to a boil over high heat. Reduce heat to low, cover and simmer for 15 to 20 minutes or until liquid is absorbed and quinoa is tender. Let stand for 5 minutes. Transfer to a large bowl and fluff with a fork. Let cool.

2. Gently stir broccoli, tomatoes, artichokes, roasted peppers, olives and chickpeas into quinoa.

3. *Dressing:* In a small bowl, whisk together mustard and vinegar. Whisk in lemon juice, oil, 2 tbsp (30 mL) water, pepper and salt. Pour over salad and stir to combine.

Couscous Primavera

Sue Mah, Dietitian, Ontario

✔ **Kid Approved**

Use whole wheat couscous and your favorite seasonal vegetables in this side dish. Sue's daughter, Abbey, helps her chop baby carrots.

Tip

Enjoy leftovers hot or cold for lunch the next day.

Variation

For a vegetarian meal, add half a 19-oz (540 mL) can of rinsed drained chickpeas.

Serving Idea

For a simple yet impressive presentation, lightly grease a small custard cup or ramekin. Scoop couscous into the cup and press it down. Invert the cup onto a serving plate and tap lightly to remove couscous.

1 tbsp	canola oil	15 mL
1	onion, chopped	1
2	cloves garlic, minced	2
3	carrots, chopped	3
1 cup	frozen green peas, thawed	250 mL
1½ cups	reduced-sodium chicken broth	375 mL
1 cup	whole wheat couscous	250 mL

1. In a large skillet, heat oil over medium heat. Sauté onion for 3 to 4 minutes or until softened. Add garlic and sauté for 30 seconds. Add carrots and peas; sauté for 3 to 4 minutes or until carrots are fork-tender.

2. Add broth, increase heat to high and bring to a boil. As soon as it comes to a boil, turn off heat and stir in couscous. Remove from heat. Cover and let stand for 5 minutes or until liquid is absorbed. Fluff with a fork.

Nutrients per serving

Calories	134
Fat	2.2 g
Saturated fat	0.1 g
Sodium	139 mg (6% DV)
Carbohydrate	25 g
Fiber	5 g (20% DV)
Protein	5 g
Calcium	27 mg (2% DV)
Iron	1.1 mg (8% DV)

Very high in: Vitamin A

Diabetes Food Choice Values:

1   Carbohydrate
½   Fat

Makes 8 servings

Lorraine comes from Cranberry Portage, Manitoba, which is, unsurprisingly, located on a portage between two lakes where wild cranberries grow. Each year she picks several pails to freeze, and she has developed many creative uses for her bounty, including this delicious accompaniment to the Thanksgiving turkey!

Tips

To make 2 cups (500 mL) cooked wild rice, combine ½ cup (125 mL) wild rice with 1½ cups (375 mL) water in a medium saucepan with a tight-fitting lid. Bring to a boil over high heat. Reduce heat to low, cover and simmer for 1 hour or until liquid is absorbed. Fluff with a fork.

You can use rinsed drained canned mushrooms instead of fresh, if you prefer.

Nutrients per serving

Calories	112
Fat	6.1 g
Saturated fat	2.1 g
Sodium	171 mg (7% DV)
Carbohydrate	12 g
Fiber	2 g (8% DV)
Protein	3 g
Calcium	24 mg (2% DV)
Iron	0.7 mg (5% DV)

Diabetes Food Choice Values:
½ Carbohydrate
1 Fat

Poultry Stuffing

Lorraine Petryk, Manitoba

2 tbsp	butter	30 mL
½ cup	chopped onion	125 mL
¼ cup	chopped celery	60 mL
1	clove garlic, minced	1
½ cup	chopped mushrooms	125 mL
1 tbsp	chopped fresh parsley	15 mL
1½ tsp	chopped fresh rosemary	7 mL
1 tsp	poultry seasoning	5 mL
1 tsp	freshly ground black pepper	5 mL
½ tsp	salt	2 mL
2 cups	cooked wild rice	500 mL
½ cup	frozen or dried cranberries (thawed if frozen)	125 mL
½ cup	sliced almonds	125 mL

1. In a medium saucepan, melt butter over medium heat. Sauté onion and celery for 3 to 4 minutes or until softened. Add garlic, mushrooms, parsley, rosemary, poultry seasoning, pepper and salt; sauté for 1 minute.

2. Stir in wild rice, cranberries and almonds; cook, stirring, until heated through.

Muffins and Quick Breads

Today, it's common to see muffins the size of a baseball, but a healthy muffin should really be only 2 to 3 inches (5 to 7.5 cm) in diameter. The muffins in this chapter are the appropriate size, and are made with whole grains and other nutrient-rich ingredients — and, of course, they taste great! Quick breads are just that: breads that can be made quickly, which usually means no yeast is used. Rather, quick breads rely on other leavening agents such as eggs, baking soda and baking powder. Enjoy a muffin or a slice of quick bread as an occasional breakfast treat, as a mid-morning or afternoon snack, or even as part of a light lunch.

Fabulous Fiber!

Muffins and quick breads are a marvelous way to add fiber to your meal plan. Non-soluble fiber is the part of a fruit, vegetable, grain, nut or seed that your body can't digest, so it's helpful in keeping your digestive tract working well. Meats and dairy products (unless they are in some way fortified with fiber) contain little, if any, fiber.

If you buy commercially prepared muffins, do so very carefully. Many are enormous, laden with fat and sugar, devoid of whole grains and lacking in fiber. If they're packaged, be sure to read the Nutrition Facts table so you know the calories, nutrients and fiber you're getting. The best way to control the calories, fat and fiber in your muffins is to make them from scratch.

A Word About Baking Powder and Baking Soda

Many recipes for baked goods call for baking powder and/or baking soda. These are both leavening agents, but they are not interchangeable, so take care to use the right one. Be aware that both of these ingredients contain a large amount of sodium. In fact, the chemical name for baking soda is "sodium bicarbonate." And since one of the ingredients in baking powder is baking soda, it also contains plenty of sodium. Just 1 tsp (5 mL) of double-acting baking powder (the type most commonly used in recipes) contains nearly 400 mg of sodium, while 1 tsp (5 mL) of baking soda contains nearly 1,300 mg! In the recipes in this chapter, we've kept the baking powder and soda to the minimum needed to produce a delicious product.

Family Cooking Lesson

Making Muffins

To make delicious, well-shaped, healthy muffins at home, follow these simple tips.

The "Muffin Method" for Mixing Batter

To create muffins that are tender, light and moist in texture and even in shape, there's a three-step process for mixing the batter:

1. Combine the measured dry ingredients in a large bowl.
2. In another bowl, whisk together the liquid ingredients (in muffin recipes, sugar is added with the liquids even though it's measured as a dry ingredient) until blended.
3. Add the liquid ingredients to the dry ingredients and stir just until combined. (If the batter is overmixed, the muffins may be rubbery and tough, or may have air pockets or tunnels running through them.)

Adding Fiber

There are several good ways to add fiber to your muffin recipes:

- Substitute whole wheat flour for half of the white flour called for in the recipe.
- Choose recipes made with wheat bran, whole wheat flour, rye flour and/or ground or whole flax seeds.
- Add ½ cup (125 mL) chopped dried fruits, such as raisins, apricots, cranberries or blueberries; ½ cup (125 mL) chopped nuts, such as walnuts, cashews or pecans; or 2 tbsp (30 mL) seeds, such as sunflower, sesame or flax.

continued...

Managing Fat

Check that the amount of fat (butter, margarine or oil) is no greater than $1/4$ to $1/3$ cup (60 to 75 mL) for a dozen muffins. The best fat choices for heart health include canola oil, safflower oil, sunflower oil and non-hydrogenated margarine. Watch out for higher-fat added ingredients such as cheese, regular sour cream or chocolate.

Here are some good ways to reduce the fat in a muffin recipe:

- Replace half the fat with an equal amount of a puréed fruit or vegetable, such as apples, bananas, prunes, carrots, sweet potato or pumpkin.
- Substitute 2%, 1% or skim milk for whole milk.
- Reduce the amount of regular cheese by half.
- Use low-fat sour cream or low-fat plain yogurt instead of regular sour cream.

Managing Sugar

Check that the amount of sugar is no greater than $3/4$ cup (175 mL) for a dozen muffins. To reduce the sugar in a muffin recipe, use one-third less and add $1/2$ to 1 tsp (2 to 5 mL) ground cinnamon or $1/2$ tsp (2 mL) vanilla or almond extract.

Marla's Pumpkin Walnut Bran Muffins

Marla McKerracher, Dietitian, Ontario

Makes 12 muffins

Serving size: 1 muffin

✔ **Kid Approved**

Sweet cinnamon, crunchy nuts and smooth pumpkin make these muffins a winner with adults and children alike.

Tips

You can cook your own pie pumpkin to make the purée for this recipe or you can use canned pumpkin purée; just be sure not to use pumpkin pie filling, which is sweetened.

These muffins freeze well. Wrap cooled muffins individually in plastic wrap, then seal in an airtight container or freezer bag and freeze for up to 1 month.

Variation

Use 1 cup (250 mL) mashed bananas, unsweetened applesauce, drained crushed pineapple or puréed butternut squash instead of the pumpkin.

Nutrients per serving

Calories	191
Fat	8.8 g
Saturated fat	0.9 g
Sodium	143 mg (6% DV)
Carbohydrate	28 g
Fiber	5 g (20% DV)
Protein	4 g
Calcium	45 mg (4% DV)
Iron	1.9 mg (14% DV)

Very high in: Magnesium
High in: Vitamin A

Diabetes Food Choice Values:
1½ Carbohydrates
2 Fats

- **Preheat oven to 400°F (200°C)**
- **12-cup muffin pan, lightly greased or lined with paper cups**

1 cup	whole wheat flour	250 mL
1 cup	wheat bran	250 mL
¼ cup	wheat germ	60 mL
1 tsp	baking soda	5 mL
1 tsp	baking powder	5 mL
1 tsp	ground cinnamon	5 mL
¾ cup	lightly packed brown sugar	175 mL
1	egg	1
¼ cup	canola oil	60 mL
1 tsp	vanilla extract	5 mL
1 cup	pumpkin purée (see tip, at left)	250 mL
½ cup	chopped walnuts	125 mL

1. In a large bowl, combine flour, bran, wheat germ, baking soda, baking powder and cinnamon.

2. In a small bowl, whisk together brown sugar, egg, oil and vanilla until blended. Stir in pumpkin. Pour over flour mixture and stir until just combined. Fold in walnuts.

3. Divide batter evenly among prepared muffin cups. Bake in preheated oven for 16 to 18 minutes or until tops are browned and a tester inserted in the center of a muffin comes out clean. Let cool in pan on a wire rack for 10 minutes, then transfer to rack to cool completely.

Makes 12 muffins

Serving size: 1 muffin

Nancy crafted this recipe nearly two decades ago from one that called for fortified infant cereal. Her children were young at the time, but they enjoy these muffins to this day. The muffins were a huge hit with our taste testers too!

Tip

These muffins freeze well. Wrap cooled muffins individually in plastic wrap, then seal in an airtight container or freezer bag and freeze for up to 1 month.

Variation

Use your favorite fruit, such as raspberries or chopped peaches, in place of the blueberries.

Nutrients per serving

Calories	175
Fat	6.4 g
Saturated fat	0.8 g
Sodium	104 mg (4% DV)
Carbohydrate	28 g
Fiber	4 g (16% DV)
Protein	5 g
Calcium	70 mg (6% DV)
Iron	1.9 mg (14% DV)

Very high in: Magnesium
High in: Zinc

Diabetes Food Choice Values:
1½ Carbohydrates
1½ Fats

Blueberry Bran Muffins

Nancy Morgan, Ontario

- **Preheat oven to 400°F (200°C)**
- **12-cup muffin pan, lightly greased or lined with paper cups**

1½ cups	wheat bran	375 mL
½ cup	all-purpose flour	125 mL
½ cup	wheat germ	125 mL
1 tsp	baking powder	5 mL
½ tsp	baking soda	2 mL
½ cup	lightly packed brown sugar	125 mL
2	eggs, beaten	2
1 cup	1% milk	250 mL
¼ cup	canola oil	60 mL
¼ cup	fancy molasses	60 mL
1 cup	fresh or frozen blueberries	250 mL

1. In a large bowl, combine bran, flour, wheat germ, baking powder and baking soda.

2. In a medium bowl, whisk together brown sugar, eggs, milk, oil and molasses until blended. Pour over flour mixture and stir until just combined. Fold in blueberries.

3. Divide batter evenly among prepared muffin cups. Bake in preheated oven for 15 to 17 minutes or until tops are firm to the touch and a tester inserted in the center of a muffin comes out clean. Let cool in pan on a wire rack for 10 minutes, then transfer to rack to cool completely.

Makes 18 muffins

Serving size: 1 muffin

✔ **Kid Approved**

This recipe was created by Jennifer's great-aunt, and Jennifer now bakes these muffins with her young son. He loves to help — Jennifer measures, and he pours and mixes!

Tip

If you don't have buttermilk, add 1 tbsp (15 mL) vinegar or lemon juice to 1 cup (250 mL) regular milk and let stand for a few minutes.

Nutrients per serving

Calories	154
Fat	5.4 g
Saturated fat	0.7 g
Sodium	122 mg (5% DV)
Carbohydrate	24 g
Fiber	3 g (12% DV)
Protein	4 g
Calcium	38 mg (3% DV)
Iron	1.2 mg (9% DV)

High in: Magnesium

Diabetes Food Choice Values:

1½ Carbohydrates

1 Fat

Apricot Oatmeal Bran Muffins

Jennifer House, Dietitian, Alberta

- **Preheat oven to 375°F (190°C)**
- **Two 12-cup muffin pans, 18 cups lightly greased or lined with paper cups**

½ cup	wheat bran	125 mL
½ cup	boiling water	125 mL
1½ cups	whole wheat flour	375 mL
1 cup	quick-cooking rolled oats	250 mL
⅓ cup	wheat germ	75 mL
1 tsp	baking soda	5 mL
¼ tsp	salt	1 mL
½ cup	lightly packed brown sugar	125 mL
1	egg	1
1 cup	buttermilk	250 mL
⅓ cup	canola oil	75 mL
1 cup	chopped dried apricots	250 mL

1. In a small bowl, stir together wheat bran and boiling water; set aside.

2. In a large bowl, combine flour, oats, wheat germ, baking soda and salt.

3. In a medium bowl, whisk together brown sugar, egg, buttermilk and oil until blended. Pour over flour mixture, along with bran mixture, and stir until just combined. Fold in apricots.

4. Divide batter evenly among prepared muffin cups. Bake in preheated oven for 16 to 18 minutes or until a tester inserted in the center of a muffin comes out clean. Let cool in pans on a wire rack for 10 minutes, then transfer to rack to cool completely.

Makes 12 muffins

Serving size: 1 muffin

Just like mayonnaise, these muffins are made with real, simple ingredients. They can be enjoyed as a dessert or even with breakfast!

Oatmeal Berry Burst Muffins

Hellmann's Mayonnaise (www.hellmanns.ca)

- **Preheat oven to 400°F (200°C)**
- **12-cup muffin pan, lightly greased or lined with paper cups**

1½ cups	all-purpose flour	375 mL
¾ cup	quick-cooking rolled oats	175 mL
2 tsp	baking powder	10 mL
½ tsp	salt	2 mL
½ tsp	ground cinnamon	2 mL
½ cup	packed brown sugar	125 mL
1	egg	1
1 cup	2% milk	250 mL
½ cup	light mayonnaise	125 mL
1 cup	fresh or frozen raspberries or blueberries (or a combination)	250 mL

1. In a large bowl, combine flour, oats, baking powder, salt and cinnamon.

2. In a medium bowl, whisk together brown sugar, egg, milk and mayonnaise until blended. Pour over flour mixture and stir until just combined. Fold in berries.

3. Divide batter evenly among prepared muffin cups. Bake in preheated oven for 20 to 25 minutes or until tops spring back when lightly touched. Let cool in pans on a wire rack for 10 minutes, then transfer to rack to cool completely.

Nutrients per serving

Calories	170
Fat	4.5 g
Saturated fat	1.0 g
Sodium	230 mg (10% DV)
Carbohydrate	29 g
Fiber	2 g (8% DV)
Protein	4 g
Calcium	65 mg (6% DV)
Iron	1.1 mg (8% DV)

High in: Folate

Diabetes Food Choice Values:

2 Carbohydrates
1 Fat

Makes 12 muffins

Serving size: 1 muffin

This recipe features some of Canada's signature ingredients, baked into a delicious muffin.

Tip

Warming the oats with the maple syrup moistens the oats and helps them absorb the maple flavor.

Nutrients per serving

Calories	225
Fat	8.8 g
Saturated fat	1.0 g
Sodium	100 mg (4% DV)
Carbohydrate	33 g
Fiber	1 g (4% DV)
Protein	4 g
Calcium	55 mg (5% DV)
Iron	1.4 mg (10% DV)

High in: Folate

Diabetes Food Choice Values:

2   Carbohydrates

2   Fats

Streusel-Topped Maple Oatmeal Muffins

Caroline Dubeau, Dietitian, Ontario

- **Preheat oven to 375°F (190°C)**
- **12-cup muffin pan, lightly greased or lined with paper cups**

¾ cup	quick-cooking rolled oats	175 mL
½ cup	pure maple syrup	125 mL
¼ cup	packed brown sugar	60 mL
2	eggs	2
⅓ cup	canola oil	75 mL
1 tsp	vanilla extract	5 mL
1¼ cups	all-purpose flour	375 mL
1 tsp	baking powder	5 mL
½ tsp	baking soda	2 mL
½ cup	low-fat plain yogurt	125 mL

Streusel Topping

¼ cup	quick-cooking rolled oats	60 mL
2 tbsp	packed brown sugar	30 mL
1 tbsp	pure maple syrup	15 mL
1 tbsp	canola oil	15 mL

1. In a microwave-safe bowl, combine oats and maple syrup. Microwave on High for 1 minute. Set aside.

2. In a large bowl, using an electric mixer on high speed, beat brown sugar, eggs, oil and vanilla for 2 minutes. Stir in half the flour, along with baking powder and baking soda, until just combined. Stir in yogurt until blended. Stir in oat mixture and the remaining flour until just combined.

3. Divide batter evenly among prepared muffin cups.

4. *Topping:* In a small bowl, combine oats, brown sugar, maple syrup and oil. Sprinkle evenly on top of muffins.

5. Bake in preheated oven for 15 to 20 minutes or until tops spring back when lightly touched. Let cool in pan on a wire rack for 10 minutes, then transfer to rack to cool completely.

Karen loves dates, so she created this muffin to satisfy her cravings!

Tip

These muffins freeze well. Wrap cooled muffins individually in plastic wrap, then seal in an airtight container or freezer bag and freeze for up to 1 month.

Variation

Use a 7½-oz (213 mL) jar of baby food puréed squash instead of the applesauce.

Serving Idea

Add a fresh pear and a serving (1½ oz/45 g) of Canadian cheese for a lovely lunch. Don't forget to drink some water!

Nutrients per serving

Calories	252
Fat	10.0 g
Saturated fat	1.1 g
Sodium	151 mg (6% DV)
Carbohydrate	39 g
Fiber	5 g (20% DV)
Protein	5 g
Calcium	74 mg (7% DV)
Iron	1.8 mg (13% DV)

Very high in: Magnesium

Diabetes Food Choice Values:

2½ Carbohydrates

2 Fats

Oatmeal, Date and Nut Muffins

Karen Kuzik, Dietitian, New Brunswick

- **Preheat oven to 400°F (200°C)**
- **12-cup muffin pan, lightly greased or lined with paper cups**

½ cup	quick-cooking rolled oats	125 mL
½ cup	buttermilk	125 mL
1½ cups	whole wheat flour	375 mL
¼ cup	ground flax seeds (flaxseed meal)	60 mL
1 tsp	baking powder	5 mL
1 tsp	baking soda	5 mL
1 tsp	ground cinnamon	5 mL
½ tsp	ground nutmeg	2 mL
¼ cup	lightly packed brown sugar	60 mL
1	egg	1
¼ cup	vegetable oil	60 mL
¼ cup	fancy molasses	60 mL
1 cup	unsweetened applesauce	250 mL
1 cup	chopped dates	250 mL
½ cup	chopped walnuts	125 mL

1. In a small bowl, combine rolled oats and buttermilk. Let stand for 5 minutes.

2. In a large bowl, combine flour, flax seeds, baking powder, baking soda, cinnamon and nutmeg.

3. In a medium bowl, whisk together brown sugar, egg, oil and molasses until blended. Stir in applesauce and oat mixture. Pour over flour mixture and stir until just combined. Fold in dates and walnuts.

4. Divide batter evenly among prepared muffin cups. Bake in preheated oven for 16 to 18 minutes or until tops are firm to the touch and a tester inserted in the center of a muffin comes out clean. Let cool in pan on a wire rack for 10 minutes, then transfer to rack to cool completely.

Makes 18 muffins

Serving size: 1 muffin

Fresh muffins on a Saturday morning are a tradition at Joan's home. These are sure to become one of your favorites.

Tips

Joan likes to assemble the wet and dry ingredients in separate bowls on Friday night, so it takes her less than a minute to finish the prep work in the morning. Be sure to refrigerate the wet ingredients.

These muffins freeze well. Wrap cooled muffins individually in plastic wrap, then seal in an airtight container or freezer bag and freeze for up to 1 month.

Variation

Substitute dried cherries or dried blueberries for the cranberries.

Nutrients per serving

Calories	162
Fat	4.9 g
Saturated fat	0.5 g
Sodium	109 mg (5% DV)
Carbohydrate	27 g
Fiber	2 g (8% DV)
Protein	3 g
Calcium	34 mg (3% DV)
Iron	1.1 mg (8% DV)

High in: Folate

Diabetes Food Choice Values:

1½ Carbohydrates

1 Fat

Orange Cranberry Flax Muffins

Joan Rew, Dietitian, Manitoba

- **Preheat oven to 375°F (190°C)**
- **Two 12-cup muffin pans, 18 cups lightly greased or lined with paper cups**

¾ cup	dried cranberries, coarsely chopped	175 mL
1½ cups	orange juice, divided	375 mL
2 cups	all-purpose flour	500 mL
¾ cup	whole wheat flour	175 mL
½ cup	ground flax seeds (flaxseed meal)	125 mL
½ cup	granulated sugar	125 mL
2 tsp	grated orange zest	10 mL
2 tsp	baking powder	10 mL
1 tsp	baking soda	5 mL
1	egg, beaten	1
¼ cup	canola oil	60 mL

1. In a small bowl, combine cranberries and ¼ cup (60 mL) of the orange juice. Set aside.

2. In a large bowl, combine all-purpose flour, whole wheat flour, flax seeds, sugar, orange zest, baking powder and baking soda.

3. In a medium bowl, whisk together egg, oil and the remaining orange juice until blended. Pour over flour mixture and stir until just combined. Fold in cranberry mixture.

4. Divide batter evenly among prepared muffin cups. Bake in preheated oven for 16 to 18 minutes or until tops are firm to the touch and a tester inserted in the center of a muffin comes out clean. Let cool in pans on a wire rack for 10 minutes, then transfer to rack to cool completely.

Crunchy hazelnut topping is a great texture pairing with tender peaches.

Tip

Buckwheat flour comes in light or dark. The darker flour will make the batter quite brown.

Nutrients per serving

Calories	197
Fat	7.6 g
Saturated fat	0.8 g
Sodium	129 mg (5% DV)
Carbohydrate	29 g
Fiber	2 g (8% DV)
Protein	4 g
Calcium	35 mg (3% DV)
Iron	1.5 mg (11% DV)

High in: Magnesium and folate

Diabetes Food Choice Values:

2 Carbohydrates

1½ Fats

Peachy Buckwheat Muffins with Hazelnut Crunch

Mary Sue Waisman, Dietitian, Nova Scotia

- **Preheat oven to 375°F (190°C)**
- **12-cup muffin pan, lightly greased or lined with paper cups**

Hazelnut Crunch

½ cup	finely chopped hazelnuts	125 mL
2 tbsp	lightly packed brown sugar	30 mL
¼ tsp	ground cinnamon	1 mL

Muffins

1 cup	buckwheat flour	250 mL
1 cup	all-purpose flour	250 mL
1 tsp	ground cinnamon	5 mL
½ tsp	baking powder	2 mL
½ tsp	baking soda	2 mL
½ tsp	ground nutmeg	2 mL
¼ tsp	salt	1 mL
½ cup	lightly packed brown sugar	125 mL
2	eggs	2
3 tbsp	canola oil	45 mL
1 tsp	vanilla extract	5 mL
1½ cups	diced fresh peaches	375 mL

1. *Hazelnut crunch:* In a small bowl, combine hazelnuts, brown sugar and cinnamon. Set aside.

2. *Muffins:* In a large bowl, combine buckwheat flour, all-purpose flour, cinnamon, baking powder, baking soda, nutmeg and salt.

3. In a medium bowl, whisk together brown sugar, eggs, oil and vanilla until blended. Pour over flour mixture and stir until just combined. Fold in peaches.

4. Divide batter evenly among prepared muffin cups. Sprinkle hazelnut crunch evenly over muffins.

5. Bake in preheated oven for 15 to 17 minutes or until tops are firm to the touch and a tester inserted in the center of a muffin comes out clean. Let cool in pans on a wire rack for 10 minutes, then transfer to rack to cool completely.

Garden Patch Muffins

Vincci Tsui, Dietitian, Alberta

- **Preheat oven to 350°F (180°C)**
- **12-cup muffin pan, lightly greased or lined with paper cups**

¾ cup	whole wheat flour	175 mL
¼ cup	ground flax seeds (flaxseed meal)	60 mL
1 tsp	baking soda	5 mL
1 tsp	ground cinnamon	5 mL
½ tsp	ground nutmeg	2 mL
⅔ cup	granulated sugar	150 mL
1	egg	1
¼ cup	unsweetened applesauce	60 mL
1 cup	shredded carrots	250 mL
1 cup	shredded zucchini, squeezed of excess moisture	250 mL
½ cup	chopped pecans	125 mL

1. In a large bowl, combine flour, flax seeds, baking soda, cinnamon and nutmeg.

2. In a small bowl, whisk together sugar and egg until blended. Stir in applesauce. Pour over flour mixture and stir until just combined. Fold in carrots, zucchini and pecans.

3. Divide batter evenly among prepared muffin cups. Bake in preheated oven for 20 to 25 minutes or until a tester inserted in the center of a muffin comes out clean. Let cool in pan on a wire rack for 10 minutes, then transfer to rack to cool completely.

Makes 12 muffins

Serving size: 1 muffin

Here's the perfect way to use fresh herbs and leftover corn on the cob.

Tip

Be sure the corn is dry and the kernels are separated before toasting it.

Variation

If you like heat, add 1 tbsp (15 mL) finely diced jalapeño pepper to the flour mixture or add ½ tsp (2 mL) hot pepper sauce to the egg mixture.

Serving Idea

Serve warm alongside a bowl of Light and Easy Chicken Chili (page 181).

Nutrients per serving

Calories	168
Fat	5.0 g
Saturated fat	0.7 g
Sodium	106 mg (4% DV)
Carbohydrate	27 g
Fiber	2 g (8% DV)
Protein	5 g
Calcium	56 mg (5% DV)
Iron	0.8 mg (6% DV)

High in: Folate

Diabetes Food Choice Values:

1½ Carbohydrates
1 Fat

Savory Herbed Cornmeal Muffins

Mary Sue Waisman, Dietitian, Nova Scotia

- **Preheat oven to 350°F (180°C)**
- **12-cup muffin pan, lightly greased or lined with paper cups**

1 cup	cooked corn kernels (from about 1 large cob)	250 mL
1¼ cups	cornmeal	300 mL
¾ cup	all-purpose flour	175 mL
¼ cup	finely chopped fresh chives	60 mL
2 tbsp	chopped fresh basil	30 mL
2 tbsp	chopped fresh cilantro	30 mL
1 tsp	baking powder	5 mL
½ tsp	baking soda	2 mL
½ tsp	chili powder	2 mL
½ tsp	freshly ground black pepper	2 mL
¼ cup	granulated sugar	60 mL
2	eggs	2
1 cup	low-fat plain yogurt	250 mL
3 tbsp	canola oil	45 mL

1. Heat a medium skillet over medium-high heat. Toast corn, stirring occasionally, for 2 to 3 minutes or until slightly blackened in spots. Transfer to a large bowl and let cool for a few minutes.

2. Add cornmeal, flour, chives, basil, cilantro, baking powder, baking soda, chili powder and pepper to corn and stir until blended.

3. In a medium bowl, whisk together sugar, eggs, yogurt and oil until blended. Pour over cornmeal mixture and stir until just combined.

4. Divide mixture evenly among muffin cups. Bake in preheated oven for 17 to 19 minutes or until tops are firm to the touch and a tester inserted in the center of a muffin comes out clean. Let cool in pan on a wire rack for 10 minutes, then transfer to rack to cool slightly.

Mom's Super-Moist Banana Loaf

Melissa Fuerst, Dietitian, Manitoba

- **Preheat oven to 350°F (180°C)**
- **Two 9- by 5-inch (23 by 12.5 cm) metal loaf pans, greased**

2½ cups	whole wheat flour	625 mL
1½ tsp	ground cinnamon	7 mL
1¼ tsp	baking powder	6 mL
1¼ tsp	baking soda	6 mL
1 tsp	ground nutmeg	5 mL
½ tsp	salt	2 mL
¼ tsp	ground cloves	1 mL
½ cup	granulated sugar	125 mL
2	eggs	2
⅔ cup	buttermilk	150 mL
2 tbsp	vegetable oil	30 mL
1½ cups	mashed ripe bananas	375 mL
⅔ cup	unsweetened applesauce	150 mL

1. In a large bowl, combine flour, cinnamon, baking powder, baking soda, nutmeg, salt and cloves.

2. In a medium bowl, whisk together sugar, eggs, buttermilk and oil until blended. Stir in bananas and applesauce. Pour over flour mixture and stir until just combined.

3. Pour batter into prepared loaf pans, dividing equally. Bake in preheated oven for 40 to 45 minutes or until a tester inserted in the center comes out clean. Let cool in pans on a wire rack for 10 minutes, then transfer to rack to cool completely.

Makes 1 loaf, 12 slices

Serving size: 1 slice

This unique pairing of cranberries and bananas works like a charm! It's great warm from the oven or served the next day with a little vanilla yogurt.

Tip

To avoid lumps, make sure the bananas are very ripe and well mashed.

Serving Idea

This loaf is the highest in fat of our three quick breads. Consider having just half a slice as a morning snack, along with some fresh apple slices and a cup of herbal tea.

Nutrients per serving

Calories	255
Fat	10.5 g
Saturated fat	1.4 g
Sodium	294 mg (12% DV)
Carbohydrate	38 g
Fiber	2 g (8% DV)
Protein	4 g
Calcium	48 mg (4% DV)
Iron	1.1 mg (8% DV)

Very high in: Vitamin D

Diabetes Food Choice Values:

2½ Carbohydrates
2 Fats

Cranberry Banana Nut Bread

Esther Archibald, Dietitian, New Brunswick

- **Preheat oven to 350°F (180°C)**
- **9- by 5-inch (23 by 12.5 cm) metal loaf pan, lightly greased and floured**

1 cup	all-purpose flour	250 mL
¾ cup	whole wheat flour	175 mL
1 tsp	baking powder	5 mL
1 tsp	baking soda	5 mL
¼ tsp	salt	1 mL
¾ cup	granulated sugar	175 mL
½ cup	non-hydrogenated margarine	125 mL
1	egg	1
1 tsp	vanilla extract	5 mL
1 cup	mashed ripe bananas	250 mL
½ cup	low-fat plain yogurt	125 mL
¾ cup	dried cranberries	175 mL
½ cup	chopped sliced almonds	125 mL

1. In a bowl, combine all-purpose flour, whole wheat flour, baking powder, baking soda and salt.

2. In a large bowl, using an electric mixer on high speed, beat sugar and margarine until light and fluffy. Beat in egg and vanilla. Stir in bananas and yogurt until well blended. Add flour mixture and beat on low speed until just combined. Stir in dried cranberries and almonds.

3. Pour batter into prepared pan. Bake in preheated oven for 45 to 55 minutes or until a tester inserted in the center comes out clean. Let cool in pan on a wire rack for 10 minutes, then transfer to rack to cool until just warm or let cool completely.

Makes 1 loaf, 12 slices

Serving size: 1 slice

Jennifer inherited this recipe from her grandmother, who likely created it during the Great Depression, when fat was hard to come by and nothing was wasted, not even orange rind!

Tip

This is a very dense loaf. It's full of flavor and is most delicious served warm. The next day, serve it toasted for breakfast with your favorite jam.

Variation

Use raisins or dried cranberries instead of currants.

Nutrients per serving

Calories	206
Fat	5.7 g
Saturated fat	0.5 g
Sodium	205 mg (9% DV)
Carbohydrate	37 g
Fiber	3 g (12% DV)
Protein	4 g
Calcium	53 mg (5% DV)
Iron	1.7 mg (12% DV)

High in: Folate

Diabetes Food Choice Values:

2   Carbohydrates

1   Fat

Orange Nut Bread

Jennifer House, Dietitian, Alberta

- **Preheat oven to 350°F (180°C)**
- **9- by 5-inch (23 by 12.5 cm) metal loaf pan, lightly greased**
- **Blender or food processor**

2 cups	all-purpose flour	500 mL
1 cup	dried currants	250 mL
½ cup	chopped walnuts	125 mL
½ cup	granulated sugar	125 mL
¼ tsp	salt	1 mL
2 tsp	baking powder	10 mL
1 tsp	baking soda	5 mL
1	large orange (unpeeled), quartered and seeded	1
¾ cup	boiling water	175 mL
2 tbsp	canola oil	30 mL
1 tsp	vanilla extract	5 mL

1. In a large bowl, combine flour, currants, walnuts, sugar, salt, baking powder and baking soda.

2. Place orange quarters in food processor. Pour in boiling water and process for about 15 seconds or until finely minced. Add oil and vanilla; process for 5 seconds or until blended. Pour over flour mixture and stir until just combined.

3. Pour into prepared loaf pan and let stand for 15 minutes.

4. Bake in preheated oven for 1 hour or until a tester inserted in the center comes out clean. Let cool in pan on a wire rack for 10 minutes, then transfer to rack to cool slightly.

Desserts

When you're planning a special meal, you'll likely want to include a luscious dessert. In this chapter, we've included dozens of nutritious options with incredible flavor, made with wholesome ingredients such as fresh and dried fruits, nuts and whole grains. You'll even find recipes made with black beans, carrots and barley — non-traditional dessert ingredients, perhaps, but you won't believe how delicious they are! Of course, there are times when only an ooey-gooey, rich dessert will do. Just keep in mind that these can add an enormous amount of calories, often with few nutrients. Enjoy a few bites and save the rest for another time, or share your dessert with a friend or family member. (If it's your birthday, by all means have a piece of cake guilt-free!)

Flavorful Fruit for Dessert

Fruit is often considered a breakfast item or a snack; rarely is it seen as a dessert, except perhaps in pies, cobblers and crisps. But with its natural sweetness, fruit is a terrific replacement for rich desserts laden with fat and sugar. You can poach pears, roast peaches, bake apples, serve dried fruits on a cheese platter or make fresh fruit parfaits with yogurt cheese — or you can serve a colorful fresh fruit salad all on its own, for simple, classic elegance. Fruit is used in many inventive ways in the dessert recipes in this chapter, so experiment and find your favorites!

Trans Fats in Baked Products

Industrially produced trans fats are created by a chemical process when hydrogen is added to unsaturated fats. Research has shown that these fats not only increase your "bad" cholesterol, but may also reduce your "good" cholesterol. Of all fats, they are the ones that most increase the risk of heart disease. Industrially produced trans fats have no known health benefits.

Commercially prepared baked products, such as cookies, pastry and pies, have traditionally included trans fats, but recently, many Canadian food manufacturers have been working to eliminate trans fats from their products. You can identify whether a product contains trans fats by looking under Fat in the Nutrition Facts table. The value given for trans fats should either be 0 or, at the very least, as low as possible.

Family Cooking Lesson

Roasting and Grilling Fruits

Many fruits, including peaches, nectarines, pears and apples, are well suited to roasting. The high temperature caramelizes the natural sugars, producing a rich, intense flavor. See our recipes for roasted peaches (page 359) and roasted pears (page 360).

One of the simplest desserts for barbecue night is grilled fruit. Once you've cooked the main meal, clean the grill to remove any residue. Cut fruit into long pieces or chunks and thread them onto skewers. Grill for a few minutes on each side, just until heated through. Serve drizzled with honey or your favorite dessert sauce. Crowd-pleasing grilled fruits include pineapple, mango, apple and pear.

Preparing desserts at home allows you to control the ingredients you use, thereby ensuring that you avoid trans fats. For example, choose non-hydrogenated margarine for baking and use clear oils, such as canola, sunflower, grapeseed, olive or peanut, for cooking. Steer clear of hydrogenated hard margarines and baking fats.

By the way, it's a myth that you can produce trans fats at home by heating olive oil to a high temperature. Olive oil has a low smoke point, so if it's heated to a high temperature, it can break down or burn, but no trans fats are produced in the process.

Family Cooking Lesson

Making a Cheese Tray

Making a cheese tray is simple and you can use your imagination and creativity. It's lots of fun to prepare. Remember, the cheese is always the star.

What You Need

2 or 3 varieties of cheese
Nuts, fresh fruit, dried fruit, candied fruit, chutneys or jams
A variety of breads and/or unsalted crackers
Serving tray
Cheese knives

Cheese Tray Tips

- When choosing your cheeses, make sure to include a variety of textures. Try firm cheese, such as Cheddar or Gouda; soft cheese, such as Brie or Camembert; semi-soft cheese, such as Havarti, Oka or Saint-Paulin; and/or blue-veined cheese, such as Gorgonzola or Bleu Bénédictin.

- Include both a mild cheese, such as Brie, and a stronger cheese, such as blue cheese or aged Cheddar.

- If you're serving the cheese tray after dinner, allow for $1\frac{1}{2}$ to 2 oz (45 to 60 g) of cheese per person. If you plan to serve it as an appetizer, purchase 3 to $3\frac{1}{2}$ oz (90 to 105 g) per person.

- Take cheese out of the refrigerator at least 45 minutes before serving to let it come to room temperature.

- Choose your serving tray: a platter, a cheeseboard, an elegant white porcelain dish, a wooden cutting board — the possibilities are endless.

- Arrange cheeses decoratively on the tray and place a knife for each cheese nearby. Scatter nuts, fresh fruit, dried fruit and/or candied fruit between the cheeses. If serving chutney or jam, place each nearest the cheese it complements best. For example, fig jam makes a delicious accompaniment to blue cheese.

- Serve with a variety of breads, such as baguette, nut bread and pumpernickel, and/or crackers. Make sure to choose unsalted crackers to emphasize the taste of the cheese.

Source: Adapted from "How to Make a Cheese Tray," www.dairygoodness.ca, with permission from the Dairy Farmers of Canada.

Sugar

Sugars have been used to enhance the flavor of food for centuries. Although tooth decay is the only health issue proven to be linked to sugar intake, Canadians are advised to choose sugars in moderation as part of a balanced diet based on *Canada's Food Guide*. It's important to keep an eye on your sugar intake because sugar provides food energy (calories) but few other nutrients.

Artificial sweeteners make food sweeter but don't contain any real food energy (calories). They have a different chemical makeup than sugars, and they don't generally affect blood glucose levels. But don't be fooled — a product that is artificially sweetened and provides fewer calories is not necessarily a healthy choice. For example, while diet pops have no sugar or calories, neither do they contain any nutrients. The same can be said for artificially sweetened cookies or candies.

Oven Rack Placement

Placement of oven racks is important when baking to make sure products do not get too dark on top (if on the highest rack) or on the bottom (if on the lowest rack). The middle of the oven is usually best. If you need to bake several pans at once, you may want to rotate them from one rack to another halfway through to ensure that all products bake evenly.

Is Chocolate Good for Me?

Research is a great thing. It revealed that cocoa beans contain flavonoids, phytonutrients that may have health benefits. The higher the amount of cocoa solids, the higher the amount of flavonoids. Trouble is, we don't know if chocolate products confer any health benefits, precisely how much chocolate is needed to reap these benefits or at what cost in calories or fat. As you chocolate fans wait for these important answers, recognize that most chocolate-containing foods are high in calories, fat and sugar; therefore, portions should be reasonable. Satisfy your chocolate cravings in a healthy way: add a few semisweet chocolate chips to a healthy muffin batter or melt a small square of dark chocolate to use as a dip for fresh berries. Unsweetened cocoa powder does not contain any fat or sugar, so stir a little bit into low-fat milk.

Makes 22 to 24 cookies

Serving size: 1 cookie

✔ Kid Approved

Shauna created this recipe to use two wonderful stone-ground ancient grains and to avoid buying boxed cookies. Shauna's kids love to measure the ingredients and pour them into the mixing bowl.

Tips

Stone-ground flours give a grainier texture to cookies than refined flours. Look for them at health food or natural foods stores or well-stocked supermarkets.

For the most even baking, bake one sheet at a time. If you do bake both sheets at once, place one in the upper third of the oven and one in the lower third. Switch their positions halfway through.

Nutrients per serving

Calories	112
Fat	5.5 g
Saturated fat	1.7 g
Sodium	89 mg (4% DV)
Carbohydrate	16 g
Fiber	1 g (4% DV)
Protein	2 g
Calcium	13 mg (1% DV)
Iron	0.5 mg (4% DV)

Diabetes Food Choice Values:

1   Carbohydrate
1   Fat

Ancient Grains Chocolate Chip Cookies

Shauna Lindzon, Dietitian, Ontario

- **Preheat oven to 350°F (180°C)**
- **Baking sheets, greased or lined with parchment paper**

½ cup	lightly packed brown sugar	125 mL
⅓ cup	non-hydrogenated margarine	75 mL
¼ cup	ground flax seeds (flaxseed meal)	60 mL
¼ cup	granulated sugar	60 mL
1	egg	1
1 tsp	vanilla extract	5 mL
¾ cup	stone-ground Kamut flour	175 mL
¾ cup	stone-ground spelt flour	175 mL
½ tsp	baking soda	2 mL
¼ tsp	salt	1 mL
1 cup	semisweet chocolate chips	250 mL

1. In a large bowl, using an electric mixer on high speed, cream brown sugar, margarine, flax seeds and granulated sugar for 1 minute. Beat in egg and vanilla until blended. Add Kamut flour, spelt flour, baking soda and salt; mix until well blended. Stir in chocolate chips.

2. Drop by tablespoonfuls (15 mL) about 2 inches (5 cm) apart on prepared baking sheets. Bake in preheated oven for 12 to 15 minutes or until bottoms are lightly browned. Let cool on pans on a wire rack for 5 minutes, then transfer to rack to cool completely.

Roasted Vegetable Pasta
(page 280)

Indian-Spiced Cauliflower,
Potatoes and Chickpeas (page 300)

Oven-Baked Sweet Potato Fries
with Curry Mayo (page 307)

Cranberry Banana Nut Bread (page 330)

Peachy Buckwheat Muffins
with Hazelnut Crunch (page 326)

Lemon and Lavender Tea Cookies (page 337)

Mini Praline Cheesecakes
(page 345, variation)

Carrot and Almond Cake
(page 348)

Pretty as a picture and perfect for afternoon tea, these are delightful served at a baby or wedding shower.

Tips

To make lavender sugar, combine 1 cup (250 mL) granulated sugar and 2 tbsp (30 mL) dried culinary lavender (make sure it hasn't been sprayed or treated). Place in an airtight container and store at room temperature for 2 weeks, shaking the container occasionally to distribute the lavender and infuse the flavor. Before use, strain the sugar to remove the lavender.

For the most even baking, bake one sheet at a time. If you do bake both sheets at once, place one in the upper third of the oven and one in the lower third. Switch their positions halfway through.

Nutrients per serving

Calories	78
Fat	2.6 g
Saturated fat	0.4 g
Sodium	65 mg (3% DV)
Carbohydrate	13 g
Fiber	0 g (0% DV)
Protein	1 g
Calcium	22 mg (2% DV)
Iron	0.4 mg (3% DV)

Diabetes Food Choice Values:

1	Carbohydrate
½	Fat

Lemon and Lavender Tea Cookies

Mary Sue Waisman, Dietitian, Nova Scotia

- **Preheat oven to 325°F (160°C)**
- **2 baking sheets, greased**

2 cups	all-purpose flour	500 mL
¼ cup	lavender sugar (see tip, at left)	60 mL
1 tbsp	baking powder	15 mL
⅓ cup	non-hydrogenated margarine	75 mL
1	egg, beaten	1
½ cup	2% milk	125 mL
2 tsp	lemon extract	10 mL
1 tbsp	dried lavender buds (optional)	15 mL

Frosting

1 cup	icing sugar	250 mL
2½ to 3 tbsp	2% milk	22 to 45 mL
2 tsp	non-hydrogenated margarine	10 mL
1 tsp	lemon extract	5 mL

1. In a large bowl, combine flour, lavender sugar and baking powder. Using a pastry blender or two knives, cut in margarine until mixture resembles coarse crumbs.

2. In a small bowl, whisk together egg, milk and lemon extract. Pour over flour mixture and stir just until a stiff dough forms (do not overmix).

3. Drop by tablespoonfuls (15 mL) about 2 inches (5 cm) apart on prepared baking sheets. Bake in preheated oven for 8 to 10 minutes or until bottoms are golden. Transfer to a wire rack and let cool completely.

4. *Frosting:* In small bowl, combine icing sugar, milk, margarine and lemon extract to form a smooth, thin frosting.

5. Drizzle frosting over cooled cookies and sprinkle with lavender buds (if using).

> Lavender is best known for its use in fragrances and bath products, but in small amounts, it is delightful in food. It's one of the herbs often featured in the blend herbes de Provence.

Makes 42 to 48 cookies

Serving size: 1 cookie

The chewiness and crunch of the fruit and nuts in the meringue is a pleasant surprise.

Tips

If you are using a stand mixer, use the whisk attachment to beat the egg whites.

Cream of tartar is helpful for stabilizing beaten egg whites.

The key to smooth meringues is slow addition of the sugar, scraping the bowl occasionally so that all the sugar gets incorporated.

This recipe can be cut in half.

Variation

Substitute ½ cup (125 mL) chocolate chips for the cherries and ½ cup (125 mL) finely chopped dried apricots for the pistachios.

Meringue Drops with Dried Cherries and Toasted Pistachios

Mary Sue Waisman, Dietitian, Nova Scotia

- **Preheat oven to 250°C (120°C)**
- **2 baking sheets, lined with parchment paper**

4	egg whites, at room temperature	4
½ tsp	cream of tartar	2 mL
¼ tsp	salt	1 mL
1¼ cups	granulated sugar	300 mL
1 tsp	vanilla extract	5 mL
½ cup	finely chopped dried cherries	125 mL
½ cup	lightly toasted finely chopped pistachios (see page 139)	125 mL

1. In a large bowl, using an electric mixer on high speed, beat egg whites, cream of tartar and salt until soft peaks form. Add sugar, 2 tbsp (30 mL) at a time, beating for 30 seconds to 1 minute after each addition to ensure sugar is fully incorporated, scraping sides of bowl occasionally. Beat until stiff glossy peaks form. Stir in vanilla. Gently fold in cherries and pistachios.

2. Drop by heaping tablespoons (15 mL) about 2 inches (5 cm) apart on prepared baking sheets. Bake in upper and lower thirds of preheated oven, switching halfway through, for 25 to 30 minutes or until dry to the touch. Turn oven off and leave meringues in oven for 3 to 4 hours or overnight to dry completely.

Nutrients per serving

Calories	34
Fat	0.6 g
Saturated fat	0.1 g
Sodium	17 mg (1% DV)
Carbohydrate	7 g
Fiber	0 g (0% DV)
Protein	1 g
Calcium	5 mg (0% DV)
Iron	0.1 mg (1% DV)

Diabetes Food Choice Values:
½ Carbohydrate

Makes 1 dozen cookies

Serving size: 1 cookie

✔ **Kid Approved**

Kori created this recipe to satisfy her apple-loving family. Kori's young cousin helps by measuring out the ingredients and dropping the dough onto the baking sheet — a perfect task for kids, as the cookies don't have to look perfect.

Tip

These cookies freeze well. Layer between waxed paper or parchment paper in an airtight container and freeze for up to 3 months.

Variation

Use ¾ cup (175 mL) raisins instead of the apple and omit the chocolate chips.

Nutrients per serving

Calories	140
Fat	6.1 g
Saturated fat	1.5 g
Sodium	85 mg (4% DV)
Carbohydrate	19 g
Fiber	2 g (8% DV)
Protein	3 g
Calcium	15 mg (1% DV)
Iron	1.0 mg (7% DV)

Diabetes Food Choice Values:

1	Carbohydrate
1	Fat

Apple and Toasted Oatmeal Cookies

Kori Kostka, Dietitian, Ontario

- **Preheat oven to 350°F (180°C)**
- **Baking sheet, greased**

1½ cups	toasted quick-cooking rolled oats (see box, below)	375 mL
½ cup	all-purpose flour	125 mL
½ tsp	ground cinnamon	2 mL
¼ tsp	ground nutmeg	1 mL
¼ tsp	baking soda	1 mL
¼ cup	lightly packed brown sugar	60 mL
¼ cup	non-hydrogenated margarine	60 mL
1	egg	1
¼ tsp	vanilla extract	1 mL
1	apple, peeled and finely chopped	1
¼ cup	semisweet chocolate chips	60 mL

1. In a large bowl, combine oats, flour, cinnamon, nutmeg and baking soda.

2. In a medium bowl, using an electric mixer on high speed, cream brown sugar and margarine for 1 minute or until light and fluffy. Beat in egg and vanilla until blended. Stir in oat mixture, apple and chocolate chips.

3. Drop by tablespoonfuls (15 mL) about 2 inches (5 cm) apart on prepared baking sheet. If desired, use a floured fork to flatten slightly. Bake in preheated oven for 12 to 15 minutes or until center of cookies springs back when lightly pressed. Transfer to a wire rack and let cool completely.

> ### How to Toast Oats
> Preheat oven to 350°F (180°C). Spread oats on a baking sheet. Bake in preheated oven for 3 minutes, flip with a spatula and bake for 3 minutes. Watch to make sure they don't burn.

Serving size: 1 cookie

✔ **Kid Approved**

This recipe was developed by Irene's family in the early 1900s, when money was scarce, and has been passed down through the generations. Irene's family has always enjoyed the cookies with skim milk, not for health reasons, but because they sold the cream from the milk to make butter.

Tips

As the name implies, these cookies are tougher than many, but pleasantly so. In fact, the texture makes them perfect accompaniments to a glass of milk or a cup of tea.

For the most even baking, bake one sheet at a time. If you do bake both sheets at once, place one in the upper third of the oven and one in the lower third. Switch their positions halfway through.

Nutrients per serving

Calories	71
Fat	0.3 g
Saturated fat	0.1 g
Sodium	83 mg (3% DV)
Carbohydrate	16 g
Fiber	0 g (0% DV)
Protein	1 g
Calcium	21 mg (2% DV)
Iron	0.8 mg (6% DV)

Diabetes Food Choice Values:

1   Carbohydrate

Toughies

Irene Doyle, Dietitian, Prince Edward Island

- **Preheat oven to 350°F (180°C)**
- **Baking sheets, greased**

3½ cups	all-purpose flour	875 mL
1 tsp	ground ginger	5 mL
1 tsp	ground cinnamon	5 mL
½ tsp	ground cloves	2 mL
½ tsp	salt	2 mL
2 tsp	baking soda	10 mL
1 cup	fancy molasses	250 mL
¼ cup	hot water	60 mL
1 tbsp	white vinegar	15 mL
1 cup	lightly packed brown sugar	250 mL
2	eggs	2

1. In a medium bowl, combine flour, ginger, cinnamon, cloves and salt.

2. In a small bowl, combine baking soda, molasses and hot water. Stir in vinegar.

3. In a large bowl, using an electric mixer on high speed beat brown sugar and eggs for 1 minute or until well combined. Beat in flour mixture alternately with molasses mixture, making three additions of flour and two of molasses, until well combined.

4. Drop by tablespoonfuls (15 mL) about 2 inches (5 cm) apart on prepared baking sheets. Bake in preheated oven for 10 to 12 minutes or until center of cookies springs back when lightly pressed. Transfer to a wire rack and let cool completely.

Shefali enjoys nuts and dried fruits. Together with unique spices, this recipe is a lovely blend of both.

Tip

Nuts contain a lot of oil and can burn easily. Check them often while they're toasting.

Variations

Add ½ cup (125 mL) crispy rice cereal and/or ½ cup (125 mL) chocolate chips with the nuts in step 3.

Use any combination of nuts you like; try hazelnuts, pecans, peanuts or macadamia nuts.

Serving Idea

These are tasty as a sweet on their own, but are also delicious on a cheese tray alongside a soft cheese, such as Brie.

Nutrients per serving

Calories	80
Fat	3.8 g
Saturated fat	0.6 g
Sodium	2 mg (0% DV)
Carbohydrate	12 g
Fiber	2 g (8% DV)
Protein	2 g
Calcium	15 mg (1% DV)
Iron	0.5 mg (4% DV)

Diabetes Food Choice Values:

½ Carbohydrate
1 Fat

Date and Nut Pinwheels

Shefali Raja, Dietitian, British Columbia

● **Preheat oven to 325°F (160°C)**

⅓ cup	whole almonds	75 mL
⅓ cup	shelled pistachios	75 mL
⅓ cup	unsalted cashews	75 mL
8 oz	pitted dates, coarsely chopped (about 1½ cups/375 mL)	250 g
1 tsp	ground cardamom	5 mL
8 to 10	saffron threads, crushed (optional)	8 to 10
1 tbsp	unsweetened shredded coconut	15 mL

1. Place almonds, pistachios and cashews on a baking sheet and toast in preheated oven for about 15 minutes or until lightly browned. Let cool, then finely chop.

2. In a small saucepan, combine dates and 2 tbsp (30 mL) water. Heat over low heat, stirring often, for 6 to 8 minutes or until a soft paste forms.

3. Stir nuts, cardamom and saffron (if using) into date paste until well combined. Set aside until cool enough to handle.

4. Spoon nut mixture onto a sheet of waxed paper and shape into a roll, 8 to 9 inches (20 to 23 cm) long and 1½ inches (4 cm) thick. Sprinkle coconut all over roll. Wrap in waxed paper and refrigerate for at least 4 hours, until firm, or overnight. Cut into ½-inch (1 cm) slices.

Dates come from the date palm tree, which is native to the Middle East and Mediterranean regions; some are also grown in California. There are many varieties of dates, one of the most popular being the Medjool variety. Medjool dates hail from Morocco and are prized for their sweet, soft flesh.

✔ **Kid Approved**

These make a great treat for a Halloween party, especially if you let kids in on the baking fun: they can measure, add and stir all ingredients.

Variations

Replace the cranberries with ⅓ cup (75 mL) mini semisweet chocolate chips and ⅓ cup (75 mL) chopped pecans.

Replace the pumpkin purée with applesauce and the cranberries with raisins. Add ½ tsp (2 mL) each ground cloves and nutmeg to the flour mixture.

Nutrients per serving

Calories	89
Fat	2.9 g
Saturated fat	0.4 g
Sodium	89 mg (4% DV)
Carbohydrate	15 g
Fiber	1 g (4% DV)
Protein	1 g
Calcium	12 mg (1% DV)
Iron	0.5 mg (4% DV)

Diabetes Food Choice Values:

1   Carbohydrate
½   Fat

Cranberry Pumpkin Cookies

Noelle Tourney, Saskatchewan

- Preheat oven to 375°F (190°C)
- Baking sheets, greased

1½ cups	all-purpose flour	375 mL
1 tsp	baking powder	5 mL
1 tsp	ground cinnamon	5 mL
¾ tsp	baking soda	3 mL
¼ tsp	salt	1 mL
⅔ cup	granulated sugar	150 mL
⅓ cup	non-hydrogenated margarine	75 mL
1	egg	1
1 tsp	vanilla extract	5 mL
⅔ cup	canned pumpkin purée (not pie filling)	150 mL
⅔ cup	dried cranberries	150 mL

1. In a large bowl, sift together flour, baking powder, cinnamon, baking soda and salt.

2. In another large bowl, using an electric mixer on high speed, cream sugar and margarine until light and fluffy. Beat in egg and vanilla until well blended. Beat in pumpkin. Stir in flour mixture until well blended. Fold in cranberries.

3. Drop by tablespoonfuls (15 mL) about 2 inches (5 cm) apart on prepared baking sheet. Bake in preheated oven for 10 to 12 minutes or until center of cookies springs back when lightly pressed. Transfer to a wire rack and let cool completely.

✔ **Kid Approved**

Here's a creative and delicious way to add a few beans to your day.

Tip

Sprinkle a little icing sugar on each brownie before serving.

Variations

Use red kidney beans instead of black beans.

For a delicious almond flavor, use 1 tbsp (15 mL) vanilla extract and 1 tsp (5 mL) almond extract.

Nutrients per serving

Calories	195
Fat	7.9 g
Saturated fat	1.1 g
Sodium	172 mg (7% DV)
Carbohydrate	29 g
Fiber	4 g (16% DV)
Protein	4 g
Calcium	38 mg (3% DV)
Iron	1.2 mg (9% DV)

Diabetes Food Choice Values:

2 Carbohydrates
1½ Fats

Black Bean Brownies

Adrienne Penner, Ontario

- **Preheat oven to 350°F (180°C)**
- **Food processor or blender**
- **9-inch (23 cm) square metal baking pan, greased**

1	can (19 oz/540 mL) black beans, drained and rinsed	1
3	eggs	3
⅓ cup	canola oil	75 mL
2 tbsp	vanilla extract	30 mL
1¼ cups	granulated sugar	300 mL
½ cup	unsweetened cocoa powder	125 mL
1½ tsp	baking powder	7 mL

1. In food processor, purée beans, eggs, oil and vanilla for 1 to 2 minutes or until smooth.

2. In a large bowl, combine sugar, cocoa and baking powder. Pour in bean mixture and stir until smooth.

3. Pour batter into prepared baking pan. Bake in preheated oven for 30 minutes or until a tester inserted in the center comes out clean. Let cool completely in pan on a wire rack.

> Most of the world's supply of vanilla comes from two islands off the east coast of Africa, Madagascar and Reunion. The characteristic long brown pod comes from a vine of the orchid family. Pure vanilla extract is generally quite expensive, mainly because the hand pollination of the orchids is very labor-intensive.

✔ **Kid Approved**

These chewy fruit-nut squares make a healthy bake sale treat.

Tips

Individually wrap squares in plastic wrap and store at room temperature for up to 5 days or freeze for up to 1 month.

These are also great for breakfast when you're short on time. Take along a square, a ¾-cup (175 g) container of yogurt and a banana for a portable breakfast.

Kids love to bake, and this is a great recipe to involve them in.

Variations

Use pecans, peanuts or cashews instead of almonds.

Use a combination of dried cranberries, raisins and dried apples instead of apricots.

Nutrients per serving

Calories	144
Fat	5.4 g
Saturated fat	0.5 g
Sodium	50 mg (2% DV)
Carbohydrate	22 g
Fiber	2 g (8% DV)
Protein	3 g
Calcium	19 mg (2% DV)
Iron	1.0 mg (7% DV)

Diabetes Food Choice Values:

1½ Carbohydrates

1   Fat

Almond Apricot Squares

Heather McColl, Dietitian, British Columbia

- **Preheat oven to 375°F (190°C)**
- **Food processor or blender**
- **17- by 12-inch (43 by 30 cm) rimmed baking sheet, lined with parchment paper**

3 cups	large-flake (old-fashioned) rolled oats	750 mL
¾ cup	sliced almonds	175 mL
3 cups	unsweetened puffed-grain cereal, such as whole wheat puffs	750 mL
2 cups	chopped dried apricots	500 mL
¼ cup	all-purpose flour	60 mL
½ tsp	salt	2 mL
1	package (12 oz/340 g) soft silken tofu, drained	1
1	egg	1
1 cup	liquid honey	250 mL
½ cup	canola oil	125 mL
1 tbsp	vanilla extract	15 mL
	Grated zest of 1 lemon	

1. Spread oats and almonds on a baking sheet. Bake in preheated oven for 8 to 10 minutes or until fragrant and light golden in color. Transfer to a large bowl. Stir in puffed cereal, apricots, flour and salt. Reduce oven temperature to 350°F (180°C).

2. In food processor, purée tofu, egg, honey, oil, vanilla and lemon zest until smooth. Make a well in the center of the oat mixture and pour in tofu mixture; fold until just combined.

3. Using a spatula, spread cereal mixture evenly on prepared baking sheet. Bake for 35 to 40 minutes or until firm in the center and golden brown. Let cool completely in pan on a wire rack before cutting into squares.

A mini muffin pan
makes for easy service
and portion control in
these delightful mini
cheesecakes.

Tip

This recipe doubles easily.
Bake in top and bottom thirds
of oven and rotate pans
partway through baking.

Variations

Make mini strawberry
cheesecakes instead. Omit the
pecans, use granulated sugar
instead of brown, use lemon
juice instead of vanilla and top
with a hulled strawberry.

If you don't have a mini
muffin pan, you can make
12 larger cheesecakes in a
12-cup muffin pan. Increase
the baking time to 15 to
18 minutes.

Mini Praline Cheesecakes

Melanie Ksienski, Dietitian, Alberta

- Preheat oven to 350°F (180°C)
- 24-cup mini muffin pan, lined with paper cups
- Food processor

1/3 cup	chopped pecans	75 mL
8 oz	light cream cheese	250 g
2/3 cup	lightly packed brown sugar	150 mL
1	egg	1
2 tsp	vanilla extract	10 mL
12	pecan halves, cut in half	12

1. Divide chopped pecans evenly among muffin cups. Set aside.

2. In food processor, process cream cheese and brown sugar for about 15 seconds or until well blended. Scrape down sides of bowl. Add egg and vanilla; process until well blended.

3. Divide cheese mixture evenly among muffin cups. Bake in preheated oven for 10 minutes or until set and small cracks form on tops of cheesecakes. Top each with 1 pecan piece. Let cool in pan on a wire rack. Cover and refrigerate for at least 3 hours, until chilled, or for up to 12 hours.

Nutrients per serving

Calories	123
Fat	7.3 g
Saturated fat	2.7 g
Sodium	71 mg (3% DV)
Carbohydrate	12 g
Fiber	0 g (0% DV)
Protein	3 g
Calcium	37 mg (3% DV)
Iron	0.7 mg (5% DV)

Diabetes Food Choice Values:
1/2 Carbohydrate
1 1/2 Fats

Makes 9 servings

✔ **Kid Approved**

A strong arm and a wooden spoon work well to make this German dessert the old-fashioned way! In Germany, this cheesecake does not have a crust, but Julia added one to suit Canadian tastes.

Tip

For ease in cutting, you can line the pan with foil, leaving a 1-inch (2.5 cm) overhang on each side. When the cheesecake has cooled completely, use the foil to lift it out of the pan, then place it on a flat surface to slice it.

Nutrients per serving

Calories	292
Fat	13.2 g
Saturated fat	4.6 g
Sodium	286 mg (12% DV)
Carbohydrate	32 g
Fiber	0 g (0% DV)
Protein	12 g
Calcium	106 mg (10% DV)
Iron	1.2 mg (9% DV)

High in: Vitamin D and vitamin B$_{12}$

Diabetes Food Choice Values:

2 Carbohydrates
1 Meat & Alternatives
2 Fats

Quarkkuchen (Fluffy Cheesecake)

Julia Besner, Dietitian, New Brunswick

- **Preheat oven to 325°F (160°C)**
- **9-inch (23 cm) square metal baking pan, greased**

1½ cups	graham wafer crumbs	375 mL
¼ cup	non-hydrogenated margarine, melted	60 mL
¾ cup	granulated sugar	175 mL
3	eggs	3
8 oz	light cream cheese, at room temperature, cut into 1-inch (2.5 cm) pieces	250 g
1 lb	quark cheese	500 g
3 tbsp	freshly squeezed lemon juice	45 mL
1 tbsp	vanilla extract	15 mL

1. In a medium bowl, combine graham crumbs and margarine. Press into bottom of prepared pan.

2. In a large bowl, beat sugar and eggs until smooth. Add cream cheese and beat for 1 to 2 minutes or until well incorporated. Stir in quark, lemon juice and vanilla until well incorporated. Pour evenly over crust.

3. Bake in preheated oven for 50 minutes or until edges turn slightly golden and center is almost set. Let cool completely in pan on a wire rack. Cover and refrigerate for at least 4 hours, until chilled, or overnight for best results. Cut into squares.

> Quark is a soft, fresh, unripened cheese made from cow's milk. Its flavor and texture are similar to those of sour cream. It's used widely in Europe and is available in many grocery stores in Canada. Some local Canadian cheesemongers also make quark. It adds a delightful texture to cheesecake.

✔ **Kid Approved**

Not just for dessert, this moist cake makes an ideal treat for morning tea or contribution to a school bake sale.

Tip

If you mix 1 to 2 tbsp (15 to 30 mL) of the flour with the blueberries before you add them, they are less likely to fall to the bottom of the cake. This works when you're making muffins, too.

Variation

Use raspberries or blackberries instead of blueberries.

Nutrients per serving

Calories	283
Fat	15.0 g
Saturated fat	2.0 g
Sodium	227 mg (9% DV)
Carbohydrate	33 g
Fiber	2 g (8% DV)
Protein	6 g
Calcium	72 mg (7% DV)
Iron	1.5 mg (11% DV)

Very high in: Folate
High in: Vitamin D

Diabetes Food Choice Values:
2   Carbohydrates
3   Fats

Blueberry Yogurt Cake

Tamara Cohen, Dietitian, Quebec

- **Preheat oven to 350°F (180°C)**
- **8-inch (20 cm) square metal baking pan, greased**

1 cup	chopped walnuts	250 mL
1/3 cup	lightly packed brown sugar	75 mL
1 tsp	ground cinnamon	5 mL
1/2 tsp	ground nutmeg	2 mL
1 1/4 cups	all-purpose flour	300 mL
1 tsp	baking powder	5 mL
1/4 tsp	baking soda	1 mL
1/4 tsp	salt	1 mL
1/3 cup	granulated sugar	75 mL
1/4 cup	non-hydrogenated margarine	60 mL
2	eggs	2
1 tsp	vanilla extract	5 mL
1/2 cup	low-fat plain or vanilla-flavored yogurt	125 mL
1 cup	blueberries	250 mL

1. In a small bowl, stir together walnuts, brown sugar, cinnamon and nutmeg. Set aside.

2. In a medium bowl, combine flour, baking powder, baking soda and salt.

3. In a large bowl, using an electric mixer on high speed, cream granulated sugar and margarine until light and fluffy. Beat in eggs and vanilla until well blended. Stir in yogurt. Stir in flour mixture until just blended. Gently fold in blueberries.

4. Spread half the batter in prepared baking dish. Sprinkle with half the walnut mixture. Spread the remaining batter on top. Sprinkle the remaining walnut mixture evenly over top.

5. Bake in preheated oven for about 40 minutes or until a tester inserted in the center comes out clean. Let cool completely in pan on a wire rack.

Carrot and Almond Cake

Susan Eredics, British Columbia

- **Preheat oven to 350°F (180°C)**
- **13- by 9-inch (33 by 23 cm) metal baking pan, greased, bottom lined with parchment paper**

2¾ cups	ground almonds	675 mL
1¾ cups	finely grated carrots	425 mL
¾ cup	fine dry bread crumbs	175 mL
1¼ tsp	baking powder	6 mL
1 tsp	ground ginger	5 mL
½ tsp	ground nutmeg	2 mL
½ tsp	ground cinnamon	2 mL
6	eggs, separated	6
1¼ cups	granulated sugar	300 mL
2 tsp	grated lemon zest	10 mL
3 tbsp	freshly squeezed lemon juice	45 mL

Cream Cheese Glaze

¼ cup	light cream cheese, softened	60 mL
¼ cup	butter, softened	60 mL
½ tsp	vanilla extract	2 mL
1½ cups	icing sugar, sifted	375 mL
	Water or milk, if necessary	

1. In a medium bowl, combine almonds and carrots. Stir in bread crumbs, baking powder, ginger, nutmeg and cinnamon. Set aside.

2. In a large bowl, using an electric mixer on high speed, beat egg whites until stiff peaks form (do not overbeat). Set aside.

3. In another large bowl, using electric mixer on high speed, beat egg yolks and sugar for 2 minutes or until thick and a ribbon trail forms when beater is lifted. Stir in lemon zest and lemon juice. Stir in carrot mixture until well blended. Gently fold in egg whites until fully incorporated.

Nutrients per serving

Calories	254
Fat	12.4 g
Saturated fat	3.2 g
Sodium	108 mg (5% DV)
Carbohydrate	32 g
Fiber	2 g (8% DV)
Protein	6 g
Calcium	71 mg (6% DV)
Iron	1.2 mg (9% DV)

High in: Magnesium and vitamin A

Diabetes Food Choice Values:

2   Carbohydrates
2½ Fats

4. Pour batter into prepared baking pan. Bake in preheated oven for 30 to 35 minutes or until a tester inserted in the center comes out clean. Let cool completely in pan on a wire rack. Invert cake onto a large plate and remove parchment paper.

5. *Glaze:* In a medium bowl, using electric mixer on high speed, beat cream cheese and butter until smooth. Beat in vanilla. Gradually add icing sugar, beating until smooth and of glaze consistency. If too thick, add $\frac{1}{2}$ to 1 tsp (2 to 5 mL) water or milk. Drizzle over cooled cake.

> Under the skin of citrus fruit is a white spongy layer called the pith. It's very bitter, so when you're zesting citrus fruits, be careful not to include any pith in your zest.

Tip

Unlike many traditional carrot cakes, this one does not rise in the middle only to settle in later. Rather, it bakes evenly, so be sure to spread the batter evenly in the pan.

✔ **Kid Approved**

Who doesn't like chocolate? Enjoy this impressive tower at your next birthday celebration.

Tip

If you use paper cups in the muffin pan, remove them from cupcakes before assembling the tower.

Nutrients per serving

Calories	237
Fat	13.5 g
Saturated fat	3.3 g
Sodium	102 mg (4% DV)
Carbohydrate	27 g
Fiber	1 g (4% DV)
Protein	4 g
Calcium	64 mg (6% DV)
Iron	1.4 mg (10% DV)

Diabetes Food Choice Values:

2	Carbohydrates
2½	Fats

Chocolate Lava Cupcake Tower

Caroline Dubeau, Dietitian, Ontario

- **Preheat oven to 350°C (180°C)**
- **12-cup muffin pan, lightly greased or lined with paper cups**

1 cup	all-purpose flour	250 mL
1 tsp	baking powder	5 mL
¼ tsp	baking soda	1 mL
½ cup	packed brown sugar	125 mL
2	eggs	2
½ cup	canola oil	125 mL
¼ cup	unsweetened cocoa powder	60 mL
1 tsp	instant coffee granules (or 1 tbsp/ 15 mL brewed coffee)	5 mL
1 tsp	vanilla extract	5 mL
¾ cup	low-fat plain yogurt	175 mL

Lava Icing

⅓ cup	packed brown sugar	75 mL
½ cup	sweetened flaked coconut	125 mL
2 tbsp	unsweetened cocoa powder	30 mL
2 tbsp	butter or canola oil	30 mL
2 tbsp	2% milk	30 mL

1. In a small bowl, combine flour, baking powder and baking soda.

2. In a large bowl, using an electric mixer on high speed, beat brown sugar, eggs and oil for 3 minutes. Add cocoa, coffee and vanilla and beat for 1 minute. Stir in flour mixture alternately with yogurt, making two additions of flour and one of yogurt.

3. Divide batter evenly among prepared muffin cups. Bake in preheated oven for 18 to 20 minutes or until tops spring back when lightly touched. Let cool in pan on a wire rack for 10 minutes, then transfer to rack to cool completely.

4. *Icing:* Meanwhile, in a small saucepan, combine brown sugar, coconut, cocoa, butter and milk. Bring to a boil over medium-high heat, stirring constantly. Boil for 2 minutes. Remove from heat and let cool completely.

5. On a large serving plate, arrange cupcakes in a tower, with four on the base, four on the second level, three on the next level and one on top. Pour icing over tower. Serve immediately.

After cocoa butter is extracted from roasted and cracked cocoa nibs, a dark brown paste, called chocolate liquor, remains. This paste is dried and crushed to produce unsweetened cocoa powder. Dutch cocoa (often called Dutch-process cocoa powder) has been treated to help counteract cocoa powder's natural acidity. The two types of cocoa powder are not interchangeable, so make sure to use the one called for in your recipe. Also, be sure not to use sweetened cocoa mix (used to make hot or cold chocolate beverages) when a recipe calls for unsweetened cocoa powder.

Variations
Coffee is often added to chocolate because it heightens the chocolate flavor. But you can omit the coffee granules if you prefer.

For a more grown-up flavor, replace the vanilla extract with almond extract.

Serving Idea
Serve this cupcake tower alongside a platter of fresh fruit at your next birthday gathering; that way, guests can choose their preferred dessert.

✔ **Kid Approved**

Pouding chômeur, a classic dessert from Quebec, was one of the first recipes Caroline prepared on her own as a child, borrowing her mom's cookbook to find the recipe. Traditionally, it's a batter baked in a maple syrup or brown sugar sauce to create a delicious, moist cake. This version has less sugar and includes some whole wheat flour and apples to give it a healthy twist.

Tips

Make the apple slices as thin as possible to ensure that they cook properly.

If you don't have maple syrup, use brown sugar diluted in 1 cup (250 mL) of water and add 1 tsp (5 mL) maple extract.

Nutrients per serving

Calories	227
Fat	7.1 g
Saturated fat	0.8 g
Sodium	68 mg (3% DV)
Carbohydrate	38 g
Fiber	1 g (4% DV)
Protein	3 g
Calcium	72 mg (7% DV)
Iron	1.1 mg (8% DV)

High in: Riboflavin

Diabetes Food Choice Values:
2½ Carbohydrates
1½ Fats

Pouding Chômeur with a Twist

Caroline Dubeau, Dietitian, Ontario

- Preheat oven to 375°F (190°C)
- 8-inch (20 cm) square glass baking dish

1 cup	pure maple syrup	250 mL
3	apples, peeled and thinly sliced	3
1 cup	all-purpose flour	250 mL
½ cup	whole wheat flour	125 mL
2 tsp	baking powder	10 mL
¼ cup	granulated sugar	60 mL
⅓ cup	canola oil	75 mL
1	egg	1
1 tsp	vanilla extract	5 mL
1 cup	2% milk	250 mL

1. Pour maple syrup and ½ cup (125 mL) water into baking dish and mix well. Spread apple slices evenly on top (do not mix).

2. In a bowl, combine all-purpose flour, whole wheat flour and baking powder.

3. In another bowl, whisk together sugar and oil. Whisk in egg and vanilla until smooth. Stir in flour mixture alternately with milk, making three additions of flour and two of milk. Pour evenly over syrup and apples (do not mix).

4. Bake in preheated oven for 40 minutes or until a tester inserted in the center comes out clean. Serve warm or cold.

Chocolate Orange Almond Tart

Tanya Lorimer-Charles, Nova Scotia

- **9-inch (23 cm) springform pan**

Crust

1½ cups	chocolate cookie crumbs	375 mL
⅓ cup	melted butter	75 mL
¼ cup	slivered almonds, toasted (see page 139) and chopped	60 mL
½ tsp	ground cinnamon	2 mL
½ tsp	grated orange zest	2 mL
½ cup	orange marmalade	125 mL

Filling

8 oz	bittersweet (dark) chocolate, chopped	250 g
1 cup	whipping (35%) cream	250 mL
2 tbsp	orange-flavored liqueur	30 mL
2 cups	assorted berries	500 mL

1. *Crust:* In a medium bowl, combine cookie crumbs and butter. Stir in almonds, cinnamon and orange zest. Press into bottom of pan. Spread orange marmalade over crust. Set aside.

2. *Filling:* Place chocolate in a medium heatproof bowl. In a medium saucepan, bring cream to a simmer over medium heat. Remove from heat and pour over chocolate. Let stand for 2 minutes. Stir to blend, then let stand until chocolate is melted. Stir until smooth. Stir in liqueur until incorporated.

3. Pour filling over crust. Refrigerate for at least 4 hours, until chocolate is firm, or for up to 12 hours. Slice and serve with berries.

Pumpkin Pie Tarts with Ground Almond Crust

Judy Campbell-Gordon, Dietitian, Quebec

- **Preheat oven to 400°F (200°C)**
- **Eight ½-cup (125 mL) heatproof ramekins, greased**
- **2 baking sheets**

½ cup	ground almonds	125 mL
2	eggs, beaten	2
1¼ cups	canned pumpkin purée (not pie filling)	300 mL
½ cup	sweetened condensed milk	125 mL
1 tsp	ground cinnamon	5 mL
½ tsp	ground ginger	2 mL
¼ tsp	ground cloves	1 mL
¼ tsp	ground nutmeg	1 mL

1. Place 4 ramekins on each baking sheet. Divide ground almonds among prepared ramekins.

2. In a medium bowl, whisk together eggs, pumpkin, milk, cinnamon, ginger, cloves and nutmeg until well blended. Divide evenly among ramekins.

3. Bake in preheated oven for 10 minutes. Reduce oven temperature to 350°F (180°C) and bake for 12 to 15 minutes or until mostly set (the middle of the tarts should still jiggle slightly). Let cool completely in ramekins on a wire rack.

Nutrients per serving

Calories	129
Fat	6.1 g
Saturated fat	1.7 g
Sodium	42 mg (2% DV)
Carbohydrate	15 g
Fiber	2 g (8% DV)
Protein	5 g
Calcium	90 mg (8% DV)
Iron	1.1 mg (8% DV)

Very high in: Vitamin A

Diabetes Food Choice Values:

1   Carbohydrate
1   Fat

This trifle is lightened up with angel food cake, but it's still big on flavor.

Variations

Use instant vanilla or banana pudding instead of white chocolate.

Replace half the orange juice with ¼ cup (60 mL) orange-flavored liqueur.

Whip ½ cup (125 mL) whipping cream to use as a replacement for the light whipped topping. Keep in mind that the fat content of the recipe will be higher if you do this.

Fresh Berry Trifle

Brigitte Lamoureux, Dietitian, Manitoba

- **Trifle bowl**

1	package (4-serving size) instant white chocolate pudding	1
1	10-inch (25 cm) angel food cake, torn into 1- to 2-inch (2.5 to 5 cm) cubes	1
½ cup	unsweetened orange juice	125 mL
5 cups	assorted berries (blueberries, raspberries, blackberries, strawberries)	1.25 L
1 cup	light whipped topping	250 mL

1. Prepare pudding according to package directions.

2. Place half the cake cubes in bottom of trifle bowl. Drizzle with half the orange juice. Spread half the pudding over cake and arrange one-third of the berries on top. Repeat layers of cake, juice, pudding and berries. Cover with whipped topping and top with the remaining berries.

3. Cover and refrigerate for at least 4 hours, until chilled, or for up to 12 hours.

Nutrients per serving

Calories	151
Fat	2.2 g
Saturated fat	1.4 g
Sodium	287 mg (12% DV)
Carbohydrate	30 g
Fiber	3 g (12% DV)
Protein	4 g
Calcium	100 mg (9% DV)
Iron	0.5 mg (4% DV)

Very high in: Vitamin C
High in: Folate

Diabetes Food Choice Values:

2   Carbohydrates
½   Fat

Makes 8 servings

Creamy lemon curd and sweet berries are happily nestled in these crisp meringue crowns.

Tips

Room temperature egg whites produce a better foam than cold egg whites.

The meringues can be baked up to 3 days in advance. Store in an airtight container at room temperature until ready to use.

Nutrients per serving

Calories	199
Fat	7.2 g
Saturated fat	2.2 g
Sodium	129 mg (5% DV)
Carbohydrate	29 g
Fiber	1 g (4% DV)
Protein	6 g
Calcium	102 mg (9% DV)
Iron	0.5 mg (4% DV)

High in: Vitamin D and vitamin B$_{12}$

Diabetes Food Choice Values:

2 Carbohydrates
½ Meat & Alternatives
1 Fat

Meringue Crowns with Ricotta Lemon Curd and Blueberries

Mary Sue Waisman, Dietitian, Nova Scotia

- Preheat oven to 400°C (200°F)
- 2 baking sheets, lined with parchment paper
- Double boiler

Meringue Crowns

2	large egg whites, at room temperature	2
¼ tsp	cream of tartar	1 mL
Pinch	salt	Pinch
½ cup	granulated sugar	125 mL
½ tsp	lemon extract	2 mL

Ricotta Lemon Curd

4	egg yolks	4
⅓ cup	granulated sugar	75 mL
2 tbsp	grated lemon zest	30 mL
⅓ cup	freshly squeezed lemon juice	75 mL
2 tbsp	non-hydrogenated margarine	30 mL
1 cup	light ricotta cheese	250 mL
2 cups	blueberries	500 mL
8	sprigs fresh mint	8

1. *Meringues:* On each prepared baking sheet, trace four 3-inch (7.5 cm) circles with a pen or pencil. Turn parchment over so marks are on the bottom. Set pans aside.

2. In a large bowl, using an electric mixer on high speed, beat egg whites, cream of tartar and salt until soft peaks form. Add sugar, 2 tbsp (30 mL) at a time, beating for 30 seconds to 1 minute after each addition to ensure sugar is fully combined with egg whites, scraping sides of bowl occasionally. Beat until stiff glossy peaks form. Fold in lemon extract.

3. Divide meringue evenly among circles on baking sheets, spreading to the entire width of each circle. With the back of a spoon, make a small indentation in the center of each (to hold the filling) and draw meringue upward on the outer edge, forming several peaks ("crown" tips).

4. Place baking sheets in preheated oven and immediately reduce oven temperature to 250°C (120°C). Bake for 30 minutes. Turn oven off and leave meringues in oven for at least 3 to 4 hours or overnight to dry completely.

5. *Curd:* In the top of a double boiler set over simmering water, whisk egg yolks and sugar for 1 minute. Whisk in lemon zest and lemon juice. Cook, whisking constantly, for 3 to 4 minutes or until mixture is thick and coats the back of a spoon. Remove from heat and stir in margarine, 1 tbsp (15 mL) at a time, letting the first blend in before adding the second. Let cool for 10 minutes.

6. Fold ricotta cheese into curd mixture. Transfer to a bowl, place plastic wrap directly on surface of curd and refrigerate for at least 4 hours, until chilled, or for up to 24 hours.

7. Place 1 meringue on each dessert plate. Divide curd among meringues and top each with berries and a mint sprig.

> There are several ways to make meringue. This is the classic French method, in which the meringue is baked. Cream of tartar helps to stabilize the egg white foam.

Variation
Fill meringues with yogurt cheese (see step 1, page 96) topped with fruit.

Dessert tofu is the base for this delicious mousse.

Variation
Use two drained 10-oz (284 mL) cans of unsweetened mandarin oranges in place of the blackberries.

Crêpes with White Chocolate Mango Mousse and Fresh Blackberries

Mary Sue Waisman, Dietitian, Nova Scotia

● **Food processor**

3 oz	white chocolate, chopped	90 g
1	package (10 oz/300 g) orange-mango-flavored silken tofu	1
2 tbsp	orange-flavored liqueur	30 mL
6	crêpes (see recipe, page 53)	6
1½ cups	blackberries	375 mL
1 tbsp	icing sugar	15 mL

1. In a microwave-safe bowl, melt white chocolate on Medium (50%) power for 1½ minutes, stirring once halfway through. If not yet melted, microwave on Medium (50%) for 30 seconds or until melted. Let cool to room temperature.

2. In food processor, purée tofu until smooth. Add cooled chocolate and liqueur; purée for 30 to 40 seconds or until smooth. Transfer to a medium bowl and refrigerate for about 2 hours or until firm.

3. Lay 1 crêpe flat on a work surface. Layer ¼ cup (60 mL) mousse down center of crêpe. Fold bottom edge of crêpe over mousse, then fold top edge over bottom edge. Transfer to a serving plate, seam side down. Repeat with the remaining crêpes. Top with blackberries and dust with icing sugar. Serve immediately.

Nutrients per serving

Calories	231
Fat	7.1 g
Saturated fat	3.4 g
Sodium	73 mg (3% DV)
Carbohydrate	35 g
Fiber	3 g (12% DV)
Protein	7 g
Calcium	118 mg (11% DV)
Iron	1.1 mg (8% DV)

High in: Folate

Diabetes Food Choice Values:
2   Carbohydrates
1½   Fats

Summer never tasted so good! Peaches and raspberries flavored with a hint of almond make for a divine combination.

Tips

Check the sweetness of the peaches. If they are very sweet, reduce the brown sugar to ¼ to ⅓ cup (60 to 75 mL).

Amaretti cookies are small, crisp, almond-flavored cookies traditionally served with coffee or liqueur after dinner in Italy. Look for them in specialty grocery stores and some large supermarkets.

Variation

Replace the almond liqueur with chilled ice wine or unsweetened apple juice.

Roasted Peaches and Raspberries with Crushed Amaretti

Mary Sue Waisman, Dietitian, Nova Scotia

- **Preheat oven to 450°F (230°C)**
- **13- by 9-inch (33 by 23 cm) glass baking dish, greased**

½ cup	lightly packed brown sugar	125 mL
1 tsp	ground cinnamon	5 mL
½ tsp	ground nutmeg	2 mL
2 lbs	peaches, sliced	1 kg
2 cups	raspberries	500 mL
2 tbsp	almond-flavored liqueur (optional)	30 mL
½ cup	crumbled amaretti cookies	125 mL

1. In a small bowl, combine brown sugar, cinnamon and nutmeg.

2. Place peaches in a single layer in prepared baking dish. Sprinkle with brown sugar mixture and scatter raspberries over top. Roast on top rack of preheated oven for 20 minutes or until juices ooze.

3. Divide fruit mixture among eight dessert dishes. Top each with a drizzle of almond liqueur (if using) and sprinkle with cookies.

Nutrients per serving

Calories	126
Fat	1.3 g
Saturated fat	0.7 g
Sodium	19 mg (1% DV)
Carbohydrate	30 g
Fiber	4 g (16% DV)
Protein	2 g
Calcium	28 mg (3% DV)
Iron	0.8 mg (6% DV)

Diabetes Food Choice Values:
1½ Carbohydrates

Makes 6 servings

The sweet, maple-flavored pears are nicely complemented by a sprinkling of chocolate and some crunch from hazelnuts.

Tip

For best results, choose pears that are ripe but firm and not overripe.

Variation

Substitute 1 oz (30 g) dark chocolate for the semisweet.

Maple-Roasted Pears with Shaved Chocolate and Toasted Hazelnuts

Mary Sue Waisman, Dietitian, Nova Scotia

- **Preheat oven to 450°F (230°C)**
- **13- by 9-inch (33 by 23 cm) glass baking dish, greased**

4	red Bartlett pears, peeled and sliced	4
2 tbsp	pure maple syrup	30 mL
1 oz	semisweet chocolate	30 g
½ cup	toasted chopped hazelnuts (see page 139)	125 mL

1. Scatter pear slices in prepared baking dish and drizzle with maple syrup. Bake in preheated oven for 10 to 15 minutes or until pears are tender when pierced with a knife.

2. Divide pears and juices among six dessert dishes. Shave one-sixth of the chocolate over each and sprinkle with hazelnuts.

Nutrients per serving

Calories	155
Fat	7.4 g
Saturated fat	1.3 g
Sodium	2 mg (0% DV)
Carbohydrate	24 g
Fiber	4 g (16% DV)
Protein	2 g
Calcium	26 mg (2% DV)
Iron	0.8 mg (6% DV)

Diabetes Food Choice Values:

1   Carbohydrate
1½ Fats

Makes 4 servings

Here's a perfect dessert for a fall evening, after a meal of pork or chicken. Pears, blue cheese and walnuts are a classic flavor combination.

Wine-Poached Pears Filled with Blue Cheese and Toasted Walnuts

Mary Sue Waisman, Dietitian, Nova Scotia

2 cups	Riesling wine	500 mL
2	firm ripe red Bartlett pears	2
4 tbsp	crumbled blue cheese	60 mL
4 tbsp	toasted finely chopped walnuts (see page 139)	60 mL

1. In a medium saucepan, bring wine to a boil over high heat. Meanwhile, peel pears, cut in half lengthwise and scoop out cores. Add pear halves to saucepan. Reduce heat to low, cover and simmer for 20 to 30 minutes or until pears are tender when pierced with a knife. Using a slotted spoon, transfer pears to a plate.

2. Return wine to medium-high heat and bring to a boil. Boil gently until reduced by about three-quarters.

3. Place 2 tbsp (30 mL) reduced wine in each of four shallow dessert bowls or dishes. Place a pear half, cored side up, in center. Sprinkle with blue cheese and walnuts.

> Riesling is a white wine known for its fruity aroma and flavor. Much of the world's Riesling grapes are grown in Germany and Alsace, but some are now grown in Australia, the United States and Canada.

Nutrients per serving

Calories	150
Fat	7.3 g
Saturated fat	2.0 g
Sodium	124 mg (5% DV)
Carbohydrate	13 g
Fiber	3 g (12% DV)
Protein	3 g
Calcium	69 mg (6% DV)
Iron	0.7 mg (5% DV)

Diabetes Food Choice Values:

1 Carbohydrate
2 Fats

Who said dessert had to be complicated? A quick broil of summer's freshest berries, scented with cinnamon and served with chilled yogurt and crunchy nuts, makes a perfect ending to a rich meal.

Tip

Don't crowd the berries in the pan or they won't broil evenly.

Variation

Use a fruit-flavored yogurt, such as strawberry or blueberry.

Broiled Strawberries with Cool Vanilla Yogurt

Mary Sue Waisman, Dietitian, Nova Scotia

- Preheat broiler, with rack set 4 inches (10 cm) from the heat
- 8- or 9-inch (20 or 23 cm) square glass baking dish

4 cups	whole strawberries, hulled	1 L
¼ cup	lightly packed brown sugar	60 mL
½ tsp	ground cinnamon	2 mL
2 cups	low-fat vanilla-flavored yogurt	500 mL
⅓ cup	toasted chopped hazelnuts (see page 139)	75 mL

1. Place strawberries in a single layer, tip side up, in baking dish. Sprinkle with brown sugar and cinnamon. Broil for 5 to 6 minutes or until berries start to release their juices and sugar starts to caramelize.

2. Divide berries and juices among six dessert dishes. Top with yogurt and sprinkle with hazelnuts.

Nutrients per serving

Calories	175
Fat	5.7 g
Saturated fat	1.3 g
Sodium	51 mg (2% DV)
Carbohydrate	29 g
Fiber	3 g (12% DV)
Protein	5 g
Calcium	138 mg (13% DV)
Iron	1.0 mg (7% DV)

Very high in: Vitamin C and riboflavin

High in: Magnesium and vitamin B_{12}

Diabetes Food Choice Values:

1½ Carbohydrates

1 Fat

Apples with Maple Custard Sauce

Caroline Dubeau, Dietitian, Ontario

● **Double boiler**

1 tbsp	butter	15 mL
6	cooking apples (such as Cortland), peeled and cut crosswise into 8 thick slices	6
2 tbsp	granulated sugar	30 mL
2 tbsp	freshly squeezed lemon juice	30 mL
1 tbsp	vanilla extract	15 mL
Maple Custard Sauce		
3	egg yolks	3
$\frac{1}{4}$ cup	pure maple syrup	60 mL
1 cup	2% milk, warmed	250 mL

1. In a large nonstick skillet, melt butter over medium heat. Sauté apples, sugar, lemon juice and vanilla for 2 minutes. Reduce heat to medium-low, cover with a tight-fitting lid and simmer, stirring once, for 15 to 20 minutes or until apples are soft.

2. *Sauce:* Meanwhile, in a medium heatproof bowl, using an electric mixer on high speed, beat egg yolks and maple syrup for 3 minutes or until pale yellow. Using a wire whisk, gently stir in warm milk. Set bowl over a saucepan of simmering water or transfer mixture to the top of a double boiler and cook, whisking continuously, for 6 to 8 minutes or until sauce is just thick enough to coat the back of a spoon. Transfer to a cool bowl and let cool. Serve warm or cover and refrigerate for up to 1 day and serve cold.

3. Divide apples among eight small dessert cups and spoon maple custard sauce over top.

Nutrients per serving

Calories	137
Fat	4.2 g
Saturated fat	1.9 g
Sodium	27 mg (1% DV)
Carbohydrate	24 g
Fiber	1 g (4% DV)
Protein	2 g
Calcium	57 mg (5% DV)
Iron	0.4 mg (3% DV)

Diabetes Food Choice Values:
1½ Carbohydrates
1 Fat

Makes 4 to 6 servings

✔ Kid Approved

Who would have thought — vegetables for dessert! Gajrela (pronounced *guj-RAY-la*) is a classic Indian dish that traditionally uses milk or cream and ghee (clarified butter). This lower-fat, healthier version also has a quicker cooking time.

Tips

Be sure to stir as directed so the mixture does not scorch.

This is a great recipe for kids to help with. Except for shredding the carrots, they can make it on their own (with supervision). They particularly like to stir the gajrela while it's cooking and watch it transform from liquid to dry.

Gajrela tastes good warm or chilled, with a scoop of vanilla frozen yogurt on the side.

Nutrients per serving

Calories	133
Fat	2.1 g
Saturated fat	1.2 g
Sodium	102 mg (4% DV)
Carbohydrate	24 g
Fiber	2 g (8% DV)
Protein	5 g
Calcium	166 mg (15% DV)
Iron	0.7 mg (5% DV)

Very high in: Vitamin A

Diabetes Food Choice Values:
1½ Carbohydrate

Gajrela

Bimaljit Dhatt, Ontario

4 cups	shredded carrots (about 12 oz/375 g)	1 L
1 cup	1% milk	250 mL
½ cup	lightly packed brown sugar	125 mL
½ tsp	ground cardamom	2 mL
¾ cup	light ricotta cheese	175 mL
2 tbsp	raisins (optional)	30 mL
2 tbsp	lightly toasted sliced almonds (optional)	30 mL

1. In a medium saucepan, bring ½ cup (125 mL) water to a boil over high heat. Add carrots, reduce heat to medium-high and boil, stirring often, for 2 minutes. Add milk and boil gently, stirring often, for 15 to 20 minutes or until mixture is almost dry (milk may appear curdled).

2. Reduce heat to medium-low and stir in brown sugar, cardamom and ricotta. Cook, stirring constantly, for 5 minutes. Stir in raisins (if using). Serve warm, sprinkled with almonds (if using).

Barley is often overlooked in desserts, but this one provides great nutrition and warms your tummy on a cold day.

Tips

Although only a tiny amount is used, the anise seed adds greatly to the flavor, so don't be tempted to leave it out. If you like the flavor, add more the next time you make this.

If you prefer, you can use 2 tbsp (30 mL) sucralose brown sugar blend instead of the brown sugar.

Variation

Mix and match nuts and dried fruits in this dessert. Try pistachios, cashews or pecans instead of almonds, and dried cranberries, blueberries or cherries instead of raisins.

Serving Idea

Serve leftovers for breakfast, along with unsweetened canned peaches.

Nutrients per serving

Calories	153
Fat	2.4 g
Saturated fat	0.9 g
Sodium	30 mg (1% DV)
Carbohydrate	30 g
Fiber	2 g (8% DV)
Protein	4 g
Calcium	89 mg (8% DV)
Iron	1.2 mg (9% DV)

Diabetes Food Choice Values:

2	Carbohydrates
½	Fat

Sweet Barley

Anya Myers, Dietitian, Nunavut

1 cup	pearl barley	250 mL
Pinch	ground anise seed	Pinch
2 tbsp	lightly packed brown sugar	30 mL
2 tbsp	chopped almonds	30 mL
1 tbsp	golden raisins	15 mL
2 cups	2% milk	500 mL

1. In a large pot with a tight-fitting lid, combine barley, anise and 3 cups (750 mL) water. Bring to a boil over high heat. Reduce heat to low, cover and simmer for 35 minutes or until liquid is absorbed. Fluff with a fork.

2. Stir in brown sugar, almonds, raisins and milk. Divide among eight dessert dishes. Serve warm.

Barley isn't a traditional dessert ingredient, but here, sweetened with maple syrup, it makes a delicious pudding. Leftovers make a delicious breakfast!

Tip

To make 2 cups (500 mL) cooked pearl barley, combine 2/3 cup (150 mL) barley and 2 cups (500 mL) water in a medium saucepan with a tight-fitting lid. Bring to a boil over high heat. Reduce heat to low, cover and simmer for 35 minutes or until liquid is absorbed. Fluff with a fork.

Variations

Use soy beverage instead of milk.

Replace the cherries with your favorite dried fruit, such as raisins, cranberries or blueberries.

Maple Barley Pudding

Edie Shaw-Ewald, Dietitian, Nova Scotia

- **Preheat oven to 350°F (180°C)**
- **8-inch (20 cm) square glass baking dish, greased**

2	eggs, beaten	2
1 tsp	ground cinnamon	5 mL
1 tsp	ground cardamom	5 mL
Pinch	salt	Pinch
1½ cups	2% milk	375 mL
½ cup	pure maple syrup	125 mL
1 tsp	vanilla extract	5 mL
2 cups	cooked pearl barley, cooled (see tip, at left)	500 mL
½ cup	dried cherries	125 mL

1. In a large bowl, whisk together eggs, cinnamon, cardamom, salt, milk, maple syrup and vanilla. Stir in barley and cherries. Pour into prepared baking dish.

2. Bake in preheated oven for 55 minutes or until set. Serve warm or cold.

Nutrients per serving

Calories	174
Fat	2.5 g
Saturated fat	1.0 g
Sodium	76 mg (3% DV)
Carbohydrate	34 g
Fiber	2 g (8% DV)
Protein	4 g
Calcium	103 mg (9% DV)
Iron	1.1 mg (8% DV)

High in: Riboflavin

Diabetes Food Choice Values:

2   Carbohydrates
½   Fat

Makes 6 to 8 servings

How easy is it to create a versatile, refreshing dessert? Simply whirl two ingredients in a food processor, then top with fresh berries.

Tip

To make fruit parfaits, use tall parfait glasses. Layer in a half-serving of mousse, followed by a half-serving of berries. Repeat layers.

Serving Idea

Serve in stemmed glasses for a buffet table.

Mango Mousse

Claude Gamache, Dietitian, Quebec

- **Food processor**

1	bag (20 oz/600 g) frozen mango chunks, thawed and drained	1
1/2 cup	low-fat vanilla-flavored yogurt	125 mL
1 cup	sliced strawberries	250 mL
1 cup	blueberries	250 mL

1. In food processor, purée mango and yogurt for 1 minute or until smooth.

2. Divide mousse among serving bowls. Top with strawberries and blueberries and serve immediately, or cover and refrigerate for up to 12 hours, then top with berries before serving.

Nutrients per serving

Calories	80
Fat	0.6 g
Saturated fat	0.2 g
Sodium	11 mg (0% DV)
Carbohydrate	19 g
Fiber	2 g (8% DV)
Protein	1 g
Calcium	32 mg (3% DV)
Iron	0.1 mg (1% DV)

Very high in: Vitamin C

Diabetes Food Choice Values:
1   Carbohydrate

Canned lychees taste like sweet grapes and take on a whole new texture when whirled into this smooth sorbet.

Tip

This recipe contains a raw egg white. If the food safety of raw eggs is a concern for you, use the pasteurized liquid egg whites instead.

Variation

Replace the lychees with canned mandarins, mangos, peaches or pears. If desired, replace the lime zest and juice with lemon zest and juice.

Lychee Sorbet

Christina Blais, Dietitian, Quebec

- **8-inch (20 cm) square baking pan**
- **Food processor**

1	can (19 oz/540 mL) lychee fruit	1
2 tbsp	white corn syrup	30 mL
½ tsp	grated lime zest	2 mL
1 tbsp	freshly squeezed lime juice	15 mL
1	egg white (or 2 tbsp/30 mL pasteurized liquid egg whites)	1
1 tbsp	vodka, Triple Sec or Cointreau (optional)	15 mL
	Fresh mint leaves	

1. Drain the lychees, reserving half the juice. In a bowl, combine reserved juice, corn syrup, lime zest and lime juice. Pour into baking pan and stir in lychees. Freeze for 3 to 4 hours or until frozen solid.

2. Remove pan from freezer. Using a sharp knife, score mixture into squares and transfer to food processor. Pulse 10 to 15 times or until mixture is crumbly. With the motor running, through the feed tube, add egg white and vodka (if using); process until very smooth.

3. If not quite solid enough to serve immediately, transfer to a plastic container, cover and freeze until firm. Scoop into serving dishes and garnish each with a mint leaf.

Nutrients per serving

Calories	68
Fat	0.0 g
Saturated fat	0.0 g
Sodium	35 mg (1% DV)
Carbohydrate	17 g
Fiber	0 g (0% DV)
Protein	1 g
Calcium	11 mg (1% DV)
Iron	0.1 mg (1% DV)

Diabetes Food Choice Values:

1   Carbohydrate

This fruity ice is sweet, tart and spicy all at once — perfect as a palate cleanser or a light dessert.

Tip

If desired, scrape the mixture with a fork every hour for 3 to 5 hours while it's freezing; this will promote the formation of ice crystals.

Pomegranate, Ginger and Clove Granita

Mary Sue Waisman, Dietitian, Nova Scotia

- **13- by 9-inch (33 by 23 cm) metal baking pan**

½ cup	granulated sugar	125 mL
1 tbsp	grated gingerroot	15 mL
1 tsp	ground cloves	5 mL
4 cups	unsweetened pomegranate juice	1 L
¼ cup	pomegranate seeds	60 mL
8	fresh mint sprigs	8

1. In a large saucepan, combine sugar, ginger, cloves and pomegranate juice. Bring to a boil over high heat, stirring to dissolve sugar. Reduce heat to medium-low and simmer for 5 minutes to allow flavors to infuse juice. Strain, if desired.

2. Pour juice into baking pan. Freeze for at least 6 hours, until solid, or overnight.

3. Scrape the mixture with a fork to create a shaved ice texture. Portion into serving bowls and top with pomegranate seeds and a sprig of mint.

Nutrients per serving

Calories	121
Fat	0.4 g
Saturated fat	0.1 g
Sodium	12 mg (1% DV)
Carbohydrate	30 g
Fiber	0 g (0% DV)
Protein	0 g
Calcium	16 mg (1% DV)
Iron	0.1 mg (1% DV)

Diabetes Food Choice Values:

2   Carbohydrate

✔ Kid Approved

Homemade frozen pops are easy and fun to make and even better to eat! Kelly's family is always so anxious to eat them that they try to pull them out of the molds before they are frozen and end up pulling out the sticks!

Tips

There is no need to use a blender; in fact, it's better to make this by hand, as chunks of banana add to the texture.

Be sure to choose 100% unsweetened juice, not just in this recipe but always!

Variation

Vary the juice and yogurt to your liking, but always use the banana for the best texture.

Frozen Tropical Vacation Pops

Kelly Hajnik, Ontario

● **Frozen pop molds or paper cups with sticks**

2	ripe bananas, mashed	2
1 cup	low-fat coconut-flavored yogurt	250 mL
1 cup	unsweetened orange juice	250 mL

1. In a bowl, combine bananas, yogurt and juice until well blended.

2. Pour banana mixture into molds and insert sticks. Freeze for at least 4 hours, until solid, or for up to 5 days.

Nutrients per serving

Calories	49
Fat	0.6 g
Saturated fat	0.3 g
Sodium	12 mg (1% DV)
Carbohydrate	10 g
Fiber	0 g (0% DV)
Protein	1 g
Calcium	32 mg (3% DV)
Iron	0.1 mg (1% DV)

Diabetes Food Choice Values:
½ Carbohydrate

✔ Kid Approved

Classic banana split flavors blend together to make a smooth and refreshing beverage.

Tip

Using frozen fruit means there's no need to add ice to this smoothie.

Variation

Use white milk instead of chocolate milk, substitute raspberry-flavored yogurt and replace the strawberries with frozen unsweetened raspberries.

Serving Idea

Garnish the glasses with cut fresh fruit.

Nutrients per serving

Calories	211
Fat	3.1 g
Saturated fat	1.8 g
Sodium	120 mg (5% DV)
Carbohydrate	39 g
Fiber	1 g (4% DV)
Protein	8 g
Calcium	250 mg (23% DV)
Iron	0.5 mg (4% DV)

High in: Vitamin D and vitamin B_{12}

Diabetes Food Choice Values:
$2\frac{1}{2}$ Carbohydrate

Banana Split Smoothie

Adapted from Dairy Farmers of Canada (www.dairygoodness.ca)

● **Blender or food processor**

2 cups	1% chocolate milk	500 mL
2 cups	low-fat strawberry-flavored yogurt	500 mL
1 cup	frozen unsweetened strawberries	250 mL
1	banana	1

1. In blender, combine chocolate milk, yogurt, strawberries and banana; purée until smooth. Pour into glasses and serve immediately.

About the Nutrient Analysis

COMPUTER ASSISTED nutrient analysis of the recipes was performed by Info Access (1988) Inc., Toronto, Ontario, using the Nutritional Accounting component of the CBORD Menu Management System. The nutrient database was the 2007b Canadian Nutrient File, supplemented when necessary with documented data from reliable sources.

The analysis was based on:

- imperial weights and measures (except for foods typically packaged and used in metric quantities);

- the larger number of servings (i.e., the smaller portion) when there was a range;

- the smaller ingredient quantity when there was a range;

- the first ingredient listed when there was a choice of ingredients.

Unless otherwise stated, recipes were analyzed using canola oil, non-hydrogenated margarine, 2% milk, 1% yogurt and long-grain rice. A pinch of salt and salt to taste were calculated as $1/8$ tsp. It was assumed that, prior to eating, meat was trimmed of external fat and skin was removed from poultry. Optional ingredients and garnishes in unspecified amounts were not included in the calculations.

Nutrient Information on Recipes

- Except for fat, saturated fat and iron, nutrient values have been rounded to the nearest whole number.

- Percent Daily Value has been assigned for sodium, fiber, calcium and iron according to the criteria established for nutrition labeling (*2003 Guide to Food Labelling and Advertising*, Canadian Food Inspection Agency). For all nutrients, 5% DV or less is a little; 15% DV or more is a lot.

- All recipes have been evaluated as "very high in" or "high in" vitamins (A, thiamin, riboflavin, niacin, B_6, folate, B_{12}, C and D) and minerals (magnesium and zinc) according to the criteria established for nutrition labeling (*2003 Guide to Food Labelling and Advertising*, Canadian Food Inspection Agency). For all vitamins and minerals except vitamin C, a serving that supplies 25% of the Daily Value (DV) is "very high in" those nutrients and a serving that supplies 15% is "high in" those nutrients. For vitamin C, a serving that supplies 50% of the Daily Value (DV) is "very high in" vitamin C and a serving that supplies 30% is "high in" vitamin C.

Diabetic Food Choice Values

Diabetic Food Choice Values were assigned based on the Canadian Diabetes Association's *Beyond the Basics: Meal Planning for Healthy Eating, Diabetes Prevention and Management* system. Carbohydrate Choices assumed 15 g of available carbohydrate per choice. Recipes containing vegetables generally assumed only 1 vegetable serving per recipe; additional carbohydrate was included in the Carbohydrate Choice assignment. Meat & Alternatives Choices generally assumed 7 g of protein and a range of 3 to 5 g fat per Choice, although the portion sizes and specific nutrient values of ingredients were also considered. Fat Choices were based on 5 g of fat per assignment. Because there is an element of judgment in assigning Choices, there may be more than one reasonable assignment for a recipe.

Resources

The authors of this book wish to gratefully acknowledge those organizations from which supporting data was used in the book to help showcase and highlight Canadian food and nutrition:

Statistics Canada
Health Canada
Agriculture and Agri-food Canada
Dietitians of Canada

as well as commodity boards that support and promote food produced in Canada.

Library and Archives Canada Cataloguing in Publication

Waisman, Mary Sue (Mary Suzanne), 1957-
      Dietitians of Canada Cook! : 275 recipes celebrate food from field to table / Mary Sue Waisman.

Includes index.
ISBN 978-0-7788-0261-7

      1. Cooking, Canadian. 2. Low-fat diet—Recipes. 3. Nutrition. I. Title.

TX715.6.W24 2011   641.5'638   C2010-907373-8

Index